# Innocents Return Abroad: Exploring Ancient Sites in Western Turkey

Jack Tucker

Copyright © 2012 Jack Tucker

All rights reserved.

ISBN: 1478343583
ISBN-13: 978-1478343585

# DEDICATION

Dedicated to my grandfather Ernest E. Tucker, for inspiring me to write, and to the many people who have supported me in this endeavor. In particular to my parents Ernest and Elizabeth, and to my brother Gregory, as well as my friends including especially Roy Patterson and Allan Hollis for their generous assistance in editing, revising and improving this text.

# CONTENTS

|  | Acknowledgments | I |
|---|---|---|
| I | Introduction | 1 |
| II | Ancient Region of Troad | 5 |
| III | Ancient Region of Mysia | 20 |
| IV | Ancient Region of Aeolia | 39 |
| V | Ancient Region of Ionia | 40 |
| VI | Ancient Region of Lydia | 108 |
| VII | Ancient Region of Caria | 118 |
| VIII | Ancient Region of Lycia | 171 |
| IX | Ancient Region of Pamphylia | 230 |
| X | Ancient Region of Pisidia | 249 |
| XI | Ancient Region of Phrygia | 275 |
| XII | Ancient Region of Bithynia | 299 |
| XIII | Constantinople | 304 |
| AI | Historical Figures | 345 |
| AII | Deities | 348 |
| AIII | Origin of Days and Months | 350 |
| AIV | List of Maps | 351 |

# ACKNOWLEDGMENTS

Samuel Clemens, commonly known as Mark Twain, inspired this travel guide with his <u>Innocents Abroad</u> published in 1869. The escapades of the 19th century European adventurers Heinrich Schliemann, Carl Humann, Sir Charles Newton, John Turtle Wood, Sir Charles Fellows, Felix Texier, and Otto Benndorf are awesome. The meticulous and well-written works of the eminent Turkish archeologist Ekrem Akurgal, as well as many other scholars (see bibliography), have been essential in preparing this work. All errors and omissions are entirely the fault of the author, who would be most grateful for any corrections or suggestions sent to <u>tuckjack2@yahoo.com</u> via email.

# I INTRODUCTION

This guidebook is entitled <u>Innocents Return Abroad</u>, named after the book <u>Innocents Abroad</u> by Samuel Clemens, more commonly known as Mark Twain, who visited the Middle East and published it in 1869. Mark Twain accompanied a large group of American travelers on the *Quaker City,* a retired naval ship used in the Civil War, along the Mediterranean coast to Constantinople, proceeding to the Black Sea and then following the Turkish coast to stop at Smyrna (Izmir) and visit Ephesus. Clearly much has changed since then. Twain and his compatriots called upon Russian Czar Alexander II at Yalta and visited ancient sites within the multi-national Ottoman Empire. However, "innocents" is still an appropriate title because many westerners, particularly Americans, remain profoundly unaware of what can be seen in Turkey and its relevance to our own heritage.

This volume, envisioned as the first of five, covers more than 60 ancient sites in western Turkey. Like Mark Twain, many modern tourists arrive in western Turkey by cruise ship and visit popular ancient sites, particularly Ephesus. However, the 21$^{st}$ century traveler has many other options not available to Mark Twain in 1867. Twain wrote a good bit about transport challenges, such as difficult donkeys, in the Ottoman territories. Nowadays a non-Turkish speaker can rent a car and, using a GPS, drive directly to any of the ancient sites listed here. Although this book describes the most popular sites where busloads of tourists arrive daily, it also includes many seldom-visited sites, often in picturesque rural areas far from main roads.  One of the joys of traveling in Turkey is that crime is virtually nonexistent and remote sites can be visited without fear.  At less visited sites, signage and onsite information is often inadequate or nonexistent, making it difficult for modern visitors to fully appreciate the rich background and fascinating stories that accompany these remarkable places.  Many images and stories widely recognized by an ancient audience require some explanation for modern visitors.  This book fills that void, describes visible structures, where to find them and their historical significance.  To indicate more information is available in a relevant text box about particular individuals, deities or historical events, the names are underlined, for example Aphrodite.  These text boxes are designated with different fonts: one for **factual, historical references,** another font for theological or miraculous stories.

Most of us are well aware of the fundamental Greco-Roman legacy to the western world.  The role of ancient city-states in developing democratic and representative forms of government is widely acknowledged, as is our linguistic and cultural heritage.  Our culture, art and architecture are largely derived from this tradition.  Ancient sites in Greece and Italy are widely known, strongly associated with this tradition and frequently visited.  Why then read about or visit ancient sites in Turkey?  In fact, this region was within the dynamic eastern portion of the Roman Empire, which contained the bulk of the economy and population.  In about 750 BCE the blind poet Homer composed the Iliad and the Odyssey, the earliest major works of western literature, on the western shore of Asia Minor, the peninsula of Asian Turkey, sometimes referred to as Anatolia.  Homer first defined the Greek gods, who have remained with us in art and literature.  It was in Asia Minor where Christianity was transformed from a minor Jewish cult into a major force in world history.  That ideological transformation is recorded in the ancient sites described here.  Many specific, less widely recognized legacies exist.  For example, the days of the week and months of the year we use on a daily basis were devised during this period based on Babylonian astrology and the prevalent polytheism (see Appendix AIII).

This guidebook covers those ancient sites active during the thousand years from 200 BCE through 800 CE.  During this period the Roman Empire reached its apex, Judaism was fundamentally transformed, Christianity arose and eventually became the official imperial ideology, and Islam was born. In the year 525 the Christian monk Dionysius Exiguus devised the BC/AD system of years to replace an earlier system based on the names of rulers, including those who persecuted Christians. He used "Anni Domini" or year of our lord (AD) for years after the year he calculated as the birth year of Jesus and "Before Christ" or BC for years before that date. In this book the religiously neutral terms Before the Common Era (BCE) in place of BC and Common Era (CE) in place of AD are used.

Social and religious developments from before the year 800 are very much with us in the modern world and shape our day-to-day perceptions. The vast majority of people living in the Americas, Europe, Africa, the Middle East and much of Asia conceive of themselves in some sense as Christian, Muslim, or Jewish. Fifty to a hundred years ago, many intellectuals and reformers were inspired by materialistic or economic-based utopian concepts as cures for social ills and inequality. More recently in the 21$^{st}$ century as Soviet style collectivism and central planning lost their appeal, many intellectuals and social reformers have come to view religion as the cure for social injustice and inequality. Particularly in the Middle East, religious political parties are increasingly influential. Few westerners realize the extent to which Islamic beliefs and practices are derived from much older Judaism and Christianity. Despite a Turkish national myth that all Turks arrived in mass from Central Asia, the vast majority of present day Turks had Roman Christian ancestors who gradually converted to Islam. The ancient sites of Asia Minor help us understand the syncretism (combining) of religious belief and the essential commonality of the three great Abrahamic religions. Given the fact that Islam was established in western Turkey after 800, most sites covered in this volume are pre-Christian, Jewish or early Christian monuments, although three important Islamic sites dating back to before 800 are included.

This volume covers eleven distinct ancient regions of western Asia Minor: Troad, Mysia, Aeolis, Ionia, Lydia, Caria, Lycia, Pamphylia, Pisidia, Phrygia, and Bithynia, as well as the city of Constantinople (modern Istanbul). Each region includes a brief historical summary and lists the sites. Then sites are described, together with relevant stories and references and the GPS coordinates. For simplicity, this volume uses Greek names for the Greco-Roman gods because the geographic area covered in this volume was Greek speaking. The term "late Roman" is used in place of Byzantine because, although Greek-speaking, the empire based in

Constantinople after the 4$^{th}$ century considered itself fully Roman in origin and culture. Also for simplicity, the directions East (E), West (W), North (N) and South (S) are represented with single letters.

Many history students sometimes feel they are studying an abstract subject involving innumerable dates and places unconnected to the modern world. For many, direct experience with the visible world is more memorable and believable than simply reading abstract written words. Unlike the 19$^{th}$ century American readers of Mark Twain, now we can use Google Earth to actually see and virtually tour each of these ancient sites without leaving home. For most sites the alignment of ancient structures, such as theatres and temples, is visible on Google Earth. To use this free software, simply go to Google.earth.com and download the software. Then take the GPS coordinates listed with any of the ancient sites described in this book, plug them into the search bar in the upper left corner, and watch the world spin. Use the slider bar on the right side of the Google Earth image to adjust the magnitude for maximum visibility. Refer to the maps for each site to identify ancient structures you can see on Google Earth. Looking directly at these sites adds a new dimension of realism and relevance to the study of ancient history.

# II ANCIENT REGION OF TROAD

Troad is a mountainous peninsula in NW Asia Minor bordered by Mysia to the E, Aeolis to the S, Aegean Sea to the W and the narrow, 60 km long strait known as the Dardanelles to the N. The 12<sup>th</sup> century BCE city-states in Troad were mentioned in the Iliad, Homer's classic tale of the Trojan War. Homer used oral poetry with a formulaic dictation, which preserved the names of individuals, names and actions from the late Bronze Age through four illiterate centuries. During the 7<sup>th</sup> century BCE Troad came under Lydian rule and in 547 BCE was incorporated into the Persian Empire. In 482 BCE Persian King Xerxes built a bridge of boats across the Dardanelles to invade Greece. A storm destroyed the first boat bridge, so Xerxes beheaded the first set of builders and had a second, more solid bridge built. In an amusing aside in chapter 33 of Innocents Abroad, Mark Twain recommends the US government adopt this approach to deal with shoddy contractor work. In 334 BCE Alexander the Great crossed the Dardanelles from Thrace, defeated the Persians and seized control. Successive Macedonian generals ruled the region after Alexander's death until after the battle of Magnesia in 190 BCE, when the Romans awarded Troad to the Kingdom of Pergamum, their stalking horse in Asia Minor. Troad was among the territories the king of Pergamum bequeathed to Rome in 133 BCE. St. Paul is known to have visited the region at least four times during his missionary journeys. Extant sites in Troad include the ancient Hellenistic cities of **Troy**, **Alexandria Troas** and **Assos** where Aristotle once resided.

The Trojan War: Homer's Iliad covers concluding episodes in the ten-year Trojan War between Mycenae and Troy. The gods themselves took sides in the epic struggle: Hera, Athena, and Poseidon supported the Greeks; Aphrodite, Apollo, and Ares (Mars) favored the Trojans. Stories of the principal characters are complicated and interrelated. For example, Priam, King of Troy during the war, was the youngest son of the previous Trojan King Laemedon. At an earlier time, Zeus kidnapped Ganymedes, another son of King Laemedon. While Ganymedes tended sheep on Mount Ida, Zeus assumed the form of an eagle and carried him away to Mount Olympus.

Ganymedes became the cupbearer of Zeus and attained immortality. To compensate Laemedon for the loss of his son, Zeus sent Hermes with a gift of two snow white horses so swift they could run over water. Later when Poseidon and Apollo offended Zeus, he compelled them to go to Troy and build huge walls around the city at the behest of King Laemedon, who promised to reward them but failed to do so. When Laemedon refused to compensate the gods, Apollo sent a plague to Troy and Poseidon sent a sea monster. Oracles promised deliverance if Laemedon would sacrifice his beautiful daughter Hesione to the sea monster. In desperation Laemedon chained his naked daughter on the rocky coast to await the monster. At this moment Hercules happened to arrive and promised to save her in return for the two snow-white horses Laemedon had received from Zeus. Laemedon agreed, and Heracles slew the monster. Once again, however, Laemedon proved an ingrate and refused to turn over the horses. Enraged, Hercules together with his friend Telamon, a Greek prince, attacked and captured Troy, and killed Laemedon and all his sons except the youngest, Podarces, who was sold into slavery. Hercules gave Laemedon's daughter Hesione to Telamon and later allowed her to ransom her brother Podarces in exchange for a golden veil. From this time on Podarces was known as Priam, from the Greek word primai 'to buy'. Hesione and Telamon had a son Teucer, half-brother of Telamon's older son Ajax. Priam became King of Troy as a young man and had twelve daughters and fifty sons, including Hector, his eldest who was a great warrior, as well as Paris, his handsomest son.

Meanwhile several gods sought to wed the attractive goddess Thetis until a prophecy revealed that her son would be greater than and would displace his father. Zeus determined the best solution would be for Thetis to wed a mortal man, since humans generally are pleased when their sons do better than they do and know their time is limited. Thetis, however, was less than pleased at the degrading prospect of marrying a mortal. To compensate Thetis, Zeus agreed to host an elaborate wedding party and invited all gods and goddesses except for Eris, goddess of strife and conflict. Eris, unhappy to be excluded, crashed the wedding and threw a golden apple onto the wedding table addressed to the most beautiful woman. Hera, Athena and Aphrodite all reached for the apple. Zeus, reluctant to decide who should get the apple, delegated the decision to Paris, the son of Trojan King Priam. Each goddess in turn attempted to bribe Paris and win the contest. Hera offered Paris political control over several cities. Athena offered Paris military success. Aphrodite offered Paris the opportunity to wed the most beautiful woman in the world. Paris voted for Aphrodite and was awarded Helen, a daughter of Zeus from a mortal woman, who was already married to Menelaus, brother of Agamemnon, King of Mycenae in mainland Greece.

Paris went to Mycenae as a guest and then, in the worst possible violation of the guest-host relationship, abducted Helen and took her back to Troy. This act precipitated the Trojan War because family honor compelled Agamemnon to assemble a host of Greek warriors to regain Helen. Agamemnon's army included the renowned heroes Achilles, Odysseus (Ulysses to Romans) and Ajax. Achilles was the son of a Greek king and a sea nymph who had rendered him invulnerable, except for his heel, when she dipped him in the river Styx as an infant. He was the strongest and most ferocious of the Greek warriors. Ajax was son of King Telamon of Salamis, and was second only to Achilles in strength and military prowess. The Greek army assembled at Aulis but the wind failed and they were unable to sail. Agamemnon had offended the goddess Artemis and only when he had sacrificed his beautiful daughter Iphigenia were they able to sail to Asia Minor. Troy, assisted by allies from Asia Minor and Thrace, withstood the Greek siege for ten years. Teucer served as a skilled archer and fired arrows from behind the giant shield of his brother Ajax. Altogether Teucer slew thirty Trojans during the war, including many one particular day when Hector led an attack to push the Greeks back to their ships. Enraged, Hector threw a huge rock at Teucer, injuring him and forcing him to retire from the battle. Finally Hector fell in single combat against Achilles, who was infuriated after Hector killed his closest friend Patroclus. After Hector's death, Penthesilea, queen of the Amazons, and Memnon, King of the Ethiopians, came to the defense of Troy. Achilles killed the Amazon queen but then fell in love with her as she lay dying. Paris, guided by Apollo, managed to hit Achilles in the heel with an arrow and kill him. At a point when Zeus appeared on the verge of favoring the Trojans, Hera managed to borrow Aphrodite's girdle of irresistibility and seduced Zeus, so he fell asleep and did not give victory to the Trojans. Ajax went mad with jealousy when Agamemnon awarded the armor of the dead Achilles to Odysseus. Ajax later committed suicide with a silver sword Hector had once given him as a gift. After Ajax committed suicide, Teucer guarded his body and insisted on a proper burial. Even after the Greeks killed Paris, the Trojans refused to surrender Helen and end the conflict.

Finally Odysseus, cleverest of the Greeks, suggested they

pretend to depart. With the help of Athena, the Greeks built and left behind a huge wooden horse with soldiers hidden inside, including Odysseus, Menelaus and Teucer. Despite the warnings of Cassandra, who could see the future but was fated not to be believed, the Trojans were fooled, brought the horse into their city and were slaughtered. The Trojan women were sold into slavery in Greece. Menelaus intended to kill Helen but confronted with her beauty could not. Despite their victory, the Greeks suffered. Agamemnon returned home only to be killed by his wife Clytemnestra and her lover. Odysseus was delayed for many years and lost his crew. Teucer, when he returned home to his father at Salamis, was blamed for the loss of Ajax, his armor and his body, and was expelled from the island. As he departed Salamis Teucer declared "nil desperandum" (never give up) and set out on the vast ocean. Eventually Teucer settled in Cyprus and founded the town of Salamis named after his homeland.

**Troy** (39° 57' 24.43" N, 26° 14' 26.86" E) is the ancient city made famous from Homer's Iliad. Historians believe the Trojan War took place in the 12$^{th}$ century BCE. Over the last century and a half excavations have revealed nine Trojan cities built over each other in succession from Troy I in 3000-2400 BCE through to Troy VII in 1300-1000 BCE, contemporaneous with the Iliad, up to Troy IX, the Ilium of the 1$^{st}$ century BCE. Modern geological methods used to reconstruct the Trojan coastline in 3000 BCE confirm the basic accuracy of Homeric geography. Ancient Greeks and Romans accepted the historicity of the Trojan War. Alexander the Great visited Troy in 334 BCE and made sacrifices at the tombs of the Homeric hero Achilles. The followers of Alexander built a large temple at Troy in honor of Athena. Roman Emperor Augustus visited Troy in 20 BCE, founded a new city of Ilium at the site and restored the Temple of Athena. Troy was particularly significant to Romans because they traced their ancestry to the Trojan Aeneas, who fled the city after its defeat. Aeneas was the son of Aphrodite (Venus to Romans) and was the basis of the claim of divine descent for the Julian dynasty of Julius Caesar and Augustus. Augustus commissioned Virgil to write the Aeneid, the classic Roman foundation story based on the journey of Aeneas from Troy to Rome. This descent enabled Romans, like the Greeks, to claim an ancient lineage from the gods. In 124 Emperor Hadrian visited and rebuilt the tomb of Ajax.

Virgil's Aeneid was written in 29-19 BCE at the request of Emperor Augustus. It tells the story of Aeneas, who personifies persistence, self-denial, and obedience to the gods. Aeneas was a son of the goddess Aphrodite and Anchises, a mortal Trojan prince. One day Aphrodite came to Anchises disguised as a beautiful maiden. Anchises, overcome with desire, made love with her and only later realized her identity. He was terrified the gods would destroy him for having slept with a goddess. Aphrodite, who deeply regretted having been with a mortal man, reassured him that everything would be alright as long as he kept the incident quiet and claimed that their child Aeneas was the offspring of a common nymph.

Aeneas was a cousin of King Priam and a courageous warrior, second only to Hector. During the Trojan War, Aeneas was seriously wounded and would have died if Aphrodite had not come to his rescue. Apollo then protected Aeneas, removing him from the battle to his temple where Leto and Artemis healed Aeneas and made him even stronger. On another occasion, Apollo urged Aeneas to fight Achilles in single combat. Again Aeneas was almost killed, but Poseidon rescued him, despite favoring the Greeks, because he knew Aeneas was destined for greatness. When Troy finally fell, the gods ordered Aeneas to flee the city. Aeneas fled with his son Ascanius and even carried away his aging father Anchises on his shoulders, but lost his wife in the confusion. With a small band of Trojan survivors, Aeneas sailed for six years, wandering through Thrace, Crete, and Sicily, before finally being shipwrecked on the African coast near Carthage. There Aeneas met and fell in love with Queen Dido, a Phoenician princess from Tyre who had been driven out of her native land by her evil brother Pygmalion, and gone on to found Carthage. Dido proposed that the Trojans settle in her land and that she and Aeneas reign jointly. Although Aeneas loved Dido and was happy with this arrangement, Zeus and Aphrodite sent the messenger god Hermes to remind Aeneas of his responsibilities and compel him to proceed on his journey. Aeneas, forced to choose between love and duty, reluctantly sailed away. When Dido learned that the Trojans had departed secretly, she ordered a huge fire built, fatally stabbed herself with a sword Aeneas had given her, and jumped into the fire. Much later, when Aeneas visited Tartarus, the underworld of the dead, he saw Dido but she refused to forgive or even acknowledge him.

Aeneas sailed on until he finally reached Latium, a land in Italy ruled by King Latinus. Aeneas allied himself with King

Latinus, and then worked out a marriage alliance whereby Aeneas married Latinus' daughter, Lavinia. King Turnus of the Rutulians also wanted Lavinia, so war broke out and was only settled when Aeneas killed Turnus in single combat. The family of Julius Caesar and Augustus was descended from Aeneas through his son Ascanius. Romulus and Remus, twin brothers suckled by a female wolf, were both descendants of Aeneas via their mother Rhea Silvia, making Aeneas progenitor of all the Roman people. Therefore Romans, like the Greeks, were descended from the gods.

**Troy Site**: Over the centuries Troy was abandoned, and by the 19th century the whereabouts of the site was unknown. Until the German archeologist Heinrich Schliemann rediscovered the site of ancient Troy in 1871 many regarded Homer's Iliad as an imaginary tale. Today, the entrance to the ruins is marked by a large wooden horse erected by the Turkish Ministry of Tourism based on images found on ancient coins. Although extant remains are limited, the site is well maintained with circular

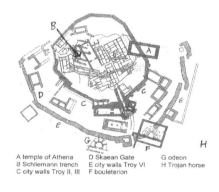

A temple of Athena  D Skaean Gate  G odeon
B Schliemann trench  E city walls Troy VI  H Trojan horse
C city walls Troy II, III  F bouleterion

*Troy*

walkways and signs showing which level (city) of ancient Troy is where. On the S edge of the site the Roman bouleuterion and odeon date from the most recent level, the Ilium of Augustus. (In ancient city-states the boule was a group of citizen representatives who assembled at a hall-like building known as a bouleuterion. An odeon was originally a place meant for singing, similar to but much smaller than a theatre, usually covered with a roof for improved acoustics.) Outlines of the temple of Athena built at the time of Alexander and rebuilt by Augustus are on the N edge of the site. From Troy VI of the Iliad are remains of the weak W wall; the Scaean Gate on the W edge of the site is where Hector and Achilles are said to have fought in their famous last encounter; and the sloping E wall that Patroclus, closest friend of Achilles, tried to scale. Archeological excavations continue under the direction of Professor Ernst Pernicka from the University of Tübingen in Germany, and involve the University of Cincinnati and the University of Pennsylvania in the United States. Further information about the archeology of Troy is available in both English and German on the excellent University of Tübingen website: http://www.uni-tuebingen.de//uni/aft/

**Heinrich Schliemann (1822-1890), an incredible rags to riches character from Germany, was "discoverer" of ancient Troy. Since childhood Schliemann had been fascinated with Homer's Iliad and Odyssey. Convinced of his intuitive, instinctive ability to find ancient artifacts, he traveled to Turkey in search of Troy. During two attempts in 1871–73 and 1878–9, Schliemann found and excavated the site now known as Troy II. Although his methodology is now widely criticized, he demonstrated that the ancient city of troy was an historical reality, not a literary fantasy. In May 1873, Schliemann discovered a horde of two gold diadems, 56 gold earrings and 8,750 golden rings and diamonds, as well as a large amount of silver and copperware. He concealed these artifacts, which he mistakenly called "Priam's Treasure," from his workers and the Ottoman government and smuggled them out of the country. Schliemann's young Greek wife occasionally appeared in public wearing this ancient jewelry. During the Russian occupation of Berlin after WW II, "Priam's Treasure" was stolen from Berlin, but eventually resurfaced in Russian museums.**

**Alexandria Troas** (39° 45' 7" N, 26° 9' 32" E) was an important ancient port city on the Aegean Sea near the modern village of Dalyan. This Hellenistic city named for Alexander the Great was founded in 300 BCE and became a major trading center due to its man-made harbor and location at the W entrance to the Dardanelles between the Aegean and the Sea of Marmara. Emperor Augustus made the city an official Roman colony. During his second missionary journey, St. Paul had a vision here, which persuaded him to go directly to Macedonia to proselytize. As recounted in the New Testament, when St. Paul visited Alexander Troas on his third missionary journey and preached a long sermon, a young man named Eutychus (meaning Fortunate) fell asleep while listening and fell from a three-storey windowsill. St. Paul picked up Eutychus, carried him back upstairs, and assured the crowd the boy would completely recover, which he did. In the 4$^{th}$ century Emperor Constantine I considered making this thriving city his new capital, but opted instead for the more defensible town of Byzantium on the Golden Horn.

**Alexandria Troas Site**: A modern road divides the heavily overgrown ruins of Alexandria Troas near the coast where visitors can see remnants of baths, an odeon, a theatre, a stadium and the necropolis. (A necropolis is a "city of the dead" or ancient cemetery, generally located outside the city walls, where relatives would meet at tombs of the deceased to honor their memory.) The circuit of the old city walls, fortified with towers at regular intervals, still can be traced. The harbor originally had two large basins, which are now largely filled in. Not far away is an ancient quarry (39° 44' 28" N, 26° 14' 30" E) where visitors can see incomplete columns *in situ* (meaning in the original place), partially carved out of the underlying granite but for some reason not completed and removed. Up in the nearby mountains is the 7th century BCE city of Neandria (39° 43' 21' N, 26° 16' 45" E), from where one of the Macedonian successors of Alexander the Great, Antigonus, took the people needed to populate Alexandria Troas. Extant ruins at Neandria include substantial intact city walls.

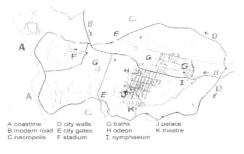

A coastline  D city walls  G baths  J palace
B modern road  E city gates  H odeon  K theatre
C necropolis  F stadium  I. nymphaeum

*Alexandria Troas*

**Alexander the Great was born July 20, 356 BCE, son of Macedonian King Philip II and his Greek queen Olympias, who claimed she was impregnated, not by her husband Philip, but rather by Zeus in the form of a snake. In the ancient world Zeus was often envisioned taking animal forms to impregnate mortal women. The day Alexander was born, the temple of Artemis (Diana to Romans) at Ephesus burned down, supposedly because the goddess was away to witness his birth. Philip had transformed Macedonia into a strong military power, which dominated the Greek city-states. Although the Greeks regarded Macedonians as barbarians with a separate language and culture, Alexander was raised using Greek, which he later established as the language of his empire. Aristotle served as Alexander's personal tutor for philosophy, science, and literature when he was 13-18 years old. Homer's Iliad and the story of Achilles particularly fascinated Alexander. At age 18 Alexander commanded a Macedonian force and destroyed a seemingly invincible Greek military unit. Relations were strained between Philip and Alexander over dynastic succession questions and**

plans to invade Persia without Alexander. In 336 BC, a knife-wielding noble killed Philip at a royal wedding. The assassin was killed instantly, which made it impossible to ascertain whether others were involved.

The army proclaimed Alexander, aged 20, as king, which prompted Greek cities led by Thebes to assert their independence. Alexander marched to the gates of Thebes and demanded they reconsider, but the city refused. Alexander attacked Thebes, brutally killed more than 6,000 men, destroyed the city and sold 30,000 survivors into slavery. His severity discouraged further Greek resistance. In 334 BCE, Alexander crossed the Dardanelles with an army of 30,000 infantry and 5000 cavalry, including 7000 Greeks allies. At Troy he worshipped and made ritual sacrifices at the shrine of Achilles. Then at the nearby Granicus River, the Macedonians confronted a Persian imperial force of 40,000, half of whom were Greek mercenaries. At a critical point in the battle, Cleitus, one of the Macedonian officers, cut off the arm of the Persian commander just as he was poised to kill Alexander. As the battle intensified the Persians fled while the Greek mercenaries were slaughtered, with only about 2,000 survivors sold into slavery. Alexander seized the Persian treasury at Sardis and proceeded S along the coast, welcomed by the Greek-speaking population. Only Miletus and Halicarnassus, with strong Persian garrisons, resisted. Alexander used land forces to capture Miletus, avoiding the powerful Persian fleet. In Caria he enlisted popular support by taking up the cause of deposed Carian queen Ada, then successfully besieged Halicarnassus. The Persians withdrew by sea, burning the city as they departed.

All along the Greek-speaking coast Alexander expelled Persian-installed tyrants and gained popular support. In 333 BCE, Alexander went N to the Phrygian capital at Gordium and cut the famous Gordian Knot. In the SE of Asia Minor he finally encountered Persian King Darius III at Issus. Although the Persians greatly outnumbered his men, fighting the battle in a mountain pass significantly reduced their numerical advantage. Alexander led his men to a brilliant victory, and tens of thousands of Persians and Greek mercenaries were killed as Darius panicked and fled, leaving behind his mother, wife, and daughters. Alexander seized Persian treasure and supplies at Damascus, and proceeded S along the coast to Tyre, a well-fortified island city his men besieged for seven months. The Macedonians built an enormous stone pier to connect Tyre to the mainland, battered down the walls, killed 7,000 defenders outright and sold the remaining 30,000 inhabitants into slavery. Alexander continued to Gaza where embittered local resistance delayed him for two months but was forcefully crushed. Then he entered Egypt welcomed as a liberator after 200 years of oppressive Persian rule. Alexander made a pilgrimage to Siwa, the remote desert temple abode of the oracle of Amon-Ra, the chief god of the Egyptian pantheon of deities. Amon-Ra had evolved from the original creator Amon and the sun god Ra and during this period the Greeks identified Amon-Ra with Zeus. The oracle at Siwa confirmed Alexander was son of Zeus Amon-Ra, destined to rule the world.

In mid-331 BCE Alexander returned to Tyre, received reinforcements and headed N toward Babylon to confront Darius. The Macedonians confronted a huge polyglot Persian army on the plains of Gaugamela (near modern Irbil, Iraq) on October 1, 331 BCE. When Alexander and his cavalry aimed straight at Darius, he again panicked and fled, at which point the Persian army disintegrated. Darius was later killed by one of his own nobles, Bessus, who claimed the Persian throne. Alexander found Darius' body and gave him a royal funeral. For the next three years the Macedonians gradually overcame local resistance throughout the Persian Empire as far as Afghanistan and Tajikistan, gaining complete control by 328 BCE. Alexander married the Sogdian princess Roxane, strengthening his local support. He began to wear Persian clothes and adopt Persian mannerisms, which greatly irritated his Macedonian followers. They particularly disliked proskynesis. (Proskynesis was the traditional Persian practice of prostrating oneself before a social superior, bowing down, groveling and crawling along the ground.) Alexander also recruited and trained young Persian soldiers in Macedonian military tactics, which alarmed his Macedonian followers. During a drunken banquet at Samarkand in 328 BCE Cleitus argued with Alexander, reminding the king of how he had saved his life, and noting that much of Alexander's present glory was owed to his father Philip. Enraged, Alexander killed him with a spear. The historian Callisthenes, a nephew of Aristotle, had accompanied Alexander's army to write about and publicize Alexander's heroic deeds. Callisthenes protested against proskynesis, fell out of favor and was later executed for participating in an alleged conspiracy.

In 326 BCE Alexander invaded Punjab. The Macedonians crossed the heavily defended Hydaspes (modern Jhelum) River, and attacked King Porus with his army of fierce Indian defenders equipped with war elephants, which the Macedonians had never seen. The Macedonians triumphed, but this difficult victory over only 22,000 Indians convinced the common soldiers that they had gone far enough. They refused to march further E across the Ganges River. Alexander reluctantly agreed to turn back, and floated his army on a flotilla of perhaps a thousand rafts for seven months down the Hydaspes and Indus Rivers to the Indian Ocean. At the coast Alexander made the disastrous decision to march W through the Gedrosian Desert in mid-summer; thousands perished during the 60-day trek. Finally back in Susa in 324 BCE, Alexander celebrated his victories, took a daughter of King Darius, Statira, as a wife, and ordered his 80 most senior officers to each marry noble Persian ladies. In Babylon Alexander contracted a violent fever, which killed him twelve days later on June 10, 323 BCE at the age of 33. When his closest followers asked who should succeed him, the dying Alexander had replied "the strongest."

In just eleven years, 335-324 BCE, Alexander had marched 35,000 km, conquered the vast Persian Empire, and fundamentally altered the course of history by infusing Greek thought over this huge territory. His Macedonian successors eventually split the empire into the four kingdoms ruled by: Seleucus in Asia; Ptolemy in Egypt; Lysimachus in Thrace; and Cassander in Macedonia and Greece. As Alexander's ornate sarcophagus returned toward Macedonia, the clever Ptolemy seized the sarcophagus and took it to Alexandria in Egypt, where it was displayed for hundreds of years. Subsequent Roman emperors greatly admired Alexander as the ultimate military genius and tried their best to emulate him.

Professor Elmar Schwertheim of the University of Münster in Germany and a team of archeologists excavated Alexandria Troas. Additional information is available in German at: http://www.uni-muenster.de/AsiaMinor/projekte/grabung-at/

**Assos** (39° 29' 28" N, 26° 20' 13" E) is located up a steep slope above the small coastal town Behramkale. In the 1$^{st}$ millennium BCE settlers from the nearby island of Lesbos (now in Greece) founded Assos. The 4$^{th}$ century BCE was a period of great prosperity for Assos when Hermeias, a former slave and student of Plato, ruled the city, as well as the rest of the Troad peninsula. Hermeias actively encouraged philosophers to move to the city. In 348 BCE Aristotle came to Assos, and established a school where he taught for three years. In 334 BCE Alexander the Great, a student of Aristotle, expelled the Persians. Alexander's successors exercised nominal sovereignty over the city and were acclaimed benefactors. However, these Macedonian monarchs did not exercise absolute authority because the city's highly defensible position and towering walls secured its autonomy. In 241-133 BCE the Kingdom of Pergamum ruled Assos, after which it was incorporated into the Roman Empire. Returning to Jerusalem on his third missionary journey in 55, St. Paul walked alone from Alexandria Troas to Assos, where he rejoined colleagues and sailed on to Lesbos.

**Aristotle (384-322 BCE) was born 55 km E of modern-day Thessaloniki in Greece, son of a court physician in Macedonia. He was first trained in medicine and then, at age seventeen, went to Athens where he studied at Plato's Academy for twenty years. Although a gifted student, Aristotle disputed Plato's belief in ideal form and preferred acquiring knowledge from empirical observation and direct experience. He was not appointed to head the Academy when Plato died in 347 BCE. Instead Aristotle went to Assos in 348 BCE to the court of Hermeias, a friend and former student at the Academy, who had become the ruler. Aristotle established a school of philosophy and expanded his research into marine biology. He remained at Assos for three years and married Pythias, the niece and adopted daughter of Hermeias. Sadly this idyllic situation came to an end when the Persians re-conquered Troad in 345 BCE and crucified Hermeias. Aristotle and his wife fled to Lesbos.**

**In 343 BCE Philip II of Macedon invited Aristotle to become tutor to his thirteen-year old son, the future Alexander the Great. Aristotle believed monarchy could be justified if the virtue of the king and his family were greater than that of the rest of the citizenry. For five years he instructed young Alexander about ethics, political theory and the wider world. Although Greeks had long regarded Macedonians as a barbarian people, Philip II and his son Alexander adopted a standard Greek language at court and sought to establish Macedonia as an integral part of the Greek world. Aristotle, undoubtedly influenced by his experience with the Persians at Assos, adopted an ethnocentric view and encouraged Alexander to contemplate eastern conquest. He is believed to have told Alexander to be a "leader" of the Greeks and treat them as "friends and relatives" but act as a "despot" toward barbarians and treat them as "beasts or plants."**

Alexander succeeded his father as ruler of Macedonia in 336 BCE and launched his attack on the Persian Empire two years later. In 335 BCE Aristotle returned to Athens and established a school of philosophy, known as the Lyceum, dedicated to Apollo. His students studied many subjects and assembled a vast library. During 335-323 BCE in Athens Aristotle composed most of his works, only a third of which are believed to have survived. His known works include tracts on logic, philosophy, ethics, physics, biology, psychology, politics, and rhetoric. He sought to develop a universal method of reasoning by which to learn as much as possible about the real world. Many of Aristotle's observation-based works remained the leading authority in their fields for 2000 years.

Prior to the invasion of Asia Minor, Aristotle had arranged for his nephew, Callisthenes of Olynthus, to serve as Alexander's court historian. During the first years of Alexander's campaign, Callisthenes lauded his brilliance, but as time went on, became increasingly skeptical as Alexander became more despotic and adopted the trappings of Persian royal authority. He was incensed with Alexander's demand that all who came before him, including Greeks, perform the servile proskynesis ceremony, i.e., crawling along the ground. Like Aristotle, Callisthenes was contemptuous of Alexander's claims of divinity. Alexander, increasingly paranoid near the end of his life, executed Callisthenes as a traitor and sent threatening letters to Aristotle. Back in Athens, Aristotle was regarded as a Macedonian representative of Alexander. When Alexander died suddenly in 323 BCE, the pro-Macedonian government in Athens collapsed. Aristotle fled the city to his mother's estates on a remote island off the coast, saying he would not give the Athenians another opportunity to sin against philosophy, as they had when they condemned Socrates to death. Aristotle died of natural causes within a year.

During the Medieval period scholars rediscovered and adopted much of Aristotle's work. They reconciled his work with Christianity and Aristotelian philosophy became the official philosophy of the Roman Catholic Church. Ironically, during the Renaissance many scientific discoveries were initially rejected because they were not contained in the writings of Aristotle, although his work was based on first-hand observation. Aristotle, together with his predecessors Socrates and Plato, was a founding figure in western philosophy.

**Assos Site**: Note the modern statute of Aristotle at the town entrance. The archeological site entrance is above the mosque at the highest point in town along the late Roman walls. On the acropolis 238 m above sea level are foundations of an early Doric order temple (14 x 30 m) dedicated to Athena in 530 BCE. Six of the original 38 temple columns remain. Down and W of the acropolis stands a well preserved 4$^{th}$ century BCE city wall and gate complete with 14 m high towers. Through the gate an ancient paved road leads NE to a large 2nd century BCE gymnasium (52 x 52 m) adjacent to ruins of a 5th-6th century church to the NE, followed by a 2nd-3rd century BCE agora complete with Hellenistic period shops and a two-storey Doric colonnade to the N.

*Temple of Athena*

(An agora was the market and assembly place of an ancient city-state, generally surrounded with columns and sometimes enclosed within a building. A colonnade is a long sequence of columns joined to a superstructure above.) Next along the road is an ancient bouleuterion (21 x 21 m). Further S toward the ocean is a 3rd century BCE Greek theatre for up to 5,000 spectators. W of the gate outside the city walls is a large Greco-Roman necropolis in which the oldest identified tomb dates back to the 7th century BCE.

The American Archeology Institute was involved in excavating the site in the late 19th century. Professor Nurettin Arslan from Çanakkale Onsekiz Mart University currently directs archeological excavations at Assos and an excellent website describes ongoing work: http://assosarchproject.com/english/index_eng.html

**The Doric order, developed in the western Dorian region of Greece in the 6th century BCE, is the earliest and simplest of three primary orders ancient builders used for designing temples and public buildings: Doric, Ionic and Corinthian. The Doric column could stand on bare floor and was topped by a plain convex disk capital and a square block cut from a single piece of marble. The vertical shaft of the Doric column contained twenty parallel concave carved ridges, known as to as fluting. (Fluting refers to shallow groves running vertically up the shaft of a column with parallel carved niches.) The columns supported an entablature. (An entablature refers to the upper horizontal superstructure of a classical building.) The lower part of an entablature was the architrave. (An architrave is the beam or lintel resting on and**

connecting the columns.) On top of the architrave was a frieze. (A frieze is the area above the architrave decorated with reliefs or sculptures.) The Doric order originated in wooden temples and retained a design of three vertical bands separated by grooves above the center of every column, which appeared like the head of a wooden beam. In Doric order buildings the grooved motif alternated with square panels, either plain or sculpted with reliefs. In contrast, in the Ionic and Corinthian orders this was an uninterrupted area of continuous reliefs. (The column capital is its head or top, wider than the shaft where the column connects to the superstructure above.) The Doric simpler capital is easy to distinguish from an Ionic or Corinthian capital. The Ionic capital has two rounded spirals, which when viewed from the end look like wrapped scrolls, and is decorated with an egg-and-dart motif. The Corinthian capital is decorated with ornate, curling, acanthus leaves. A Doric column is plainer, thicker and heavier than the other later orders. According to Vitruvius, the famous Roman architect who wrote De Architectura, the Doric column is stronger and more masculine because its thicker column diameter-to-height ratio (5-6:1) is based on the relationship between foot length and height of an average man, as opposed to the narrower proportions used in other orders. The Romans combined orders, as at the Sebasteion at Aphrodisias, and used Doric columns for the lowest level of mufti-story buildings, Ionic columns for the mid-level and more slender Corinthian columns for the upper levels. The temple of Athena at Assos is a good example of a Doric temple. Famous Doric structures elsewhere are the Parthenon on the Acropolis at Athens in Greece and the Lincoln Memorial in Washington, DC.

# III ANCIENT REGION OF MYSIA

Mysia is an ancient region in NW Anatolia bordering the Troad to the NW, Lydia to the SE, Phrygia and Bithynia to the E, and Aeolia to the S. The Mysians were Thracians who crossed over to Asia before 1200 BCE and were allied with Troy in the Trojan War. Mysia formed the heart of the Kingdom of **Pergamum** in the 3$^{rd}$ century BCE. In 133 BCE, Pergamum came under Roman rule, and Mysia became part of the Roman province of Asia (western Asia Minor).

**Pergamum** (39° 7' 59" N, 27° 11' 1" E) is an ancient city 113 km N of Izmir on high ground 400 m above a surrounding valley. After the death of Alexander the Great, Lysimachus, one of his leading successors, left a fortune (9000 talents = 234,000 kilos of gold) at Pergamum in the care of his local commander Philetaerus, a talented non-Greek of servile origin who had risen through the military ranks. When Lysimachus died in battle in 282 BCE, Philetaerus seized the treasure and used it to found the Attalid dynasty at Pergamum. In 278 BCE Bithynian King Nicomedes I transported 20,000 large, fierce Celtic Gaul warriors from northern Europe into Anatolia to serve him as mercenaries. Once established in the Gordium-Ancyra area these unruly Gauls, also known as Galatians, plundered and terrorized surrounding kingdoms and became a major security concern for Pergamum. Attalus I (241-197 BCE) of Pergamum managed to defeat a large band of these marauding Galatians, a major achievement that led the local population to regard him as a savior. This military victory was memorialized in the famous Altar of Zeus (now at the Pergamon Museum in Berlin). Attalus I was, however, less successful resisting encroachment from the Seleucid successors of Alexander, prompting him to ally Pergamum with Rome in 212

BCE during the first and second Macedonian Wars. Again under king Eumenes II (197-160 BCE) Pergamum supported Rome against Perseus of Macedonia during the third Macedonian War. In return the Romans granted Pergamum all the former Seleucid domains in Asia Minor because at this juncture of history the Roman Senate opposed any further territorial expansion. Attalid rulers transformed Pergamum into a showcase of Hellenistic art. Splendid Roman villas later uncovered at Pompeii in Italy were designed to resemble Attalid palaces. When Attalus III died without an heir in 133 BCE he bequeathed Pergamum and all its territory to Rome. Pergamum prospered under Roman rule with a $2^{nd}$ century population estimated to have been 150,000. In 1864 Carl Humann rediscovered the ancient city of Pergamum and the altar of Zeus.

**Carl Humann (1839-1896) was the son of an innkeeper in Essen, Germany who developed a strong, self-taught interest in archaeology. As a young man Humann was diagnosed with tuberculosis and moved S to work in a warmer climate, obtaining work in the Ottoman Empire as railway and road construction surveyor. In 1864 he noticed sculptural reliefs built into an $8^{th}$ century late Roman wall at Bergama. Local people used these ancient ruins as a quarry for building materials and took marble to make lime fertilizer. In 1864-1871 Humann managed to stop this destruction, carried out initial excavations, and sent his initial finds Berlin. His steadfast preservation efforts were successful because the German Empire, recently established in 1871, sought to create a world-class museum in Berlin on a par with the British Museum and the Louvre. In 1878 Humann obtained recognition from the Berlin Royal Museum and financial support for his work, as well as formal permission from the Ottoman government to excavate. He led excavations until 1886 and recovered extensive altar of Zeus friezes, which subsequently became the centerpiece of the Pergamon Museum. Carl Humann also played a major role publicizing and excavating ancient ruins at Hierapolis (1887), Magnesia on the Meander (1891-1894), Ephesus (1895), and finally Priene (1895). He was buried at a Catholic cemetery in Smyrna in 1896, and in 1967 was reinterred just S of the base of the altar of Zeus at Pergamum.**

**Pergamum Acropolis Site:** The acropolis is steep, and the cable car option makes sense for most visitors. At Pergamum the original Hellenistic structures were built from local blue-grey andesite stone, while newer Roman monuments were done in marble. Later this Roman marble was either burned in kilns by local people to make lime powder for fertilizer, or carted away to distant European museums, which left in place the city's original Hellenistic character. The first structure encountered near the upper parking lot after arriving at the upper acropolis is the Heroon dedicated to the worship of Pergamene kings. (A heroon was a Hellenistic, temple-like structure dedicated to deified king or a fallen hero.) The Heroon contained a peristyle courtyard (18 x 21 m), an antechamber where meals were eaten in honor of the deified kings, and a separate cult room. (Peristyle refers to a covered colonnade surrounding an inner courtyard or building.) Entering the acropolis via the main gate and proceeding up the stairs, visitors come to the scanty remains of four contiguous royal palaces on the right belonging, from S to N, to: Attalus II, Eumenes II, Attalus I and finally Philetaerus. During the Roman period, the W parts of these palaces were absorbed into the temple of Emperor Trajan, which extends over a large terrace and is the one fully Roman edifice remaining at Pergamum. Corinthian order columns surround the temple, and the podium is reached from a stairway in front.

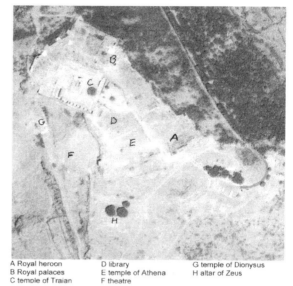

A Royal heroon  
B Royal palaces  
C temple of Traian  
D library  
E temple of Athena  
F theatre  
G temple of Dionysus  
H altar of Zeus  

*Pergamum acropolis*

The Corinthian order is distinguished by the use of two rows of stylized acanthus leaves and four scrolls (volutes) in the capital. Like the Ionic column the Corinthian column shaft has 24 vertical grooves (flutes), but its proportions are even narrower with a height 10 times the diameter at the base. The Corinthian style developed in mainland Greece in the 4th century BCE and was widely used in later centuries by the Romans. The 1st century BCE Roman architect Vitruvius claimed that a Greek sculptor named Callimachus created the Corinthian capital after he saw a woven basket overgrown by an acanthus plant over the grave of a young girl.

*Temple of Trajan*

The temple of Trajan was completed during the reign of his successor Emperor Hadrian. The surrounding frieze includes Medusa heads. Due to her petrifying gaze, Medusa was frequently depicted on temples for protection.

**Trajan (Marcus Ulpius Nerva Traianus) reigned as Roman emperor 98-117.** Born in 53 in Spain, Trajan rose through the ranks of the Roman army during the reign of Emperor Domitian. His father was Governor of Syria in 76-77. Trajan commanded a Roman army along the German frontier and crushed a major revolt in 89. In 96 Emperor Domitian was assassinated and succeeded by the unpopular senator Nerva. To appease the army, Nerva adopted the popular Trajan as heir. Nerva died early in 98, and Trajan was acclaimed emperor. Trajan governed fairly, freed people wrongly imprisoned under Domitian and returned confiscated property. In 101 Trajan attacked Dacia (modern Romania) and completely conquered the territory by 106. In 107 Trajan also seized the Arab Nabatean Kingdom. During this period Trajan corresponded with Pliny the Younger, his governor of Asia, and told him not to harass the Christians unless they were openly practicing the religion – a relatively tolerant "don't ask, don't tell" policy.

In 113 Trajan attacked the Persians and expanded Roman territory to the maximum extent ever reached. In 115 Trajan turned S into Mesopotamia and conquered Nisibis. In 116, one Roman army crossed the Tigris into Adiabene; a second Roman army followed the river S, capturing Babylon. Trajan himself sailed down the Euphrates, dragged his fleet overland into the Tigris, captured Seleucia and finally took the Parthian capital of Ctesiphon. Trajan continued S to the Persian Gulf and famously lamented that he was too old to follow Alexander the Great and conquer India. In 116 Trajan defeated a Parthian army and re-conquered Seleucia, formally deposing the Parthian king Osroes I. However, Roman soldiers behind the front lines failed to conquer the fortress city of Hatra on the Tigris and a Jewish rebellion known as the Kitos War erupted with active Parthian support. While leading this campaign Trajan became gravely ill, dying late in 117 en route back to Rome. The Senate deified Trajan, and his adopted son Hadrian succeeded him.

Medusa, once a priestess of Athena, had been an attractive mortal woman with beautiful hair. Poseidon, god of the sea, developed a passion for Medusa and had sexual intercourse with her on the floor of a temple to Athena. The virgin goddess Athena, enraged by this desecration of her temple, changed Medusa into a horrific monster with snakes for hair and a glance that would turn men to stone. After Medusa had been a fearsome monster for years and had killed countless innocents, brave young Perseus, a mortal son of Zeus, vowed to bring back her head. Hermes gave him a curved sword and a pair of winged sandals; Athena gave him a polished bronze shield, which served as a mirror, and the helmet of invisibility of Pluto.

*Medusa*

Thus armed, Perseus set forth for Medusa's cave. Eventually he found her remote lair in a deep cave surrounded by stone men and beasts. Perseus hid until Medusa slept. Then he gradually approached wearing the invisibility helmet and walking backwards while looking at her reflection in the shield. He cut off her head with the sword of Hermes.

At Pergamum between the temple of Trajan and the temple of Athena are the remains of the library established by Eumenes II with three rooms plus a large reading hall that once contained 200,000 volumes. To protect scrolls and books from moisture, a double wall surrounded the library and shelves were set 50 cm away from the wall. According to ancient sources, the Egyptian Ptolemies were so jealous of the Pergamum library that they stopped exporting papyrus, prompting the Pergamenes to use a new substance made from fine calfskin called "pergaminus" to make books, from which the word "parchment" was derived. After Julius Caesar badly damaged the library of Alexandria in 48 BCE, Mark Antony, as Roman ruler in the E, is believed to have given the contents of the Pergamum library to Cleopatra as a wedding present in 41 BCE.

The temple of Athena, once the most important shrine in ancient Pergamum, dates back to the $3^{rd}$ century BCE. Only the temple foundations remain, just above the theatre. King Eumenes II built a monumental entrance to the temple of Athena with an upper storey using Corinthian columns, a lower storey with Doric columns, and in between the Greek inscription "King Eumenes to Athena, Bringer of Victory." This monumental gate (now at the Pergamon Museum in Berlin) displays an upper frieze of garlands supported by heads of bulls alternating with eagles. Further along, a frieze emphasizes military victory by depicting captured weapons, such as the oval shields of the Galatians and round shields of the Syrians. A $6^{th}$ century late Roman church was built over the N half of the temple. From the temple of Athena a narrow tunnel leads to the theatre.

The attractive theatre of Pergamum is quite steep and provided 10,000 spectators with a panoramic view of the valley below as well as the stage and the city above. The theatre dates back to the 3$^{rd}$ century BCE and is divided by two diazomas into three sections. (A diazoma is a horizontal walkway, which separates lower and upper tiers of seats in ancient theatres.) The king's box is located just above the middle of the lower diazoma. The temple of Dionysus, built against the cliff, is adjacent to the theatre stage where such temples dedicated to the god of wine and ecstasy were often located. The original 3$^{rd}$ century BCE temple was restored in marble during the 211-217 reign of Emperor Caracalla.

*Pergamum Theatre*

Proceeding S from the theatre, the visitor comes to the five-stepped base where the Altar of Zeus once stood. This altar was the Attalid centerpiece of the acropolis, depicting the epic battle between the Olympian gods and the Titans for control over the universe – the Titanomachy. Eumenes II built this altar in 170 BCE to symbolize Pergamum's victory over the marauding Galatians as a triumph of order over chaos. The 133 m long altar frieze was originally painted, with more than a hundred larger-than-life figures, many adorned in gold and bronze. On the W side a wide flight of marble stairs led up to an open court enclosed in a colonnaded stoa. (A stoa is a covered walkway lined with columns, often with shops and located around the central marketplace.) An altar for burning

*Altar of Zeus (Pergamon Museum in Berlin)*

offerings to the gods stood inside the court. In the mid 6$^{th}$ century early Christians broke the altar into pieces to use in a defensive wall, in which they were preserved. Near the altar base at Pergamum stands the tomb of Carl Humann, the German railroad engineer who spotted the pieces of the Altar of Zeus in the wall, recognized their historic importance, and saved them from destruction by sending them to Berlin.

The Titanomachy was a divine war. Unlike his five siblings, Zeus was hidden away by his mother and not swallowed by his father Cronus (Saturn to Romans). After reaching adulthood, Zeus forced his father Cronus to disgorge his siblings. After their release these Olympic gods, along with allies they managed to gather, challenged the elder gods for control over the universe. Zeus, Poseidon, and Pluto received weapons from the three Cyclopes to help in the war: Zeus the thunderbolt, Pluto the Helm of Darkness, and Poseidon the trident.

The war lasted for ten

*Titanomachy (Berlin)*

years and ended with the victory of the younger Olympian gods. Following their victory, Zeus and his two brothers, Poseidon and Pluto, drew lots for realms to rule. Zeus received the sky, Poseidon the seas, and Pluto the underworld of Tartarus.

A smaller frieze on a wall inside the Altar of Pergamum depicted the life of Telephos, son of Hercules and founder of Pergamum.

Telephos was the founder of Pergamum and a son of Hercules and princess Auge, daughter of the Greek King Aleus of Tegea. The Telephos frieze dates back to 165 BCE and depicts his life story in framed chronological episodes delineated with columns, pillars, and trees. Aleus had heard an oracle predicting that a son of Auge would kill one of Aleus' own sons. To prevent this scenario Aleus installed his daughter Auge as priestess at the temple of Athena in Tegea, a position requiring perpetual virginity. During a visit to Tegea, Hercules fell in love with Auge and seduced her. Upon discovering that his daughter was pregnant, the furious Aleus exposed the baby to die on Mount Parthenium and cast his daughter out to sea alone in a small boat to drown. Instead, Auge crossed the Aegean Sea and landed at Mysia in Asia Minor. Teuthras, king of Mysia, discovered Auge when she landed, found her charming and adopted her as his daughter. As a priestess of Athena, Auge established her worship in Mysia.

Meanwhile the baby Telephos survived on Mount Parthenium because a lioness suckled him and various nymphs took care of him through the intercession of Hercules. When Telephos grew up, he made his way to Tegea and encountered some local youths who queried him about his origins. When he admitted his ignorance, one youth in particular taunted him. Infuriated, Telephos grabbed him by the hair and threw him a great distance, inadvertently killing the youth, who turned out to be Lycurgus son of Aleus and, unbeknownst to Telephos, his own uncle. To avoid the vengeance of Aleus, Telephos quickly left Greece and crossed the Aegean Sea to Asia Minor. Eventually Telephos arrived in Mysia at a time when the kingdom faced foreign invasion. King Teuthras welcomed Telephos who agreed to take up arms in defense of Mysia. His courageous actions so impressed Teuthras, who had no son, that he decided to make Telephos his heir and insisted he marry his adopted daughter Auge. She was secretly opposed the match, wishing to remain faithful to the memory of Hercules, so she took a sword to the wedding bed, intending to kill Telephos. After an enormous snake miraculously appeared in the bed between them, the frightened Auge confessed her murderous intention and told Telephos the story of her seduction by Hercules. At this point they recognized each other as mother and son.

Despite not consummating the marriage with Auge, Telephos eventually became king of Mysia and founder of Pergamum. Telephos married Hiera, a princess of the Amazons allied with Mysia and Troy. Not long after their marriage, a Greek raiding party arrived at Mysia and Telephos led the local forces against them. In the fighting the Greeks killed the Amazon Hiera, after which the heart-broken Telephos called a temporary truce to hold her funeral. After fighting resumed Telephos killed many of the Greeks but was seriously wounded in battle at the river Kaikos when Dionysus caught him in a grapevine and Achilles struck him with his spear. Although Telephos managed to drive away the Greeks, he was unable to recover from his wound. Finally he consulted the Oracle at Delphi and was told, "He that wounded shall also heal." In desperation Telephos dressed up like a beggar and went to Mycenae in search of Achilles and the cure for his wound. To force the issue, Telephos went to the house of king Agamemnon, seized his infant son Orestes, and demanded that Achilles cure his wound in return for the baby Orestes. Although the Greek commanders were willing to cooperate because they believed they could get to Troy with Telephos as a guide, Achilles declared he was no doctor and had no idea how to cure Telephos. Odysseus, however, figured out that the deeper meaning of the oracle referred to the spear of Achilles rather than the warrior himself. They applied a little rust from the spear to the wound each day and soon it was healed. As agreed, Telephos guided the Greeks to Troy but then refused to switch sides and join the attack, instead returning home to Pergamum.

Although many tourists only visit the Pergamum acropolis, much more awaits further down the hill along an ancient road. S of the altar is the upper agora. An agora was the assembly place and market of an ancient city-state, generally surrounded with columns and sometimes enclosed within a building. Along the right (W) of the road are ruins of a Roman era bath complex. Next is an interconnected bath-heroon complex dedicated to Diodorus Pasporos, a prominent 1st century Pergamene citizen who managed to persuade the Romans to reduce reparation payments imposed after the Mithradatic wars. The complex includes reliefs along its walls depicting weapons, fighting cocks, and a helmet.

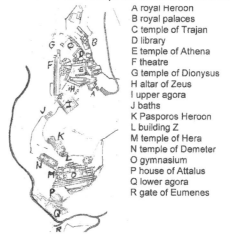

A royal Heroon
B royal palaces
C temple of Trajan
D library
E temple of Athena
F theatre
G temple of Dionysus
H altar of Zeus
I upper agora
J baths
K Pasporos Heroon
L building Z
M temple of Hera
N temple of Demeter
O gymnasium
P house of Attalus
Q lower agora
R gate of Eumenes

In 180-160 BCE King Eumenes II erected a large two-level state guesthouse, now known as Building Z, in the steep hillside with a central court and surrounding halls. During the 2nd century elaborate mosaic floors were added. In 178 an earthquake covered the floors with debris and preserved the mosaics, which are now protected by a modern shelter. In the center a large mosaic depicts Dionysus as a child held by Silenus. The Dionysian theme continues in the next room with a mosaic containing sixteen octagons depicting theatre masks, maenads (female followers of Dionysus) and satyrs. (Satyrs had the upper body of men, horns on their heads, the lower body of goats, and loved wine, women, song and roaming freely in wooded mountains.)

*Pergamum*

**Silenus was a companion and tutor to Dionysus. He was a satyr of the forest with the ears, tail and legs of a goat. A**

notorious consumer of wine, he was usually drunk and had to be supported by satyrs or carried by a donkey. Silenus was the oldest, wisest and most drunken of the followers of Dionysus. When intoxicated, Silenus possessed great knowledge and prophetic power.

Following the main road from the Pergamum acropolis further down, the visitor comes to the 2$^{nd}$ century BCE temple of Hera, wife of Zeus, built by King Attalus II. This Doric temple faced S, and its front stairway, and foundations with columns remain in place, with a stairway in front.

Hera (Juno to Romans) is queen of the Olympian gods, wife and sister of Zeus. Hera is the goddess of marriage and childbirth, and takes special care of married women. She sits on a golden throne beside Zeus and when she enters the chamber of the gods, all stand in deference. The children of Hera and Zeus are Ares, god of war; Hebe, goddess of youthfulness; Eileithyia, goddess of childbirth; Eris, goddess of discord; and Hephaestus, god of workmanship. When Hephaestus was born, Hera was so disgusted with his ugliness that she threw him off Mount Olympus, which is why he is lame. As first lady of Olympus, Hera always has a vengeful eye out for Zeus' frequent marital infidelities and seeks revenge on his many lovers and their offspring. When Hera discovered that Zeus had impregnated Leto, she prevented her daughter Eileithyia, goddess of childbirth, from assisting her. Fortunately for Leto, it was easy to deliver Artemis, the first of her twins, on her own. Artemis then served as midwife during the much more difficult birth of Apollo.

On another occasion when Zeus was involved with a beautiful young nymph named Io, Hera became suspicious. To avoid detection, Zeus turned Io into a beautiful white heifer. Still suspicious, Hera demanded the heifer as a present, which Zeus granted her to maintain his appearance of innocence. As soon as Hera got hold of Io, she chained her to a sacred olive tree and ordered Argus to keep constant watch on her to ensure that Zeus would not come near. Argus was a giant with one hundred eyes, the perfect watchman because he would always have some eyes awake and watchful. Zeus then commanded Hermes to kill Argus. Hermes, disguised as a shepherd, put all of Argus' eyes asleep by slowly reciting the tale of Pan and Syrinx, and then killed him with a stone. When Hera learned Argus was dead, she took his eyes out and placed them in the peacock's plumage. Hera then sent a gadfly to sting poor Io and drive her far away across the Bosphorus to Egypt.

The story of Hercules, which means "fame of Hera," is intimately connected with Hera. Zeus impregnated the mortal woman Alcmene by taking the form of her husband. When Alcmene was in labor, Hera instructed her daughter Eileithyia, goddess of childbirth, to prevent the birth by crossing her legs. As Alcmene was near death, her clever servant Galanthis figured out what was happening. Galanthis then fooled Eileithyia, telling her the baby had been already born. The startled goddess jumped up and unclasped Alcmene's legs, which enabled Hercules to be born. Upon realizing the deception, Hera turned Galanthis into a weasel. Later Zeus tricked Hera into nursing the infant Heracles; discovering his true identity Hera angrily pulled him off her breast, and a spurt of her milk formed the Milky Way. Throughout his life Hera continually obstructed Hercules. When he finally came to Olympus as an immortal god, the two reconciled and Hercules married Hera's daughter Hebe, goddess of youthfulness. During the Trojan War, Hera, furious that Paris had chosen Aphrodite as the fairest despite Hera's offer to make him ruler of Europe and Asia, favored the Greeks. Hera was the leading supporter of Jason and the Argonauts in their quest for the Golden Fleece, although she eventually became disenchanted with Jason due to his treatment of Medea.

To the W lies Pergamum's temple of Demeter, first built by Philetaerus to accommodate about 800 people, with a large rectangular terrace and unusual Aeolic palm leaf capitals on Doric columns. Next can be seen the large 2$^{nd}$ century BCE gymnasium, built on three terraces with an upper gymnasium for young men, a middle gymnasium for adolescent boys and a lower gymnasium used for male children. Archeological excavation shows that to the E a part of the middle gymnasium contained a 2$^{nd}$ century imperial cult section dedicated to the emperor, as well as to Hermes and Hercules, gods associated with physical prowess. Continuing down the ancient main street past the lower gymnasium, visitors pass remains of the house of Consul Attalus to the right, which contains ancient floor mosaics and wall murals. (In the Roman Republic Consul was the supreme office of power held by two individuals simultaneously for one year.) In the early 2$^{nd}$ century BCE Eumenes II built a second lower agora to accommodate Pergamum's growing population and prosperity, a public marketplace that became the center of the city's commercial activity. Inscriptions uncovered at the lower agora include regulations governing construction and maintenance of roads, cisterns, fountains and houses.

The **Pergamum temple of Serapis** (39° 7' 19" N, 27° 11' 1" E) stands far down from the acropolis in the modern town of Bergama. The temple is a vast redbrick hulk known locally as Kizil Avlu (Red Hall). This temple was erected during the time of Emperor Hadrian (117-138) when worship of Serapis and his consort Isis was quite popular. The large rectangular temple (60 x 26 m) stands 19 m high, adjacent to two huge domed rotundas. The original monumental entrance was via four central columns of the portico leading to the main building through a huge bronze door. (A portico is a porch with a roof over a walkway supported by columns leading to the entrance of a building.) Religious ceremonies were conducted inside in semi-darkness where a 10 m high statue of Serapis stood in the center of a podium surrounded by water. A passage through the podium and up the middle of the base enabled priests to

*Temple of Serapis*

speak to worshippers as if the words were coming directly from the statue. The temple towers flanking the main building had courtyards with pools used for ablutions at each end, flanked by stoas on three sides. The roofs of these stoas were supported by twice-life-size column-statues of atlantes or caryatids. (Atlantes are male column statues derived from the titan Atlas who supported heaven at the ends of the earth; caryatids are female column statues derived from the ancient Greek women of Caryae who danced with a high, round basket-like hat on their heads.)

Atlas was the powerful Titan who supported the heavens. Earlier Atlas had sided with the Titans in their war against the Olympians, the Titanomachy. When the Titans were defeated, many were confined to Tartarus, but Zeus condemned Atlas to stand at the western edge of Gaia, the Earth, and hold up Ouranos, the Sky, on his shoulders, to prevent the two from resuming their primordial embrace. Later, out of pity, Athena showed Atlas Medusa's head, which turned him into the stone mountains in North Africa, known as the Atlas mountain range.

During the 1st century, John the Apostle ordained Saint Antipas as the first bishop of Pergamum. In the New Testament Book of Revelation St. John mentioned the Christian church at Pergamum as one of the original Seven Churches. At this temple of Serapis in 92 St. Antipas was a victim of an early clash between Christians and Serapis worshippers. He was martyred when an angry mob burned him alive in the "brazen bull," a device used to burn incense, which represented the bull Apis. During the 5th century, Christians converted the main building into a church dedicated to the Apostle John and replaced the E wall with an apse. (An apse is the semi-circular recessed area at the end of a church, where holds the altar and where clergy are seated during services.) The temple of Serapis rotunda to the N currently houses a mosque. The German Archeological Institute has worked on this structure: http://www.dainst.org/en/project/pergamon-red-hall?ft=all

Serapis was a syncretistic god introduced in Alexandria derived from Osiris, Egyptian god of the underworld and consort of Isis, and Apis, an Egyptian bull-deity representing strength and fertility. Following the death of Alexander the Great in 323 BCE, his military successors took control of different parts of his empire. Ptolemy I Soter (323-283 BCE) was the first Macedonian king to rule Egypt. Ptolemy sought common religious symbols and beliefs to bring together his Greek and Egyptian subjects and promote his own legitimacy. According to tradition, the dying Alexander consulted Serapis at Babylon in 323 BCE. Although a cult of Osirapis, an agricultural god in the form of a sacred bull embodying principles of life after death, had long existed in the Egyptian city of Memphis, Ptolemy deliberately expanded, supported and embellished Osirapis with Greek divine attributes and made him into Serapis. Under Greek influence, Serapis changed from a mummified human with the head of a bull into a completely anthropomorphic form with long hair and a long beard, wearing a Greek tunic, seated on a throne with the three-headed dog Cerberus at his feet. On his head Serapis wore a basket of corn measure, representing fertility. Greeks attributed Serapis with the power over the sun of Helios and Apollo; the fertility and natural growth powers of Dionysus; the sovereignty over the underworld of Pluto; and the healing arts of Asclepius. Serapis appeared to mortals in dreams. He became widely popular throughout the major cities of Mediterranean world as his cult quickly spread following the trade routes from Alexandria to as far away as Britain. Outside Egypt Serapis replaced Osiris as the consort of the highly popular and widely worshipped Isis. In Rome, Serapis was worshiped at a 1<sup>st</sup> century BCE sanctuary of Isis. Worship of Isis and Serapis became particularly popular with Romans late in the 1<sup>st</sup> century. The largest and most famous center of the worship of

*Serapis (Antalya Museum)*

Serapis was at his great temple in Alexandria, considered a world wonder and a major pilgrimage site. The Serapis Temple possessed a library of as many as 300,000 volumes, an annex of the Great Library of Alexandria. Worship of Serapis continued until 385 when a Christian mob, led by the Patriarch, destroyed the ancient temple of Serapis at Alexandria.

The 4th century BCE **Pergamum Asclepium** (39° 7' 9" N, 27° 9' 56" E) lies SW of the acropolis and the town of Bergama. (An asclepium was an ancient hospital complex devoted to the healing and physical recovery of patients and dedicated to the god Asclepius.) The highly influential physician Galen worked at the Pergamum Asclepium for many years.

**Galen, the most famous physician of the Roman Empire, was born in 129 at Pergamum into an upper class Pergamene family. He began studying medicine at age 16 at Pergamum, and studied for twelve years at Smyrna, Corinth and Alexandria. When Galen returned to Pergamum at age 28, the Asclepium high priest appointed him surgeon for gladiators, which gave him considerable practical experience treating patients. Galen strongly believed in the ability of the human body to restore itself and based his treatment on improved diet, exercise and baths. He contributed significantly to medical knowledge of circulatory and nervous systems. In 162 Galen went to Rome and eventually became court physician for co-emperors Marcus Aurelius and Lucius Verus. His prolific writing is one of the main sources of information about the ancient world and his medical texts remained in use in Europe until the 17th century. Galen was of the opinion that Christian martyrdom was "irrational."**

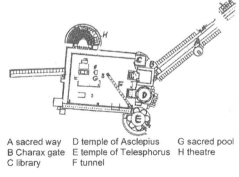

A sacred way   D temple of Asclepius   G sacred pool
B Charax gate  E temple of Telesphorus  H theatre
C library      F tunnel

*Pergamum Asclepium*

**Pergamum Asclepium Site:** Most extant ruins date from the time of Emperors Hadrian in 117-138 and Antoninus Pius in 138-161. More marble survived here than on the acropolis because the low-lying site was buried. The approach to the

Asclepium is along the sacred way, an 820 m long colonnaded street. The sacred way ends at a monumental gate decorated with Corinthian columns built by Pergamene consul Claudias Charax in 142. The square-shaped remains of the library stand to the N of the gate where a statue of Emperor Hadrian was discovered (now at Bergama Museum). S of the gate is the circular, domed temple of Asclepius with interior angular niches for statues of health-related deities, such as Hygeia. Further S is the two-storey circular temple of Telesphorus treatment center, divided into six sections with large stone basins on the ground floor. Patients received treatments including massage, mud baths, medicinal herbs and application of ointments. From here an 80 m long tunnel runs diagonally to the sacred pool in the center of the enclosure.

**Hygeia and Telesphorus:** Hygeia was the goddess of health, cleanliness and sanitation. While her father Asclepius was directly responsible for healing, she was responsible for preventing sickness and maintaining good health. Our word "hygiene" is derived from her name. The god Telesphorus, meaning accomplisher, was a dwarf who always wore a cap and symbolized recovery from illness.

*Asclepium Sacred Way*

Telesphorus was originally a Celtic god whom the Galatians brought to Anatolia in the 3$^{rd}$ century BCE. Asclepius adopted him at Pergamum and his fame spread throughout the Roman Empire.

To the W is the theatre, built for 3500 people and used during festivals of Asclepius. The complex once employed many caretakers, bath attendants and ritual singers, all managed by a hereditary priesthood. Patients bathed in sacred spring water and recounted their dreams to

*Asclepium Theatre*

priests who developed cures based on this input. After completing their treatment, patients left Asclepius money, sacrificial animals, cakes and votive offerings, such as terracotta models representing healed body parts.

Asclepius was god of medicine and healing; his name literally means, "to cut open." He was a son of Apollo and a mortal woman Coronis, whom Artemis killed when she was pregnant because she took another lover besides Apollo. Artemis rescued the unborn Asclepius from his dying mother's womb and carried him to the centaur Chiron. (A centaur is a being with the head, arms and upper body of a man with the lower body and four legs of a horse.) Chiron, known as a great healer, was also highly regarded as a tutor. Chiron raised Asclepius and instructed him in the art of medicine. Asclepius had six daughters: Hygeia (hygiene), Iaso (medicine), Aceso (healing), Aglaea (healthy glow), Panacea (universal cure) and Meditrina (serpent-bearer). The rod of Asclepius, a snake-entwined staff, was derived from the Phoenician Eshmun and remains to this day the symbol of medicine. From about 350 BCE onwards, belief in Asclepius became popular and pilgrims flocked to healing temples of Asclepius, known as Asclepieia, for treatment. Hippocrates, known as the father of medicine, began his work at the Asclepium located on the Greek island of Kos. The original Hippocratic Oath began with the words "I swear by Apollo the Physician and by Asclepius and by Hygeia and Panacea and by all the gods"... The Asclepium at Pergamum was one of the leading hospitals in the ancient world. Ritual purification was followed by offerings or sacrifices to Asclepius. Non-venomous snakes, which appeared to be reborn when they shed their skin, were sacred to Asclepius, and lived at the Asclepieia where the sick and injured slept. The snakes were commonly used in healing rituals. The healing cult of Asclepius was a major rival to early Christianity with its emphasis on faith healing in the name of Jesus. This may explain why early Christians reviled snakes.

Considerable information about Pergamum is available in English on the websites of Berlin's Pergamon Museum and the German Archeological Institute:
http://www.smb.museum/smb/standorte/index.php?p=2&objID=27&n=15

http://www.dainst.org/en/project/pergamon?ft=all

# IV ANCIENT REGION OF AEOLIA

Aeolia lies along the W coast bordered by Mysia to the N and Ionia to the S. Early Greek settlers speaking an Aeolic dialect arrived after the Trojan War. According to tradition, they were descendants of Agamemnon. The most powerful of twelve ancient Aeolian League cities was **Cyme**, whose ruins are still visible. Lydia ruled Aeolia until Cyrus the Great defeated Croesus in 547 BCE and incorporated the region into the Persian Empire. Aeolia was part of the territory Pergamum bequeathed to Rome in 133 BCE.

**Cyme** (38° 45' 34" N, 26° 56' 8" E) is 40 km S of Bergama near the village of Namurt Limani on the Aegean coast. Cyme, the largest and most important of the Aeolian cities, provided essential naval support to Persian Emperors Darius and Xerxes during their $5^{th}$ and $4^{th}$ century BCE campaigns against the Greeks. The Persian survivors of the Battle of Salamis in 480 BCE returned to Cyme. Aphrodite was worshipped at Cyme from the founding of her temple in the $4^{th}$ century BCE until the $2^{nd}$ century BCE.

**Cyme Site:** Today Cyme is a modest, partially excavated site located near a container-shipping port directly on the coast. On a hilltop to the N are remains of a small, Ionic style temple dedicated to Isis and Osiris. Visitors see remains of a large building and two rows of columns standing on low ground near the road. Much has been pilfered over the centuries and only the cavea remains from the theater on the side of a hill. (The cavea was the seating area for spectators in an ancient theatre.) W of the theater two harbor piers lie 1-2 m underwater in the harbor. Heavy vegetative cover makes it difficult to explore. The Italian Archeological Mission to Cyme in Aeolia provides additional information about this site in Italian at: http://www.kyme.info/joomla/

# V ANCIENT REGION OF IONIA

Ionia is a mountainous coastal area S of Aeolia and N of Caria with fertile valleys, named after Ionians from mainland Greece who settled before 1000 BCE.  Merchants and mercenaries from Ionia established trade and worked in the Near East where they acquired the alphabet (from Phoenicia), iron technology, sculpture (from Egyptian funerary decorations), and masonry.  During the $7^{th}$-$6^{th}$ centuries BCE important Ionian cities developed and prosperity grew, as demonstrated by a dramatic increase in the number of stone temples.  Common interests led twelve of these cities to form the Ionian League: **Miletus**, **Priene**, **Ephesus**, **Teos**, **Phocaea**, **Erythrai**, Lebedus, Colophon, Clazomenae, Chios, Myus, and Samos.  To this day important structures remain from the first six Ionian League cities listed.  **Didyma,** an important prophecy center second only to the Oracle at Delphi, was managed by Miletus.  Similarly, Colophon maintained an important prophecy center at **Claros**.  Although the city of **Magnesia ad Maeandrum** was located within Ionia, it was not included in the early Ionian League because the original settlers were Aeolians.

Lydian King Croesus conquered Ionia and was in turn defeated by Cyrus the Great of Persia in 546 BCE.  Miletus led an Ionian rebellion against Persian rule in 499-494 BCE supported by Athens.  The Persians brutally suppressed the revolt and burned Miletus in 494 BCE.  Then Persia launched a retaliatory war against Athens, which ultimately led to the defeat of Persia in 479 BCE.  In 449 BCE the Persian Empire formally gave up sovereignty of the Ionian Greeks.  Although nominally independent, the Ionian cities fell increasingly under the control of Athens and the Delian League.  Following the Peloponnesian War between Athens and Sparta, the Ionian Greeks returned to Persian rule in 386 BCE.  After 334 BCE Alexander the Great permanently expelled the Persians and conquered their territories. After the death of Alexander, Ionia was ruled by various Macedonian successors and then by Pergamum. Under Roman rule after 133 BCE, many Ionian cities supported rebel Mithridates VI of Pontus in 88-63 BCE. When Rome eventually defeated Mithridates many Ionian cities were forced to pay reparations and lost political influence. Ionian cities suffered greatly during the Roman civil wars but prospered when Emperor Augustus restored stability after the Battle of Actium in 31 BCE. Ionia is well known in popular literature; for example scenes from Harry Sidebottom's excellent *Warrior of Rome* series take place at extant sites here.

**Phocaea**, modern Foça (meaning seal), was the most northern Ionian city with two natural harbors containing small islands. According to Herodotus, Phocaeans were the first Greeks to make long distance sea-voyages. In the 6$^{th}$ century BCE settlers from Phocaea founded colonies at Massalia (Marseilles, France), Alalia (Corsica, France), Emporion Empúries, Spain) and Elea (Velia, Italy). Although little remains of 

*Persian Tomb*

ancient Phocaea, the 4$^{th}$ century BCE **Persian tomb** (38° 39' 37" N, 26° 49' 2" E) stands 7 km E of Foça along the main road. Known locally as Tas Kule or rock tower, this funerary monument was carved directly out of solid rock. The structure has a lower 2.7 m high rectangular storey (9 x 6 m) surmounted by a second 1.9 m high storey (3 x 3 m). Although ancient Lycian tombs had two stories, the front entrance pattern is more Lydian, and unlike Lycian tombs, an entranceway leads to a small chamber opening into the funerary chamber on the ground floor. Four steps between the two levels suggest strong Persian influence. Most archeologists believe this hybrid monument was built for a Persian aristocrat or a local ruler serving the Persians.

**Erythrai** (38° 22' 53" N, 26° 28' 52" E), modern Ildiri, is a small, seldom visited site 20 km NE of Çeşme on a small peninsula overlooking the sea. Erythrai was established on this site from at least the 4$^{th}$ century BCE. The city's shifting of alliances back and forth between Persia and the Greeks is reflected in inscriptions found at the site. Although one 4th century BCE inscription calls Persian governor Mausolus a benefactor of Erythrai, the city is known to have signed a mutual defense treaty with Hermeias, the ruler of Assos and an opponent of Persia (later killed by the Persians). In 334 BCE Alexander the Great freed the city from Persian rule and, like the other Ionian cities it was later ruled by Pergamum and then Rome. Erythrai flourished under Roman rule until a series of earthquakes hit the region in the 1st century.

**Erythrai Site:** Extant ruins include a 4-5 m thick Hellenistic wall on the landward side dating back to the early 3$^{rd}$ century BCE. The remains of a theatre are visible in the N slope of the acropolis. In the 1960s the prominent Turkish archeologist Professor Ekrem Akurgal of Ankara University excavated the site. This work is described in English and Turkish at:
http://www.izmirturizm.gov.tr/dosya/1-279926/h/cesme-son.pdf

**Teos** (38° 10' 38" N, 26° 47' 4" E), near modern Sigacik 18 km SW of Seferihisar, was founded in the 9$^{th}$ century BCE on a narrow isthmus between two natural harbors. The city was famous for its wine and worship of Dionysus, the patron deity of drama as well as wine and agriculture. In the 3$^{rd}$ century BCE the Ionian actors at Teos established a guild, which provided actors for the theatres all over Asia Minor. Teos assisted the Romans against the Macedonian Seleucids and initially prospered under Roman rule, but gradually declined due to commercial competition from Smyrna.

**Teos Site:** Buildings at Teos are made from a local blue-grey limestone. The principal structure at the site was a huge temple of Dionysus (19 x 35 m), built by Hermogenes in 130 BCE and restored during the $2^{nd}$ century reign of Emperor Hadrian. The Ionic temple of Dionysus at Teos strongly resembled the much

*Temple of Dionysus at Teos*

earlier temple of Athena at Priene built by Pythius except that the cella or sacred chamber is only slightly larger than the entranceway. (The cella was the sacred, windowless inner chamber of a temple.) The influential Roman architect Vitruvius greatly appreciated the design of this temple and lauded Hermogenes in his written work, which had a major impact on architectural style throughout the empire.

**Marcus Vitruvius (70-15 BCE) was a famous Roman architect who wrote De Architectura dedicated to the Emperor Augustus and known today as The Ten Books on Architecture. He asserts that a structure must be solid, useful, and beautiful. Vitruvius strongly endorsed the rules on symmetry and proportion Hermogenes applied to the Temple of Dionysus at Teos. He particularly admired Hermogenes' use of so-called Eustyle Intercolumniation, i.e., requiring that spacing between columns be exactly 2.25 times the column diameter, and that the Ionic column height be 9.5 times the column diameter. For Vitruvius, harmonious and symmetrical relations among the components of**

**a temple are fixed so that changing one element requires proportionate change everywhere.**

Under the Romans the Teos temple of Dionysus was re-consecrated to the imperial cult of Tiberius. Near the temple an ancient main street has been uncovered. The Roman odeon lies NE of the temple of Dionysus, SE of the theatre. Amidst the heavy vegetation, sections of $3^{rd}$ century Hellenistic walls to the W of the temple of Dionysus are still visible. The remains of the stage and cavea of $2^{nd}$ century BCE theatre stand on the SW side of the acropolis. To the NE of the acropolis are the largely buried remains of the gymnasium where an ancient inscription specified remuneration for teachers.

At the **Teos Harbor Site** (38° 10' 17" N, 26° 47' 25" E) remnants of an ancient Roman pier can still be seen. Dr. Numan Tuna of the Middle East Technical University is excavating Teos: http://tacdam.metu.edu.tr/index.php@option=com_content&task=view&id=18&Itemid=58

**Claros** (38° 0' 15" N, 27° 11' 34" E), 32 km N of Kusadasi, was a religious site with an ancient temple of Apollo with an oracle, similar to those at Delphi and Didyma. According to tradition Mopsus, a celebrated seer and son of Apollo from the mortal daughter of the ancient seer Tiresias, founded the oracle at Claros. The accuracy of Mopsus' prophesies was celebrated in the ancient Greek saying, "it's more certain than Mopsus" for something of absolute certainty. Unlike the oracles at Didyma and Delphi, the oracle at Claros was always male. Although oracles held office for only one year, temple priests and poetic verse composers were appointed for life. The temple was built around a sacred fresh water spring. The oracle would sit in a room below the temple cella (inner chamber) and divine a prophecy after drinking the holy water. Advice seekers waited on stone benches in an outer chamber and received prophecies written in poetic verse. The Claros temple dates back to the 7th century BCE and was mentioned by Homer. According to tradition, Alexander the Great established Smyrna (modern Izmir) after he consulted with the oracle at Claros about a dream. In the year 18 the popular general Germanicus, grandson of Augustus and adopted son of Tiberius, consulted the oracle and was warned correctly that his death was imminent.

**Germanicus Julius Caesar (15 BCE – 19 CE), commonly known as Germanicus, was a member of the Julio-Claudian dynasty. He was grandson-in-law and great-nephew of Emperor Augustus, brother of Emperor Claudius and father of Emperor Caligula. Germanicus was extremely popular among Roman citizens and considered the likely heir of Augustus. However, in the year 4 Augustus was persuaded by his wife Livia to appoint his stepson Tiberius, her son from her first marriage, as his successor. As a compromise, Augustus insisted that Tiberius adopt Germanicus as a son and name him heir. Germanicus held several successful military commands, and was an inspired leader, loved by his soldiers. After the death of Augustus in 14 rebellious soldiers demanded that Germanicus become Emperor; Germanicus demurred, put down the rebellion and stayed loyal to Tiberius. Despite Germanicus' repeated successes as supreme commander in Germania, Emperor Tiberius recalled his nephew and sent him to a command in Asia. In 18 Germanicus conquered Cappadocia and Commagene. Then on a visit to Antioch the following year Germanicus died suddenly, apparently poisoned.**

**Claros Site:** The 2nd century BCE propylon stood at the S edge of the site was where visitors embarked by ship to a colonnaded sacred way lined with statues to the temple of Apollo. (A propylon was a monumental gateway styled after the entrance

*Claros*

to the acropolis in Athens). Inscriptions carved on the columns named worshippers from throughout the Roman world, as well as youths chosen to sing hymns to Apollo. The 4th century BCE temple was built on a five-step platform (26 x 46 m) with eleven Doric columns along the long side, six along the short side. Two columns remain on the N side. Because the temple lies below the water table, many of the ruins are now submerged. Inside the sacred chamber of the temple were large statues (8 m high) of Apollo, his sister Artemis and their mother Leto. Parts of these statues now stand NW of the temple. A large altar (19 x 9 m) stands 30 m E of the temple of Apollo. Between the temple and the altar are four rows of iron rings fixed on heavy blocks used to tie down a hundred cattle for a large-scale, simultaneous animal sacrifice. Two separate altars, one dedicated to Apollo and the other to Dionysus, were sometimes placed on top of the main altar. A sundial dedicated to Dionysus stood nearby. To the S of the main temple a smaller 6th century BCE Ionic temple was dedicated to Artemis. Although archeologists from the University of Izmir in Turkey are now primarily responsible for the site, French archeologists played a leading role in earlier excavations and an excellent French diplomatic mission website describes this work in English at: http://www.diplomatie.gouv.fr/en/global-issues/education-research/archaeology/archaeology-notebooks/ancient-east/turkey-claros/


**Ephesus** (37° 56' 8" N, 27° 20' 45" E), one of the largest and most important cities of the 1st-2nd century Roman Empire, lies 3 km SW of modern Selçuk. These extensive remains include grand buildings constructed at private expense by leading citizens as a reflection of civic pride and social status. In 560 BCE Lydian King Croesus conquered Ephesus but was soon superseded by Persia. A rebellion against Persia at Ephesus in 498 BCE precipitated the Greco-Persian wars. After Alexander defeated the Persians and established Macedonian rule, one of his successors, Lysimachus, ruled Ephesus and moved the city to its present location to avoid flooding. Lysimachus built the first 8 km long wall around the city, most of which is gone although an ancient square watchtower, known as Saint Paul's prison, remains on a low hill to the W. After the demise of the Macedonians, Ephesus was ruled first by Pergamum, and later Rome. Under Roman rule after 133 BCE, many citizens of Ephesus supported the rebellion led by Mithridates VI and slaughtered a large number of resident Romans in 88 BCE. When Augustus became emperor in 27 BCE, he made Ephesus the capital of the Roman province of Asia. Ephesus reached its peak prosperity during the $1^{st}$-$3^{rd}$ centuries with a population of about 250,000. With a population only surpassed by Rome, Alexandria and Antioch, Ephesus became the most important commercial center in W Anatolia.

Ephesus became an early Christian center during the mid-$1^{st}$ century. St. John and the Virgin Mary settled in Ephesus in the year 37, and John is believed to have written his Gospel at Ephesus. Ephesus was one of the seven cities he addressed in the New Testament Book of Revelation, indicating the strength of its Christian community. St. Paul lived in the city 52-54 working with the Christian congregation and organizing missionary activity in the hinterlands. Paul's conflict with local artisans whose livelihood depended on selling religious trinkets to pilgrims visiting the temple of Artemis forced him to leave town. Even after he was imprisoned in Rome in 62, Paul continued to write letters to the Christian community at Ephesus.

Emperor Constantine I rebuilt much of the city and erected new public baths. In 406 St. John Chrysostom, the energetic Christian patriarch of Constantinople, led a mob armed with hammers to destroy the temple of Artemis. Chrysostom also managed to usurp the authority of the Ephesus bishops and establish the Virgin Mary as the patroness of Constantinople, instead of Ephesus despite her earlier residence. An earthquake in 614 heavily damaged the town. Over the centuries the commercial importance of the city steadily declined as the harbor silted up, despite repeated attempts at dredging. Now the former harbor is 6 km inland. Ephesus declined further after Arab raiders under Muslim Caliph Muawiyah I sacked the city in 654-655.

Mark Twain devoted Chapter 40 of Innocents Abroad to Ephesus. When he visited in 1867, John Turtle Wood had only recently begun his work and the city still was largely unexcavated. The most striking difference was the sense of isolation and abandonment Twain described, quite a contrast to the throngs of daily visitors nowadays. Twain wrote, "We shall never know what magnificence is, until this imperial city is laid bare to the sun." He would doubtless be impressed at how much more the modern visitor can see.

**John Turtle Wood (1821–1890) was the British engineer and archaeologist who first rediscovered Ephesus. In 1858, Wood designed railway stations for the Smyrna-Aydin railroad in the Ottoman Empire. Wood was well aware of the New Testament account of Saint Paul being shouted down the followers of Artemis, and her temple being regarded as one of the Seven Wonders of the ancient world. He became determined to rediscover the temple, which had been lost for at least five hundred years. In 1863 Wood began a full-time search with a modest expense allowance from the British Museum in return for property rights to his discoveries at Ephesus. Wood started excavations at the Greco-Roman ruins of the main city, and partially excavated the odeon, the tomb of Saint Luke, and the theatre. In Innocents Abroad at the beginning of Chapter 41, Mark Twain refers to what must have been Wood as "the English company who have acquired the right to excavate Ephesus... need to be protected and deserve to be," which prevented his American group from carrying away souvenirs. In 1867 Wood found a Greek inscription at the theatre, which referred to carrying statuettes on festival days from the temple of Artemis, through the Magnesian gate to the theatre. Using this information, he traced the ancient paved road back from the Magnesian gate and found a temple wall. Wood excavated the site, and, on December 31, 1869, rediscovered the temple of Artemis under seven m of sediment. Early Christians had thoroughly destroyed the temple and little remained, although Wood found various sculptures and**

**architectural fragments, which he sent to the British Museum. In 1874 Wood returned to London where he was acclaimed discoverer of Ephesus, elected a fellow of both the Royal Institute of British Architects and the Society of Antiquaries, and awarded a British government pension of £200 per annum.**

In listing stories related to Ephesus, Mark Twain noted that this area was where Artemis was born, Syrinx was transformed into a reed, Antony and Cleopatra held court, Saint Paul preached, Mary Magdalene died, and the Virgin Mary lived out her life together with the Apostle John. As Twain pointed out, the nearby Meander River even contributed a word to our language.

Syrinx was a nymph and a follower of Artemis, known for her chastity. Pursued by the amorous Pan, god of the forest, she ran to the edge of a river and begged to be delivered from her pursuer. In answer to her prayer, much like Daphne, she was transformed into the hollow water reeds along the river. The frustrated Pan cut the reeds and fashioned them into a flute-like musical instrument, which made a haunting sound and came to be known as a syrinx. Syrinx is also the origin of our word "syringe."

Mary Magdalene was one of Jesus' most celebrated disciples, a woman with a controversial reputation whom Jesus cleansed of "seven demons." She was known as Mary Magdalene because she was from the Galilean town Magdala. She was prominent during the final days of Jesus and was present at the crucifixion after many had fled. Mary Magdalene witnessed the burial of Jesus, the discovery that his tomb was empty, and the Resurrection. Pope Gregory the Great first asserted five hundred years after her death that she had been a reformed prostitute. Mary Magdalene is patroness of "wayward women" and "Magdalene houses" were established to reform female prostitutes. The $2^{nd}$-$3^{rd}$ century Acts of Philip suggest Mary Magdalene was a close companion of Jesus, and that following the crucifixion she accompanied other early Christian leaders to Asia Minor. She is believed to have been present, along with St. Bartholomew, at the crucifixion of the Apostle Philip at Hierapolis. In 886 her relics were transferred from Ephesus to Constantinople.

The **Ephesus temple of Artemis** (37° 56' 58.7" N, 27° 21' 50.83" E), known as one of the Seven Wonders of the ancient world, was a colossal structure and the leading temple to the goddess, first built around 550 BCE. The temple was enlarged under Lydian rule when King Croesus donated 36 columns with relief sculptures. The scant ruins of this structure are located apart from the main Ephesus ruins on the edge of the nearby town of Selçuk.

*Temple of Artemis with Tomb of St. John and Iyas Bey Mosque (background)*

At Ephesus Artemis was venerated as a fertility goddess, complete with bull testicles as symbols of male virility, as well as bees and flowers. Most scholars believe worship of the mother goddess Cybele at Ephesus gradually evolved into worship of Artemis and eventually into the Virgin Mary during the Christian era. By coincidence, a publicity-seeking madman named Herostratus burned down the Temple of Artemis on the night that Alexander the Great was born in 356 BCE. When Alexander liberated Ephesus from Persia in 334 BCE, he triumphantly entered the city and offered to finance rebuilding the temple, which would have been rededicated to both Artemis and Alexander himself. The citizens demurred, claiming one god should not build a temple to another. In the mid-4$^{th}$ century BCE the citizens of Ephesus rebuilt the large Ionic temple (105 x 55 m) on a platform (3 m high) over the older foundations.

Artemis was the patron goddess of Ephesus, and her temple was the central point of worship. She personified Ephesus on the city's ancient coins as well as in early treaties with other cities, and her preeminence is confirmed in numerous surviving inscriptions. Ephesians conducted innumerable feasts and processions in honor of Artemis, and thousands of pilgrims visited her temple, just as thousands of Jews made the pilgrimage to Jerusalem. Pilgrims to the temple of Artemis were a major source of revenue for local residents, as confirmed when angry silversmiths attacked St. Paul for threatening their livelihood. In the Roman era, the largest celebration of the virgin goddess Artemis was the three-day Nemoralia or Festival of Lights. Participants washed their hair and dressed it with flowers, then assembled at night by candlelight. Hunting dogs were also adorned with flowers, and the hunting or killing of wild beasts was forbidden. For women and slaves it was a day of rest, dancing and singing. Worshippers formed long processions carrying torches and candles, writing prayers on ribbons and tying them to trees. On August 15, the third day of the Nemoralia, worshippers of Artemis celebrated her ascension as the queen of heaven.

Adherents of Artemis were undoubtedly serious rivals and competitors of the early Christians. In 401 a mob of Christians led by Saint John Chrysostom completely destroyed the temple of Artemis. Columns from this temple were later used in constructing the Hagia Sophia in Constantinople. At present all that remains of this once magnificent temple are foundations and one standing column.

*Artemis*

**Artemis (Diana to Romans) is goddess of nature, hunting, fertility and childbirth. She is**

portrayed as a huntress accompanied by a deer, goddess of wild as well as domestic animals. Artemis danced, usually accompanied by her nymphs, in mountains, forests, and marshes. She remained the eternal virgin. Her symbols included the golden bow and arrow, the hunting dog, the stag, and the moon. Artemis is the twin sister of Apollo and daughter of Zeus and Leto. At the time of her birth Hera was furious with Zeus, because he had secretly impregnated the goddess Leto. Hera therefore prevented the other goddesses from helping Leto in childbirth. Leto gave birth to Artemis at the grove of Ortygia near Ephesus where the House of the Virgin Mary would one day stand. The newborn Artemis then helped her mother Leto cross from Asia Minor to the island of Delos, where although only one day old she served as midwife while Apollo was born. This was the beginning of Artemis' role as guardian of young children and patron of women in childbirth. Hephaestus, craftsman of the gods, made a silver bow and arrows for Artemis. Pan, god of the forest, provided her with dogs. Four stags with golden antlers pulled the chariot of Artemis.

According to tradition, Amazons established the worship of Artemis at Ephesus. From the Anatolian mother goddess Cybele she inherited eunuch priests and bees as her symbol. Like her brother Apollo, Artemis was a divinity of healing who could alleviate the sufferings of mortals. However, their arrows could also bring sudden death and plague. Niobe, for example, paid a high price when she claimed superiority to the goddess Leto because she had fourteen children. At an early age Artemis asked her father Zeus, to grant her eternal virginity. Her companions, as well as the priests and priestesses devoted to her service, vowed to live pure and chaste lives. Transgressions were severely punished. Among Artemis' occasional hunting companions was Orion, a son of Poseidon. Orion was a man of gigantic proportions and a famed hunter. On one occasion, unable to restrain himself, Orion tried to rape the virgin goddess. Artemis summoned a scorpion, which killed Orion and his dog. Orion became a constellation in the night sky, his dog became the star Sirius, and the scorpion became the Scorpio constellation. On another occasion the hunter Actaeon met his death because he encountered the goddess naked while she was bathing. Once Zeus seduced and impregnated the nymph Callisto, a virgin companion of Artemis, by taking the form of Artemis herself. The enraged Artemis showed no mercy. She first turned Callisto into a bear, then shot an arrow and killed her.

One day Artemis sent a huge boar to ravage Calydon because King Oeneus had forgotten to dedicate appropriate harvest sacrifices to her. A hunt for the boar was organized. The Amazon huntress Atalanta drew first blood from the boar, and the renowned hunter Meleager killed it but then lost his own life. In another incident, the giants Otus and Ephialtes, enormous and ferocious sons of Poseidon, intended to attack Mount Olympus and seize Hera and Artemis. Other gods feared the giants, but Artemis changed herself into a deer and jumped between them, prompting them to kill each other with their spears.

During the Trojan War Artemis, like her brother Apollo, sided with the Trojans against the Greeks. While the Greek fleet gathered at Aulis to depart Greece for Asia Minor, Artemis becalmed the winds. A seer advised Agamemnon that the only way to appease Artemis was to sacrifice his daughter Iphigenia, which he agreed to do. Artemis snatched Iphigenia from the sacrificial altar at the last moment before her death, and she became a priestess of Artemis. During the course of fighting at Troy, divine allies of the Greeks and Trojans engaged each other in combat. The powerful goddess Hera, wife of Zeus, struck Artemis on the ear with her own quiver, causing the arrows to fall out and Artemis to flee crying to her father Zeus. Meanwhile her mother Leto gathered up Artemis' bow and arrows. Artemis, Leto, and Apollo all helped to heal Aeneas, progenitor of the Romans, after he was severely wounded on the battlefield. The three secretly healed Aeneas at a temple of Apollo and enabled him to escape burning Troy with his aged father, his son and a few followers.

The **Ephesus Tomb of Apostle John** (37° 57' 10" N, 27° 22' 3" E) in the nearby town of Selçuk is the burial site of the Apostle John. According to tradition, Jesus at the crucifixion asked John to take care of his mother the Virgin Mary. John was buried in a small Christian church on this hilltop, which was replaced by a wooden topped basilica in the 4th century. As early as the 2nd century the tomb became a major Christian pilgrimage site. The present Church of St. John the Theologian is a large structure (130 x 60 m) Emperor Justinian built in the 6th century.

*Tomb of Apostle John*

The entrance to this cruciform (cross-shaped) church with six domes was from an atrium to the W. The square-shaped atrium was surrounded with porticos on three sides, and the outer side was turned into a promenade. Blue marble pillars with the monograms of Justinian and his wife Theodora on the capitals separated the nave from the aisles. (The nave is the central lengthwise aisle of a church, the central approach to the altar. If a church has other aisles comparable to the central nave, it is said to have more than one nave.) Three naves were topped with six domes, the largest of which was over the tomb of St. John. The tomb was raised on two steps under the central dome and is now clearly marked with four columns and a marble slab. On the E side were bays arranged in a semicircle used by priests during ceremonies. N of the tomb is a 10th century fresco depicting Christ in the center, with Saint John on the right. Defensive walls were built around the church in the 8th-9th centuries at a time of Arab raids. Down the hill from the church of Apostle John is an ornate 14th century Selçuk mosque.

**John the Apostle was first a disciple of John the Baptist and later one of the twelve apostles of Jesus, together with his brother James. Before that John and James were humble fishermen at Lake Genesareth. According to the New Testament John was one of the closest eyewitnesses to the life**

and work of Jesus. Apostles Peter, James and John were the only witnesses to three miracles Jesus performed: the raising of the daughter of Jairus from death; the Transfiguration, when Jesus became radiant on the mountain; and the Agony in the Garden of Gethsemane after the Last Supper, when Jesus discussed his imminent death with God. John sat next to Jesus at the Last Supper. John remained near Jesus at the foot of the cross on Calvary with the Virgin Mary, and a group of pious women. After the Ascension of Jesus, John, together with Peter, assumed the leadership role in early Christianity. Following the stoning of Saint Stephen in the year 34 and subsequent persecution, John and Mary fled Jerusalem with a community of believers and moved to the more tolerant and heterogeneous city of Ephesus. John's leadership role for the early Christian community in Asia Minor expanded after both Paul and Peter were martyred in Rome under Emperor Nero. During the First Jewish-Roman War, Roman authorities exiled John to nearby Patmos in 69-70, where he wrote the New Testament Book of Revelation. After the war was over, John was released. He returned to Ephesus, where he wrote the Gospel of John and the Epistles (meaning letters) of John. John ministered to Christians for another 25 years, then died in Ephesus during the reign of Emperor Nerva 96-98. He was the only Apostle to die of natural causes. His burial place was a major Christian pilgrimage site for centuries. As Mark Twain notes in Innocents Abroad, many believed sacred dust rising from St. John's grave had miraculous curative properties.

From 1954 to 1977 Professor Paulo Verzone of Istanbul Technical University and the Italian Archeological Mission worked on the Church and tomb of Apostle John as described at: http://www.archmuseum.org/Gallery/Photo_15_3_archeology3 ephesos.html?Page=1

The **House of the Virgin Mary** (37° 54' 44" N, 27° 19' 58" E), 7 km from Selçuk, was the last home of the Virgin Mary, mother of Jesus, in 37-48. On the site of the house today is a cruciform church with a central dome incorporated into the walls of a $6^{th}$ century building. A red line distinguishes the restored parts from the original structure, parts of which archeologists date back to the

1st century. Visitors enter the church via an arched portico with flanking niches, then a vaulted narthex (front lobby) from where a raised portal leads to the nave and apse. The niche in the E wall is regarded as a shrine. According to tradition, water from the nearby fountain at the Roman era cistern has

*House of Virgin Mary*

curative powers because the Virgin Mary drank its water during her last days on earth. Anne Catherine Emmerich, a German nun subsequently recognized as a saint, played a key role in the 19th century Christian rediscovery of the House of the Virgin Mary. Emmerich was bedridden with stigmata -- bodily pain in locations corresponding to the crucifixion wounds of Jesus -- and was believed able to diagnose and cure the diseases of others. She had a series of visions in 1818-24 about the life of the Virgin Mary, recounted to a poet named Clemens Brentano who transcribed them as The Life of the Blessed Virgin Mary published in 1852. Although Emmerich had never been to Turkey, one vision was said to describe precisely the extant House of the Virgin.

*Virgin Mary*

According to tradition, a Catholic priest used the book in 1881 to find the house exactly as described. Three recent popes visited this house: Paul VI on July 26, 1967; John Paul II on November 30, 1979; and Benedict XVI on November 29, 2006. The Virgin Mary is mentioned several times in the Koran, and Muslims also regard the House of Mary as a sacred place.

**Virgin Mary at Ephesus:** After the crucifixion, Mary accompanied the Apostle John and other early Christians to Ephesus. In the earliest Christian tradition, churches were named for people who lived and worked at them, and the first church dedicated to the Virgin Mary is in Ephesus. Local villagers, descendants of the Christians of Ephesus, have an ancient belief that this was the Virgin's last residence, which they celebrate with a pilgrimage every August 15. When the Third Ecumenical Council met at Ephesus in 431, its formal concluding declaration stated that the Apostle John and the Virgin Mary had lived at Ephesus. Although Jerusalem also claims to be the Virgin Mary's final resting place, the doctrine of the Dormition (falling asleep) or Assumption of Mary and her bodily resurrection before being taken up to heaven may resolve the ambiguity. According to tradition, when her time came the Archangel Gabriel revealed to Mary that her departure would occur three days later. The apostles, scattered throughout the world, were miraculously transported to her side, perhaps in Bethlehem, when she died. Mary was buried in Gethsemane and when the Apostles returned to the grave, her body was gone, leaving a sweet fragrance. An apparition confirmed that Jesus had taken her body to heaven to be reunited with her soul. Catholic and Orthodox Christian churches celebrate the Assumption (Dormition) of the Virgin Mary on August 15, commemorating her ascension body and soul as the queen of heaven. As Christianity spread beyond Jerusalem to areas where other gods and goddesses were worshipped, the faith adopted the attributes of other belief systems. In place of the virgin goddess Artemis, the Virgin Mary became increasingly popular in 3$^{rd}$ century Ephesus. Mary assumed many of Artemis' titles, such as "Queen of Heaven" and her veneration occurs on August 15, the same date Artemis was venerated.

The Ephesus Cave of the Seven Sleepers (37° 56' 37" N, 27° 21' 14" E) relates to the story of the Seven Sleepers considered saints by Catholics, Orthodox Christians and Muslims. This site became a major early Christian pilgrimage site where archeologists have discovered a large Christian cemetery with numerous inscriptions of prayers dedicated to the Seven Sleepers.

**The Seven Sleepers were seven youths, persecuted because of their monotheistic Christian beliefs during the 3$^{rd}$ century persecutions of Emperor Decius. They found refuge in a cave near Ephesus and slept soundly for 170 years. When they**

awoke and went into town they found, to their astonishment, crosses everywhere and a Christian population. To their amazement they learned that the reigning emperor, Theodosius II, was himself a Christian. These seven saints, named John, Maximian, Constantine, Mortian, Malchus, Serapion, and Dionysus, then died and were buried at the site where a church later was constructed in their honor. Although their story was popular among Christians during the 7th-8th centuries, it later fell out of favor. However, the story of the Seven Sleepers is preserved in the Koran, where it served as a reminder of the triumph of monotheism despite the fact that it took place before Islam. The story of the Seven Sleepers is an article of faith for those

*Cave of the Seven Sleepers*

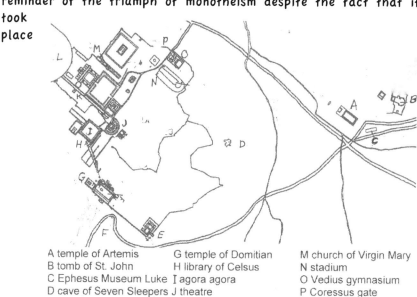

A temple of Artemis
B tomb of St. John
C Ephesus Museum Luke
D cave of Seven Sleepers
E Magnesian gate
F tomb of St. Luke
G temple of Domitian
H library of Celsus
I agora agora
J theatre
K Arcadian Way
L ancient harbor
M church of Virgin Mary
N stadium
O Vedius gymnasium
P Coressus gate

*Ephesus & Selçuk*

who believe the Koran is the unabridged word of God. This story inspired Washington Irving to write <u>Rip Van Winkle</u>. In <u>Innocents Abroad</u>, Mark Twain transforms the story into an amusing tale of juvenile delinquency.

The **main city of Ephesus** had three entrances: the Magnesian Gate (37° 56' 8" N, 27° 20' 45" E) to the SE; the Coressus Gate (37° 56' 45" N, 27° 20' 31" E) near the stadium toward the N; and the Harbor Gate for arrival by sea. Visitors either enter the site from the 1st century BCE Magnesian Gate and walk downhill through the city, or enter from the Coressus Gate entrance to the N and walk uphill. In the 19th century <u>John Turtle Wood</u> found a pillar carved with bull and cross at the small circular structure to the W, on the other (S) side of the main street from the Magnesian Gate, which he and local tradition claimed was the tomb of <u>St. Luke</u>.

Saint Luke the Evangelist lived 1-84 and was a close companion of St. Paul during his missionary campaigns. Although not an eyewitness to Jesus' ministry, Luke went to Jerusalem and became an early non-Jewish follower of Jesus. In his youth he studied Greek philosophy, art, and medicine. Born and raised in Antioch on the Orontes, Luke was a scholarly Greco-Syrian physician and well-educated writer. He wrote the <u>New Testament</u> Gospel of Luke and the Acts of the Apostles, and was known as the first icon painter. Luke remained an unmarried, committed Christian until he was martyred at age 84. In 357 his relics were transferred to Constantinople. Saint Luke is the patron saint of artists, physicians, surgeons, and students.

At Ephesus the 2nd century E Bath Gymnasium complex is immediately N of the Magnesian Gate with a palaestra at the entrance. (A palaestra was a large exercise area used for wrestling, often part of a gymnasium.) During excavations, statues of the gods <u>Asclepius</u>, <u>Aphrodite</u>, <u>Dionysus</u>,

### Upper Ephesus City

A Tomb of St. Luke  D Odeon  G Memmius Monument
B state agora  E Prytaneum  H Polio Fountain
C Temple of Julius Caesar  F Bassus Nympaheum  I Temple of Domitian

Hygeia, and Pan were found here at the 2$^{nd}$ century Baths of Varius in the center of the structure, surrounded on three sides by halls for physical exercise and games. Mosaics in the 40 m long corridor date to the 5th century. To the W are ruins of the large Basilica (168 x 16 m) built during the reign of Augustus. Statues of Augustus and Livia were uncovered here at the entrance to the 1$^{st}$ century state agora, which is immediately adjacent to the S of the Basilica up four steps. This large agora (160 x 58 m) had stoas on three sides. In the center of the state agora was a small 1$^{st}$ century temple of Isis (15 x 22 m), where a statue of Mark Antony was discovered. The temple façade contained statues of Odysseus and the Cyclops, now displayed in the Ephesus Museum in Bergama. This temple collapsed during the reign of Augustus and was not re-built, which is not surprising because Cleopatra was strongly associated with Isis.

A water reservoir in the corner of the agora was supplied from the Pollio Aqueduct. The Sextilius Pollio fountain, erected in 93, had a large pool and concave marble façade. (A Proconsul was a Roman provincial governor). SW of the state agora are remains of a two-storey nymphaeum named after Gaius Laecanius Bassus, proconsul (governor) 80-81. (A nymph is a female nature spirit often associated with particular springs or natural water sources. A nymphaeum was a man-made monumental fountain, dedicated to the nymphs, which supplied water from aqueducts to urban populations). This particular nymphaeum was supplied with water from a long Roman aqueduct and decorated with depictions of Tritons and the Muses.

The Muses are nine daughters of Zeus and Mnemosyne, the goddess of memory, who inspire artists, poets, philosophers, musicians and scientists. Their leader is the god Apollo, and they sit near the throne of Zeus to sing about the origin of the world and glorious deeds of great heroes. Each Muse has a particular interest: Calliope, epic poetry; Clio, history; Euterpe, flutes and lyric poetry; Thalia, comedy and pastoral poetry; Melpomene, tragedy; Terpsichore, dance; Erato, love poetry; Polyhymnia, sacred poetry; and Urania, astronomy. From them we derive the modern words: amuse, museum, music and mosaic, as well as the name calliope for a musical instrument.

Next down the hill is the odeon, used for municipal council meetings, plays and concerts, which seated 1500 people. It was built in about 150, paid for by wealthy local residents Publius Vedius Antoninus and his wife Flavia Papiana. The temple of Divus Julius and Dea Roma stands next to the odeon, built in 29 BCE when Augustus granted the city the right to construct a shrine dedicated to Dea Roma, the patron goddess of Rome, and Divus Julius, the deified Julius Caesar.

**Julius Caesar (Gaius Julius Caesar) was born July 12, 100 BCE in Rome. Although his aristocratic family claimed direct descent from Aeneas, and hence Aphrodite, in politics Caesar sided with populist reformers. His aunt Julia had married Marius, an influential Roman politician who eliminated property**

qualifications for military service and reduced the influence of the land-owning aristocracy. In 83 BCE the powerful Roman general Sulla led a successful counter-revolution and ordered Caesar to divorce his wife, who was related to Marius. Caesar demurred, lost much of his property but not his life due to the intervention of influential relatives. In 81 BCE, to escape Sulla, Caesar served in the Roman military first in Greece, where he was commended for saving another soldier in combat, then on an anti-piracy campaign in the region of Cilicia in SE Asia Minor. When Sulla died in 78 BCE, Caesar returned to Rome and started his political career gaining notoriety as a public prosecutor of Sulla's henchmen.

En route to study oratory at Rhodes, Caesar was captured by pirates and held for ransom for 40 days. The pirates demanded a ransom of 20 silver talents, but Caesar declared he was worth much more and insisted they ask for 50 talents. Much to their amusement, he stated he would return to punish them. The ransom was paid; Caesar was released, organized an expedition, caught up with the pirates and executed them all. Caesar's next task was to organize a volunteer force in 74 BCE to defend Romans in Asia when the third Mithradatic War broke out. Early in his career in 69-60 BCE Caesar served first as quaestor in Spain, then as aedile in Rome, and finally as Proconsul (governor) of Roman Spain, where he significantly enhanced his military reputation and his financial position. (A quaestor was a senior Roman financial administrator; an aedile an administrator responsible for maintaining public buildings, the grain market, and staging public festivals and games.) Returning to Rome in 60 BCE, Caesar brought together two powerful rivals, the esteemed general Pompey and the richest man in Rome, Crassus, to form a ruling triumvirate. Early in 59 BCE, Pompey sealed the alliance by marrying Caesar's only child, Julia. Caesar served as consul, the highest political position, in 59 BCE and secured Senate appointment as governor of Gaul for five years. He obtained Senate ratification of Pompey's long-delayed political settlement of the E, cancelled tax demands on farmers and allocated public land to fathers of three or more children.

In 58 BCE, Caesar went to Gaul for eight years, where he commanded more than 50,000 men in a brilliant campaign of conquest in what is now France and Belgium. In 55-54 BCE,

Caesar even made two expeditions to Britain. In 52 BCE the Gauls staged a massive revolt led by Vercingetorix. Eventually the Gallic force moved into the fortified hill town of Alesia (near modern Dijon). Caesar besieged the town, surrounded it with a ring of fortified trenches with an outer trench to defend against Gallic reinforcements. Despite the arrival of as many as 250,000 Gallic warriors as reinforcements, the disciplined Romans stood their ground. During a massive Gallic attack, Caesar joined the hand-to-hand combat in person and rallied his forces. Caesar's cavalry suddenly emerged in a surprise attack from behind, and the Gauls dissolved into disorder and defeat. The captured Gauls were sold into slavery en masse. Vercingetorix was paraded through the streets of Rome in Caesar's triumph and then ritually strangled.

In a personal tragedy with major political consequences Caesar's daughter Julia died in childbirth in 54 BCE, which severed the family connection between Pompey and Caesar. Pompey, increasingly alarmed at Caesar' success in Gaul, turned against Caesar. Crassus died in 53 BCE fighting the Persians at Carrhae in Syria during a misconceived military disaster. In 52 BCE the Senate, anxious to limit Caesar's growing power, enacted legislation to name a new governor in Gaul and leave Caesar legally liable for exceeding his authority. Then in 49 BCE the Senate ordered Caesar to relinquish command of his army. Instead Caesar crossed the Rubicon River, the demarcation line between Gaul and Italy, and marched his battle-hardened army into Rome.

Pompey, now aligned with the pro-republican senators, but with insufficient troops in Italy to confront Caesar, withdrew to the E to raise funds and recruit men. After seizing control in Rome and being elected consul for 48 BCE, Caesar attacked Pompey's supporters and their legions in Spain, where most of the men defected to his side. Caesar then pursued Pompey to Greece and at the battle of Pharsalus in 48 BCE decisively defeated Pompey, who fled to Egypt. The young Egyptian pharaoh, seeking favor with Caesar, treacherously assassinated Pompey as he disembarked. Caesar arrived in Alexandria, punished Pompey's assassins and remained for nine months beguiled by Cleopatra and entangled in an Egyptian dynastic struggle. Caesar impregnated Cleopatra and his only son, Caesarion, was born nine months later. Caesar returned to Rome after fighting a brief war at Zela in Asia Minor where he "came, saw and conquered" Pharnaces, son of Mithridates VI.

After two more victorious campaigns against republican forces in Spain and Africa, Caesar returned to Rome to rule. He expanded Roman citizenship in the Italian peninsula, established Roman settlements in the provinces, reformed the tax laws, drained large tracts of marshland, enlarged the Senate to make it more representative, rebuilt Carthage and Corinth, and reformed the calendar. Caesar scandalized Rome by welcoming Cleopatra, his foreign queen, to stay with him in Rome. In February 44 BCE Caesar was named dictator for life; less than a month later on March 15, aristocratic conspirators led by Marcus Junius Brutus and Gaius Cassius cornered Caesar in the Senate and stabbed him 23 times. Their action changed the course of history and condemned Rome to 13 more years of civil war.

Beyond his military and political exploits, Caesar was a highly literate writer; his surviving works include The Gallic War: Seven Commentaries written in 51 BCE and Civil War, an account of the 49-48 BCE conflict with Pompey. Even the name Caesar became synonymous with the term for ruler in German as Kaiser, in Russian as Tsar, and in Arabic and Turkish as qayṣar.

Past the temple Divus Julius was the prytaneum, a $3^{rd}$ century BCE Doric structure rebuilt during the reign of Augustus. (A prytaneum was the political center of the city, somewhat like a city hall, which contained the altar of Hestia.) Religious ceremonies were held around a four-cornered pit containing a perpetually burning sacred fire.

Hestia (Vesta to Romans), meaning hearth, was one of the original twelve Olympian gods and sister of Zeus and Hera. She is the virgin goddess of the hearth, domesticity, architecture, and family unity. Every family hearth was her altar. She received the first offering of every sacrifice in the household. The hearth fire in an ancient household was not allowed to go out except as part of an elaborate purification ceremony. For the city of Ephesus, priests, known as Curetes, were responsible for guarding and maintaining this sacred fire at Hestia's official sanctuary. The main extant street of ancient Ephesus is named for this priestly order. In Rome the chaste all-female College of Vestal Virgins carried out this function.

*Temple of Domitian*

Further along the main street is the temple of the Emperor Domitian, built on a raised terrace in 89-90, dedicated to the imperial cult. The approach to the temple was up a monumental stairway, still partially visible N of the terrace. The façade of the temple had eight columns in front. The altar was decorated with weapons representing defeated enemies. The temple included a statue (5 m high) of the Emperor Domitian of which only the head and left arm survive because, upon hearing of the unpopular emperor's assassination, a jubilant mob at Ephesus broke apart the statue. Underneath the temple is a museum of inscriptions, which can be visited by appointment.

**Emperor Domitian (Titus Flavius Domitianus) reigned as Roman emperor 81–96 and was known for conducting a reign of terror. He was born in 51 as the second son of Emperor Vespasian. During civil war in 69, Domitian remained unharmed in Rome, but escaped into hiding when the forces of his father's rival Vitellius stormed the capital. On Vespasian's death in 79, Domitian's older brother Titus became emperor. Domitian was jealous of his more talented older brother and may have had a hand in Titus' untimely death in 81. Domitian curried popular favor with free food, gladiatorial shows and games, in which he sometimes took part in person. He significantly increased the pay of the army to retain its support. Domitian rebuilt damaged buildings in Rome and launched a major road building campaign in Asia Minor. An ardent supporter of traditional Roman religion, Domitian built temples, reestablished religious ceremonies, and tried to enforce morality by law. In Germania, Domitian annexed the territory between the Rhine and the Danube and then fortified**

the Rhine-Danube border. In 85 the Dacians on the lower Danube (modern Rumania) invaded the empire, and an entire Roman legion was lost in the fighting. The war ended in 88 in a compromise, which left the Dacians in place and paid them for "protecting" the frontier.

The aristocracy hated Domitian because of his ostentation and cruelty. Domitian insisted on being addressed as "master and god," surrounded himself with spies and informers, and put to death at least twelve senators of consular rank. Following an attempted rebellion among the Roman forces in Germania in 89, Domitian ordered numerous executions and conducted a reign of terror 93-96.

He also confiscated the property of his victims. The execution of his cousin Flavius Clemens in 95 convinced his closest associates that no one was safe. Two Praetorian commanders conspired with the emperor's wife and managed to kill Domitian on Sept. 18, 96. His successor senator Nerva, who took over the government at once, also was involved in the murder. The Roman aristocracy despised Domitian because of his reign of terror and the Senate formally condemned the memory of Domitian and ordered his name removed from monuments. The temple at Ephesus was officially rededicated to Vespasian and Titus.

*Domitian*

At Ephesus the Memmius monument, built on the N side of Domitian Square in 30-50, honors the family of Lucius Cornelius Sulla, the Roman general who defeated Mithridates VI of Pontus in 87 BCE and established himself as the dictatorial ruler of Rome. The monument was intended to remind residents of the folly of the Mithradatic rebellion, which many in Ephesus had initially supported. The Memmius Monument was built in the shape of a four-sided victory crown, with four steps leading up to the pedestal on all sides and hand-carved stonework at the base of each arch. On the monument the Roman general Sulla, his son Gaius and his grandson Memmius are depicted as soldiers wearing togas.

Lucius Cornelius Sulla was a Roman general and dictator during the Roman Republic period. In 107 BCE Sulla served under the famous general Gaius Marius in a North African war against Numidian King Jugurtha. Sulla cleverly managed to capture Jugurtha and end the war. In 104-101 BCE he served under Marius in war again and was so successful that Marius became jealous and resentful. Sulla wisely returned to Rome and lived quietly until 93 BCE when he was elected praetor. In 92 BCE, the Senate sent Sulla to Asia Minor to suppress the rebellious Mithridates VI of Pontus, and restore a local Roman ally as ruler of Cappadocia. Sulla defeated Mithridates and fulfilled his mission, then returned to Rome and assumed a leading role within the city's conservative aristocracy.

*Memmius Monument*

In 91 BCE Sulla defeated a rebellion among the Samnites, Italian allies of Rome, during the Social (Italic) War. Then he was elected consul in 88 BCE. At this time Mithridates VI of Pontus, under the guise of Greek nationalism, rebelled again and slaughtered 80,000 Latin speakers in Asia Minor. Although the Senate chose Sulla to lead a counterattack against Mithridates, his old rival the demagogue Gaius Marius also demanded the command and popular riots ensued. In response, Sulla broke with precedent and led his army into Rome, and expelled Marius and his populist supporters from the city. In 87 BCE Sulla left Italy for Greece and Asia Minor where he spent four years successfully pursuing Mithridates and accumulating enormous plunder. In 84 BCE, Sulla concluded a peace agreement with Mithridates, which recovered all conquered territory but allowed Mithridates to remain in control of Pontus. Although Marius had died in 86 BCE, his populist supporters had gained control of Rome during Sulla's absence, confiscated Sulla's property, and declared him a public enemy. In 83 BCE Sulla returned to Rome with 40,000 veterans seeking vengeance, supported by most of the Roman aristocracy, including Gnaeus Pompeius, later known as Pompey the Great. Over the next year Sulla defeated the remaining Marius supporters as well as the resurgent Italian Samnites. Sulla became dictator of Rome and issued "proscription" edicts exhibited at the forum, which declared his opponents to be outlaws, sentenced them to death, and confiscated their properties. Sulla rewarded his veterans and informants with confiscated land. In 79 BCE Sulla retired from public office and died a year later. Although Sulla restored order at a time of chaos and defeated external military threats, the precedent of his dictatorial rule undoubtedly hastened the fall of the Republic and the end of pluralistic government in Rome.

Across from the Memmius Monument is a marble relief of a flying Nike, goddess of victory, which was formerly part of the Hercules Arch. This 4<sup>th</sup> century Nike holds a wreath and a palm branch, both symbols of victory.

*Nike*

**Nike (Victoria to Romans) is the Winged Goddess of Victory. Nike was a close companion of Zeus and Athena, serving as divine charioteer in the Titanomachy or war against the older deities. She is the goddess of strength, speed, and victory who rewards victors on the battlefields with fame and glory.**

Proceeding down the main street in Ephesus visitors come to the 2<sup>nd</sup> century Hercules Arch reliefs, reassembled at this point in the 4<sup>th</sup> century to form a victory arch. Further along is the Fountain of Trajan (12 m high), built in 104, which once had a pool in front flanked with columns and a large statue of Trajan (only one foot remains), as well as statues of Aphrodite, Dionysus and a satyr. On the other side of the street the spacious terrace houses for the wealthy residents were built into the slope in the 1<sup>st</sup> century and continuously occupied until the 7th century. These restored houses, decorated with mosaics and frescoes, provide visitors with unique insight into daily provincial life in the ancient empire. The roof of one house served as the terrace of the one above, rather like an upscale modern apartment complex. These residences had indoor plumbing, including water supplied for individual baths, and heating systems. Walls and floors were painted or covered with mosaics displaying theatrical scenes taken from stories about gods and mortals. For example, inside the first house is a scene from the story of Orestes.

Orestes was the son of Clytemnestra and Agamemnon of the house of Atreus descended from Niobe. Orestes was absent from Mycenae when his father, Agamemnon, returned from the Trojan War and was murdered by his wife Clytemnestra and her lover Aegisthus. Years later, Orestes returned and with his sister Electra avenged his father by slaying his mother and Aegisthus. Orestes went crazy after he killed his mother, and was pursued by the Erinyes – monstrous spirits meant to punish violations of family decency. Athena conducted a matricide trial of Orestes during which Apollo argued that his actions were justified. Orestes was finally acquitted.

Another mosaic in the same rooms shows the desperate struggle between Hercules and the river god Achelous.

Achelous was the deity of the Achelous River, the largest river of Greece, and the strongest of all river deities. Deianeira, daughter of King Oeneus of Calydon, was so incredibly beautiful that both Hercules and Achelous wanted her. Despite the ability of Achelous to change himself into a serpent, bull-headed man, or a bull, Hercules was able to defeat him in the contest and win Deianeira. During the fighting, Hercules broke off one of Achelous' horns, which became the cornucopia. (The cornucopia or horn of plenty was a symbol of agricultural abundance, overflowing with vegetables, fruits and nuts.)

In the second terrace house visitors can see a fresco of Ariadne and Dionysus surrounded with luxuriant plants and animals.

Ariadne, meaning most holy, was daughter of King Minos of Crete, and granddaughter of the sun god Helios. At this time, Athens was required to send to their death in Crete seven young men and women each year. The Minotaur, a bull-like monster, would devour the young people. Determined to end this barbaric human sacrifice, the Athenian Theseus arrived as part of the sacrificial group. Ariadne fell in love with Theseus and surreptitiously gave him a sword to defend himself and a ball of red fleece thread to escape the Minotaur's labyrinth. Theseus succeeded in killing the Minotaur and fled Crete with Ariadne. However, Theseus then abandoned Ariadne on the island of Naxos while she was sleeping. The god Dionysus then appeared on Naxos and married Ariadne eventually bringing her to Olympus as an immortal.

Another wall fresco depicts a scene from the ancient play *Sikyonios* by Menander.

**Menander (342-291 BCE) was a popular Athenian playwright, who wrote more than a hundred comedies, only one of which survived in its entirety into modern times. *Sikyonios*, or "The Man from Sikyon," survives only in fragments but the essential plot can be discerned. A military officer named Stratophanes purchased a four-year old girl and her family's servant on the slave market after pirates had kidnapped them. This was not an unrealistic scenario in the ancient world where robbers often kidnapped traveling citizens and sold them into slavery. Stratophanes was kind to his household help and did not abuse either the girl or her family servant. When she was old enough to marry, both Stratophanes and his neighbor Moschion fell in love with her. As the story developed, the girl found out she was a citizen of Athens and obtained her freedom. Stratophanes and his friend Theron tried to persuade an old man to claim to be her father so that he could give Stratophanes permission to marry her. Theron unsuccessfully attempted to bribe the old man, who then discovered he actually was her father. Stratophanes and his rival Moschion discovered they were really brothers. The play ended with a double wedding for Stratophanes and Theron and a double recognition of parents and long lost children.**

Other frescoes and mosaics depict Tritons, Eros and the philosopher Socrates sculpted in a sitting position with a baton in his hand.

Triton is the messenger of the sea, son of Poseidon and the Nereid Amphitrite. He carries a trident and blows on a conch shell to calm or raise ocean waves. His offspring, known as Tritons, were half fish and half human, i.e., mermaids and mermen.

**Socrates, father of philosophy, was born in Athens in 469 BCE, son of a stone sculptor and a midwife. The Athenians had recently defeated a Persian invasion and the Delian League was developing into an Athenian empire. During Socrates' youth Athens was dominated by the populist leader Pericles, who created people's courts, promoted arts and literature, built the Parthenon and supported democratic government. Socrates' father died when he was in his early teens, leaving him a modest inheritance that enabled him to devote himself to philosophical dialogue.**

**Socrates was an ugly, peculiar looking man with bulging eyes, and a flat, upturned nose. He wore his hair long, walked around unwashed and barefoot. All his life he refused to accept money for teaching and claimed an inner voice told him what to do. Socrates had enough money to own a suit of armor, and served as a citizen soldier (hoplite) in the Athenian army. After two years of military training, he went in 432 BCE to help put down the rebellion of a smaller city. In a battle on the way home Socrates distinguished himself by saving the life of the wounded Alcibiades. On another occasion during the Peloponnesian War, Socrates behaved bravely when his unit faced a cavalry charge. In 418 BCE he married Xanthippe and eventually had three sons.**

**Socrates spent most of his adult life in the agora talking with people he encountered about ethical issues. His approach was to destroy the illusion that people already fully understood the world and to goad them into accepting their own ignorance as a vital first step in discovering essential concepts governing human life. Socrates would approach an interlocutor in an attitude of assumed ignorance, ask a question, apparently for his own information, and then follow up with questions, until the other person would recognize and admit his own ignorance. Then Socrates would ask another series of questions, each designed to clarify and define the subject, often related to moral character in**

terms of moderation, courage, love, and reverence. According to tradition, Chaerephon, a friend of Socrates, asked the oracle of Apollo at Delphi whether anyone was wiser than Socrates and was told "no one." Socrates took this to mean that since he himself knew very little, no one else did either, but that questions could lead to greater understanding.

Socrates never wrote anything, and his legacy is based entirely on the accounts of others. Xenophon, the soldier and historian who wrote <u>Anabasis</u> about the Greek march home through Persia, reported that he never knew anyone who tried harder to find out what each of his companions knew than Socrates. Socrates is most well known from the works of Plato, a favored student who was only 25 years old when Socrates died. Scholars believe Plato's earliest Socratic dialogues most faithfully represent the real Socrates.

Socrates' leading detractor was the comic playwright Aristophanes. In his 423 BCE play *Clouds*, Socrates is presented as an eccentric stalking the streets of Athens, rolling his eyes at unintelligent remarks and continually gazing up at the clouds. In a somewhat sinister aside in the 438 BCE play *Birds*, Aristophanes describes a gang of pro-Sparta aristocratic youths as "Socratified." Although some historians consider Socrates apolitical, he was neither a democrat nor an egalitarian. Many people wonder why in 399 BCE a jury in democratic Athens would sentence a seventy-year-old philosopher to death. During the tumultuous period of the Peloponnesian War with Sparta, Athenian democracy was twice overthrown. On both occasions, the anti-democratic ringleaders were close friends of Socrates: Alcibiades in 411-410 BCE and Critias in 404-403 BCE. These brief periods of tyrannical rule and social conflict were highly disruptive, with perhaps 1,500 leading democrats summarily executed. Then in 401 yet another anti-democratic uprising occurred, but was suppressed.

In 399 BCE Socrates was accused of impiety and subversion of moral traditions. His daylong trial took place in a people's court at the agora with a jury of 500 male citizens chosen by lot. Socrates often had said gods would not lie or do wicked things, but the Olympian gods as commonly understood were quarrelsome and vindictive. However, the most compelling argument against Socrates was that he was responsible for educating Critias, who became the cruelest and most blood thirsty of the tyrants. Socrates denied responsibility, refused to retract anything he had ever said or apologize for anything he had done. 280 jurors voted that he was guilty; 220 jurors voted for acquittal. Once the guilty verdict was determined, each side had the opportunity to propose a punishment and the jurors would decide. The accusers proposed the punishment of death, expecting the defense would propose exile, which likely would have been accepted. Instead, Socrates proposed his punishment should be to eat free meals at the public dining hall. The jury then voted 360 for the death penalty, 140 for a large fine. Socrates was condemned to drink the poison hemlock, and he met his fate with calmness and dignity.

Further down on the other side of Curetes Street is the temple of Hadrian, dedicated in 118 to the emperor as well as to Artemis and the people of Ephesus. At the first decorative arch Corinthian columns support a frieze head of a crowned Tyche.

*Medusa on Hadrian Temple*

Tyche (Fortuna to Romans) governed the destiny and prosperity of individual cities. She is a goddess of fate, the personification of luck, sometimes appearing with the cornucopia or horn of plenty. Many ancient cities venerated their own specific versions of Tyche. She is often depicted wearing a crown like the walls of a city.

The second arch over the main portal of the temple of Hadrian contains a figure of Medusa, intended to keep away evil spirits, surrounded by acanthus leaves. Inscribed names of the emperors Hadrian, Galerius, Maximian, Diocletian, and Constantine, confirm that their statues once stood in this temple. Two friezes restored in the 4th century represent the founding of Ephesus when

Androclus killed the boar. The friezes also depict Hercules, Theseus, and the Amazons with the gods Athena, Apollo, and Artemis. Most surprisingly a fourth panel on the right, dating back to the 4<sup>th</sup> century, shows Emperor Theodosius I together with his wife and son. In 381, this same Christian Emperor Theodosius I outlawed non-Christian cults throughout the empire, which suggests his image together with the Olympian gods was carved before that transition year in the religious history of Ephesus.

**Theodosius I (Flavius Theodosius Augustus) reigned 379-395. He was the last Roman Emperor to rule over a united empire. Theodosius was born in 347 in NW Spain where his parents, and even his grandparents, are believed to have been Christians. His father, Flavius Theodosius, was a noted general. Serving with his father, Theodosius participated in campaigns against the Picts and Scots in Britain in 368-369, against the Alemanni in Gaul in 370, and against the Sarmatians in the Balkans in 372-373. He served as a military commander in Moesia on the lower Danube and defeated the Sarmatians in 374. Then disaster struck when his father was executed for treason; Theodosius withdrew into exile in Spain. After Visigoths slaughtered Emperor Valens and his army at Adrianople in 378, Emperor Gratian recalled Theodosius from exile and sent him to confront the Visigoths. Theodosius was so militarily successful that Gratian elevated him to the rank of Augustus (as a subordinate co-ruler) of the E in 379.**

**Out of necessity Theodosius developed a policy of dealing with the Germanic tribes pouring in from the N by granting them land and provisions in return for having their soldiers serve in the Roman military as needed. In 382 Goths were permitted to live in Thrace within the Empire and retain their own ruler and laws. The unintended result was the creation of separate nations within the Empire, which endangered internal stability and contributed to its decline. At a time of a shortage of military manpower, these Germans provided Theodosius with fierce and skilled fighters and gave him an initial advantage in responding to potential usurpers to the W.**

**Before 391 Theodosius tolerated traditional non-Christian religious practices and rituals, as had his Christian predecessors, and entrusted adherents of the old cults with high imperial**

offices. In 391, however, he decreed laws effectively prohibiting non-Christian worship, forbidding visits to non-Christian religious sites and outlawing adornment or use of images representing the old gods. Although Theodosius had earlier supported preservation of temples and statues of the gods as useful public buildings and works of art, at this time he was increasingly influenced by Christian leaders and officially permitted the destruction of famous non-Christian temples, such as the Serapeum in Alexandria. Although bands of monks and Christian officials had long taken the law into their own hands to destroy centers of non-Christian worship, now such actions had the emperor's tacit approval. Theodosius refused to restore the Altar of Victory in the Roman Senate and ended the Olympic games.

In 383, Emperor Gratian was killed in a rebellion, and Theodosius supported his brother and successor, Valentinian II, as Roman emperor in the W. After Theodosius fought two bloody civil wars in quick succession against usurpers, he assigned Arbogast, one of his leading military commanders, to Rome to assist Valentinian II. When Valentinian II died under questionable circumstances, Arbogast installed Flavius Eugenius, a former rhetoric teacher with close connections to the pagan aristocracy of the Senate, as puppet emperor in the W. Theodosius, however, refused to accept Eugenius, ostensibly because of his pagan ties, and promoted his own son Honorius as Emperor in the W. Eugenius, although nominally a Christian, rallied believers in traditional, non-Christian religion. He set up ancient altars again, including the Altar of Victory at Rome, and led his soldiers under the standard of Hercules Invictus. In 394 Theodosius and his army, including many recent Germanic recruits, defeated Arbogast near Aquileia and executed the usurper Eugenius, while Arbogast committed suicide. With the defeat of Arbogast and Eugenius, Theodosius effectively reunited the empire under one ruler for the last time. When Theodosius died less than six months later in January 395, the empire was divided between his sons Honorius and Arcadius.

Further along on the NE side of the main street in Ephesus are the three-storey Scholastikia Baths. In the 5$^{th}$ century a prominent Christian woman named Scholastikia paid for these buildings to be extensively reconstructed and her headless statue remains *in situ*. After this remodeling the baths could accommodate up to a thousand customers and even contained a library. An adjacent two-storey brothel was built in the 1st century with a large hall on the ground floor and several small rooms for customers upstairs. A small bronze figure of Priapus, a rustic fertility god depicted with an enormous permanent erection, was found at the brothel and can be seen at the Ephesus Museum in Selçuk. The adjacent latrine to the W was constructed over a channel with an uninterrupted flow of water and was designed to accommodate large numbers of people.

The tomb of Arsinoë IV of Egypt, across the street from the Scholastikia Baths, is the final resting place of the rival and younger sister of Cleopatra VII. This octagonal tomb was surrounded with Corinthian columns, had a pyramid-shaped roof and dates back to 50-20 BCE. In 1926 the body of a 15–20 years old woman was found in the burial chamber. Despite the fact that there was no inscription, most archeologists have concluded this is Arsinoë's tomb based on its octagonal shape (like the Lighthouse of Alexandria), Egyptian-style columns and the historical record. Arsinoë IV lived in Ephesus and was murdered while seeking sanctuary at the temple of Artemis.

**Cleopatra VII Philopator (69 BCE–30 BCE) and Arsinoë IV (62-41 BCE) were members of the dynasty descended from Ptolemy, the Macedonian general who seized Egypt upon the death of Alexander the Great. Cleopatra became joint monarch at age 18, together with her ten-year old brother Ptolemy XIII when her father died in 51 BCE. Arsinoë was her youngest sister. In 48 BCE a cabal of courtiers deposed Cleopatra and made her brother Ptolemy XIII sole ruler. At this time, Pompey was losing the civil war with Julius Caesar and decided to flee to Alexandria where once he had supported Cleopatra's father. Instead of helping his father's old friend, 13-year-old Ptolemy VIII sat on a throne facing the harbor and watched as Pompey disembarked from a ship and was murdered by a duplicitous Roman officer. Although the young Pharaoh and his minders had attempted to curry favor, Caesar was horrified when presented with Pompey's severed head two days later and angrily seized control of Alexandria.**

**Cleopatra had herself secretly smuggled into the palace inside a carpet to meet with Caesar alone. She was 21 years old, became**

Caesar's lover and nine months later, in 47 BCE, gave birth to Caesar's only known son, Caesarion (little Caesar). Meanwhile Cleopatra's sister Arsinoë IV escaped Alexandria with her supporters, and was proclaimed Pharaoh by a rival Egyptian army. After months of armed conflict Caesar managed, upon receiving Roman reinforcements, to crush the Egyptian opposition, drown Ptolemy XIII in the Nile, and place Cleopatra on the throne. Caesar captured Arsinoë IV, transported her to Rome to appear in his 46 BCE Triumph parade, but spared her life. Arsinoë was granted sanctuary at the temple of Artemis in Ephesus.

Cleopatra and her entourage were staying at one of Caesar's properties in Rome when Roman senators assassinated him on March 15, 44 BCE. Cleopatra returned home and supported the Caesarian party against the Republicans during the ensuing civil war. After the Republican defeat, Mark Antony in 41 BCE summoned Cleopatra to Tarsus. Cleopatra arrived in unprecedented regal style, seduced Mark Antony and persuaded him to eliminate her rival sister Arsinoë IV. In 41 BCE Mark Antony had Arsinoë executed on the steps of the temple of Artemis in Ephesus, a scandalous violation of the sanctuary rules. On 25 December 40 BC, Cleopatra gave birth to twins fathered by Antony. Antony married Cleopatra according to the Egyptian rite despite the fact that he was already married to Octavian's sister. Then Antony and Cleopatra had another child. In 34 BCE, Antony proclaimed Cleopatra and Caesarion co-rulers of Egypt and Cyprus and assigned other E Roman provinces to their joint offspring. Octavian cleverly used these actions against Antony, and portrayed him as under the control of an eastern despot and no longer Roman. In 33 BCE Antony and Cleopatra lived together at Ephesus while she funded his military preparations. Then the Roman Senate declared war on Egypt. At the naval battle in 31 BCE Octavian's forces decisively defeated Antony and Cleopatra. After the suicide of Antony and Cleopatra, Octavian's forces murdered Caesarion, but the three children of Cleopatra and Antony were taken back to Rome and raised in the imperial household.

The Hellenistic era heroon of Androclus, Athenian founder of Ephesus, stands next to the Tomb of Arsinoë, as confirmed by a nearby inscription. Androclus also is depicted on a 2$^{nd}$ century frieze in the Hadrian temple.

Androclus, son of the King of Athens, was searching for a place to establish a colony of Athenians under pressure from invading Dorians in the 10$^{th}$ century BCE. An oracle of Apollo had prophesized that a fish and a boar would show the location for the new settlement. While Androclus was frying a fish in a pan, it fell from the pan, created a commotion and startled a boar hiding in the nearby bushes. Androclus pursued the frightened boar and established the city of Ephesus at the place where he caught and killed the boar.

Consul Gaius Julius Aquila built the Library of Celsus at Ephesus in 110 to honor his father, Celsus Polemaenus, governor of the Roman province of Asia 105-107. The tomb of Celsus, in a crypt below the large central niche, was discovered undisturbed by archeologists in 1904. His body was in a lead coffin inside a marble sarcophagus decorated with garlands, rosettes, representations of Nike, and erotes. (Erotes are winged spirits associated with love and desire, offspring of Aphrodite.) The body was returned to where it was found. The two-storey library façade rests on a concave podium reached via nine steps to three entrances flanked with Corinthian columns.

*Library of Celsus with gate of Mazaeus and Mithridates (right)*

Side columns are smaller than center columns for visual effect. Four female statues (originals in Vienna at the Ephesus Museum) in niches on the first level symbolize: Sophia (wisdom), Arete (excellence), Ennoia (insight) and Episteme (knowledge). Aquila bequeathed a considerable sum of money in his will to maintain the library and acquire books. The library, carefully reconstructed from original pieces, once contained 12,000 scrolls within the walls of its inner chamber. An air gap between inner and outer walls protected the scrolls from damage due to humidity or temperature change. A menorah with seven branches carved along one of the library stairs attests to the presence of the early Jewish community.

During excavations a relief commemorating the victory of Lucius Verus over the Parthians was found in a pool in front of the library. This Parthian Monument of Ephesus is one of the most important 2nd century Roman reliefs from Asia Minor. Although no longer *in situ*, much of the relief can be seen at the Ephesus Museum in nearby Selçuk, while the bulk of the relief is on display at the Ephesus Museum in Vienna. The massive relief commemorates the victory of Roman Emperor Lucius Verus, who visited Ephesus and married here during the 161-166 Parthian Campaign. The reliefs have a total length of about 70 m.

**Lucius Verus reigned as Roman co-emperor with Marcus Aurelius 161-169. He was born in 130, son of a senator whom Emperor Hadrian had designated as his successor. When the father of Lucius Verus died before Hadrian, the emperor designated Antoninus Pius as successor, but stipulated that Lucius Verus and Hadrian's nephew Marcus Aurelius would be the heirs of Antoninus Pius. When Antoninus Pius died in 161, the Senate favored Marcus Aurelius over his 31-year old joint heir and was prepared to anoint him sole emperor. Marcus Aurelius, however, insisted that his adopted brother Lucius Verus serve as joint emperor. For the first time, Rome was ruled by a diarchy. The Parthian monarch, Vologases IV, taking advantage of transition uncertainty in Rome, overthrew a Roman client king in Armenia and seized control of the buffer state, a frequent point of enmity between the two rival superpowers. Vologases installed Pacorus, an Arsacid dynast like himself, as king of Armenia. In response a Roman legion under Severianus marched from Cappadocia into Armenia, but was trapped by the Parthians at Elegia, just past the frontier, and massacred in just three days. The Parthians then invaded Roman territory and inflicted further**

defeats on the Roman army in Syria.

To bolster morale and underscore Roman determination to confront the Parthian threat, Marcus Aurelius in 162 prevailed upon his co-ruler Lucius Verus to head E to oversee the war. Lucius Verus proceeded slowly to Corinth and Athens, where he celebrated the Eleusinian Mysteries. Lucius Verus stopped in Ephesus and then proceeded along the S coast of Asia Minor to Antioch where he spent most of the campaign. To compensate for Lucius Verus' lack of military experience, Marcus Aurelius appointed a seasoned general, Avidius Cassius, as commander in Syria, and his best field commanders to the campaign. Fortunately for the Romans, Lucius Verus sensibly delegated his authority to these capable generals and used his influence to obtain critical military supplies. While in Antioch Lucius Verus found a talented "woman of perfect beauty" named Panthea from Smyrna, which appears to have prompted Marcus Aurelius to accelerate plans for him to marry. In early 164 in the middle of the war, Lucius Verus went to Ephesus and married Marcus Aurelius' daughter Lucilla, not yet fifteen.

*Lucius Verus*

The steadfast Romans conducted a methodical five-year (161-166) campaign. After beating back Parthian attacks, Roman forces retook the Armenian capital Artaxata and took the offensive in Mesopotamia. The Parthians retreated to Nisibis, but the city was besieged and captured. A second Roman force moved down the Euphrates, and fought a major battle at Dura Europas. By the end of 165 the Romans proceeded down the Tigris River and reached Seleucia on the right (W) bank and Ctesiphon on the left (E). Ctesiphon was occupied and the royal palace burned down; Seleucia was sacked. In 166 Vologases IV capitulated, ceded the W of Mesopotamia to Rome and acknowledged Gaius Julius Sohaemus, a Roman senator of Arsacid ancestry, as king of Armenia. Following this Roman victory Lucius Verus passed through Sardis and donated a large structure to the resident Jewish community, perhaps for services rendered during the war.

Lucius Verus returned to Rome, took the credit for the military successes, and celebrated a joint triumph with Marcus Aurelius in October 166. Sadly the victorious Roman army brought back a terrible plague from the E, likely smallpox, which killed as many as five million people (about 10% of the population) over the next 15 years. In 168 the two emperors left Rome and went N to the Danube to confront threatening Germanic tribes. Returning to Italy a year later, Lucius Verus fell ill, probably from smallpox, and died at the age of 38.

At Ephesus the Gate of Mazaeus and Mithridates is the triple-arch entrance (16 m high) to the agora from the

Lower Ephesus City

| | | |
|---|---|---|
| A Terrace Houses | D Trajan Fountain | G Main Agora |
| B Church of Virgin Mary | E Library of Celsus | H Theatre |
| C Marble Way | F Serapis Temple | I Arcadian Way |

Celsus Library built in 3-4 BCE by two wealthy freedmen (former slaves). Mazaeus and Mithridates dedicated the gate in both Latin and Greek to Emperor Augustus, his wife Livia and their son-in-law Agrippa. Inside the gate a $3^{rd}$ century inscription sets a price ceiling for bread. This $3^{rd}$ century BCE commercial agora was in the large open area (110 x 110 m) between the theater and the harbor surrounded with stoas. It was lined with shops on three sides. The two-storey Doric colonnade on the E side dates back to the reign of Emperor Nero. At the center of the agora were a sundial-water clock and statues of prominent citizens. In the SW corner are steps leading to $2^{nd}$ century ruins of a temple of Serapis where eight massive marble columns 1.5 m in diameter remain. Most historians view this temple as evidence of strong trade relations with Egypt, a major grain exporter in the $2^{nd}$ century. In the $4^{th}$ century the Serapis temple was converted into a Christian church. The Marble Way runs between the theatre and the Library of Celsus, paved with large marble slabs during the 5$^{th}$ century. It was once part of a Sacred Way that led from the theatre to the temple of Artemis. Ancient water and sewer channels ran underneath. Deep ruts in the street surface confirm heavy ancient wheeled traffic. A raised 8 m high Doric colonnade parallel to the street on the W side was built for pedestrians during the reign of Nero and decorated with

*Marble Way*

reliefs of gladiatorial combat. Along the Marble Way the carved head of a woman, a heart and a foot is an advertisement, perhaps the first in history, for the brothel. At the entrance of the theatre is a 2$^{nd}$ century BCE Hellenistic fountain set between two Ionic columns. The large theatre (145 m wide, 30 m high) held 25,000 spectators. The second storey of the three-level theatre was built during the 1$^{st}$ century reign of Nero, the third level during the 2$^{nd}$ century reign of Septimius Severus. The slope of the theatre increases for the higher rows of seats to ensure spectators higher up had a good view of the stage. The Emperor's box is near the center stage. It was here that St. Paul famously decried false gods, particularly Artemis, precipitating an angry riot of silversmiths who depended on the sale of Artemis idols for their livelihood. During Roman times this open-air theater was used for gladiatorial contests, as revealed with recent archaeological evidence of a large gladiator graveyard nearby. A Greek inscription on an archway between the theatre and the Marble

Way reads, "Long live the Christian Emperors and the Greens," referring to one of the main chariot racing teams.

The Arcadian Way, or Harbor Street, is an 11 m wide colonnaded street running 600 m from the theater to the harbor, which silted

*Ephesus Theatre: Scene of Artemis supporters riot against St. Paul*

up long ago. It was raised and rebuilt in marble during the reign of Emperor Arcadius (395-408). On each side were covered pedestrian walkways (5 m wide) paved with mosaics and lined with shops. In the $5^{th}$ century, fifty streetlights lined the Arcadian Way – a luxury only found here, at Antioch, and in Rome itself. During the reign of Emperor Justinian in the $6^{th}$ century statues of the Four Evangelists (Mathew, Mark, Luke and John) were placed in the midpoint of the street where the pedestals can still be seen to this day. To the N $2^{nd}$ century ruins of the harbor baths-gymnasium, built during the reign of Domitian and restored by Constantine II, constitute the largest structure (160 x 170 m) at Ephesus. Facing the entrance are pools and a façade decorated with wreathed bulls heads. The hall on the N side was dedicated to imperial cult worship of the emperor, and a hall on the S side was used for lectures and meetings. The city had one of the most advanced aqueduct systems in the ancient world, with multiple aqueducts of various sizes used to supply different areas of the city.

In the early 4th century, the long thin building (260 x 30 m) close to the harbor became the first church dedicated to the Virgin Mary. Austrian archeologists led by Otto Benndorf rediscovered this Church of Mary in the 1890s. The structure was first built in the 2nd century as part as 280 m long stoa complex, transformed into a church decorated with marble slabs from other buildings in about 400. The Church of Mary is sometimes called the Double Church because it is believed that one side was dedicated to the Virgin Mary, while the other was dedicated to St. John. On the N side of the church stands a well-preserved baptistery with a central pool. ( A baptistery in early Christian architecture was a separate structure built around a baptismal font or pool. Most baptisteries date from after 325, when large numbers of adults converted to Christianity following the example of Emperor Constantine, but before the 9th century when infant baptism became commonplace.)

*Church of the Virgin Mary*

In the early 5th century Bishop Nestorius of Constantinople believed no union was possible between the human and the divine and preached against using the term "Mother of God" to refer to the Virgin Mary. In response in 431 Emperor Theodosius II called the Third Ecumenical Council at Ephesus, which was held in the Church of the Virgin Mary. The 245 bishops present condemned the views of Nestorius as heresy and banished him. Mary was formally declared "Mother of God." Near the lower entrance lie the 2nd-3rd century ruins of the Vedius gymnasium and the stadium. This stadium was the venue of gladiatorial contests and a place where many early Christians were martyred before the days of Emperor Constantine.

**Otto Benndorf (1838-1907)** was a German-Austrian archaeologist who played a leading role in excavating Ephesus. Benndorf was an accomplished academic archeologist who taught at the universities of Zurich, Munich, Prague and finally Vienna from 1877. Among his students were Friedrich Nietzsche and Michael Rostovtzeff, a prominent Russian-American archeologist. Together with Carl Humann Benndorf organized early excavations at Ephesus starting in 1895. Initially these excavations built on the work of John Turtle Wood at the temple of Artemis, but then expanded to discover other important structures such as the Ephesus agora, Library of Celsus, and Church of the Virgin Mary. Benndorf founded the Austrian Archaeological Institute in 1898 and continued as its director until his death. Largely due to his work, Austrian archeologists established a strong presence at Ephesus and a powerful legacy at the Ephesus Museum in Vienna.

The Austrian Archeological Institute has an excellent website covering Ephesus in depth at:
http://www.oeai.at/index.php/excavation-history.html

The website of the Museum of Ephesus in Vienna is:
http://www.khm.at/en/collections/ephesos-museum

*Magnesia*

**Magnesia on the Meander** (37° 51' 8" N, 27° 31' 41" E), located 19 km SE of Ephesus and 24 km N of Miletus, is on the W side of a major Turkish road, which cuts through the site. Magnesia is on the banks of the Lethacus River, a small tributary of the Meander River upstream from Ephesus. The city was named Magnesia after colonists from the original Magnesia in northern Greece, and called "on the Meander" to distinguish it from Magnesia ad Sipylum. According to an inscription found at the site, a prophecy of Apollo led the first settlers to Leukophryene (white eyebrows) the daughter of a local king who betrayed her city to the Magnesians. Although Magnesia lay within Ionia, it was not accepted into the Ionian League because its settlers were Aeolians rather than Ionians. Lydians and then later Persians conquered and ruled Magnesia. Destroyed by invading Cimmerians in the mid-7$^{th}$ century BCE, the city slowly recovered and became the residence of a Persian satrap (governor) in the 6$^{th}$ century BCE. A temple of Artemis was first built in the 6$^{th}$ century BCE at the foot of Mount Thorax and after 392 BCE the entire city of Magnesia was transplanted to the more defensible area near the temple. Alexander the Great visited in 334 BCE and expelled the Persians. According to tradition, a theophany occurred when Artemis appeared and the oracle at Delphi declared Magnesia holy ground. In 208 BCE representatives from Magnesia went all over the Hellenistic world seeking recognition for new quadrennial Pan-Hellenic games at the city to honor Artemis. As numerous inscriptions at Magnesia attest, seventy Hellenistic cities and monarchs from as far afield as Sicily and Persia agreed to participate. In 87 BCE Magnesia resisted Mithridates VI of Pontus for which Roman general Sulla rewarded the city with political autonomy.

**Magnesia on the Meander Site**: The city walls, cut by the modern highway, date back to 620-630 in the late Roman period. Many previously excavated structures at this extensive but seldom-visited site have been reburied under river silt. Ruins are still visible of the large Artemis temple, originally built in the 6$^{th}$ century BCE, then redesigned and rebuilt by Hermogenes of Alabanda in 220 BCE. The temple stood on a large platform (41 x 67 m) facing W surrounded with 15 Ionic columns along the long side, eight along the short. The foundations of the altar remain. At Magnesia Hermogenes designed the earliest known example in Asia Minor of an architrave (main beam or lintel over a door) decorated with a continuous 175 m long frieze. The subject of the frieze is an Amazonomachy, and it depicts Greek warriors and Amazons engaged in violent fighting with rearing horses, dueling individuals and wounded fighters collapsed on the ground. This iconography resembles the 4$^{th}$ century BCE Amazonomachy at the Mausoleum of Halicarnassus. Attractive fragments of this Amazonomachy frieze remain *in situ* atop the columns in what was the temple of Artemis, later transformed into a Christian church. Much of the Magnesia Amazonomachy now can be seen in Istanbul, Berlin and particularly Paris, where 43 panels of the frieze make up the largest group of architectural sculptures at the Louvre.

Amazonomachy depicts the power struggle between the sexes in violent physical terms. One of the twelve labors of Hercules was to recover the girdle of the Amazon queen Hippolyta, which she had obtained

*Amazonomachy*

from her father Ares, god of war. Theseus, founder of Athens, accompanied Hercules on his journey. When Hercules arrived in the remote northern land of the Amazons, Hippolyta met with him, learned the purpose of his visit and initially agreed to hand over her girdle. However, Hera, always jealous of Hercules, spread the rumor that Hercules and Theseus had come to abduct the queen. The Amazons attacked, forcing Hercules and Theseus to defend themselves and escape. Hercules took Hippolyta's girdle and Theseus seized the queen and carried her off to Athens as a reluctant trophy. The abduction of Hippolyta eventually led to a retaliatory Amazon invasion of Attica. However, by this time Theseus had impregnated Hippolyta, who bore him a son named Hippolytus. The Amazon army besieged Athens, demanded the return of Hippolyta and her girdle. Hippolyta, who by this time had fallen in love with Theseus and intended to remain in Athens, attempted to arrange a peace but was accidently killed by an Amazon archer. With the death of their queen, the Amazons withdrew from Attica after suffering heavy losses. To ancient Greeks Amazons represented savagery and their defeat was a triumph of civilization and the natural order. The Amazon image is derived from the nomadic Scythians from the steppes of Ukraine and Russia, frequent enemies of the Greeks, and Amazons were often depicted in Scythian dress. Archaeological evidence confirms that Scythian women participated in warfare.

At Magnesia a 1st century monumental gateway (propylon) leads to the large colonnaded agora (188 x 99 m). A 2nd century BCE temple of Zeus, similar to the temple of Artemis but smaller (16 x 7 m), once stood to the S of the agora. To the S lie partially buried remnants of a 3rd century theatre built into the hillside with capacity for 3,000 spectators. Near the center of the site is a 2nd century gymnasium-baths complex. Further to the S are buried remains of a horseshoe-shaped Roman stadium, which once had capacity for 28,000 people. Reliefs found here depicted captured armor, helmets and shields, suggesting gladiatorial games were held in this stadium. On the E side of the highway is another 2nd century gymnasium-baths complex. Since 1985 archeologists from the University of Ankara have excavated Magnesia. Professor Orhan Bingöl is Magnesia site director and comprehensive information is available in English at the website: http://magnesia.org/index.htm

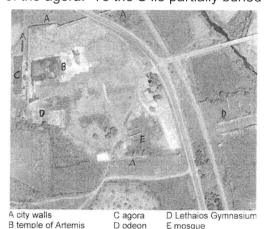

A city walls  C agora  D Lethaios Gymnasium
B temple of Artemis  D odeon  E mosque

*Magnesia*

**Priene** (37° 39' 33" N, 27° 17' 49" E) is situated in a pine forest on the edge of Mount Mycale near the modern village Güllübahce (rose garden), 40 km S of Kuşadası and 25 km N of Miletus. By the 8th century BCE the Ionian League met regularly at a temple of Poseidon at Priene. In about 540 BCE the Persians captured Priene. The city took part in the subsequent Ionian revolts led by Miletus against Persian rule (499–494 BCE). In 350 BCE the city was rebuilt at its present site with support from Athens along the lines recommended by Hippodamus. Paved streets intersected at right angles to form equal-sized city blocks with a distinct central area reserved for public buildings on level terraces connected by stairways up steep slopes. In 334 BCE Alexander the Great resided in Priene during his lengthy siege of Persian-ruled Miletus. Alexander contributed to the temple of Athena and the house where he stayed became a temple. The growth of Priene was severely constrained by its mountainous location and the maximum population was only about 6000. The extensive site commands a panoramic view of the surrounding valley, which was seacoast in the 4th century BCE. Priene faced a perennial problem because the Meander River silted up its harbor and by the 1st century BCE Priene no longer had a nearby seaport. Although Priene was incorporated into the Roman Empire in 129 BCE, it was not prosperous enough to be rebuilt under the Romans and therefore retains its older Hellenistic character. During the late Roman period Priene had a Jewish community and a substantial enough Christian community to have a bishop. The city gradually declined and was abandoned

A city walls  F temple of Athena  K temple of Asclepius
B site entrance  G Alexander house  L bouleterion
C Egyptian temple  H synagogue  M prytaneum
D theatre  I Cybele sanctuary  N gymnasium
E temple of Demeter  J agora  O stadium

*Priene*

completely after the arrival of the Turks in the 13<sup>th</sup> century.

**Priene Site**: The ruins are enclosed within largely intact 4<sup>th</sup> century BCE city walls (6 m high), with towers and three principal gates. The city was built on successive terraces that rise up a steep hill connected with stairs. Priene was laid out in an orderly grid plan: six main streets run E-W intersecting 15 evenly spaced cross streets at right angles. The town was divided into 80 blocks, each 47 x 35 m, of which 30 were for temples and official building, 50 devoted to private residences. Most of the residential blocks were on the W side of town. Affluent houses were four to a block; common houses were eight per block. Official buildings and temples would fit exactly on one, two or three blocks and generally open onto the E-W streets above the agora. Buildings faced S to receive more sun in the winter less in summer. Water flowed in from the mountain via an aqueduct and was distributed throughout the city, providing many houses with indoor plumbing. Private houses usually contained a rectangular courtyard, enclosed by living quarters and storerooms, which opened to the street via a narrow entranceway. Visitors approach up a steep slope from the E through the old city walls.

The remains of a 3<sup>rd</sup> century BCE temple of the Egyptian gods Serapis, Isis, Harpocrates and Anubis are SW of the main gate on the E edge of the city. The stone foundation (47 x 31 m) of the temple included a 5 m high terrace wall and a stone altar. Inscriptions found at the site name the gods and specify detailed worship rituals. One inscription states that unless an Egyptian priest supervised these rituals a financial penalty would be incurred, which demonstrates how foreign the cult must have been to local people.

Isis is the goddess of motherhood, magic and fertility, an ideal mother and wife, as well as patron of nature. Her consort Osiris began as a pharaoh who taught Egyptians the arts of civilization, particularly agriculture. Set was Osiris' evil and jealous brother who conspired to assassinate Osiris and seize power. Set secretly made a wooden sarcophagus exactly the right size for Osiris. At a royal party, Set managed to fool Osiris into getting into the coffin, which he and his accomplices then slammed shut, sealed with lead, and threw into the Nile. Upon realizing that Osiris was gone, Isis went looking for him. She eventually learned that the coffin had floated down the Nile River and along the Mediterranean coast to Byblos in Phoenicia (Lebanon) where it became embedded in the trunk of a cedar tree. The cedar tree was made into a pillar at the King of Byblos' palace. Isis managed to retrieve the coffin and open it, but Osiris was already dead. Isis brought his body back to Egypt and hid it. Out hunting one night, Set came across the hidden body of Osiris. Enraged, he tore the body into fourteen pieces and scattered them throughout the land. Once again Isis set out to look for the body parts of Osiris, but she could only find 13 of the 14 parts because a fish had eaten his phallus. Isis made him a new one out of gold and sang until Osiris came back to life long enough to impregnate her. Afterwards he died again, but this time he had a proper burial. Isis gave birth to Horus at the Nile Delta and then fled with her newborn to escape the wrath of Set. Isis protected and raised Horus until he was old enough to defeat Set and become Pharaoh of Egypt. Ancient Egyptians believed that the Nile River flooded every year because of Isis' tears of sorrow for losing Osiris. Each year religious rituals reenacted the death and rebirth of Osiris. Isis was depicted holding her young child, Horus, with a crown and a vulture. The iconography of Isis as mother and protector of Horus was strikingly similar to Christian depictions of the Virgin Mary holding baby Jesus. During the formative stage of Christianity, worship of Isis was widely popular throughout the Roman Empire. As in early Christianity, the story of Osiris, Isis and Horus involves a trinity. Although of divine origin, Osiris suffered death and mutilation at the hands of evil. After a great struggle he arose to become king of the underworld and judge of the dead. Ancient Egyptian followers of Osiris and Isis believed in resurrection. In death a person would face judgment by a tribunal of divine judges. Those who had lived in

*Isis (Antalya Museum)*

righteousness would be welcomed into the Kingdom of Osiris. Those who had not would face a devourer and be denied eternal life. Isis came close to being a universal goddess worshipped throughout the Mediterranean world. Scholars believe early Christians sometimes worshipped before depictions of Isis and Horus as representations of the Virgin Mary and Jesus. Given these basic similarities, early Christians naturally regarded the cult of Isis as a rival and a threat.

Harpocrates is a manifestation of the god Horus as a Child. Horus was the son of Isis and Osiris. Osiris was the original god-king of Egypt, who became the god of the underworld. Horus was the nephew of Set, Osiris's brother. When Set murdered Osiris and contested Horus's inheritance, i.e., the royal throne of Egypt, Horus became Set's enemy. Horus battled Set and was finally victorious, avenging his father and assuming rule over the earth. Pharaohs of Egypt were reincarnations of Horus. Under Ptolemaic rule, Serapis was identified with Osiris as the consort of Isis and father of Horus. Harpocrates is represented as a child with his finger pressed upon his lips. For Greeks and Romans he became the god of silence and secrecy. For this reason, his statue was placed at the entrance of temples where mysteries were celebrated and secret rituals practiced.

Anubis, the Egyptian god of mummification, has the body of a man with the head of a jackal. Anubis is a son of Osiris, the god of the underworld, and Nephthys, the consort of Osiris' brother Set. One night Nephthys tricked Osiris, getting him drunk and pretending to be Isis. The result of this illicit union was Anubis. He invented embalming and, at one point, even embalmed the dead Osiris and preserved him to live again as god of the underworld. Anubis cares for the dead and guides souls to the underworld. He tests the dead for their knowledge of the gods and their faith. Anubis places the heart of the deceased on scales of justice during the Judging of the Heart procedure. If the heart is lighter than a feather, the soul lives forever in the underworld. If not, Ammit the destroyer, a creature with the head of a crocodile, shoulders of a lion and hindquarters of a hippopotamus, devours the heart.

Visitors to Priene can continue W two blocks to the well-preserved 4th century BCE theatre on the right. Although the stage area was modified and expanded under Roman rule, the essentially Hellenistic architecture of horseshoe-shaped seating area with capacity for 5,000 remains intact. Five majestic 2nd century BCE marble chairs with lion claws on the arms and legs were reserved for leading dignitaries. In the late Roman period, the S edge of the theatre stage area was converted into a bishop's church with a central nave and two aisles. The 4th century BCE temple of Demeter and Persephone lies three blocks N on a much higher terrace above the rest of the city. The large sanctuary (45 x 18 m) was entered from the E and contains fragments of walls and columns, and a Roman period altar to the right.

*Priene Theatre*

*Temple of Athena built by Pythius*

The magnificent temple of Athena lies in the center of Priene and was the largest and most important building in the city. Pythius of Priene built the temple in the mid 4th century BCE and it became a highly influential example of a structure designed in the Ionic order.

**The Ionic order was strongly preferred by Pythius of Priene, the architect responsible for the temple of Athena at Priene as well as the Mausoleum at Halicarnassus (tomb of Mausolus). The Roman architect Vitruvius mentions the Commentaries of Pythius, now lost, which was used to train architects for centuries. Pythius criticized problems and inconsistencies in the Doric order and was a major proponent of the Ionic order for erecting temples and public buildings. The Ionic order originated in the Greek-speaking cities along the Aegean coast of Asia Minor in the mid-6th century BCE. An Ionic column capital is decorated with a**

carved egg-and-dart motif and what appear to be rolled scrolls (volutes), adapted from Phoenician and Egyptian designs. Without the Doric wood end motif in the entablature above the columns, the Ionic frieze can hold a continuous band of reliefs. Another difference is that an Ionic column has 24 vertical grooves (flutes) along the shaft, as compared to only 20 for the Doric. Most importantly an Ionic column is narrower with a height 9-10 times the base diameter, as opposed to the proportions of a Doric column 5-6 times the base. The famous 6th century BCE temple of Artemis at Ephesus was built in the Ionic order, as was the temple of Apollo at Didyma. The style and innovation Pythius used in designing the temple of Athena at Priene was widely replicated throughout the Hellenistic world.

The temple of Athena rested on a three-stepped rectangular platform (37 x 20 m). A large porch (pronaos) on the E side, longer than in earlier temples, led to a cella where at the W end a 6.5 m high statue of Athena stood on a pedestal, helmeted with goatskin, spear and shield, holding Nike in her right hand. The cella was exactly twice as large as the pronaos. For the first time, Pythius added a porch at the rear of the temple. The temple was surrounded with 34 Ionic columns, each with a diameter one tenth of their height, eleven on the long side, and six on the short side, as well as two columns each at the pronaos and back porch. Five columns still stand. Traces or red and blue paint found on the structure confirm it was brightly painted in ancient times. The mid-2nd century BCE altar to the E side of the temple included a Titanomachy relief (now in Istanbul), a smaller scale version of the Great Altar of Zeus at Pergamum. When Alexander the Great resided in Priene in 334 BCE, he agreed to pay for the ongoing temple construction as attested in a famous inscription from the Priene temple, which reads, "King Alexander has dedicated this Temple to Athena Polias." Visitors can see the original inscription at the British Museum:

http://www.britishmuseum.org/explore/highlights/highlight_image.aspx?image=k63220.jpg&retpage=18026

Much later during Roman rule a monumental gateway was built connecting the temple to the street in front. In the 1st century the temple was rededicated to both Athena and Emperor Augustus.

Athena (Antalya Museum)

Athena (Minerva to Romans) is a daughter of Zeus and Metis. Athena is goddess of reason, strategic warfare, and justice. Upon learning that Metis could produce offspring greater than he, Zeus swallowed Metis whole. Sometime later Zeus was afflicted with an extreme headache. With the help of Hephaestus, Zeus' head was temporarily opened and out sprang the fully-grown Athena, dressed in the gown and helmet of her mother. Athena is usually portrayed wearing body armor with her helmet, carrying a shield and a lance. During the Titanomachy, Athena slew the fearsome giant Pallas. She represented the disciplined, strategic side of war, as opposed to the violent savagery and wholesale slaughter of Ares, the god of war. Athena protected the state from external enemies and supported only civilized, prudent military undertakings likely to have favorable results. Her companion is Nike, the goddess of victory. Her shield bears the defensive image of the Medusa head with its petrifying power.

Athena serves as a caring mentor for worthy heroes such as Hercules, Odysseus and Bellerophon, but never takes a lover. Athena is the enforcer of rules of sexual modesty and Medusa was punished for violating those rules. Because Tiresias encountered Athena naked in her bath, she punished him by making him blind. However, Athena later pitied him and gave him the ability to understand the language of the birds, and hence the gift of prophecy. Beyond her military role, Athena is also goddess of civilization and industry, as opposed to Artemis, goddess of nature and hunting. Athena encourages practical peacetime pursuits and crafts. In her contest with

Poseidon to be the chief deity of Athens, her advocacy of olive tree cultivation won over the population. Athena tamed horses, allowing men to use them. She also invented the flute but discarded it and cursed it when the other Olympians made fun of her. Later the hapless satyr Marsayas picked it up and was punished for his impudence. Athena was also renowned as goddess of spinning. On one occasion, a Lydian girl named Arachne, who was a master spinner, had the temerity to claim her work was superior to that of Athena. The furious Athena changed Arachne into a spider condemned to spin forever. Athena maintains the authority of the law in support of justice and order. During the trial of Orestes for matricide, Athena broke the deadlock and established the precedent that a tied jury vote results in acquittal.

In Priene the House of Alexander the Great is on the main street leading to the W gate one block down from the temple of Athena. Alexander lived in this house in 334 BCE during the prolonged siege of Miletus, and it was later converted into a temple dedicated to his memory. At this house were found a small marble likeness of Alexander and an inscription admonishing that only the pure, dressed in white should enter (both are now in Berlin). The $4^{th}$-$7^{th}$ century Priene Synagogue, just above the House of Alexander, was first discovered in the late $19^{th}$ century but initially was considered a Christian house church. The synagogue was built into an older Hellenistic house and consisted of a main hall with two rows of columns forming a small basilica, of which only one remains in place. In 1928 archaeologists correctly identified the building as a synagogue because they found a niche for Torah scrolls in the E wall. (The Torah refers to the first five books of the Old Testament.) There were also two carved stone menorahs found at the site: one with a lulav (palm branch), shofar (ram's horn) and etrog (citron) and another with two peacocks, a lulav and an etrog. Priene is one of the few sites in Asia Minor where the exact location of an ancient synagogue has been identified.

**Sukkot, lulav and etrog:** Sukkot or the Feast of Ingathering is a harvest holiday stipulated in the Old Testament Book of Leviticus and celebrated on the 15th day of the month of Tishrei, which falls in late September-October. Sukkot recalls the time when Jews would build huts, known as sukkah, near their fields during the harvest. On the first day of the 7-8 day holiday work is forbidden and holiday meals are eaten inside the sukkah, which symbolizes the fragile dwellings where the Israelites lived during their forty years in the wilderness after fleeing Egypt. Each day Jews recite a blessing using four natural items: the lulav (date palm frond), hadas (myrtle bough), aravah (willow branch) and etrog, a citrus fruit similar to a lemon in appearance and taste, but with little juice. The lulav, myrtle and willow are held in one hand while the etrog is held in the other. The worshipper brings his hands together and waves the items up and down in all four directions to attest to God's mastery of creation and to pray for adequate rainfall during the coming year.

At Priene a Cybele sanctuary once occupied a spot further W next to the W Gate along the S side of the main road. The large $3^{rd}$ century BCE agora (76 x 35 m) is several blocks E along this main road from the W Gate and forms the center of the city. Doric porticoes surrounded the agora on three sides and an altar dedicated to Hermes stood in the center. The $2^{nd}$ century BCE Ionic temple of Asclepius, which was previously misidentified as a temple of Zeus, is directly to the E of the agora. Pythius designed this temple in the same Ionic style as the Temple of Athena, but on a significantly smaller scale (8.5 x 13.5 m). A statue of Asclepius once stood to the S, the altar (5 x 4 m) was to the E, and there was portico on the N side. Ruins of a fortress and church built in the $13^{th}$ century lie on the NE corner. The square-shaped, $2^{nd}$ century BCE bouleuterion (20 x 21 m) stands directly N of the Asclepius temple and only seated 640 in ten rows of seats under a wooden roof. In the center was a marble altar decorated with bulls' heads and laurel leaves. Next door to the bouleuterion was the prytaneum (city hall) where the sacred fire of Hestia was kept. The large stadium (190 x 18 m) lies on a terrace 60 m below the main city, but within the walls and accessible via a stairway to the SW. The upper and lower gymnasiums are adjacent to a stadium to the W. All three date back to the $2^{nd}$ century BCE. The German Archeological Institute is largely responsible for excavations at Priene: http://www.dainst.org/en/project/priene?ft=33%2B162

**Miletus** (37° 31' 50" N, 27° 16' 33" E), 25 km S of Priene, is an ancient city near the mouth of the Meander River. Miletus, the leading city in Asia Minor during the 10th-5th centuries BCE, was a major port city with four natural harbors. Now it lies 8 km from the Aegean Sea due to silting from the Meander River. Homer recounts in the Iliad how Miletians fought as Trojan allies in the Trojan War. Miletus established colonies around the Mediterranean and Black Seas. In the late 5th century BCE the Miletian alphabet, obtained from the Phoenicians, was adopted by Athens and became the standard Greek alphabet. In 499 BCE Miletus led the Greek rebellion against the Persians, which prompted the Persians to destroy Miletus five years later. The city was rebuilt in 479 BCE with streets laid out in the grid pattern that the city planner, Hippodamus of Miletus, advocated. Over time Miletus gradually declined as its harbors turned into swampland.

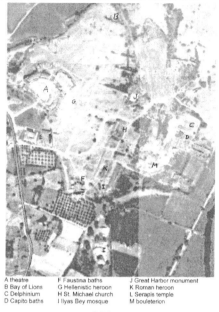

A theatre    F Faustina baths    J Great Harbor monument
B Bay of Lions    G Hellenistic heroon    K Roman heroon
C Delphinium    H St. Michael church    L Serapis temple
D Capito baths    I Ilyas Bey mosque    M bouleterion

*Miletus*

**Hippodamus of Miletus (498–408 BCE) was the father of urban planning who developed a grid pattern with straight streets intersecting at right angles to form quadrilateral city blocks. He was a brilliant urban planner, political theorist, and eccentric who made his own clothes and wore long hair. Hippodamus emphasized social order and rationality in contrast to the arbitrary, chaotic and confused development common to most ancient cities. Hippodamus first applied this geometric approach in 479 BCE when he oversaw the reconstruction of his home city Miletus following the Persian destruction. Miletus was the grid plan prototype with public spaces and buildings in the city center, blocks created by streets and side streets crossing at right angles. Hippodamus even aligned buildings and streets so that**

the flow of mountain and sea breezes would help cool the town during the hot summers.

At the request of his friend Pericles, the Athenian leader, Hippodamus went to Athens in 475 BCE and designed the new harbor town of Piraeus. In 443 BCE Hippodamus accompanied Athenian settlers to Thurii in Italy as the new colony's architect. His town planning concepts were also applied at Priene, Ephesus and Rhodes. Eventually these grid plans were replicated throughout the Roman Empire. Aristotle, in his classic work Politics, outlines Hippodamus' concept of three social classes: warriors, craftsmen and farmers, as well as three related types of urban land usage: religious (temples), public (markets,

*Miletus Theatre*

infrastructure, administration) and private (dwellings, farms). Hippodamus envisioned an ideal city with about 10,000 free male inhabitants or a total population of about 50,000. From Hippodamus came the earliest notions of patent law as a means for society to reward individuals who create socially useful items and make practical innovations.

**Miletus Site:** The lower parts of the extensive Miletus site are subject to flooding. The enormous theatre (140 m wide, 30 m high), which was once directly on the coastline but now sits on the river's floodplain, is the first building visitors see. The original Hellenistic theatre was greatly expanded under Roman rule in about 100 to reach a capacity of 15,000. Ancient inscriptions still visible reserve seats for particular groups. For example, the third row of seats from the bottom says, "Reserved for the goldsmiths of the Blue Team," referring an important chariot-racing team in the late Roman Empire. Another inscription marked seats for "Jews and god-worshippers," which is believed to refer to Jews and non-Jewish monotheists, among the first Christian converts. S of the theatre is a 15th century caravanserai. To the E of the theatre is the round Hellenistic heroon, built in honor of a currently unknown hero. To the NE is the Great Harbor Monument, first erected to honor Pompey for eliminating coastal pirates, and

*Great Harbor Monument*

subsequently modified to celebrate Augustus' victory at Actium. The monument depicts a triton with a dolphin and is partially submerged. The Great Harbor Monument is where, according to the New Testament Book of Acts, St. Paul spoke encouraging words to the Ephesian Elders in the year 57, when he told them that he would see them no more. It was here that St. Paul quoted Jesus to the effect that, "It is more blessed to give than to receive." Near the NW corner of the Harbor Monument are is a ruined Roman structure identified as a synagogue. The Harbor Monument was once on the edge of the Bay of Lions, but now stands in a swamp. In ancient Miletus, during times of danger a chain would be laid across this bay between two lion statues to prevent hostile ships from entering. One of these lions is still visible on the W side of the former bay. To the E was the harbor with a row of shops and a 160 m long Doric stoa or covered walkway on the S side. To the E of the stoa lies the low, largely submerged 6th century BCE Delphinium, a temple representing Apollo as a dolphin, the form he used to guide the first settlers to Miletus. From the Delphinium an ancient Sacred Way led 15 km to Didyma. Next, to the S, are large 1st century baths built by

Vergilius Capito, governor of Roman Asia under Emperor Claudius. Later 15th century Selçuk baths stand in front. The marshland between these structures was once the N and S agora.

Further S is the 7th century Church of Saint Michael, built over a temple of Dionysus, with a modern building built to cover its rather limited mosaics. Nearby to the SW is the early 14th century Ilyas Bey Mosque. NW of the church are the 2nd century BCE bouleuterion ruins, and a 2nd century Roman nymphaeum.

*Serapis*

Between the bouleuterion and Ilyas Bey Mosque are impressive remains of the 3rd century temple of Serapis. Although most of the structure is covered with vegetation, the pediment still depicts Serapis with rays of sun radiating out from his head. (The pediment is the triangular section above an ancient building supported with columns, often decorated with sculptures and reliefs.) To the W are the impressive and well preserved 2nd century Baths of Faustina, wife of Emperor Marcus Aurelius. Within the bath complex is a reclining figure – the Meander River God. During 19th century excavations the Market Gate of Miletus was discovered and transported to Germany where it can now be seen at the Pergamon Museum in Berlin:

*Menander River God*

http://www.smb.museum/smb/kalender/details.php?objID=17477&typeId=10

Professor Volkmar von Graeve of Ruhr-University in Bochum, Germany as well as other Austrian and German archeologists, have done considerable work at this important site as described in English and German:

http://www.oeai.at/index.php/miletusartemis-chitone.html

http://www.dainst.org/en/project/miletos?ft=33%2B162

**Didyma** (37° 23' 6" N, 27° 15' 22" E) was an ancient religious sanctuary, which contained a temple and oracle of Apollo. Zeus chose this venue for his tryst with Leto, which produced the twins Apollo and Artemis (Didyma means twin). Branchus was a son of Apollo and a mortal woman from Miletus, who received prophetic abilities from Apollo and introduced his worship at Didyma. Branchus' descendants, the Branchides, were an influential clan of prophets and priests who administered the temple. Although the oracle at Didyma dates back to even before the Ionians arrived in the 10th century BCE, its prominence and renown grew significantly after Lydian King Croesus became a major benefactor in the 5th century BCE. Didyma became the second most renowned oracle in the Hellenistic world after Delphi. Didyma was not a town, but rather a large religious sanctuary belonging to Miletus and approached from that city via a 15 km long Sacred Way. The final stretch of this sacred road was lined with statues of lions, priests, and priestesses. In 1857-1858 Sir Charles Newton recovered some of these statues for the British Museum, an example of which is a sculpture of an individual ruler named Chares dedicated to Apollo:

http://www.britishmuseum.org/explore/highlights/highlight_objects/gr/m/marble_statue_of_chares.aspx

In 494 BCE the Persians destroyed Didyma sanctuary, expelled the priests, and carried away an ancient bronze statute of Apollo. The sacred spring dried up and the oracle was silenced for more than 150 years. After 334 BCE the sacred spring flowed again after Alexander the Great and the Macedonians re-consecrated the oracle and rebuilt the temple on a much larger scale. Each year beginning in the $2^{nd}$ century BCE a Pan-Hellenic festival was held at the temple. According to ancient sources the oracle successfully predicted: that Alexander would defeat the Persians; that Macedonian general Seleucus I Nicator would become king but should avoid crossing in Europe (where he was assassinated); and that Trajan would become Roman emperor. Some sources claim that during the $3^{rd}$ century the Didyma oracle recommended Diocletian's persecution of Christians. By the $4^{th}$ century belief in the oracle of Apollo dwindled with the rise of Christianity, which regarded oracles as work of the devil. In the $5^{th}$ century Emperor Theodosius II built a church within the temple courtyard, effectively shutting down the oracle as incompatible with Christian faith.

The god Apollo, together with his twin sister Artemis, was the offspring of the goddess Leto and Zeus. Hera, queen of the gods, tried to prevent their birth and sent the serpent Python to attack Leto. When he was four days old, Apollo went after the Python to avenge its attack on his mother. He went straight to Mount Parnassus, chased the Python to the oracle at Delphi, entered the sacred precinct with the oracle priestess, and killed the Python with his arrows. Apollo then took over responsibility for the oracle at Delphi. The oracle priestess was known as the Pythia, in honor of the Python. Apollo was only able to speak truth and could foretell the future with unerring accuracy, which is why oracles are attributed to him.

As punishment for killing the Python at this sacred spot, Zeus ordered Apollo to work for one year as a servant and shepherd for King Admetus of Pherae. The king, who did not know Apollo's true identity, turned out to be a kind and pious man who treated him well. Admetus was very interested in marrying Alestis, a highly desirable princess with many suitors. To find Alestis the best possible husband, her father set the seemingly impossible task of yoking a boar and a lion to the same chariot as a condition for obtaining the princess. In his capacity of servant, Apollo yoked the two together and Admetus married Alestis. At the end of his year of servitude, Apollo used his gift of prophecy to look into the future and learned that Admetus was fated to die soon. However, Apollo could intercede with the fates and avoid an early death for Admetus, if another would willingly take his place. To the surprise of Admetus, neither of his elderly parents was willing to make this sacrifice, but his young wife Alestis immediately agreed. Once the deed was done, Admetus deeply regretted having allowed Alestis to die in his place. Later Hercules visited Admetus and was so deeply impressed with his hospitality and sense of justice that he was determined to help him. Hercules found and wrestled with Thanatos, the demi-god of death, until he released Alcestis, and then Hercules led her back to the mortal world and to her husband Admetus.

Daphne, meaning laurel, was a water nymph and daughter of the river god Peneus. One day Eros struck Apollo with a golden arrow and caused him to fall in love with Daphne. Sadly Daphne was struck with a lead arrow, which made her afraid of love, so when Apollo pursued and overtook her, the terrified Daphne called out to her father for help. To save her, Peneus turned his daughter into a laurel tree. Apollo, deeply saddened by his loss, decreed that from now on the laurel wreath would be a symbol of victory.

The silver arrows of Apollo and his twin sister Artemis were known for their ability to bring plague and sudden death, as that visited upon the children of Niobe. However, Apollo could also treat and cure illness. On one occasion Apollo fell deeply in love with the beautiful mortal woman Coronis and impregnated her. Coronis was by nature a sexually promiscuous woman. Apollo assigned a white raven to keep an eye on her while he attended to his many other responsibilities. When the white raven soon reported that Coronis was two-timing him, the furious Apollo blamed the messenger and turned the raven black, the color of mourning. Emotionally unable to destroy Coronis himself, he asked his sister Artemis to take care of it for him. Artemis killed Coronis for her adultery, but delivered and saved her baby who became Asclepius, god of medicine and healing.

Ever since the baby Hermes invented the lyre and gave it to Apollo in return for the stolen cattle, Apollo has been an accomplished musician. As leader of the Muses, he was god of music. The satyr Marsayas found a flute discarded by Athena and became such an expert flutist that he foolishly challenged Apollo to a musical competition. King Midas was chosen as one of the judges and Marsayas had the audacity to win the first round. Apollo ultimately triumphed and punished Marsayas severely for having the hubris to challenge a god. Apollo also turned the ears of King Midas into donkey ears because he had initially preferred the music of Marsayas.

*Temple of Apollo at Didyma*

On one occasion, Apollo was so smitten with Cassandra, the beautiful daughter of King Priam of Troy, when she fell asleep in his Trojan temple that he gave her the gift of prophecy. Apollo fully expected her, in return, to gladly become his lover, but sadly she refused. Furious at this rejection, Apollo then fated Cassandra to never be believed despite the fact that she could see the future. During the Trojan War, Cassandra warned her fellow Trojans about the Trojan Horse, but to no avail. After the fall of Troy she was raped by a Greek soldier in the temple of Athena and then carried off to

Greece as a slave of Agamemnon. Apollo favored the Trojans in the war and helped Aeneas to escape and found Rome. Apollo is god of colonists and his priests at Delphi, Didyma and elsewhere often gave divine guidance as to where and when colonial expeditions should be undertaken. Apollo is sometimes confused with Helios, the sun god who drives a golden chariot across the sky each day.

**Didyma Site:** This large Ionic temple rests on a huge podium (109 x 51 m) reached via a flight of stairs (3.5 m high) on the E side. Numerous well-preserved Ionic columns remain in place around the temple. Behind the temple porch was a great doorway where petitioners presented their queries. At Didyma inquiries and

*Column capital at Didyma*

answers were written. An antechamber with a 1.7 m high doorsill was the oracle archive where written copies of queries and the oracles were stored. From the E side of the temple two narrow passages lead down to the cella of the temple. At the W end of the cella is a temple within a temple, a small Ionic shrine believed to have held the statue of Apollo. A sacred spring ran through the cella, which was open to the sky but surrounded by high, thick walls. The prophetess would place her feet in the sacred spring or its water vapor. She then uttered words deliriously, which a priest would turn into hexameter verse, write down and present to the petitioner. The temple podium once also served as the wall of a stadium with benches bearing individual names. The site is

surrounded with reliefs and temple decorations, including decorative column capitals and gigantic heads of the Gorgons, Medusa and her sisters. Professor Andreas Furtwängler from the Martin Luther University at Halle-Wittenberg in Germany has conducted recent excavations at Didyma:
http://www.dainst.org/en/node/23947?ft=all

# VI ANCIENT REGION OF LYDIA

Lydia was the ancient region bordered by Aeolia and Ionia to the W, Mysia to the N, Phrygia to the E and Caria to the S. According to the ancient historian Herodotus, the ancient Mermand dynasty in Lydia began with an act of voyeurism. The reigning king of Sardis, Candaules, was so boastful of his queen's beauty that he insisted his bodyguard Gyges stand behind a curtain in royal bedroom and secretly observe the queen undress. Gyges obliged, but the queen noticed him. Later she summoned Gyges and, because her honor was besmirched, gave him a choice: he could die for causing her dishonor or he could kill the king for dishonoring her and replace him. Gyges chose the latter option and founded the Mermand dynasty, which ruled Lydia 680-547 BCE. He minted the first coins in about 650 BCE made from electrum, a mixture of gold and silver.

According to Herodotus, Lydian women, unlike Greek women, were allowed to choose their own husbands and the less affluent ones would routinely engage in prostitution before marriage to accumulate enough of a dowry to obtain a good husband. Lydia was known for rich deposits of gold, particularly in the Pactolus River where, under the direction of Dionysus, Midas washed away his golden touch. Probably for this reason, the Lydians were the first people to mint coins. In the $6^{th}$ century BCE during the reign of King Croesus, whose name is still synonymous with great wealth, Lydian conquests transformed the kingdom into an extensive empire. Croesus ruled from his magnificent capital at **Sardis**. In 547 BCE Persian King Cyrus the Great defeated Croesus and incorporated Lydia into the Persian Empire. Alexander the Great defeated Persia in 334 BCE and introduced

Greco-Macedonian rule. Rome's ally Pergamum ruled the territory from 189 BCE until 133 BCE when Lydia was included in the Roman province of Asia. **Sardis** on the Pactolus River is the principal ancient site in Lydia and was home to a large and prosperous Jewish community. The Lydians also founded the mountainous town of **Kibyra**, site of a well-preserved stadium and bouleuterion.

**Sardis** (38° 29' 18" N, 28° 2' 23" E), modern Sart, is 95 km E of Izmir (ancient Smyrna) and was the capital of ancient Lydia. Sardis was home to King Croesus and was where coins were first minted, which greatly facilitated trade and economic growth.

**Croesus: Sardis reached the peak of its wealth and power during the reign of King Croesus 560-546 BCE, and the expression rich as Croesus refers to this era. Sardis was the first city to mint coins, initially made from electrum, a naturally occurring gold-silver alloy. The ancient historian Herodotus reports that Croesus was the first ruler who managed to separate the two metals and mint pure gold and pure silver coins. The Athenian philosopher Solon was said to have visited Croesus, who asked him whom he considered the happiest man he ever met. Croesus, who believed himself to be that man, was annoyed when Solon mentioned an obscure Greek, but Solon maintained that only at death could lifelong happiness be reckoned. Although Croesus ruled almost all of W Asia Minor, he was concerned about the growing power of Persia to the E. Croesus consulted the oracle of Apollo at Delphi about whether to confront the Persians. The oracle replied that were he to attack Persia, he would "destroy a great empire." Croesus was pleased with this advice and attacked, but Persian King Cyrus the Great fought the invaders to a standstill. Croesus then withdrew to Sardis, whereupon Cyrus retaliated with a surprise winter attack. In 546 BCE the Persians conquered Sardis and captured Croesus, destroying a great empire as the oracle had prophesized. Cyrus intended to burn Croesus alive as an example to those who would defy him. However, just as the fire started Croesus prayed to Apollo and a sudden downpour extinguished the flames. Recognizing this as divine intervention, Cyrus immediately released Croesus and installed him as his**

senior advisor.

*Sardis: shops, Synagogue, Marble Hall; House of Bronzes and agora (in front)*

A large and influential Jewish community was established early in Sardis as the largest ancient Jewish synagogue yet discovered in the Diaspora confirms. The Old Testament refers to exiles from Jerusalem residing in Sepharad, Hebrew for Sardis, indicating a considerable resident Jewish population as early as the 6$^{th}$ century BCE. Some scholars even claim the term Sephardic Jew comes from Sardis. After 546 BCE Sardis was transformed into the major Persian imperial stronghold as the capital of the Persian satrapy of Sfarda. The Old Testament recounts that the edict of Haman threatened the large Jewish community in the Persian Empire at this time but Esther, as wife of the Persian ruler, together with her uncle Mordecai, saved her people from the edict. Although Greek culture predominated after Alexander the Great ended Persian rule in 334 BCE, Macedonian Seleucid kings settled Jewish military garrisons drawn from the poorer regions of Judea and Galilee as military colonists in Lydia and Phrygia, which expanded the Jewish community at Sardis and its commercial opportunities. From Sardis the Jewish community established commercial ties with coreligionists in distant cities. They developed basic principles of credit and banking, and adopted Greek as their primary language. However, the Jews at Sardis remained monotheistic and refused to worship foreign gods. They practiced circumcision and observed the Sabbath and the Law of Moses.

Direct Roman rule after 133 BCE further enhanced the prosperity of Sardis. As the ancient Roman-Jewish historian Josephus notes, the Roman governor at the time of Julius Caesar sent the

Jews of Sardis a formal letter to guaranteeing five basic rights: 1) to have a place of assembly, i.e., a synagogue; 2) to keep the Sabbath; 3) to eat kosher food; 4) to govern their own affairs; and 5) to contribute to the temple in Jerusalem. Later when a local administrator attempted to confiscate funds the Jewish community had collected to send to Jerusalem, Emperor Augustus overruled him. Scholars estimate that as much as ten percent of the Roman Empire's population was Jewish. The large Sardis synagogue demonstrates the size, importance, and civic integration of these ancient Jewish Diaspora communities.

The wealthy synagogue at Sardis attracted converts and sympathizers from the non-Jewish population. Even when circumcision and the dietary restrictions discouraged outright conversion, many non-Jewish citizens were drawn to monotheism and became known as "god-fearers." The earliest Christians were drawn from the Jewish community either as direct converts from Judaism or from the non-Jewish "god-fearers." The nascent development of Christian communities was highly dependent on the presence of local Jews and synagogues, as the strong geographic correlation between early Christian communities and established Jewish communities demonstrates. The Roman view that Jewish monotheism was legitimate enabled the first Christians to exist as a Jewish sect of Jesus followers. By the end of the 1st century, Sardis was a significant Christian center, as demonstrated by the fact that the Apostle John noted its church as one of the Seven Churches of

*Synagogue Forecourt*

Asia in the <u>New Testament</u> Book of Revelation. The 2$^{nd}$ century population is estimated to have been 100,000. After Sassanid Persians destroyed Sardis in 616, the city was largely abandoned.

**Sardis Site:** The 3$^{rd}$ century synagogue lies parallel to and N of the E-W road near the Sart village intersection. In the 3$^{rd}$ century, the S part of a gymnasium-bath complex was converted into a large synagogue. A Hebrew inscription records that Roman Emperor <u>Lucius Verus</u> gave the building to the Jewish community. The size and central location of this synagogue demonstrate the wealth and influence of the ancient Jewish community and confirm its integration into the larger community. This extensive synagogue (85 x 20 m) is the largest of any ancient Diaspora synagogue yet uncovered.

*Torah Shrine*

Inscriptions confirm that the Jews of Sardis had Greek names and most inscriptions were in Greek. One inscription near the synagogue entrance exhorts Jews to "find, open, read, observe" the commandments of God. The 25 m long forecourt to the synagogue contains a large marble basin in the center surrounded by columns. Floor mosaic panels identify ancient donors to the synagogue. The forecourt led to a long (60 m) main hall.

*Synagogue Lectern with lions and eagles*

Floors and walls were decorated with ornate mosaics and

elaborate marble designs.

Although most of the congregation stood or sat on mats on the mosaic-covered floor, the semicircular apse at the W end of the main hall had three rows of marble benches for elders.  During services for up to a thousand people, the congregation faced E toward Jerusalem.  There appears to have been no separate section for women; they may have worshipped with the men, or at different times or at home.  In front of the apse stands a large marble table used as a lectern for reading the Torah.  Thunderbolt-carrying eagles (once symbols of Zeus) support the marble table.  Double lions facing backwards and forwards flank the marble table.  These same lions once flanked a statue of Cybele in the 5$^{th}$-4$^{th}$ centuries BCE.  Archeological evidence suggests the Sardis Jews intentionally identified the traditional Sardis lion with the biblical Lion of Judah.  The marble eagle table and the lion sculptures are the only known instance of recycled pagan sculpture in a synagogue.  On the E wall of the main hall were two large square Torah shrines, which held reading scrolls.  Beneath the S shrine Hebrew inscriptions were found as well as a menorah plaque flanked by a shofar (ram horn) and a lulav (date palm frond) with rolled Torah scrolls carved under the curved branches.  Overall more than a dozen menorah representations were found at the site.

At Sardis adjacent to and S of the synagogue the 4$^{th}$ century main road was paved with marble and lined on the N side with 27 shops and a colonnade.  Six shops were marked with Jewish menorahs, and ten bore Christian crosses, while the others did not indicate religious affiliation.

*Sardis Marble Hall*

Archeologists have identified specific uses of individual shops, such as a restaurant, paint shop, hardware store, glassware shop, a shop belonging to a proprietor named Sabbatios, and a cloth dyeing business owned by Jacob, an elder in the synagogue. From the main street a side entrance leads to the synagogue. A nearby Greek inscription on the ground refers to Germanicus, the popular nephew of Emperor Tiberius who died prematurely in the year 19.

The bath-gymnasium complex is directly N of the synagogue and the main street. The restored two-storey marble court of the hall of the imperial cult stands at the edge of the palaestra and dates back to 211 when it was dedicated to Geta and Caracalla, the sons of Emperor Septimius Severus, and to their mother, Julia Domna. The "Geta" dedication was erased after Caracalla murdered his brother and became sole emperor.

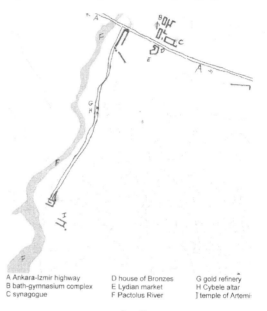

A Ankara-Izmir highway
B bath-gymnasium complex
C synagogue
D house of Bronzes
E Lydian market
F Pactolus River
G gold refinery
H Cybele altar
I temple of Artemis

*Sardis*

Beyond the Marble Court the bath-gymnasium contained rooms along an exercise hall and a heated bathhouse. The structure had patterned marble floors, walls lined with marble. The first storey is made of Ionic capitals, and the second storey is decorated with acanthus leaves. Niches in the façade held statues of gods and emperors and an arched doorway on the W side led to a large bathing pool.

*Sardis: Temple of Artemis*

A few meters S of the modern road the so-called House of Bronzes dates back to the mid-6th century. Bronze liturgical objects and an altar found here suggest this was the house of an early Christian bishop. SW of this house was an ancient Lydian marketplace dating back to 300-700 BCE. S of the highway, just to the N of the acropolis lie scant ruins of a 3rd century BCE stadium with capacity for 20,000, which was restored in Roman times. Further E and N of the highway are remains of a late Roman church, city walls and another bath complex.

From the central intersection of the modern village a paved road runs S along the E side of the Pactolus River toward the temple of Artemis. Along the road to the W are ruins of an early gold refinery dating from the time of Croesus. Gold recovered from the river was melted down, refined in furnaces and used for coins. Lydians produced the first coins, standardized pieces of metal whose value was guaranteed by the state. These coins bore no inscription but were stamped with a lion head, the emblem of Sardis. Cybele presided over this activity from her stone altar, which faced E flanked by crouching lions and dated back to the 7th century BCE. Sardis became a major trading center in part because its coinage greatly facilitated commerce.

The **Sardis temple of Artemis** (38° 28' 46" N, 28° 1' 50" E), one km S of Sart village on the E bank of the Patroclus River, is the fourth largest ancient Ionic temple (91 x 41 m) yet discovered. At present the temple has eight columns of the E façade, two Ionic columns preserved to their full height plus numerous column bases. Although the temple dates from 334 BCE shortly after Alexander the Great liberated the city from the Persians, it was refurbished in 176 BCE. Like other Artemis temples, it faced W. To the W of the temple stands a 6$^{th}$ century BCE red sandstone altar complete with a flight of steps. During the reign of Antoninus Pius in 138-161, Sardis was given responsibility for maintaining an imperial cult temple dedicated to the worship of the emperor and his family. At this time the temple of Artemis was divided into two parts: Zeus and the Emperor Antoninus Pius were worshipped on the W side; while Artemis and Empress Faustina were worshipped on the E side. The temple was abandoned in the 4$^{th}$ century due to the spread of Christianity. In the SE corner of the temple is a small church dating back to the 4$^{th}$ century. The Metropolitan Museum of Art in New York contains many fine artifacts from the Sardis, including an Ionic column from this temple of Artemis: http://www.metmuseum.org/Collections/search-the-collections/130012942

Archeologists from Harvard University and the University of Wisconsin-Madison led by Nick Cahill have been involved in excavating Sardis: http://www.harvardartmuseums.org/study-and-research/researchcenters/sardis.dot
http://news.ls.wisc.edu/?p=655

**Kibyra** (37° 9' 33" N, 29° 29' 45" E) is a large site on the high ground above modern Gölhisar 106 km SW of Burdur. Originally a Lydian city, Kibyra became the head of a tetrapolis that included neighboring cities of Bubon, Balbura and Oinoanda in the 2$^{nd}$ century BCE. The Romans terminated the tetrapolis, incorporated Kibyra into the Roman Province of Asia, and put the other three cities into the Lycian League. Emperor Hadrian visited in 129.

**Kibyra Site:** Kibyra is spread over three hills and surrounded on three sides by a necropolis. Three large buildings dominate the extensive site. Visitors first come to a large 200 m long stadium on a lower terrace to the E. The well-preserved stadium has a panoramic view overlooking a plain and a lake. A main street or sacred road, flanked by sarcophagi, ran between the stadium and

*Kibyra Stadium*

the rest of the city. This road runs W toward the theatre past a temple with an open courtyard and an altar. The commercial agoras with small shops were located along this axis. The vast necropolis contains different burial styles and surrounds the main hill to the N, W and S. Archeologists have identified hundreds of sarcophagi, altars and underground burial chambers. The sarcophagi are carved from local limestone, many decorated with small shields, garlands, rosettes or Medusa heads. The odeon could seat 3600 and contains an ancient Medusa head and a mosaic pavement in front. The theatre is large and well preserved. The Suna & İnan Kıraç Research Institute on Mediterranean Civilizations publishes ANMED (News of Archaeology from Anatolia's Mediterranean Areas) in English and Turkish, which describes recent work of Turkish archeologists at Kibyra:

http://www.akmedanmed.com/article_en.php?catID=15&artID=287

# VII ANCIENT REGION OF CARIA

Caria means "steep country" and lies where the Taurus Mountains create numerous deep inlets along an irregular coastline, extending S from Ionia to Lycia encompassing the Bodrum Peninsula. The islands of Rhodes and Kos lie off the coast. During the 6$^{th}$ century BCE Lydia ruled Caria briefly under King Croesus until Cyrus the Great of Persia defeated him and conquered the region. In the 5$^{th}$ century BCE Greek settlers arrived along the coastline, while indigenous Carians remained in the interior. During 499-497 BCE Carian cities joined Ionia in an unsuccessful rebellion against Persian rule. After the Greeks defeated the Persians at Salamis in 479 BCE, coastal Caria fell under Athenian control and its cities joined the Delian league. Following the 431-404 BCE Peloponnesian War between Athens and Sparta, Persia regained control over Caria. In the 4$^{th}$ century BCE Mausolus governed Caria as a largely autonomous satrap (governor) and his tomb was known as one of the Seven Wonders of the ancient world. In 334 BCE Alexander the Great conquered Caria with the support of Carian Queen Ada. Following the death of Alexander his Ptolemaic and Seleucid successors struggled to control the region. After the battle of Magnesia in 190 BCE, Seleucid ruler Antiochus (III) the Great was compelled to cede Caria to nominal rule by Rhodes. After 125 BCE Caria was incorporated into the Roman Empire. Much of Caria, with the notable exception of Aphrodisias, supported Mithridates VI of Pontus during his 88-85 BCE attempts to rally Greek-speaking Asia Minor against Roman rule. During the period of Roman civil wars, the former Roman Republican Labenius invaded Caria with a Parthian army and did considerable damage. Christianity only became popular following the conversion of Emperor Constantine in the 4th century. Carian cities with significant remaining sites include: **Aphrodisias, Nyasa, Alabanda, Alinda, Herakleia, Labranda, Euromos, Iasos, Mylasa, Halicarnassus, Amos, Knidos**, and **Kaunos**.

**Aphrodisias** (37° 42′ 33 N, 28° 43′ 25 E) is a well-preserved ancient city 230 km E of Izmir, 80 km W of Denizli near the modern village of Geyre in the Meander River basin. Aphrodisias, named after the goddess Aphrodite, was for many centuries only a shrine. By the 2nd century BCE the city was laid out on a Hippodamian grid plan with central public spaces and regular city blocks (36 x 39 m) in residential areas. Unlike other city buildings, the temple of Aphrodite and the theater are not oriented along the grid axis because they predate the city grid. Aphrodisias was rewarded for remaining loyal to Rome during the Mithridatic Wars. In 85 BCE Roman dictator Sulla, on the advice of the oracle at Delphi, honored Aphrodite at Aphrodisias with a golden crown and a double axe, the traditional symbol of power in Caria. The Julia clan of Julius Caesar and Augustus Caesar claimed descent from Aphrodite, had strong ties to Aphrodisias and gave the city special privileges and tax benefits. Aphrodisias,

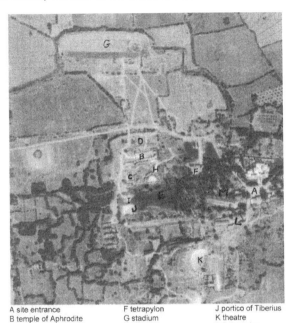

A site entrance
B temple of Aphrodite
C bishop's palace
D school of philosophy
E agora
F tetrapylon
G stadium
H odeon
I baths of Hadrian
J portico of Tiberius
K theatre
L Sebastaion
M museum

*Aphrodisias*

with about 15,000 inhabitants, became capital of Roman Caria and prospered during the 1st century BCE – 6th century CE period of Roman rule. In the mid-4th century Aphrodisias was walled for the first time as attested by the Antioch Gate dedicated to Emperor Constantius II (323-361).

*Aphrodite and Anchises at birth of Aeneas*

Aphrodite (Venus to Romans) is the goddess of love, beauty and sexuality. Aphrodite arose from the sea foam on a scallop shell where Cronus threw the severed genitals of his father Ouranos. To prevent conflict among the gods for the favors of the highly attractive Aphrodite, Zeus married her to Hephaestus, the lame god of craftsmanship. Despite this precaution, Aphrodite engaged in a number of illicit sexual relationships, particularly with Ares, (Mars to Romans) the god of war with whom she bore the child Eros (Cupid to Romans). Cupid carries a bow and arrow and is responsible for making people fall in love. Although stunningly beautiful, Aphrodite is vain, ill tempered and easily offended.

Once out of jealousy of the beauty of the mortal woman Psyche, Aphrodite commanded her son Cupid to use his golden arrows to cause Psyche to fall in love with the most unattractive man on earth. Instead, Cupid fell in love with Psyche himself. After overcoming a series of mean-spirited obstacles Aphrodite created, including a daunting trip to the underworld Tartarus, the couple were

*Aphrodite*

married and Zeus made Psyche into a goddess. To punish Aphrodite for various episodes in which she caused gods to fall in love with mortals, Zeus made her fall in love with Anchises, a young Trojan shepherd. Aphrodite disguised herself as a mortal and seduced Anchises. The union between them produced Aeneas who, following the destruction of Troy, went on to Italy and became the ancestor of the Romans. On another occasion, Aphrodite bribed the mortal Paris to judge her the fairest one of the goddesses, which precipitated the Trojan War. Erotes are children of Aphrodite, handsome, nude winged youths associated with love and sex, who form part of her retinue. Ritual prostitution was practiced in temples of Aphrodite as documented at numerous sites in Greece, North Africa, Italy and the Mediterranean. Male worshippers would have sexual intercourse with the priestesses of Aphrodite as an integral part of the religious service. The modern term aphrodisiac, meaning something stimulating sexual desire, is derived from Aphrodite.

**Aphrodisias Site:** The tetrapylon is the monumental gateway that connected the main street to the sacred way leading to the temple of Aphrodite. (A tetrapylon is a cube-shaped Roman monumental gateway built at a crossroads with four gates, one on each side.) The pediment over the columns on the W side is adorned with figures of Eros (Cupid) and Nike hunting among the acanthus leaves. Turkish born New York University professor Kenan Erim, who was instrumental in the 20$^{th}$ century excavation of Aphrodisias, lies buried near the tetrapylon. The 1$^{st}$ century BCE temple of Aphrodite in the city center was refurbished during the reign of Augustus and emphasized the city's strong connection with the Julio-Claudian dynasty. It was a large structure (8.5 x 31 m) surrounded by Ionic columns, many bearing inscriptions recording important donations to the temple. Emperor Hadrian completed work on a two-storey

*Tetrapylon*

facade to the E and porticos to the N, S, and W of the temple precinct in the 2nd century. Only 14 of these columns remain in place today. Near the temple excavators found a statue of Aphrodite of Aphrodisias from the cella. She wears a long garment, one arm stretched forward, adorned with necklaces and a crown with a diadem and a wreath of myrtle. Her garment encompasses figures symbolizing her divine identity: the Three Graces, the moon goddess Selene, the sun god Helios, Erotes, and Aphrodite herself half-naked, accompanied by a dolphin and a triton.

The Three Graces, also known as the three charities or beauties, are daughters of Zeus and the sea-nymph Eurynome, and serve as attendants of Aphrodite. They always appear together, naked, two facing forward, one facing backward. They are protectors of fine arts and plants, as well as sources of human inspiration. Euphrosyne embodies cheerfulness, mirth, merriment, and joy. Thalia represents spring blossoms, abundance, rejoicing, banquets and feasting. Aglaia is brightness, splendor and festivity. The three graces weave Aphrodite's robe and keep her spirits up. They took care of the devastated Aphrodite after she returned from the humiliation of being caught in her husband Hephaestus' trap and exposed to the other gods while in a love embrace with Ares. The Graces bathed her, anointed her with ambrosial oil, dressed her in fine clothing, and helped her regain the cheerful attitude needed to get on with her life.

*Three Graces (Antalya Museum)*

In the 5th century the temple of Aphrodite at Aphrodisias was converted into a Christian cathedral. During this enormous undertaking columns in the front and back were moved to extend the side colonnades, creating two long rows of 19 columns each. The cella of the temple was dismantled and walls containing cult statues removed. New walls were built to enclose the building, making it into a large basilica church (60 x 28 m). Walls were added at the front and rear to form a nave, and an apse was added to the E with an atrium and baptistery added to the W end. Turning the temple inside out and expanding it in this way was unique among the many known temple-to-church conversions. S of the temple-church, N of the agora is the Bishop House, a grand structure with a large audience chamber, possibly first built for the Roman governor. The 3$^{rd}$ century School of Philosophy building stood N of the temple of Aphrodite, surrounded by columns with a square pool in the center. From this area a path leads 350 m N to the stadium.

The stadium (262 x 59 m) at the N edge of Aphrodisias is among the largest and best preserved from the Roman Empire. It had 30 tiers of seats, capacity for 30,000 spectators. The stadium had two curved ends, rather than the standard one curved and one flat end, and bowed-out long sides. This form was an unusual combination of the standard U-shaped Hellenistic stadium and the oval Roman amphitheater, which resulted in an ellipse shape that enabled spectators to see the entire arena.

*Aphrodisias Stadium*

Inscriptions on the seats reserved space for particular groups and individuals. The stadium dates back to the 1$^{st}$ or 2$^{nd}$ century and was the venue for athletic competitions, imperial cult festivals and gladiatorial games. As overall security deteriorated in the mid-4$^{th}$ century, the W, N and part of the E sides of the stadium were incorporated into a defensive wall around the city.

The semicircular odeon stands to the S of the temple of Aphrodite, N of the agora, and has nine rows of intact marble seats, some with lion feet and inscriptions reserving space for particular groups, such as Jews, young men and Blue Team supporters. This 2$^{nd}$ century building was used for city council meetings,

*Agora and Baths of Hadrian*

lectures and had capacity to seat 1700 people. Statues of prominent religious and political figures, as well as major donors, both male and female, adorned the hall. One statue was a personification of Demos, representing the citizens of Aphrodisias; another was of the god Apollo seated playing the lyre.

The Aphrodisias market square was a double agora. The N agora (205 x 120 m) was surrounded with a Doric portico and is now a grassy field. The S agora (212 x 70 m) contained the 1$^{st}$ century Ionic Portico of Tiberius with friezes and dedicatory inscriptions honoring the emperor. In the center of the portico is a large pool (175 x 25 m) with a semicircular shape at the N and E ends. The 2$^{nd}$ century Baths of Hadrian, which faced the agora to the W end of the Portico of Tiberius, had two large rectangular chambers on both sides of a large central hall. An ancient inscription warned bathers against leaving valuables with their clothes.

**Tiberius (Tiberius Julius Caesar Augustus) reigned as Roman emperor 14-37. He was born in 42 BCE, son of the Roman**

aristocrat Tiberius Claudius Nero, who fled Rome in 44 BCE because of his Republican sympathies. Tiberias' mother Livia married Emperor Augustus in 39 BCE. In 20 BCE, Tiberius was sent E to serve under Marcus Agrippa, a close friend of Augustus and his leading military commander. Tiberius led a Roman force into Armenia and helped persuade the Parthians to return previously captured Roman military standards and accept Armenia as a neutral buffer state. Upon returning from the E in 19 BCE, Tiberius married Agrippina's daughter Vipsania. Tiberius then commanded Roman forces in the Alps and conquered the territory of Raetia (now in S Germany and E Switzerland). In 13 BCE, Tiberius was appointed consul, and his son, Drusus Julius Caesar, was born. Although Augustus considered Tiberius a potential successor,

*Tiberius with barbarian captive*

he was only fourth choice after Agrippa, husband of Augustus' only daughter Julia, and their two sons, Gaius and Lucius. After the unfortunate death of Agrippa in 12 BCE, Augustus forced a reluctant Tiberius to divorce his wife Vipsania and, for dynastic reasons, marry Agrippa's widow Julia. Tiberius had truly loved Vipsania and after a public spectacle in which he begged her for forgiveness, Augustus forbade Tiberius to ever even see Vipsania again.

Relations between Augustus and Tiberius deteriorated, but after the unexpected deaths of the two heirs apparent, Gaius and Lucius, Augustus reluctantly recognized Tiberius as his heir and successor. In the year 10 Tiberius was appointed coregent with Augustus. As part of the arrangement Tiberius was required to adopt his own eighteen-year-old nephew Germanicus as his heir and successor. In the year 14 at the age of 56, Tiberius became emperor when the elderly Augustus died. Relations between the Senate and Tiberius became strained because the new emperor confused and frightened the senators. Tiberius granted his popular adopted son Germanicus military command in Germany to suppress a Roman army mutiny and in 14-16 to campaign against unruly Germanic tribes. Tiberius granted Germanicus a military triumph in Rome in 17 and then sent him to secure the E frontier. In 19 Germanicus died in Antioch, where on his deathbed, he accused Piso, Roman governor of Syria and a close friend of Tiberius, of poisoning him. Germanicus' widow, Agrippina the Elder, returned to Italy with her popular husband's ashes and publicly accused Piso of murder. Piso was put on trial and forced to commit suicide.

As he became increasingly paranoid, Tiberius came to rely more and more on Aelius Sejanus, the commander of the Praetorian

*Sebasteion at Aphrodisias*

Guard. Due to his efficiency, fawning sycophancy, and unquestioning loyalty, Sejanus became the emperor's closest confidant. As a likely future emperor, Tiberius' son Drusus represented a potential threat to Sejanus. Sejanus managed seduce Drusus' wife Livilla and in 23 Livilla and Sejanus secretly poisoned Drusus, further isolating Tiberius. In 25 Sejanus asked Tiberius for permission to marry Livilla, but the emperor refused. In 26 Tiberius, strongly encouraged by Sejanus, decided to leave

Rome and live in relative seclusion on the island of Capri. Tiberius never returned to Rome. Sejanus was left in charge. He promptly arrested, convicted and imprisoned the popular Agrippina, widow of Germanicus, as well as her two sons, Nero Caesar, and Drusus Caesar. In 30 Sejanus was betrothed to Livilla's daughter. In 31 Sejanus served as consul together with Tiberius and the Praetorian commander appeared poised to become emperor. On October 18, Sejanus was summoned to the Senate to hear a formal announcement from Tiberius, which he doubtless expected would formally designate him as his heir. Instead, the letter accused him of treason and ordered his arrest. Unbeknownst to Sejanus, Tiberius had received a letter from Antonia, wife of Agrippina's youngest son Gaius (future emperor Caligula), which persuaded him to secretly remove control over the Praetorian Guard and take action against Sejanus. The Praetorian Guard summarily executed Sejanus as well as his family members and Livilla. Sadly, Agrippina and her two eldest sons remained under arrest and died in custody. Tiberius spent his last paranoid years at Capri, indulging himself in debauchery with teenage girls. In 37 Tiberius fell ill and died at his villa aged 78, perhaps suffocated on instructions from his successor Caligula.

At Aphrodisias the 1$^{st}$ century BCE theatre with its white marble seats had space for 8000 spectators. The stage building contained six rooms and inscriptions on the wall reported imperial and senatorial decrees and dedications.
According to one inscription, Julius Gaius Zoilus paid for the theatre stage building and dedicated it to Aphrodite and the people. Julius Gaius Zoilus was a slave of Julius Caesar (hence his first names) subsequently freed by Augustus. Zoilus returned to his native Aphrodisias with the prestige and rewards of imperial

*Claudius conquers Britannia*

administrative service at the highest levels. Zoilus aligned Aphrodisias with Augustus during his power struggle with Mark Antony and consistently fostered strong relations with the imperial government.

S of the museum the 1st century Sebasteion is an imperial cult temple dedicated to Aphrodite, Emperor Augustus and the people. The Sebasteion included a 14 m wide courtyard with two parallel three-storey 80 m long, 12 m high porticoes. At the E end steps led to a Corinthian style temple. The W entranceway was adorned with a statue of Aphrodite portrayed as the first mother of the imperial family. The Sebasteion made an explicit connection between Greek religious beliefs and the godlike Augustan regime in the upper storey. Aphrodite is venerated as ancestral mother of the family of Julius Caesar, Augustus, and their successors; she represented a cosmic force integrating local elites into imperial power. Each storey of the two porticos was a façade adorned with different column styles interspersed with reliefs: the first Doric, the middle Ionic and the top Corinthian. The upper two stories were decorated with two hundred large marble reliefs of single figures or 2-4 figures together in narrative scenes. The subjects of these reliefs were divided into distinct themes by the two levels. The upper storey depicted imperial subjects, while the lower storey showed figures of conquered peoples and places in the Roman Empire, each depicted as a statuesque female, ranging from Spain in the W to the Arabs and Judeans in the E. For example, one frieze shows a bare breasted, helmeted female warrior labeled "Britannia" writhing in agony under the knee of a Roman; an inscription reading "Tiberius Claudius Caesar" commemorates the Roman conquest of Britain under Emperor Claudius.

**Claudius (Tiberius Claudius Caesar Augustus Germanicus) reigned as Roman Emperor 41-54. He was born in 10 BCE, son of Nero Claudius Drusus and Antonia, daughter of Mark Antony. His father died on campaign when Claudius was only one year old, and his beloved older brother Germanicus, the popular Roman general, died under suspicious circumstances in 19. His sister Livilla was executed in 31 for conspiring against their uncle, Emperor Tiberius. Claudius survived all this court intrigue**

because no one regarded him as a threat. He suffered from physical disabilities, including a limp, a speech impediment, and an awkward tendency to drool, perhaps due to polio or cerebral palsy at an early age. Because the imperial family regarded him as an embarrassment, he was long excluded from public life. Claudius spent his childhood in seclusion and became an avid reader. In 7 the Roman historian Livy was hired as his tutor and helped him develop into a scholar. During his nephew Caligula's reign Claudius was named consul, together with the emperor, probably to avoid elevating any potential rival.

On January 24, 41, a group of imperial bodyguards assassinated Caligula and chaos ensued. German bodyguards fiercely loyal to the dead emperor went on a rampage, indiscriminately killing anyone whom they regarded as involved in the assassination. At the same time, the Praetorian Guard began looting the imperial palace and found Claudius cowering behind a curtain. The more forward-looking members of the guard realized they needed an emperor to safeguard their position, declared Claudius emperor and carried him off to their camp. The Senate initially resisted the idea, but was unable to unite around an alternative candidate and, partly out of fear of the Praetorians, two days later agreed to support Claudius. In this transition the 1st century Jewish king Agrippa I, known as Herod in the New Testament, played a key role. He had grown up at the Roman court and had been a friend of Tiberius, Claudius and later Caligula. At the end of the reign of Tiberius, Herod was imprisoned after a report reached Tiberius that he wanted him dead so that Caligula would become emperor. When Tiberius died, Emperor Caligula released Herod and placed him in power in Galilee. After the assassination of Caligula, Herod acted as intermediary between the Senate and the Praetorian Guard to ensure a smooth ascension for Claudius.

After Claudius became emperor, the health and bearing of this enigmatic ruler improved dramatically. Claudius rewarded Herod by giving him Judea and Samaria, which made him one of the most powerful Roman client kings. However, Claudius later became suspicious when Herod tried to fortify Jerusalem, and he compelled Herod to desist. When Herod died suddenly and unexpectedly in 44, his kingdom reverted to direct Roman rule. In 42 Emperor Claudius prepared to conquer Britain and further legitimize his rule as a successful military leader. Four legions with about 20,000 men attacked Britain in the summer of 43.

The British were overwhelmed and pushed back to the Thames. Future Emperor Vespasian commanded one of these legions and distinguished himself during the campaign. After the initial offensive was launched, Claudius joined the Roman troops in Britain with elephants and reinforcements, which undoubtedly shocked and awed the local population. Claudius assumed command, engaged and defeated the enemy, and took Camelodunum (Colchester), where he later established a colony of retired Roman soldiers. Eleven British tribes formally surrendered to Claudius. He then departed after 16 days. The Senate granted Claudius a triumph and his military credentials were firmly established. The annexation of Britain was the first major territorial acquisition of the empire since the reign of Augustus.

Attempting to improve relations with the aristocracy, Claudius destroyed Caligula's infamous stock of poisons and returned many properties his predecessor had confiscated. However, he remained suspicious of the Roman aristocracy, and relied heavily on Greek freedmen (former slaves) to administer the empire. Claudius expanded Roman citizenship and brought in the first non-Italian senators from Gaul. Before becoming emperor, Claudius had married Valeria Messalina, a cousin closely connected with Caligula's entourage. They had two children, a daughter Octavia and a son, later named Britannicus in honor of his father's military conquest. According to ancient accounts Messalina was a nymphomaniac who supposedly went so far as to compete with a prostitute one night to see who could have more sexual partners. In 48 Messalina went too far when she staged a marriage ceremony with one Gaius Silius, who was designated to serve as consul, when Claudius was away. Both were executed shortly thereafter. In the wake of Messalina's death, an intense scramble for influence took place as all the emperor's advisors put forward competing candidates to replace her. One soon prevailed as Claudius made the mistake of marrying Agrippina, sister of Caligula. Agrippina dominated Claudius's last years, persuading him to adopt her son Nero, marry his daughter Octavia to Nero and then designate Nero successor in place of his natural son, Britannicus. As relations frayed between Claudius and Agrippina, she fed him the poison mushrooms that killed him on October 13, 54.

At the Sebasteion of Aphrodisias on the S portico, upper storey reliefs juxtaposed traditional Greek gods with victorious Roman imperial figures. Roman emperors from Augustus to Nero are displayed as part of an Olympian pantheon and an inscription specifically calls them "Olympian god-emperors." One surviving relief depicts Emperor Nero being crowned by his mother Agripinna appearing as the goddess as Tyche (ironically Nero had Agripinna killed). Another partially defaced relief shows Nero conquering Armenia.

**Nero (Nero Claudius Caesar Augustus Germanicus) reigned as Roman Emperor 54-68. He was born in 37 to Agrippina, a sister of Emperor Caligula. When Caligula was assassinated, Agrippina was recalled from exile and eventually in 49 married her uncle, Emperor Claudius. In 51 Agrippina persuaded Claudius to designate Nero as his successor, in preference to his own younger son Britannicus, and to betroth his daughter Octavia to Nero. In 54 Agrippina, to ensure Nero's accession, poisoned Claudius. Nero, not yet seventeen, was proclaimed emperor. To eliminate a potential rival, Nero poisoned Britannicus in 55. At Aphrodisias, Nero is depicted as the conqueror of Armenia. Shortly after his accession, the Persians overthrew an Armenian king allied with Rome and replaced him with the Parthian prince Tiridates. Armenia was an important buffer state between the two superpowers and this act precipitated several years of armed conflict. Full-scale war broke out in 58 and the Romans ultimately drove the Parthians out of Armenia. When conflict flared up again in 63, Nero agreed to a**

*Agripinna as Tyche crowns her son Nero*

compromise, which lasted 50 years, whereby a Parthian would be King of Armenia, but only after being crowned as such in Rome by the Roman emperor.

In 58 Nero took Poppaea, the beautiful wife of a friend, as his mistress and turned decisively against his domineering mother. His first attempt at matricide was to build his mother an attractive boat, secretly designed to sink in the Bay of Naples. Although some of her entourage drowned, Agrippina managed to swim ashore. Upon learning she had survived, Nero ordered her stabbed her to death at her country house. Nero's marriage to Octavia was annulled. Octavia was banished to Campania, and later killed. Poppaea was given the title Augusta and her critics were executed. Nero habitually went out at night in Rome incognito with dissolute friends attacking men and assaulting women. One day pregnant Poppaea complained when Nero came home late and the enraged emperor kicked her to death.

*Nero conquers Armenia*

In Roman Britain Nero faced serious problems when Prasutagus, King of the Iceni (modern Norfolk) died in 60, and avaricious Roman officials disregarded his bequest of half his kingdom to his two daughters. When his widow, queen Boudicca objected, she was publically whipped and her two daughters were raped. The furious Iceni rose up and, joined by surrounding tribes, burned down Camulodunum (Colchester), Verulamium (St Albans), several military posts, and finally Londinium. Rebels slaughtered 70-80,000 Romans and pro-Roman Britons before the rebellion was put down.

From an early age Nero had a deep craving for popularity, considered himself an incredibly gifted artistic genius, and could not tolerate rivals. He created and participated in the Neronia, a festival encompassing music, oratory, poetry, gymnastics, and riding, which took place in 60 and 65. Enthusiastic attendance was compulsory for his entourage and in 65 the future Emperor Vespasian barely escaped with his life because he fell asleep during one of Nero's performances. Nero competed in the 67 Olympic Games as a charioteer, actor and singer, where not surprisingly he won every contest.

In July 64 Rome's Great Fire burned for six days completely destroying three of the city's fourteen districts and badly damaging seven. Although Nero assisted disaster victims, he was widely viewed as responsible. It was said he played the lyre and sang of the burning of Troy, Rome's ancestral city, as the fire raged. After the fire, Nero greatly compounded his public image problem by using the vast area between the Palatine and the Equiline hills, which fire had been utterly destroyed, to build himself a Golden Palace. This vast complex included extensive pleasure gardens and even an artificial lake. From the scale of the project it obviously could not have been done had the land not been cleared by fire, which led many to conclude Nero had set the fire deliberately. To escape blame, Nero identified the early Christians as scapegoats. Christians were widely unpopular as atheists who brought on calamities with their refusal to worship traditional gods, and with their secret meetings and cannibalistic rituals that involved drinking their savior's blood and eating his flesh. To entertain the angry mob, Christians were executed in large numbers: covered with flammable pitch and set on fire, or eaten alive by hungry animals. During this wave of persecution in 67, St. Peter was crucified upside down on the Vatican hill and St. Paul was beheaded along the Via Ostiensis. Although these horrific Christian executions engendered public sympathy, Christianity was an apocalyptic faith at this time, and a Christian faction may well have started the great fire.

In 68, as Nero became increasingly arbitrary and murderous, revolt finally began among Romans in the provinces, first in Gaul and then in Spain. After an initial uprising in Gaul was suppressed, Galba, the 71-year-old governor of Spain claimed the throne and began to march his army toward Rome. Then the Praetorian commander in Rome persuaded his men to abandon Nero. The emboldened Senate declared Nero a public enemy and sentenced him to death. Nero panicked, was rapidly abandoned by his erstwhile supporters, and committed suicide on June 9, 68.

At the Aphrodisias Sebasteion, the lower storey reliefs depicted 45 scenes involving the Greek religious figures such as Dionysus and Hercules, as well as Rome's Trojan forbearers Anchises and Aeneas. Representations included: the Three Graces, Bellerophon and Pegasus, Leda and the Swan, and Achilles and Penthesilea. Seventy of an estimated 200 reliefs have been recovered and are on display in the museum.

*Aeneas flees Troy*

Leda was the beautiful wife of King Tyndareus of Sparta. Zeus desired Leda and came to her in the guise of a swan flying into her arms seeking protection from a pursuing eagle. Zeus then seduced Leda on the same night she lay with her husband Tyndareus. As a result of this coupling, Leda produced two eggs containing human embryos. Both eggs had twins. The first egg held Helen, daughter of Zeus and most beautiful woman in the world, together with Clytemnestra, daughter of Tyndareus and future wife of Agamemnon. The other egg held the twins Castor and Pollux (known as the Dioscuri), the former mortal, the latter immortal. Later Castor and Pollux accompanied the Roman army on campaign and during battle often were seen among the cavalry. They also protected sailors and travelers at sea. Once in a dispute with two other men over a pair of desirable women, immortal Pollux killed one but the other suitor mortally wounded Castor. Pollux wept over the body of his brother because he could not accompany him to Tartarus. The Dioscuri were incorporated into ancient funeral rituals as symbols of life and death.

Penthesileia, meaning "mourned by the people," was an Amazon queen and daughter of the god Ares who joined the Trojan War on the side of Trojan King Priam. She supported the Trojans as an act of penitence for having accidently killed her sister, and arrived at a bad time for the Trojans just after the death and funeral of Hector, the great Trojan hero

*Leda with Zeus as eagle*

Achilles killed. Penthesileia and a dozen companions vigorously attacked and killed many Greek soldiers, including Machaon, a physician and son of Asclepius. She fought with Ajax but neither triumphed. Then Achilles confronted and killed her. As she was dying, Achilles lifted off her helmet, saw her beauty and fell in love with her. Another Greek soldier, Thersites, mocked Achilles' sentiment and attempted to desecrate Penthesileia's body. Achilles killed Thersites on the spot. Achilles then buried Penthesileia's body with full honors on the banks of the Xanthus River.

At the Aphrodisias museum, the list of contributors to a Jewish synagogue is the longest Jewish inscription found outside of Israel and sheds light on development of early Christianity. This 3$^{rd}$ century Greek language inscription is written on two faces of a rectangular pillar. It lists donations made by 130 individuals and notes their occupations: goldsmith, bronze-smith, clothing maker, linen worker, sausage maker, poultry worker, sweetmeat maker, stone mason, sheep dealer, carpenter and boot-maker. The list includes 52 God-fearers, i.e., non-Jewish sympathizers with Jewish monotheism, who had non-biblical names and engaged in activities forbidden by Jewish law, such as municipal government, athletics and boxing. These individuals likely formed the nucleus of the earliest Christian community at Aphrodisias.

The sculpture workshop, located N of the odeon, S of the temple of Aphrodite, was active 1$^{st}$ century BCE-5$^{th}$ century. Quarries with fine white and blue-gray marble were located just 2 km N of the city and a strong local tradition of marble sculpture developed. At the site stone-carving tools and many pieces of sculpture were discovered, including 25 well-preserved statues and 325 fragments of gods, heroes, emperors, orators, philosophers, and boxers, as well as ornamental grave reliefs. Aphrodisias was known throughout the Empire for its fine sculpture.

Professor Kenan Erim and other New York University archeologists have long done superb work on Aphrodisias as described at: http://www.nyu.edu/projects/aphrodisias/home.ti.htm

**Herakleia** (37° 30' 8" N, 27° 31' 31" E), originally known as Latmus and now Kapıkırı, is 25 km W of Miletus at a remote, scenic spot on the S slopes of Mount Latmus and the E shore of Lake Bafa. This modest city was originally a port on the SE corner of the Latmian Gulf. In the 5$^{th}$ century BCE Latmus was a member of the Delian League. In the 4$^{th}$ century BCE the Persian satrap Mausolus of Halicarnassus captured and fortified the city. At the beginning of the 3$^{rd}$ century BCE Persian influence receded and the city was reestablished 1 km to the W as Herakleia, renamed for Hercules. The new city was built on a Hippodamian grid system with walls extending from the harbor to the upper slopes of Mt. Latmus.

Hercules (Herakles to Greeks) was a son of Zeus and the mortal woman Alcmene, conceived when Zeus deceived her by assuming the form of her husband, who was away at war. Hera, wife of Zeus, particularly resented Hercules. Shortly after he was born, Hera sent two serpents to kill Hercules as he lay in his crib. Hercules throttled a snake in each hand and was found by his nanny playing with the dead snakes as if they were toys. Hercules grew to have extraordinary strength and courage, but was prone to extreme sexual desire, as well as gluttony and drunkenness. He was prone to occasional fits of uncontrollable fury. As a young man, Hercules married Megara, princess of Thebes, and had children. Once in a fit of rage, Hercules killed his own children much to his subsequent horror. The oracle at Delphi told Hercules that to redeem himself, he must labor as a slave for twelve years for his cousin King Eurystheus. In the ancient world the twelve labors of Hercules were well known and depicted on Greek and Roman coinage. The first six Labors were performed in the Peloponnesus, the center of Greek civilization: 1) kill the Nemean lion; 2) destroy the Lernaean Hydra; 3) capture the Ceryneian Deer; 4) capture the Erymanthian Boar; 5) clean the Augean Stables; and 6) kill the Stymphalian Birds. The subsequent six Labors were performed in areas increasingly remote from the known Greek world: 7) capture the Cretan Bull; 8) round up the Mares of Diomedes; 9) steal the girdle of Amazon Queen Hippolyta; 10) herd the Cattle of Geryon; 11) fetch the Apples of Hesperides; and 12) capture Cerberus.

*Hercules (Side Museum)*

The life of Hercules symbolized overcoming unknown dangers and making the world safe for Greek colonists. The strait of Gibraltar was known as the Pillars of Hercules because he placed two massive stones there to ensure the safety of ships sailing between the two landmasses. Hercules is easily recognizable in iconography and coinage wearing the lion skin headdress he obtained during his first Labor, as well as carrying an olive club. Hercules shot and killed the eagle that tortured Prometheus, as his punishment for stealing fire from the gods and giving it to mortals, and freed him from his chains. Once Hercules killed the Lion of Cithaeron at the behest of the king of Thespiae. As a reward, the king granted him one night during which Hercules was allowed to make love with any of his fifty daughters. Hercules complied, and all 50 daughters were impregnated and all 50 bore sons, an incident sometimes known as his Thirteenth Labor. Many kings of ancient Greece traced their lineage to one or another of these daughters, particularly the kings of Sparta and Macedon.

Later Hercules fought the horned river god Achelous for the mortal woman Deianeira. Upon Achelous' death, Hercules removed one of his horns and gave it to some nymphs who turned it into the cornucopia. Soon after Hercules and Deianeira wed, they were going to cross a river. The centaur Nessus offered to help Deianeira to cross the river, but then attempted to rape her. Enraged, Hercules shot and mortally wounded Nessus with a poisoned arrow dipped in the Lernaean Hydra's blood. As he lay dying, Nessus told Deianeira to collect his blood and, if she ever needed to keep Hercules faithful to her, she should put it on his clothing. Nessus did not mention that his blood was tainted by the poisonous blood of the Hydra, and would burn through the skin of anyone it touched. Eventually, Deianeira suspected Hercules of infidelity and soaked his shirt in the blood of Nessus. After Hercules put on the shirt, the cloth burned into him and the flesh was ripped from his bones. To end his suffering, Hercules built a funeral pyre and burned himself up. Hercules was then transformed into a god, joined his father Zeus on Mount Olympus, and married Hera's daughter Hebe, the goddess of youthfulness. The transformation of Hercules from a powerful man into a god undoubtedly appealed to ancient Greek and Roman rulers. Several Roman emperors associated themselves with Hercules on their coins and elsewhere to bolster their legitimacy and symbolize their strength.

By the 1st century BCE silting from the Meander River transformed the gulf at Herakleia into the large freshwater lake Bafa and ships could no longer access the city from the Aegean Sea. Herakleia was known in antiquity as the home of Endymion, the eternal sleeper. In the 7th century Christian monks fleeing Muslim Arabia gathered at

A agora  D bouleterion  G nymphaeum
B city walls  E baths  H temple of Endymion
C temple of Athena  F theatre  I Roman fortress

*Herakleia*

Herakleia and developed an important monastic center.

Endymion was a handsome young shepherd in Caria tending his flock on the slopes of Mount Latmus. One night as he lay sleeping the titan moon goddess Selene saw him and was strongly attracted. She was so enamored with Endymion that she appeared before him, kissed him, and lay with him. Soon the two fell deeply in love. Fearful of losing her mortal lover, Selene begged Zeus to grant him eternal life. Zeus finally agreed that Endymion could escape old age and death, but only by sleeping forever in a cave on Mt. Latmus. Endymion gladly agreed for the sake of Selene. Each night Selene lay with Endymion and, without once waking from his deep slumber, he impregnated her 50 times and he produced 50 daughters known as the Menae, goddesses of the lunar months. With the advent of Christianity and the arrival of numerous monks at Herakleia, the story of Endymion was reinterpreted. Now Endymion was a Christian ascetic who studied the movement of the moon for many years and finally by this means learned the secret name of God. The Endymion sanctuary at Herakleia became an early Christian pilgrimage site. Once a year Christian priests would open his tomb and the bones of Endymion would emit a strange humming sound, believed to be his attempt to pass on the secret name of God to the worthy.

**Herakleia Site**: The rectangular agora (60 x 130 m), now the schoolyard, is in the ancient city center with ruins of a two-storey row of shops along the S edge. The city is surrounded with well-preserved 3rd century BCE walls complete with towers and windows. To the W on a prominent rock outcrop stands the 3rd century BCE temple of Athena, with three high walls of finely cut blocks still in place. E of the agora are the scanty ruins of a bouleuterion. To the NE are remains of Roman baths, a theater, and a nymphaeum. S of the agora on a hill overlooking the lake stands the temple of Endymion facing SW, also not aligned with the grid due to its antiquity. The temple has an entrance hall and colonnaded forecourt, as well as cella with a horseshoe-shaped rear wall cut out of bedrock, perhaps representing the cave of Endymion. Beyond the temple toward the lakeshore are a late

Roman fort and a church, as well as tombs cut into the rock. German archeologists have worked at Herakleia as reported in German at: http://latmos-felsbilder.de/


**Kaunos** (36° 49' 33" N, 28° 37' 18" E) was a Carian port on the border of Lycia now on an inland lake 5 km from the sea. Pottery shards indicate Kaunos existed by at least the 9$^{th}$ century BCE. According to tradition, Caunos, the eponymous founder of Kaunos was the son of Apollo's son Miletos from Crete. Caunos fled his home, because he was hopelessly in love with his twin sister Byblis, and founded the city of Kaunos. Byblis shared his passion and tried to follow Caunos, only to collapse in tears and be turned into a spring by water nymphs. Although this story suggests a Greek origin, the Carians were an indigenous tribe. In 540 BCE the Persian general Harpagos conquered the region despite bitter resistance from Kaunos. After the Greek victory over Persia at the battle of Salamis in 480 BCE, Kaunos joined the Athenian dominated Delian League. In the 4$^{th}$ century BCE Persian rule was reestablished under the satraps Hecatomnos and then his son Mausolus. After Alexander the Great conquered the area in 334 BCE, the Seleucids, the Ptolemies, Rhodes, and finally Rome ruled Kaunos in succession. In 88 BCE Kaunos supported Mithridates VI of Pontus against Rome and massacred resident Roman citizens. The Romans defeated Mithridates and punished Kaunos by returning the city to rule from Rhodes, which continued well in to the 1$^{st}$ century. Kaunos was Christianized in the 4$^{th}$ century. As the Dalyan River slowly silted up, the surroundings turned to marshland and became increasingly unhealthy due to malaria. However, turtles thrive here and the nearby coast is a protected area where Giant Loggerhead turtles lay their eggs. Most visitors reach Kaunos by boat from the nearby fishing and tourist village of Dalyan, although it can be reached by road.

**Kaunos Site**: The 150 m high Kaunos acropolis was once surrounded on three sides by the sea. To the N are remnants of 4th century BCE defensive walls (8 m high) built under Persian rule. To the NE is a marshy plain, once the main harbor. The former W harbor, which could be blocked with a chain, is now the

A bath complex      C theatre      E Vespasian nymphaeum
B 6th century church      D temple of Zeus      F Capito monument

*Kaunos*

Suluklu Gol (Lake of Leeches). On the high ground near the car park are the remains of a substantial bath complex (58 x 28 m). Nearby also on the high ground stand ruins of a 6th century domed, triple-nave church (14 x 14.5 m). Down the hill from the church was a 1st century BCE temple (9.6 x 6.8 m) dedicated to Zeus, which contained a sacred stone (3.5 m high) in religious use since the 5th century BCE. The 2nd century BCE theatre, to the W of the acropolis, had 33 rows and could seat 5000. Substantial walls support the N part of the theatre, while to the S it was built into the hillside. Below the ridge lie descending terraces including the large terrace of a 2nd century BCE temple dedicated to Apollo. Further down was a 3rd century BCE stoa (94 m long) on the N edge of the agora, with a row of columns in front and a wall in back. Archeological finds here reveal a cult of sailors dedicated to Aphrodite. Archeologists also found 3rd century BCE bases for statues of Mausolus and his father Hecatomnos, who ruled the city from Halicarnassus. On the S wall of a 1st century nymphaeum dedicated to Emperor Vespasian, an inscription states that merchants could export certain items, including slaves, from Kaunos duty free.

**Vespasian (Titus Flavius Vespasianus) reigned as Roman emperor 69-79 and founded the Flavian dynasty. He was born in 9 in Italy NW of Rome into a prominent family, son of a successful tax collector and financier. Vespasian followed in the footsteps of his maternal uncle and became a senator in 25. He served under Emperor Tiberius in Thrace and then in Crete and Cyrene. In 39 Vespasian married Flavia Domitilla, a match apparently based on love rather than political calculation, and had three children, a daughter Domitilla and the future emperors Titus and Domitian. Under Emperor Claudius, Vespasian played a key role in the invasion of Britain. Vespasian led a Roman legion across the S of England, where he fought the enemy thirty times, subdued two tribes, and conquered the Isle of Wight. Emperor Claudius even granted Vespasian a formal triumph. In 51 Vespasian was elevated to the rank of Consul. In 63 Emperor Nero appointed Vespasian governor of Roman Africa. Vespasian was praised for his prudent administration and known for not abusing his position for personal financial gain. Vespasian returned to Rome and accompanied Emperor Nero on a two-year tour of Greece. In one bizarre incident in 65, Vespasian incurred Nero's wrath because he fell asleep during one of the emperor's artistic performances. Vespasian fled for his life to hide out in an obscure country town until the storm was over.**

*Nymphaeum of Vespasian*

In 67 at age 58 Vespasian was rehabilitated and sent E to quell the 66-70 Jewish Revolt. In spring of 67, Vespasian led 60,000 legionaries, auxiliaries, and allies to restore order in Judea. He moved quickly and decisively, and by October he had pacified Galilee and surrounded Jerusalem. At about this time Vespasian befriended Josephus, a Jewish prisoner of war and future Roman historian, who shrewdly predicted Vespasian would become emperor. In 68 revolts in Hispania and Gaul in the W of the empire brought about the downfall and suicide of Emperor Nero. A year of four emperors ushered in a period of chaos and civil war as first Galba, then Marcus Salvius Otho and finally Aulus Vitellius seized power only to be violently deposed because they lacked broad-based military and senatorial support.

Still engaged in the Jewish War, Vespasian carefully observed the situation and garnered support among the Roman legions in the E. First he secured the support of the governor of Syria. Then in July Roman legions in Egypt and Judea declared support for Vespasian as emperor, followed in August by the forces in Syria and along the Danube. Vespasian then sent 20,000 troops under a loyal subordinate to Italy, which defeated the forces of Vitellius at Cremona on October 24 and seized Rome on December 20, 69. The Senate proclaimed Vespasian emperor and he arrived in Rome in the late summer of 70, leaving his elder son Titus in charge of Judaea. The siege of Jerusalem, during which as many as half a million people died, finally ended on September 2, 70, although the siege of Masada continued until 73. The Romans destroyed the Jewish Temple, carrying away treasure and enslaving people for Titus's grand triumph in Rome. Vespasian proved to be a gifted administrator. He reestablished discipline in the army after the civil wars. Vespasian reformed imperial finances after the extravagance of the Nero years and the subsequent chaos. He launched major building projects, such as the Roman Coliseum, and reformed taxation to raise revenue. He increased the number of legions in the E, annexed the N of England, pacified Wales, and accelerated the Romanization of Hispania. Vespasian strengthened the Senate and the equestrian order with well-qualified candidates. In 71 Vespasian granted Titus the title Caesar and clearly designated him as his successor. Vespasian fell ill in 79 and on his deathbed even joked that he would soon become a god. He died on June 24, 79 and was duly deified by the Senate. The succession of Titus was smooth and undisputed.

At the far end of the Kaunos agora on the right stands a 2 m high monument to the family of Quintus Vedius Capito, a priest of Zeus and host of visiting dignitaries. Toward the town of Daylan in the steep cliffs above the channel are carved many elaborate $4^{th}$ century BCE temple type tombs, which appear strongly influenced by the Lycian style.

**Knidos** (36° 41' 10" N, 27° 22' 29" E) is located on the far W end of the Datca peninsula 35 km W of the town of Datca. In the $7^{th}$ century BCE Spartans founded the colony Knidos at the site of the modern town of Datca. By 546 BCE the Persians ruled Knidos. When Persian influence was on the wane in 486 BCE, Knidos joined the Delian League. In 360 BCE the citizens of Knidos relocated the city to the extreme end of the peninsula to take advantage of the fact that prevailing winds often delayed trading ships for several days at this point. Ancient Knidos had two harbors: one on the Aegean, the other on the Mediterranean, connected via a man made channel, which enabled ships to pass through upon paying a tariff to the good citizens of Knidos. The larger S harbor was enclosed with two strongly built piers, still extant. Persian control was reestablished in 386 BCE and continued until the arrival of Alexander in the 334 BCE. After Alexander, Knidos was ruled successively by the Macedonians, Rhodes and then, after 129 BCE, Rome. Knidos made the mistake of supporting Mithridates VI of Pontus and paid the price. However, overall the strategically located city prospered from improved trade and security conditions Roman rule created. The city was built on terraces rising from sea level up 305 m to a fortified acropolis.

Knidos was most famous for its statue of naked Aphrodite. For hundreds of years, Greeks had sculpted the naked male form, but never the female. Between 360 and 330 BCE Praxiteles of Athens sculpted two stunning and lifelike versions of Aphrodite, one naked and the other clothed. Knidos bravely erected the naked Aphrodite on a podium in the center of a round temple where it could be viewed from all sides, after many other cities had demurred fearing public outrage. Aphrodite of Knidos became a major ancient tourist attraction for visitors from all over the known world; the fully clothed Aphrodite at the city of Kos was much less popular. Unfortunately, the Knidos statue has been lost, likely due to the influence of censorious early Christians, but an ancient copy still exists at the Vatican museum. In the mid-19th century a British team of archeologists directed by Sir Charles Newton removed a seated statue of Demeter and a marble funerary lion, which are now on display at the British Museum.

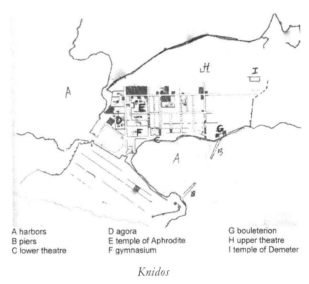

A harbors    D agora    G bouleterion
B piers    E temple of Aphrodite    H upper theatre
C lower theatre    F gymnasium    I temple of Demeter

*Knidos*

**Knidos Site**: Knidos was a planned city, built on a Hippodamian grid system with four wide parallel streets running E-W intersecting a steep, wide stairway. On the NW side of the city was the smaller N or military harbor, which was almost completely enclosed and could be shut with a chain. The larger commercial harbor to the SE was partially enclosed with two piers, which can be seen underwater. The center of the site is a large agora near the N harbor. Two large late Roman churches stood on each side of the agora. To the N of the church on the E side are the scant remains of the Doric temple of Apollo. Further N on the highest terrace to the W is a round podium believed to be the temple of Aphrodite, which held the famous statue overlooking the two harbors with an entranceway built of white marble, with heart-shaped columns.

The 3$^{rd}$ century BCE gymnasium (21 x 16 m) lies on the S side of the ancient main street on three levels descending E to W. At the gymnasium an inscription honors Artemidoros, son of Theopompos, who warned Julius Caesar of the conspiracy to murder him on March 15, 44 BCE. Artemidoros once taught philosophy here and was granted the right to be buried in the gymnasium. Near the harbor stands a Hellenistic theatre with 35 rows of seats built into the hillside for 5000 spectators. Along the shore to the E is a Roman era bouleuterion with a speaker platform. Higher up (N) is a larger theatre, difficult to make out because most of the stone was removed. To the E, past a 4$^{th}$ century BCE sundial, is the Roman era Demeter sanctuary. Up 30 m on the smooth perpendicular cliff visitors can see the carved rock opening where the famous Demeter statue sculpted in 330 BCE once sat. It can still be seen at the British Museum: http://www.britishmuseum.org/explore/highlights/highlight_objects/gr/m/marble_statue_of_demeter.aspx

*Podium for Aphrodite Statue*

A large necropolis lies outside the E walls of Knidos along the modern road. A km further SE Newton found the colossal six-ton

marble lion commemorating the 394 BCE Athenian naval victory against the Spartans at Knidos. The Knidos lion can also be seen at the British Museum:
http://www.britishmuseum.org/explore/highlights/highlight_objects/gr/c/colossal_marble_lion.aspx

In the late 1960s American archeologist Iris Cornelia Love of Long Island University discovered the circular building where the famous statue of Aphrodite stood. Archeologists working at Knidos include Professor Ramazan Özgan of Selçuk University in Konya, Turkey, and Professor Wolfgang Ehrhardt of University of Freiburg in Germany, as well as members of the British Institute of Archaeology in Ankara. Following in the footsteps of Sir Charles Newton, the current British Museum Knidos project leader is Ian Jenkins:
http://www.britishmuseum.org/research/research_projects/return_to_cnidus.aspx

**Amos** (36° 45' 24" N, 28° 16' 0" E) is 20 km S of Marmaris on the Loryma peninsula at Asarcık Hill, NW of Kumlubük Bay. Rhodes controlled the peninsula until the $2^{nd}$ century. **Amos Site**: The marked trail to the site is directly adjacent to a modern road and the city walls are visible from the parking area. This remote site affords a panoramic view of the seaside. The trail leads along the $4^{th}$ century BCE walls up to the acropolis, and to a well-preserved theatre with capacity for 1200 spectators and a three chambered stage building. Ruins include foundations of a temple and altar dedicated to Apollo with nearby statute pedestals and various inscribed blocks, including three 200 BCE rental contracts.

**Labranda** (37° 25' 7" N, 27° 49' 12" E), 14 km NE of Milas (ancient Mylasa), was a religious sanctuary built on terraces at a remote, 700 m high mountainside dedicated to Zeus Labrynthos. The word Labrys means "two-sided axe," a Carian symbol of

Zeus; the suffix "nda" means "place of." Worship of Zeus was dominant at Labranda from the 5th century BCE until the Christian era. Although Labranda was the leading religious sanctuary in Caria, it was never larger than a village. Mylasa controlled the sanctuary, appointed priests and organized religious processions to Labranda via a 13 km long sacred way. In 499 BCE Ionian and Carian cities unsuccessfully rebelled against Persian rule. After Persian King Darius I the Great defeated them, the Carians took

*Labranda: Androns (left) Temple of Zeus (center)*

refuge at the sacred precinct of Labranda, regrouped and renewed their struggle. In 497 Darius beat them again at Labranda and secured control over Caria. After the Greek victory at Salamis in 479 BCE, Persian control waned until about 400 BCE. Then the Persians appointed the local Carian prince Hetacomnus as satrap (governor) for Caria. Hetacomnus consolidated power in the region and was succeeded by his son Mausolus in 377 BCE. To accommodate Carian public opinion, Mausolus and his brother Idreius significantly upgraded and expanded the Carian religious sanctuary at Labranda. They organized elaborate festivals and athletic games. Thousands of people from all over Caria visited Labranda, made animal sacrifices dedicated to Zeus and participated in feasts and games in his honor. Zeus answered questions and gave advice via oracular eels, adorned with necklaces and earrings, kept in a pool. Answers were affirmative when the eels vigorously consumed proffered food, negative when they did not. In 355 BCE Mausolus just barely escaped an assassination attempt during the festivities at Labranda. In gratitude to Zeus for his narrow escape, Mausolus further increased his Labranda building program. The sanctuary remained active under the Romans until a major 4th century fire destroyed the complex.

**Labranda Site**: The car park is at the SE corner of the site where two marble Ionic entrances (propylea) once joined the 8 m wide, 13 km long sacred way from Mylasa. Ruins of a 4th century BCE rectangular structure fronted with four Doric columns, which once served as a treasury and later part of a Roman bath complex, stand near the entrance.

A baths   C stairway   E temple of Zeus
B Roman church   D androns   F Idrieus tomb

*Labranda*

The late Roman church adjacent to the Doric structure was undoubtedly built to hasten conversion of recalcitrant Zeus worshippers. The sacred eels were located in the ablution chamber to the SE along the lower terrace. A 12 m wide, well-preserved stairway leads up to the temple terrace and to the androns. (An andron was an ancient meetinghouse reserved exclusively for men with couches and tables used for banquets and social events.) The andron furthest S was built in Roman times; Mausolus built the adjacent andron; and his brother Idreius built the well-preserved mid-4th century BCE andron higher up, closer to the temple of Zeus. During the late Roman period an altar was installed and Christian priests used the structure.

The temple of Zeus (25 x 16 m) was first built in the 5th century BCE, and, as an inscription attests, expanded in the 4th century BCE under Idreius. An Ionic colonnade was erected around the temple. To the N of the third andron is a Doric style residence for priests dedicated by satrap Idreius to Zeus. Further up the hill (N) toward the acropolis is a 4$^{th}$ century tomb with a large front courtyard and two burial chambers one in front of the other, which contain five sarcophagi, believed to be the burial place of Idreius. To the NW are scanty remains of a stadium (176 m long) with two starting and ending stones for athletic games dedicated to Zeus. Professor Lars Karlsson of Uppsala University in Sweden directs excavations at Labranda. An excellent site description in English, Turkish and Swedish can be found at: http://www.labraunda.org/Labraunda.org/Welcome_to_Labraunda.html

**Mylasa** (37° 19′ 4″ N, 27° 46′ 19″ E), modern Milas, is a pleasant farming town, located between Bodrum and Euromos. Mylasa wielded considerable influence due to its control of Labranda, the preeminent Carian religious site. In the mid 6$^{th}$ century BCE Mylasa with the rest of Caria fell under Persian control. After the Persian defeat at Salamis in 479 BCE, Mylasa joined the Delian league until reverting to Persian control in 404 BCE. In Asia Minor, local satraps with considerable autonomy governed on behalf of the Persian King. Mylasa was capital of the Carian satrap Hecatomnus in 391-377 BCE. Under instructions from Persia, Hecatomnus gained control over Miletus, the largest Greek settlement in Asia Minor. When he died in 377 BCE, his son Mausolus succeeded him. Mausolus consolidated power and eventually moved his capital to Halicarnassus (modern Bodrum). Later in 4$^{th}$ century BCE Alexander extinguished Persian control and then the Ptolemies, the Seleucids, Rhodes and finally Rome ruled. During the Roman civil war, the former Republican Labenius sacked Mylasa in 40 BCE with a Parthian army. Mylasa was rebuilt with help from Emperor Augustus.

**Mylasa Site**: At Milas the 2nd century Battle Axe Gate or Baltali Kapi (37° 18' 58.6" N, 27° 47' 7" E) was the N gate of the walls around ancient Mylasa and the starting point of the paved sacred way leading 13 km to Labranda. The arch keystone on the outer side is

*Double-sided Axe: Symbol of Zeus*

a double axe relief, which represents Zeus. At the former Mylasa necropolis stands an intact monumental Roman tomb known as the Gümüşkesen (37° 19' 4" N, 27° 46' 19" E), meaning silver purse, which dates back to 160-180. The burial chamber stands on a high podium supporting a platform surrounded with twelve Corinthian columns holding up a pyramid-shaped roof. The interior ceiling displays impressive geometric and floral decorations. A hole in the floor of the platform enabled mourners to pour wine and honey into the burial chamber below. This monumental tomb is believed to contain many stylistic elements drawn from much larger 4th century BCE tomb of Mausolus at Halicarnassus. Milas also has a good, compact Archeological Museum with fine Roman era statuary in the garden.

*Milas Monumental Tomb*

**Iasos** (37° 16' 45" N, 27° 35' 3" E), modern Kıyıkışlacık, is 20 km W of Milas on the Gulf of Iasos opposite the town of Güllük. In 431–404 BCE Iasos was a member of the Delian League and involved in the Peloponnesian War. In 412 BCE Spartans attacked and destroyed Iasos. It was part of the Persian satrapy of Mausolus in the 4th century. In 125 BCE Iasos was incorporated into Roman Asia along with the rest of Caria and was generally prosperous under Roman rule.

**Iasos Site**: Iasos is built on a small peninsula jutting out into the sea. Near the remains of an aqueduct is a monumental temple tomb, once known as the fish market, in the style of a Corinthian temple façade on a ten-stepped platform. Iasos has two circuit walls: one with towers and gates surrounds the city on the peninsula; the other has a large gate and surrounds the landward end of the peninsula where the modern town lies. In the SW corner of the agora stands the 4th century BCE bouleuterion (22 x 26 m), rebuilt in the 1st century with seats at the edge decorated with lion paws. The remains of a stoa lie to the S of the agora. In the side of the rock to the NE is the 4th century BCE theatre together with inscriptions, such as one reserving a section of the cavea and stage for Dionysus. On the S side, towards the open sea are remains of a Roman era villa with decorative mosaics. Further on at the S extremity of the peninsula is a shrine dedicated to Demeter and Persephone with a stepped propylon or entranceway from which pilgrims could approach from the shore after disembarking from boats. The Italian Archeological Mission to Iasos has a website in Italian: http://www.associazioneiasosdicaria.org/joomla/

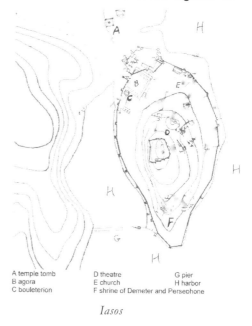

A temple tomb
B agora
C bouleterion
D theatre
E church
F shrine of Demeter and Persephone
G pier
H harbor

*Iasos*

Halicarnassus (37° 2' 24 N", 27° 25' 18" E), modern Bodrum, is a picturesque mass tourism destination located on the Ceramic Gulf. The city was originally a Dorian colony. Lydians and then Persians ruled Halicarnassus in the 6$^{th}$-4$^{th}$ centuries BCE. During the 5$^{th}$ century BCE Greek Queen Artemisia I of Halicarnassus ruled on behalf of Persia and distinguished herself at the Battle of Salamis in 480 BCE. Herodotus (484-425 BCE), known as the father of history, was a native of Halicarnassus.

**Herodotus (484-420 BCE) is known as the father of history and anthropology because of his comprehensive Histories, a narrative history of Persian Empire, its constituent tribes and the wars with the Greeks 499–479 BCE. He combines an historical method based on research and logical reasoning with traditional storytelling. Herodotus describes the Persian Empire in the order that successive Persian Kings Cyrus, Cambyses, and Darius conquered its constituent parts, and includes observations on the geography, social structure, and history of each region. Although Herodotus suggests divine retribution for human arrogance and cruelty, he emphasizes the actions and character of individuals. He reflects the Greek belief in the rule of law as opposed to tyrannical despotism, but portrays Persians and other peoples of the E with sympathy and objectivity. Herodotus was born a Persian subject in Halicarnassus, a member of a prominent Greek family. He traveled extensively for many years throughout the Persian Empire to the capital at Susa, Lydia, Phrygia, Mesopotamia, Phoenicia, Egypt as far S as Aswan, as well as Thrace, Rhodes, Cyprus, Delos, Crete, Samos, Macedonia, Scythia, the Danube, along the N coast of the Black Sea to Colchis and the Don River. Herodotus and his family were involved in a struggle against the local tyrant Lygdamis, which prompted him to leave the city in 457 BCE and move to Samos. Later Herodotus moved to Athens, where he became friends with Sophocles, the renowned Greek tragedian. Eventually Herodotus settled in Thurii, a newly established Athenian colony in southern Italy.**

Mausolus, the Carian satrap (governor) under the Persians, moved the regional capital from Mylasa to Halicarnassus in 370-365 BCE. The city was famous for the elaborate tomb of Mausolus, one of the Seven Wonders of the ancient world. Alexander the Great ended Persian rule with the conquest of

Halicarnassus in 334 BCE, but retreating Persians did enormous damage and burned down the city.

**Mausolus** was a Carian who ruled Caria as satrap (governor) 377–353 BCE on behalf of Persia. Mausolus was eldest son of Hecatomnus, a native Carian who served the Persians as satrap 395-377 BCE from Mylasa, where his tomb was recently discovered. Hecatomnus had three sons, Mausolus, Idrieus and Pixodarus and two daughters, Artemisia and Ada. In a bizarre traditional practice, Artemisa and Ada were married to their brothers Mausolus and Idrieus. Mausolus moved his capital from Mylasa to Halicarnassus, where he dredged the harbor, paved the streets, built houses and erected a fortified palace. As satrap, Mausolus exercised considerable autonomy and embraced Hellenistic culture. He constructed formidable walls with watchtowers and built a Hellenistic theatre. Mausolus, on behalf of the Persians, defeated a rebellion by Pericles of Limyra and annexed a considerable portion of Lycia. Mausolus and later his brother Idrieus went to great lengths to rebuild the primary Carian religious sanctuary at Labranda in honor of Zeus.

Mausolus is best known for his monumental tomb, from which we derive the word mausoleum. The Mausoleum of Mausolus at Halicarnassus was erected by order of his sister and widow Artemisia. Artemisia succeeded Mausolus in 353 BCE and reigned for two years, followed by Idrieus, who was in turn succeeded by his wife and sister Ada when he died in 344 BCE. In 340 BCE Ada's younger brother Pixodarus got tired of waiting and usurped her rule. When Pixodarus died in 335 BCE his Persian son-in-law was given the satrapy of Caria. Meanwhile deposed queen Ada remained in the fortified town of Alinda until Alexander the Great arrived on the scene in 334 BCE. Ada supported Alexander, giving him added legitimacy among the Carians, and was reinstated as queen of Caria with Alexander her designated heir.

**Halicarnassus Site**: Although the tomb of Mausolus no longer stands, the foundations exist and a museum on the site provides a sense of its former grandeur. The 43 m high structure consisted of: a podium, a colonnaded enclosure, a pyramid, and a pedestal with a chariot at the apex, surrounded with fine sculpture. The podium (30 x 36 m) was built from blocks of green stone cased with marble. There were 36 Ionic columns surrounding a square cella. The principal frieze was an Amazonomachy, i.e., combat between Greek men and Amazon women. Above the colonnade rose the pyramid with 24 steps leading up to a statue of Mausolus and his sister-queen Artemisia in a chariot at the apex. The Mausoleum was a cultural amalgam, which combined a Lycian style high rectangular podium, an Ionic Greek style colonnaded enclosure, and an Egyptian stepped pyramid roof. Sir Charles Newton rediscovered the Mausoleum at Halicarnassus in 1856.

A Mausoleum   C theatre   D Castle of St. Peter
B Myndus gate

*Bodrum (Halicarnassus)*

**Sir Charles Newton (1816-1894) was the son of a vicar, who studied archeology at Oxford and joined the British Museum in 1840. The British Foreign Office named Newton vice consul at Mytilene on the island of Lesbos in 1852, where his job was to find, record and obtain ancient artifacts for the British Museum. He conducted excavations at Bodrum in 1856-1857 and uncovered the large statues of the Mausolus and his wife Artemisia Newton now on display at the British Museum in Room 21:**
http://www.britishmuseum.org/explore/highlights/highlight_objects/gr/c/seated_statue_of_a_man.aspx

**Newton also made important discoveries at Didyma and directed the British team excavating at Knidos, which obtained the ancient statute of Demeter and the colossal lion, also at the British Museum. In 1862 he returned to London as curator of Greek and**

Roman antiquities. Sir Charles Newton was one of the first scholars to emphasize studying and photographing classical objects and physical ruins, instead of simply relying on historical texts to learn about the past.

To the W of the Mausoleum, the 4$^{th}$ century BCE Myndus Gate is a remnant of the ancient Halicarnassus city wall with two standing towers. To the N of the Mausoleum is the large Greco-Roman theatre, originally built in the 4$^{th}$ century BCE and expanded under the Romans to seat 13,000. The lower part of the theatre is well preserved and still used for concerts. Further N of the theatre is the necropolis with numerous Hellenistic and Roman rock-cut tombs. In the 15$^{th}$ century the citadel Alexander once besieged was transformed into the Castle of St. Peter by the Christian knights of St John using materials from the Mausoleum. This castle, surrounded with a moat, is now a museum containing ancient statuary and artifacts, including shipwrecks from the late Roman period. The Carian princess hall contains the remains of Carian Queen Ada, restored to power by Alexander the Great. Danish archeologists led by Professor Kristian Jeppesen have worked at Bodrum as described in an excellent University of Southern Denmark website:
http://www.sdu.dk/en/Om_SDU/Institutter_centre/Ihks/Forskning/Forskningsprojekter/Halikarnassos


**Euromos** (37° 22' 27" N, 27° 40' 31" E), meaning strong, is 12 km NW of Milas (the ancient Mylasa), and seldom visited despite a fine temple of Zeus. Settlement here dates back to the 6$^{th}$ century BCE. Euromos was a substantial and prosperous city, closely aligned with nearby Mylasa. The city reached its peak prosperity under Roman rule during the 1$^{st}$ century BCE-2$^{nd}$ century CE.

**Euromos Site**: The most outstanding structure at Euromos is a large 2$^{nd}$ century temple of Zeus (14 x 27 m), one of the best-preserved classical temples in Turkey. Corinthian columns surrounded the temple with 11 columns on the long side, six on the short, of which 16 remain standing and support part of an upper architrave. Most of these majestic columns are inscribed with names of donors: five contributed by state physician and magistrate Menecrates and his daughter Typhaena; seven contributed by the magistrate Leo Quintus. One of the temple blocks displays the double-sided axe symbol of Zeus. The temple entrance was on the E side through a double row of columns. Steps led into the cella to where a statue of Zeus stood. To the E of the temple are remains of a marble altar. The main city was to the N where a heavily overgrown theatre can still be made out, built into a slight hill above the plain. Nearby are a number of Carian rock-cut tombs.

*Euromos Temple of Zeus*

Zeus (Jupiter to Romans) is the King of gods and men, god of sky and thunder, most powerful of all who rules the heavens and Mount Olympus. He is guardian of political order and peace. Zeus was the child of Cronus and Rhea, youngest of six siblings.

*Donors listed on columns*

Cronus sired five children with Rhea: Hestia, Demeter, Hera, Pluto, and Poseidon, but swallowed them all as soon as they were born in an attempt to avoid his fate, which was to be overcome by a more powerful son just as Cronus had overthrown his own father. When Rhea gave birth to her sixth child, Zeus, she deceitfully gave Cronus a rock wrapped in swaddling clothes, which he promptly swallowed. Rhea hid Zeus until, as an adult, Zeus confronted Cronus and forced him to disgorge his five siblings. Then Zeus released the brothers of Cronus, including the Cyclopes, from Tartarus. In appreciation, the Cyclopes gave Zeus the gift of thunder and lightning.  Zeus, together with his brothers and sisters, overthrew Cronus and the other titans, in a war known as the Titanomachy.  The defeated titans were confined to the underworld realm of Tartarus.  Atlas, one of the titans that fought against Zeus, was punished by having to hold up the sky.  After the Titanomachy, Zeus drew lots with his elder brothers, Poseidon and Pluto, to divide the universe: Zeus received the sky and the heavens, Poseidon the oceans and rivers, and Pluto the underworld of the dead.  Zeus was brother and consort of Hera, but known for his erotic escapades with goddesses, nymphs and mortal women, during which numerous offspring were conceived.  With Hera he fathered Ares, god of war; Hephaestus, god of workmanship; and Hebe, goddess of youth.  Hera was jealous of his amorous conquests and an enemy of his mistresses and their children by him.

*Zeus (Antalya Museum)*

Zeus has a contradictory, somewhat ambiguous relationship with the human race.  He punished Prometheus severely for stealing a spark of divine fire and giving it to men, which enabled them to improve their lives and develop.  Zeus also gave mankind Pandora, the first woman, with a box she should never open but of course did, which contained all the evils of the world.  On the other hand, Zeus would sometimes visit earth in disguise and displayed tender feelings toward mankind, as in the story of Philemon and Baucis, a poor but pious couple, who killed their last goose to feed an unknown guest and were well rewarded.  Eagles are the birds of Zeus and often symbolized his presence.  His tree is the oak and priests would listen to the rustling of oak leaves to interpret the will of Zeus.

**Alabanda** (37° 35′ 31″ N, 27° 59′ 7″ E), modern Doganyurt, is 8 km W of Çine in a remote farming area. In the Carian language, "ala" meant horse and "banda" meant victory. The city was founded in the 4th century BCE on a plain at the foot of two hills to the S and controlled from a stronghold on the hill to the E. Like the rest of Caria, the city was under Persian rule and, after Alexander, subject to the rivalry between his Seleucid and Ptolemaic successors. In 190 BCE, the battle of Magnesia ended Seleucid domination and, together with the other Carian cities, Alabanda came under the nominal rule of Rhodes and later Rome. In 40 BCE, the Roman rebel Labenius and a Parthian army occupied the city. After the local citizens slaughtered Labenius' garrison, the Parthian army robbed the city of all moveable wealth. Alabanda later prospered under Roman rule.

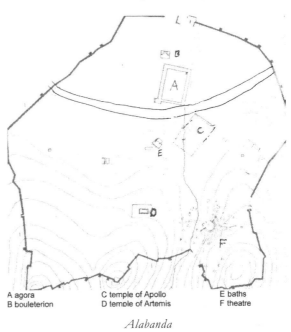

A agora  C temple of Apollo  E baths
B bouleterion  D temple of Artemis  F theatre

*Alabanda*

*Alabanda bouleutrion*

**Alabanda Site**: A modern country road bisects the widely scattered site. The ancient city walls encompassed an area of 4-5 square km on the plain and extended up the two nearby hills, where a section of wall and towers can still be seen. To the N on the side of the main road away from the village in a cornfield are the scant remains of the agora (112 x 72 m). More impressive is the rectangular bouleuterion (22 x 35) N of the agora toward the main city gate. The bouleuterion seats formed a semicircle within the rectangular structure, where one wall remains largely intact. On the village side of the main road to the S are the other ruins. Moving S toward the village to the right (W) lie remains of the large Ionic $2^{nd}$ century BCE temple of Apollo (35 x 22 m), which originally had 13 white columns along the long side, eight along the short. An inscription confirms this temple was dedicated to Apollo Isotemus (meaning equal in honor) and the Divine Emperors. Parts of a frieze depicting an Amazonomachy were recovered at the site. Further to the W lie the scant remains of Hellenistic and Roman baths. To the S at the foot of the hill in the village stands the Hellenistic theatre, which had a 90 m long façade. On the slopes of the hill S of the city stand the foundations of a $2^{nd}$ century BCE Doric temple (28 x 15 m), probably dedicated to Artemis. Although little remains, archeologists uncovered a statuette of Artemis here. Outside the walls to the W are numerous tombs in a large necropolis; some sarcophagi bear inscriptions indicating professions of the deceased. The TAY (Archaeological Settlements of Turkey) Project website provides additional information about Alabanda in English and Turkish: http://tayproject.org/TAYages.fm$Retrieve?CagNo=5247&html=ag es_detail_e.html&layout=web

**Alinda** (37° 33' 29" N, 27° 49' 43" E) was a highly defensible mountain fortress overlooking a fertile plain, and is now part of the modern town of Karpuzlu. In 334 BCE Carian Queen Ada met Alexander the Great here and eventually persuaded him to restore her to power. Following Alexander's campaign, Alinda rapidly Hellenized. By the mid 3rd century BCE the Seleucids established a garrison at Alinda.

*Alinda market building*

**Alinda Site**: Up a steep slope from the modern town is the well-preserved, 99 m long, 15 m high Hellenistic market building. This building originally had three stories, of which the lower two remain largely intact. The first level consisted of pairs of individual shops, one behind the other,

*Alinda Theatre*

which opened onto a terrace to the S. The second storey was divided with a double row of columns and formed a single long hall, lighted by a large window to the W and narrow slits in the front wall. The top storey was level with and adjoined a flat, open agora (30 x 30 m) to the N. Proceeding further up the mountain, now the domain of numerous cows, visitors come to the largely intact early $2^{nd}$ century BCE 5000-seat theatre, expanded by the Romans in the $1^{st}$ century. The theatre, heavily overgrown, faces SW and provides a panoramic view of the valley. Near the summit of the hill is a well-preserved, two-storey Hellenistic square tower from where a tunnel once led to the theatre. To the NW is a second, higher walled acropolis with cisterns, suggesting this was a stronghold to retreat to in times of danger. In the valley below stands an extended section of a Roman aqueduct with four supporting arches. Work at Alinda is described in English on the Austrian Academy of Science website:
http://www.oeaw.ac.at/antike/index.php?id=25&L=2



**Nysa on the Meander** (37° 54' 12" N, 28° 8' 42" E), 3 km N of Sultanhisar, 31 km E of Aydin, is an impressive and extensive ancient site. Although most of Caria supported Mithridates VI of Pontus during the 88-85 BCE Mithridatic Wars, the wealthy Nysaean merchant Chaerimon supported the Romans and provided the local garrison with 60,000 bushels of wheat. Mithridates put a bounty on the head of Chaerimon who sought sanctuary at the temple of Artemis at Ephesus, but was caught and executed. Nysa was known as a significant center of learning with a large library. Strabo lived and studied in Nysa, and left an account of life in the city.

**Strabo (63 BCE–23 CE) was born in Amasya, in the Kingdom of Pontus, which Pompey had recently defeated and incorporated into the Roman Empire. Members of his Georgian mother's family held important offices under Mithridates VI, the fierce opponent of Rome, but switched sides and became loyal supporters of Rome.**

As a young man Strabo went to Nysa to study under Aristodemus, a teacher of rhetoric and former tutor of Pompey's sons. In 44 BCE Strabo moved to Rome to study under Tyrannion, once a tutor of Cicero, and Athenodorus, former tutor of Augustus. Strabo developed an interest in Stoic philosophy, remained in Rome until 31 BCE and wrote his multi-volume Historical Sketches (now lost). Although culturally Greek, Strabo staunchly supported Roman imperialism and greatly admired Augustus. Strabo traveled extensively as far as Armenia to the E, the Black Sea to the N, the Italian coast opposite Sardinia to the W, and Ethiopia to the S. In 25 BCE he accompanied the Roman prefect Aelius Gallus up the Nile to Philae in Upper Egypt.

In about the year 7, when he was 57 years old, Strabo began drafting his 17-volume Geography, an encyclopedia of the ancient world from the Atlantic Ocean in the W to the Indus River in the E including: Spain, Gaul, Britain, Italy, Sicily, the Balkans, Greece, the Black Sea, and the Caspian Sea, Asia Minor, India, Persia, Assyria, Babylonia, Syria, Arabia, Egypt and Africa. His sources were his own direct observations, earlier Greek historians who accompanied Alexander the Great, and recent reports from Roman expeditions sent out by Mark Antony and Emperor Augustus. The last dateable event is the death of King Juba II of Mauretania in 23 CE. Strabo intended this work to provide practical information for statesmen on natural resources, customs, ethnology and trading patterns. He included histories of cities and states, related myths and legends, and stories of leading citizens. Strabo revered Homer and carefully identified cities listed in the Iliad. He described the journeys of Hercules as if they were recent historical events. Strabo included geological phenomena such as the Atlantic tides, volcanic landscapes in southern Italy and Sicily, fountains of naphtha near the Euphrates River, and the ebb and flow of the Nile River. Strabo even anticipated modern theories of plate tectonics in explaining observable geological features.

Nysa was known as the place where nymphs raised the baby Dionysus, as well as where Pluto abducted Persephone, daughter of Demeter. Outside the city was the Plutonium, a sacred precinct only for the sick and priests with a shrine dedicated to the gods Pluto and Persephone and a healing center in a natural cave above the shrine, known as the Charonium. At the Charonium patients would receive treatment prescribed to them or to the priests by the gods in dreams.

**Nysa Site**: A modern road runs through this accessible and well-maintained site to a car park in front of the theatre. To the W the ruins include a large, multi-storey $2^{nd}$ century library complex. Three walls remain intact.

*Nysa Library*

Bookshelves were located on either side of the reading room (15 x 13 m) with space separating them from the outer walls to keep the books dry. Scant remains of a gymnasium lie 150 m S of the library. To the W of the gymnasium are two late Roman churches built over earlier temples. Further W on the edge of the city is a necropolis. A sacred way led 3 km W from the necropolis to the Plutonium . Nysa was unusual in that it was built on both sides of a mountain stream ravine.

The large Greco-Roman theater straddled the stream to the NE of the city with a seating capacity of 8,800. The stage building is decorated with scenes of the life and revelry of Dionysius, the god of theatre and ecstasy. These reliefs provide considerable insight into the story of Dionysus because at Nysa many were preserved *in situ* and are being restored.

*Hermes brings Baby Dionysus to Nymphs*

*Baby Dionysus with Korybantes and Meander River God*

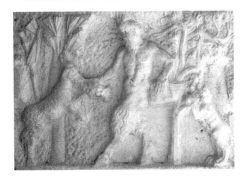

*Satyr, Goat and Panther*

Dionysus (Bacchus to Romans) was god of the grape harvest, wine, ritual madness, theatre and ecstasy. He is the son of Zeus and Semele, a mortal princess of Thebes. When Hera learned that Zeus had impregnated Semele, she disguised herself as a kindly old woman and gained her confidence. Hera persuaded the young princess to doubt Zeus and, after he had sworn by the River Styx to grant any request, Semele insisted he reveal himself to her in his true form. Zeus was compelled to appear as a god and Semele died immediately from a blast of lightning. Zeus took the embryo from Semele's lifeless body and implanted it in his own thigh. A few months later, Dionysus was born when Zeus released the baby from his thigh. Zeus instructed Hermes to take the infant Dionysus to be raised by the nymphs at the city of Nysa on the Meander. While in Nysa, Dionysus was protected by the Korybantes, dancing male warriors who would protect him at all costs. When Dionysus grew up, he discovered the culture of the vine and how to make wine. Still resentful, Hera struck him with madness, and he became a wanderer. In Phrygia the goddess Cybele cured Dionysus and he then set out to teach people how to make wine. He is often depicted as a beardless, disorderly, drunken youth. Satyrs and panthers accompanied Dionysus. The mountain nymphs who raised him became followers of Dionysus. Dionysus is a liberator whose wine, music and ecstatic dance frees followers from self-conscious fears and subverts social order. His entourage also includes wild female followers, the Maenads, who dance and drink themselves into an ecstatic frenzy, lose all self-control, shout excitedly, and engage in uncontrolled sexual behavior. His followers play wild, exciting music. Dionysus also has a wise teacher, the satyr Silenus. In later years, Dionysus even took Ariadne as a wife when Theseus abandoned her on the island of Naxos.

Once, while he was disguised as a mortal sitting beside the seashore, a ship of pirates seized Dionysus, taking him for a prince they could hold for ransom or sell into slavery. They tried to bind him with ropes, but no rope could hold him. Dionysus turned into a fierce lion killing many of the crew. Some of the sailors jumped off the ship and were turned into dolphins. The helmsman, who first recognized the god and tried to stop the crew, was spared and allowed to retain his human form. Dionysus returned to his birthplace, Thebes, to exact revenge on the ruler, his cousin Pentheus, for denying his divinity and outlawing his worship. Dionysus slowly drove Pentheus mad, lured him to the woods of Mount Cithaeron where the Maenads tore him to pieces in an ecstatic frenzy.

*Maenad*

On another occasion, King Lycurgus of Thrace imprisoned all the followers of Dionysus. In response the god created a drought, drove Lycurgus insane, bound him with vines, and precipitated a revolt, which resulted in Lycurgus being drawn and quartered. Despite these two worrisome precedents, the Roman Senate criminalized worship of Dionysus in 186 BCE because it challenged social order and traditional Roman morality.

The theatre stage building also contains reliefs related to the goddess Demeter and the abduction of her daughter Persephone at Nysa.

Demeter (Ceres to Romans) is goddess of agriculture, grain production, crop fertility, motherly relationships and seasons. The word cereal is derived from Ceres. Demeter taught humans the art of agriculture: sowing seeds, plowing, and harvesting. She presides over the cycle of life and death. Demeter often appears carrying corn or wheat, crowned with fruits or grain. One day Pluto, god of the dead, forcibly abducted Demeter's daughter Persephone, making her Queen of underworld Tartarus, the unseen realm of the dead. Demeter did not know her whereabouts and searched for her daughter all over the earth. Increasingly desperate to find her missing daughter, Demeter disguised herself as an old woman to facilitate her search. She obtained employment at the house of the mortal Celeus and his wife Metanira as a nanny for the two boys Demophon and Triptolemus. In gratitude for their generosity, Demeter intended to make Demophon immortal by burning away his mortality each night at the family hearth, but Metanira discovered and was frightened by her actions and Demeter had to depart.

*Persephone, Pluto with Eros and Satyr*

Although the virgin goddesses Athena and Artemis would seem her most likely allies, they did nothing to assist Demeter in her plight. Instead, Demeter received assistance from a most unlikely benefactor, the titan goddess Hecate, who herself had a reputation as an abductor of young women. Hecate advised Demeter to seek assistance from Helios, the all-seeing sun god.

Helios had seen it all and told Demeter Pluto was the culprit. In desperate fury, Demeter refused to return to Mount Olympus, stopping the growth of grain, fruit and all vegetation. As drought spread and people could no longer make sacrifices to the gods, Zeus became increasingly worried. He sent Hermes to ask his brother Pluto to release Persephone. Pluto reluctantly agreed, but before Persephone left she ate four pomegranate seeds, which because they were from Tartarus, require her to return to Pluto for four months every year. When Demeter welcomes her daughter in spring the earth blossoms, but when Persephone returns to her husband in autumn the earth becomes barren. Once Persephone returned, Demeter remembered the generosity of the mortal Celeus and his family. She taught their boy Triptolemus the art of successful agriculture and he became one of her original priests. Triptolemus, often depicted with ears of corn along with Demeter and Persephone, was first to learn the secret rites of Eleusinian Mysteries. (The Eleusian Mysteries began in about 1500 BCE based on the return of Persephone to the land of the living and symbolize the annual return of life to earth.) Initiates were required to be Greek speakers and never have committed murder.

*Persephone, Demeter and Triptolemus*

The Eleusian Mysteries annual rites persisted for almost two thousand years. Participation increased significantly in about 300 BCE and during the Roman period several pre-Christian emperors were initiates. The rites involved cleansing ceremonies, animal sacrifices, a religious procession of about 30 km from the Athens cemetery to the temple at Eleusis, fasting, visions following the use of a possibly psychedelic drug, and finally a highly secret viewing of sacred relics of Demeter. The Mysteries suggested initiates could experience life after death, much as corn grows again from seed. Christianity was a bitter foe of these beliefs, and Roman emperor Theodosius I closed the Eleusian temples in 392.

The theatre stage building reliefs depict Hecate (right) together with Demeter, Eros and a wild boar.

Hecate (Trivia to Romans) is an ancient titan goddess associated with three-way crossroads, graveyards, fire, moonlight, witchcraft, poisonous plant botany, and sorcery. She is queen of ghosts, a shadowy underworld figure who assisted Zeus during the Titanomachy and thus retained her powers. She wanders through the dark night, noticed only by barking dogs as she passes. Hecate kidnaps young women to assist in her nefarious activities and later transforms them into nymphs. Having assisted Demeter to recover her daughter, Hecate accompanies Persephone on her yearly journey to Tartarus.

*Demeter and Hecate*

At Nysa under the road just E of the theatre is a 150 m long fully functional ancient Roman tunnel through which the stream runs, as Strabo described. Further up the modern road on the E side of the ravine are the remains of a vast agora with several columns. Nearby to the NW is the well-preserved late 2nd century bouleuterion, a semicircular structure enclosed in a rectangle. The bouleuterion had five stairways and 12 rows of seats with capacity for 600-700 people. It was paved with limestone blocks, with a speaker rostrum and three large entrances to the S. Outside were several bullhead carvings, eight columns, a bathing pool and a marble bath. The scant ruins of an ancient Plutonium (37° 53' 48" N, 28° 6' 35" E) lie just E of the small village of Salavatli. Archeological work at Nysa is described

on the website of the University of New England in Australia:
http://www.une.edu.au/cat/sites/nysaadmeandrum.php

# VIII ANCIENT REGION OF LYCIA

Ancient Lycia is a mountainous region with fertile valleys, which lies along the Mediterranean coast E of Caria, S of Pisidia and W of Pamphylia. The Lycians were one of the so-called Sea Peoples who invaded the Hittite Empire around 1200 BCE. During the 6$^{th}$ century Persians under King Cyrus the Great conquered Lycia despite fierce Lycian resistance, notably at **Xanthus**. Lycian soldiers participated in the Persian invasion of Greece in 480 BCE. After the Persian defeat at Salamis in 480 BCE, Athens dominated much of coastal Lycia. About 400 BCE Persian control over Lycia strengthened during the Peloponnesian War between Athens and Sparta. A local prince, Pericles of **Limyra**, dominated E Lycia and came into conflict with Mausolus, the Persian satrap based in Halicarnassus. A trilingual inscription found at **Letoon** provides definite evidence of strong Carian influence in Lycia at this time. Alexander the Great conquered Lycia in 333 BCE. After his untimely death, his Macedonian successors dominated Lycia and the region was rapidly Hellenized over the course of the 4$^{th}$ century BCE. After the defeat of the Seleucids at Magnesia ad Sipylum in 188 BCE, the Romans insisted that Lycia be given to Rhodes. Under Roman protection, in 168 BCE Lycia reverted to self-government in the Lycian League, a system of representative government studied by the 18$^{th}$ century founders of the United States, particularly James Madison and Alexander Hamilton. In 43 Emperor Claudius dissolved the Lycian League and incorporated the territory directly into the Roman Empire. Lycia contains many of the finest ancient ruins in Turkey, including sites at: **Telmessos** (modern Fethiye), **Oinoanda, Tlos, Pinara, Sidyma, Xanthus, Letoon, Patara, Antiphellos** (modern Kas),

**Cyanea**, **Myra**, **Andriace**, **Sura**, **Arykanda**, **Limyra**, **Olympos**, **Chimaera** and **Phaselis**. Lycian funerary architecture includes striking wood-like carved stone sarcophagi placed on high bases, often in the center of town rather than outside the city walls, as was the norm for other civilizations. Lycians also built elaborate temple-style tombs in rock cliffs. The historic Lycian Way long distance hiking trail passes through several pristine mountain villages as it climbs 1500 m above sea level and covers 500 km from Antalya to Ovacik. The well-marked route passes many ancient sites including **Sidyma**, **Xanthus**, Pydnai, **Letoon**, **Patara**, Phellos, **Telmessos** (modern Kas), **Myra** and **Olympos**. Kate Clow's excellent book The Lycian Way provides practical trail details, site descriptions and useful cultural information.


**Telmessos** (36° 37' 7" N, 29° 7' 4" E), modern Fethiye, was incorporated into the Lycian League in the 2$^{nd}$ century BCE. Alexander the Great was strongly linked to Telmessos by a close advisor, Aristander of Telmessos, his favorite soothsayer, diviner and dream interpreter. Aristander was already ensconced at the Macedonian court in 357 BCE, when he correctly interpreted King Philip's dream regarding Olympias' pregnancy and the birth of Alexander. Aristander continued as an influential presence during Alexander's campaigns, and Aristander correctly predicted Alexander's glorious victories. Given Aristander's influence Telmessos opened its gates to Alexander immediately with no conflict. After the death of Alexander, various Macedonian successors and then Pergamum ruled Telmessos before it became an integral part of the Roman Empire. Although modern Fethiye is a major tourist town with few ancient remains, the Fethiye Museum contains ancient statuary as well as an important 4$^{th}$ century BCE trilingual inscription (Aramaic, Lycian and Greek) from **Letoon** recording establishment of a religious cult.

**Telmessos Site**: Lycian stone tombs reflect an ancient style of wooden housing with imitation stone joints and beams covered with pointed arches. Lycians developed an elaborately decorated style of sarcophagus with lids suggesting a capsized boat. For example, a Lycian sarcophagus near the waterfront next to the Post Office has a double front in two stories with square imitation house beams and an arched lid. Both sides of the lid depict rows of warriors and the ends of the lid are divided into four panels. The most famous tomb in town is a 4th century BCE Lycian rock-cut tomb on the E cliff edge of the acropolis with a Greek inscription to "Amyntas son of Hermapios."

*Cliffside Tomb of Amyntas in Telmessos*

This elaborate tomb resembles a temple with two Ionic columns on either side of the entrance of a porch façade. The inner chamber had three stone benches for the dead. In the 1850s the French adventurer Charles Texier visited this tomb and carved his name into the upper left corner of the tomb door. More Lycian tombs can be seen to the left.

**Oinoanda** (36° 48' 30" N, 29° 33' 2" E), meaning rich in wine, is a strikingly beautiful remote site 32 km NW of Elmali in the mountainous upper Xanthus River valley. In 3rd-2nd centuries BCE many people from Termessos moved to Oinoanda. The city prospered under the Romans, particularly in the 2nd-3rd centuries. Archeological evidence suggests the city was abandoned in the 9th century, perhaps after the aqueduct became unusable.

**Oinoanda Site**: Reaching the site requires stopping at the small village of Incealiler and hiking 1.5 km up a steep 300 m slope for about an hour in a remote area to an altitude of 1400 m. The city lies on a broad ridge between two high hills on terraces facing S. The summit was fortified; a well-preserved wall and two guard towers with slits for shooting arrows reaches a height of 10 m at the S end. The wall intersects a major aqueduct. The site is overgrown with attractive pine trees and other vegetation with little sign of current excavation. The paved agora in the center of the city covers a level rectangular space formerly lined with statues from which a number of bases remain. Large statue fragments can still be seen *in situ*, including the finely carved left side of a face and head with torso. To the N at the highest point is the theatre, built into a slope outside the city walls, facing S. The theatre is 42 m wide, with 21 rows of seats for 1800 people. Many tombs are visible near the city, including famous house-like Lycian stone monuments. In the cliff-face to the W are several rock-cut tombs with separate lids. The impressive 2$^{nd}$ century mausoleum of Licinnia Flavilla outside the walls to the S provides a long inscription with the genealogy of her distinguished Oinoandan family.

*Oinoanda Figure*

To the N up the hill is a flat open space known as the Esplanade where archeologists discovered blocks from the remarkable stoa where Diogenes of Oinoanda in about 120 inscribed his famous discourse on the Epicurean philosophy. This ancient text on Epicurean teaching covers 260 square m. Epicurus lived five centuries before this

*Theatre at Oinoanda*

inscription was carved. The inscription probably remained visible for 125-150 years until the blocks were broken up and used for other purposes during the early Christian era, such as rebuilding the outer defensive wall or constructing houses. The steep terrain made it impractical to remove inscribed blocks beyond the immediate area; many component parts have been rediscovered one by one.

Diogenes of Oinoanda was born in the second half of the 1$^{st}$ century into a rich, influential family. He studied rhetoric at Rhodes, where he retired each winter to escape the cold at Oinoanda. He had a wide circle of Epicurean friends and traveled to Chalcis, Athens and Thebes. Diogenes created the inscription portico when he was an old man to impart the wisdom of Epicureanism to posterity. Epicureanism was highly unpopular with many other philosophers and religious leaders and much of the original work of Epicurus has been lost. For this reason, the Diogenes inscriptions played a crucial role in understanding his doctrine. The inscription contains: a treatise on ethics, which describes how pleasure is the aim of life, virtue the means to achieve it; a treatise which discusses dreams, the gods, the origin of humans and the invention of clothing, speech and writing; a treatise on old age; letters from Diogenes to his friends, including one concerning the Epicurean doctrine of innumerable worlds; Epicurean maxims and sayings; and even letters written by Epicurus, including one to his mother on the subject of dreams. Although the translated inscription text is too extensive to quote in its entirety, the following excerpts convey a sense of the message:

We observe that most people suffer from false notions about the nature of things, and do not listen to the body when it brings the just accusation that the soul drags it to things, which are not necessary, given that the wants of the body are small and easy to obtain…. Vain fears of death and of the gods grip many men, who do not see that true pleasure does not come from the approval of the crowd, or from perfumes or ointments, but from the study of nature…. I have now reached the sunset of my life, and I am on the verge of departing from it due to old age, but before I die I wish to compose this anthem to celebrate the fullness of happiness and to help those who are benevolent and capable of receiving it…. Moreover, it is right that I seek to help the generations to come, for they too belong to us, though they are still unborn, and it is also right that I help those foreigners who may come here…. But you should know that we bring these truths, not to all people indeed, but only to those people who are benevolent and capable of receiving it. And this includes those who are called "foreigners" though they are not really so, for the compass of the world gives all people a single country and home, our earth and world…. I say both now and always, shouting out loudly to all Greeks and non-Greeks, that pleasure is the end of the best mode of life, while the virtues are in no way the end in themselves, but the means to an end…. Fears of the gods, of death, and of pain, and also desires, which exceed the limits fixed by nature; these disturbing emotions are roots of all evil, and unless we defeat them a multitude of evils will grow and consume us…. And those who are wise and choose not to do wrong, are not wise on account of the gods, but on account of thinking correctly about certain things, such as about pain and death, for indeed without exception men do wrong either on account of fear or on account of the lure of pleasure…. And the number of those who are conscientious on account of the gods, and not on account of the laws, is few, only two or three among multitudes, and not even they are steadfast in acting righteously, for they are not soundly persuaded about providence. A clear indication of the complete inability of the gods to prevent wrongdoing is provided by the nations of the Jews and the Egyptians, who, while being the most superstitious of all peoples, are the vilest of peoples…. Do not believe that all men may achieve wisdom, because not all men are capable of it. But for those men for whom wisdom is possible, such men may truly live as gods…. Such men will be capable of deriving all their necessities from agriculture, without need of slaves, for indeed we ourselves shall plow and dig and tend the plants and divert rivers and watch over the crops. Neither fear of the gods, nor of death, nor of pain, nor slavery to those desires, which are neither natural nor necessary, shall interrupt the continuity of our friendships and our shared study of philosophy, for our farming operations in a life close to Nature will provide for us all that our nature wants.

The German Archeological Institute website contains an excellent description in English about work at Oinoanda: http://www.dainst.org/en/project/oinoanda?ft=all

**Tlos** (36° 33' 13" N, 29° 25' 9" E), modern Douvar 12 km S of Kemer, is a major tourist site located on a strategic hilltop in the upper Xanthus River valley. The site is dominated by its ancient acropolis, a rocky outcrop rising from a plateau with steep cliffs covered with rock-cut tombs facing N and NE. Tlos was the oldest Lycian city dating back to before 2000 BCE, and one of the six cities forming the Lycian League. A tomb on the acropolis dating back to 350-320 BCE is associated with Bellerophon, progenitor of the Lycian royalty.

Bellerophon was a brave and handsome young man from Corinth. One day he accidently killed his own brother while out hunting. Desperate to obtain forgiveness for this grievous action, Bellerophon left home and entered the service of Proetus, king of Tiryns. King Proetus initially welcomed the young man but his queen, Anteia, fell hopelessly in love with Bellerophon at first sight. Anteia relentlessly pursued Bellerophon at every opportunity when her husband was absent. Infuriated after Bellerophon repeatedly spurned her advances on moral grounds, she falsely claimed to her husband that Bellerophon had sexually assaulted her. Rather than confront Bellerophon directly, the savvy King Proetus directed him to go to Asia Minor and enter the service of his father-in-law, King Iobates of Lycia. King Proetus gave Bellerophon a sealed letter to deliver to King Iobates, which asked that Bellerophon be put to death for having dishonored his daughter Anteia. In Lycia Bellerophon received a royal welcome on the banks of the Xanthus River and King Iobates held a feast in his honor. On his tenth day in Lycia Bellerophon remembered to deliver the sealed letter to King Iobates. The king, horrified upon reading the written accusation, felt he could not execute a guest. Instead gave Bellerophon an impossible task, which would have the same result. He asked Bellerophon to rid Lycia of the dreaded monster Chimaera. Bellerophon learned that this terrible monster had long terrorized the countryside, each night attacking and consuming women, children, and livestock.

Although not afraid of this daunting challenge, Bellerophon sought the advice of Polybius, the wisest man in Lycia. Polybius told Bellerophon about Pegasus, the white flying horse, which had emerged from the neck of Medusa when Perseus beheaded her. Polybius advised the eager young Bellerophon that he must obtain Pegasus to have any chance against Chimaera.

*Pegasus and Bellerophon (Aphrodisias Museum)*

Polybius urged Bellerophon to pray to the goddess Athena, make offerings to her and seek her help. Bellerophon went to the temple of Athena, and prayed devoutly for assistance. Athena appeared to him that night in a dream, told him where to find Pegasus and how to capture him with a golden bridle. When Bellerophon awoke, he miraculously found a golden bridle next to him. He then went deep into the forest, found the spring Athena mentioned in the dream, and waited, hidden in the bushes. After Pegasus finally arrived, Bellerophon patiently waited until Pegasus kneeled down to drink, and then silently emerged and slipped the bridle over Pegasus' head. Pegasus bolted away and flew up into the sky, desperately trying to shake off Bellerophon, but to no avail. Eventually Pegasus got used to Bellerophon and accepted him as his rider. With Pegasus at his command, Bellerophon set out to deal with Chimaera.

Long ago a fearsome half-snake, half woman creature named Echidna had mated with the monster Typhon and produced Chimaera, a fire-breathing, three-headed creature. Chimaera had the head and body of a lion in front, a second head of a snake in back on her tail and a goat-head erupting from her back. She could consciously emit gales of fire from each of these heads at will. Knowing that Chimaera emerged every night at dusk from her deep underground lair, Bellerophon and Pegasus scoured the Lycian countryside looking for flames emerging from the vicious monster or the desperate cries of her victims. Finally they spotted her. Flying above the Chimaera on Pegasus, Bellerophon rained down arrows, but these had little effect on the thick skin of the ferocious beast and her flaming breath only narrowly missed the agile Pegasus several times. Bellerophon attacked directly with a long spear, but this was burned to a crisp as he flung it and he himself was almost incinerated. At this point Bellerophon withdrew to a safe distance and observed Chimaera until she returned to her lair at daybreak. Bellerophon then spent the day forging three leaden javelins. The next evening as Chimaera emerged from her cave, Bellerophon, always astride Pegasus, bravely confronted her from above. He thrust each of the javelins down on her. After carefully calculating all the angles and acting with incredible speed, he thrust a javelin between the jaws of each head in such a way that it melted and entered her stomach as molten liquid. Chimaera was completely immobilized and weighted down after this attack. She fell back into her cave and has never emerged since although flames from her mouths can still be seen rising to the surface above her lair at the Temple of Hephaestus in Yanartaş in Lycia near Olympos.

Rather than rewarding Bellerophon for his incredible bravery and ingenuity, King Iobates sent him to singlehandedly drive back the invading Solymians and their Amazon allies. The dauntless Bellerophon obeyed without question. Mounted on Pegasus and flying high above the invading armies he rained down arrows and boulders until they surrendered and begged for mercy. Bellerophon then settled the Solymians in the mountain town of Termessos. Unimpressed King Iobates next tasked Bellerophon with stopping a vicious band of Carian pirates raiding Lycian settlements all along the coast. Bellerophon and Pegasus soon caught up with the pirates, shot burning arrows down on their ship from above and drove them away forever. Despite these brave deeds, King Iobates still felt compelled to punish Bellerophon for attempting to dishonor his daughter. In desperation the king ordered his men to seize and imprison Bellerophon. Furious at this betrayal, Bellerophon escaped and called on Poseidon to flood the Xanthus River. As the river rose steadily the desperate women of Lycia, terrified that they would lose their houses and all their possessions, came to Bellerophon and offered him sex in return for stopping the flood. This offer embarrassed Bellerophon and he immediately called off the flood without demanding anything in return. King Iobates observed his reaction and concluded that the allegations contained in the sealed letter were untrue. The king confronted Bellerophon with the letter and learned the truth. Reassured about Bellerophon's integrity and aware of his military prowess, King Iobates married his second daughter Philonoe to Bellerophon and made him heir to the throne.

For years the couple was happy, and when Iobates died, Bellerophon became king and the progenitor of the Lycian royal house. Sadly, one day hubris got the better of Bellerophon and he decided to ride Pegasus up to Mount Olympus, unbidden, to visit the gods. Zeus, offended at the audacity of the mortal Bellerophon in presuming his hospitality, sent a gadfly to sting Pegasus. Pegasus was so startled that he reared up and threw Bellerophon off his back. As Bellerophon plummeted to earth, Athena took pity on her former protégé and caused him to fall into soft marshland and survive. Covered in mud and in disgrace Bellerophon crawled back home. Zeus instructed Pegasus not to return to

A acropolis
B Bellerophon tomb
C stadium
D agora
E palaestra
F church
G baths
H theatre

*Tlos*

Bellerophon and instead honored him with a place in the Heavens as a constellation, still visible to this day. Broken hearted after losing his equine companion, Bellerophon soon died and was buried with full honors at the royal Lycian tomb at Tlos.

A Jewish community is also known to have existed at Tlos with its own magistrates. Archeologists at Tlos have recently uncovered statues of Emperor Hadrian, Emperor Antoninus Pius and his daughter Faustina the Younger, as well as the goddess Isis (all now at Fethiye Museum in Turkey). Christianity eventually triumphed and a bishop from Tlos attended the Council of Chalcedon in 415.

*Acropolis at Tlos*

**Tlos Site**: Visitors can follow a good path directly up the slope to the acropolis and the Lycian house-type rock-cut tombs cut directly into the rock, some with figures depicted. At the summit stands the fortress of a notorious 19th century Ottoman feudal lord, built over a Lycian structure, as well as a Roman era wall. To reach the Bellerophon tomb on the N face, take the lower trail to the right below the cliffs. Red arrows and a crude ladder lead up to the tomb. Faint relief figures of Bellerophon and Pegasus, as well as four other animal figures adorn the tomb exterior, above and below the entrance portals. To the SE of the acropolis is the Roman stadium with seating for 3500. Columns strewn around the area suggest a columned portico once stood to the N. Parallel to the stadium to the SE are remnants of a 150 m long, two-storey structure with large arched doors in the W wall, which was probably an agora. To the S was a palaestra (wrestling hall). Further SE was an extensive baths complex. E of the palaestra lie remains of a substantial late Roman church. Further up across the modern road on the left is a large 2$^{nd}$ century Roman theatre with 34 rows of seats supported by a structure of vaults. Inscriptions indicate that this theatre was funded from the donations of many citizens and built gradually over more than a century. A portion of the stage building still stands and theatre mask reliefs on stone blocks remain visible.

**Pinara** (36° 29' 31" N, 29° 15' 31" E), 42 km SE of Fethiye, is a large ancient Lycian city in a remote mountainous area, reached along a twisting dirt road. In the Lycian language "pinara" meant "round," referring to the 500 m high round hilltop above the city pigeonholed with dramatic rock-cut tombs. Settlement at Pinara existed as early as the 5$^{th}$ century BCE, and the city was one of the six leading members of the Lycian League. In the 4$^{th}$ century BCE it was among the first Lycian cities to submit to Alexander the Great without a fight. Eventually Pinara was annexed to the Roman Empire. The city prospered under Roman rule and became an early Christian city. Repeated Arab invasions in the 9$^{th}$ century led to the city's abandonment.

**Pinara Site**: Approaching the city visitors see a large flat-topped reddish cliff (500 m high) honeycombed on its E face with hundreds of rock-cut rectangular burial tombs. Reaching and carving these tombs required sophisticated methodology and

*Pinara cliff tombs*

equipment. On the left after the entrance on the E side of the valley before the main site, an unmarked path leads up to the mid-4th century BCE Royal Tomb with reliefs on and above the lintel of people and horses. The interior of the porch contains marvelous reliefs of four (as yet unidentified) walled cities complete with human figures, houses, gates, towers and tombs. The interior contains a single chamber with one bench at the back. To the N higher up on the lower acropolis is an impressive arched house tomb crowned with oxen horns at the peak. To the W at the base of a lower hill are the scant remains of an odeon with a portal to the E. To the N the temple of Aphrodite is known for its unusual heart-shaped columns. Carved reliefs of a penis suggest that the temple worship here involved ritual prostitution. To the W are steep steps carved into the rock leading up to the upper acropolis used for defense in times of trouble. To the E on lower ground below the cliff lie extensive ruins of a well-preserved 2nd century BCE Hellenistic theatre. The theatre could accommodate 3200 spectators. A 2005 article in AMED contains a good article on inscribed tombs at Pinara: http://www.akmedanmed.com/article_en.php?artID=84&catID=10

*Pinara Royal Tomb lintel*

**Sidyma** (36° 24′ 5″ N, 29° 12′ 18″ E) is a remote site at a small, 500 m high village of Dodurga, 55 km S of Fethiye. As early as the 5th century BCE Sidyma was mentioned on the Athenian-Delian League tribute lists. The city was prosperous and influential under Roman rule during the 1st-3rd centuries and had citizens who served as Roman consuls. The town had and still has a reputation for hospitality. While only a common soldier, the future Emperor Marcian (reigned 450-457) became seriously ill after fighting the Persians and in 422 the Roman army left him at Sidyma to convalesce. Two brothers befriended him and nursed him back to health. One day out hunting, the brothers observed a huge eagle with outstretched wings shielding Marcian as he slept. Correctly interpreting the omen, the brothers later asked Marcian what he would do for them if he ever became emperor. He replied that he would generously repay their kindness, which he did many years later as emperor.

**Sidyma Site**: This remote site is virtually untouched, and appears much as it would have to 19th century European travelers. Many of the old stone houses in the picturesque village of Dodurga, which was built over the original city center, incorporate parts of ancient structures.

*Sidyma standing tombs*

The platform under a large tree next to the mosque marks where there was once an agora. The mosque occupies the site of a Roman bath, with remnants of an aqueduct leading to the building. The clearly marked Lycian Way long-distance hiking trail passes right through the small village. Columns mark where a stoa once stood. To the N of the stoa are remains of a small ancient temple dedicated to the goddess Artemis and the emperors built during the 1st century reign of Emperor Claudius. An inscribed stone incorporated into the back of the mosque lists several deities including Zeus, Apollo, Artemis, Aphrodite, and Athena. About one hundred tombs ranging in age form the 5th century BCE to the 5th century lie scattered around the fields and village gardens. Two identical 2nd century sarcophagi with a gable-shaped roof stand on a common base, apparently belonging to a father and son of the Aristodemus family. Not far away is a large temple-type monumental tomb raised on two steps with a large upper slab still in place, decorated on the underside with attractive carved reliefs of human heads and flowers. To the N of the village the acropolis contains scant remains of a fortress and a church dating back to the late Roman period. Along the SE side of the acropolis runs an early wall (365 m long, 3 m high) with a small gate, forecourt and tower. Further above the wall is the theater with six rows of partially visible seats. The theatre faces SE and could seat 1600 people.

**Xanthus** (36° 21' 24" N, 29° 19' 6" E), modern Kınık, lies 63 km SE of Fethiye on a hillside overlooking the Eşen River in the Xanthus Valley, surrounded by the Taurus Mountains. Xanthus, meaning yellow, administered the sacred Letoon cult center 8 km to the S. Homer mentions Sarpedon, founder of Xanthus, as an ally of the Trojans during the Trojan War. In 540 BCE Xanthus resorted to desperate measures when faced with an overwhelming force of Persian invaders sent by Cyrus the Great. After an initial defeat when the outcome was inevitable, the men of Xanthus burned up their material possessions, women, children, and slaves on the acropolis and then sallied forth in a suicidal attack to kill as many Persians as possible. The entire population of Xanthus perished except for 80 families who happened to be absent and returned to gradually repopulate the city. Archeological evidence suggests fire destroyed the wooden tombs

A theatre  F Roman street  J Vespasian gate
B Lycian acropolis  G church  K Lion tomb
C Sarpedon shrine  H Nereid monument  L Payava tomb
D Harpy tomb  I city walls  M Roman acropolis
E Inscribed pillar

*Xanthus*

and temples of Xanthus again in about 470 BCE, when Cimon of Athens attacked the city to retaliate for the earlier destruction of the Athenian Acropolis by the Persians and their Lycian allies.

The Xanthians rebuilt the city in stone, established the temple of Artemis and defeated the Athenians in the next round of fighting.

*Lycian Pillar Tomb and Harpy Tomb*

In 390 BCE Lycian King Arbinas asserted control over Lycia, ruled from Xanthus, built the Nereid Monument as his tomb, and died in 370 BCE. Xanthus surrendered to Alexander the Great in 334 BCE. In 42 BCE Brutus, the assassin of Julius Caesar, came to Lycia to extort funds for his campaign against Augustus and Antony. The Lycian League refused to contribute, but was no match for the Romans. Brutus besieged Xanthus and the same gruesome history was repeated when the city refused to surrender; only Xanthian 150 men survived the carnage. Eventually Xanthus recovered and resumed its role as the leading Lycian city in the Roman Empire. Xanthus was deserted after waves of Arab raids during the 7th century.

**Xanthus Site**: A modern road runs through Xanthus and the Lycian Way reaches Xanthus from Letoon. To the W of the road stands the $2^{nd}$ century Roman theatre originally with seats for 2200. The upper rows of the cavea are missing, and the stage building is only partially standing. S of the theatre is the original $8^{th}$ century BCE Lycian acropolis on high ground with foundations of a square building in the SE corner destroyed at the time of the Persian capture and mass suicide in 540 BCE. In the NE corner of this acropolis are remains of a late Roman church and monastery, built over an earlier Roman temple. Higher up to the W are the scanty remains of a temple of Artemis, a small sanctuary with three parallel chambers, which probably contained the shrine dedicated of the Sarpedon.

Sarpedon was the courageous leader of the Lycian contingent in the Trojan War against the Greeks. He was the son of Zeus and Laodamia, the daughter of Bellerophon. Patroclus killed Sarpedon in battle. Apollo carried the body of Sarpedon back to Xanthus where he was buried with full honors. By the 5$^{th}$ century BCE a Sarpedoneia cult center was established at the Xanthus acropolis at the temple of Artemis, where athletic games were held and sacrifices made in his honor.

To the W of the Xanthus theatre are three dramatic tombs close together. Furthest S is the 1$^{st}$ century Roman pillar tomb. Adjacent to the N is the 4$^{th}$ century BCE Lycian pillar tomb supporting a sarcophagus (3.6 m high) with a pointed arch on top of a pillar (3.4 m high) made of stone blocks. The third is the famous Harpy Tomb (8.9 m high) dating back to 480-470 BCE, given its name by Sir Charles Fellows in 1838. The Harpy Tomb is a single, monolithic column rising more than 5 m high, set upon a two-stepped podium. The grave chamber was at the top of the column. Its reliefs depict the deceased in battle, and separately a man and his wife receiving homage from their children. On all four sides seated figures receive gifts. On the S and E sides are birds; on the N side a helmet; and on the W side are two seated females, three standing figures approach the one on the right, the other receives an indistinct object. On the E side are three other female figures, one apparently accompanied by a dog. The figures Sir Charles Fellows misidentified as Harpies are on the N and S sides on

*Harpy Tomb*

either side of the seated figures. They are bird-women with female heads, wings and tails, carrying children in their arms. These winged females are sirens, bird-women who carry the souls of the dead, in the form of children, to the Isles of the Blessed. The seated figures are members of the ruling family. The reliefs were originally colored, chiefly in red and blue, traces of which were visible at the time of the discovery. Crosses were painted on the back of the reliefs, suggesting that a Christian hermit once used the grave-chamber as a refuge. Concrete reproductions stand in place of the original, which is at the British Museum in London:

http://www.britishmuseum.org/explore/highlights/highlight_objects/gr/r/harpy_tomb_relief_panel.aspx

**Sir Charles Fellows (1799-1860) was an early British archaeologist and explorer who visited Lycia and explored the Xanthus river valley in 1838 when it was unknown to western Europeans. Fellows identified, described and sketched ancient ruins at Patara, Xanthus, Tlos and Pinara. At Tlos he discovered the Bellerophon tomb, and he saw the incredible cliff-tombs at Pinara. He was particularly impressed with the ancient Lycian capital of Xanthus where he discovered several 5$^{th}$ century BCE monuments including the Payava tomb, the Lion tomb, the Nereid monument, and a structure he named the Harpy tomb. The latter tomb had four female-headed figures on the four extremities of its N and S sides, with wings and bird-like tails and claws, each carrying away a female child. Fellows, well versed in Homer, understood this scene as an allusion to the story of Harpies in the Odyssey (book XX, lines 64-78) carrying away the orphaned daughters of Pandarus. (Ironically, the Lycian archer Pandarus in Homer's Iliad was transformed in later works by Chaucer and Shakespeare into a sexually degenerate character from whom the modern word "pander" is derived.) Fellow's account of this expedition, his Journal written during an Excursion in Asia Minor, was published in 1839 and generated enormous public interest. In response British Foreign Secretary Lord Palmerston obtained permission from the Ottoman authorities to take these ancient Lycian funerary monuments back to the British Museum in London. At his own expense in 1839-40, Fellows led a British**

effort supported with the British naval vessel, HMS Beacon. From Patara at the mouth of the Xanthus River twenty men dragged boats upriver for four days. In this remote country, the crew was afflicted with malaria, two men died when a supply boat capsized, and wolves ate a tethered horse during the night. After nine weeks of continuous labor at Xanthus, the sailors managed to detach the marble reliefs, pack them in 82 protected crates, and haul them back to London in two trips. After the artifacts were successfully reassembled, the British Museum reimbursed Fellows for his expenses and he was knighted in 1845. The Harpy Tomb, Payava Tomb, Nereid Monument and the sarcophagus lid of the Lion Tomb are all preserved and still can be seen at British Museum.

To the NE of the Xanthus agora along the road is the Inscribed Pillar, a 5$^{th}$ century BCE house tomb with reliefs, which recount the life and accomplishments of King Kerei in Lycian and Greek. He fought for Lycian independence from Athens during the Peloponnesian war. Kerei was a champion wrestler in his youth; sacked many cities; and slew seven Greek Hoplites (foot soldiers) in one day. This monument is famous because it is the longest Lycian inscription known, over 250 lines of text. The grave chamber from this monument is now at the Istanbul Archeological Museum.

Across the modern road from the theatre is an excavated late Roman street, once lined with shops on both sides. To the SE of the excavated road are remains of a late Roman basilica with mosaics. To the S is the Nereid monument, actually the tomb of King Arbinas built in 380 BCE. This Ionic-order temple-like structure combines Greek and Lycian architectural styles. The monument contains friezes of Greeks in battle with barbarians, and hunting. Arbinas was a 4$^{th}$ century BCE Lycian ruler who first built the temple of Leto, the Letoon. One podium frieze depicts the siege and surrender of a city. The name Nereid derives from the female Nereids or sea nymphs appearing between the Ionic columns.

**Nereids are the 50 daughters of the sea god Nereus,**

personifications of ocean waves. The best known of the Nereids were: Amphitrite, consort of Poseidon; and Thetis, wife of Peleus, king of the Myrmidons, and mother of the hero Achilles.

Although the monument base remains *in situ*, the main Nereid monument can be seen today at the British Museum: http://www.britishmuseum.org/explore/highlights/highlight_image.aspx?image=ps066824.jpg&retpage=18302

To the SE is the Hellenistic gateway to Xanthus, built during the period when Macedonian Seleucid King Antiochus III ruled the city. The 1st century Vespasian Gate stands NW of the Hellenistic Gate directly along the modern road. The Vespasian Gate was the main entrance to Xanthus and the starting point for the sacred road to Letoon. NE of the Roman basilica stood a second late Roman church. Up a trail further to the NE lies the Lion Tomb, which depicts scenes of lions and men and dates back to 550-550 BCE. Part of the sarcophagus is now at the British Museum: http://www.britishmuseum.org/explore/highlights/highlight_objects/gr/m/lion_tomb_marble_relief.aspx

NW from the Lion Tomb is the 370-360 BCE Payava Tomb, also taken to London with only the pedestal remaining *in situ*. The monument contains on one side a Lycian inscription about a Persian Satrap Autophradates meeting Payava, and a war scene relief on the other side. Reliefs on the sarcophagus lid depict four horses pulling a chariot; a Greek athlete and his bearded compatriot; a seated figure in full Persian dress receiving a delegation; and two longhaired and bearded soldiers, wearing armor and cloaks. Lion heads project from the curved roof. The top-level friezes show a bear hunt on one side, and a battle between cavalry and foot soldiers on the other. The Payava tomb can be seen at the British Museum:

http://www.britishmuseum.org/explore/highlights/highlight_objects/gr/t/the_tomb_of_payava,_a_lykian_a.aspx

French archeologists have done considerable work at both Xanthus and Letoon as described at: http://www.diplomatie.gouv.fr/en/france-priorities/education-research/archaeology/archaeology-notebooks/ancient-east/turkey-xanthos-and-the-letoon/

**Letoon** (36° 19' 55" N, 29° 17' 24" E), 4 km south of Xanthus, was the leading Lycian religious center. The principal deities of ancient Lycia were Leto and her twin offspring, Artemis and Apollo. Letoon was a sacred cult center and venue for Lycian national festivals, administered by Xanthus rather than a city in its own right. Letoon was the assembly place for the Lycian League.

A temple of Leto   C temple of Apollo   E monastery
B temple of Artemis   D nymphaeum   F theatre

*Letoon*

Archaeological finds date back to the 7<sup>th</sup> century BCE. Alexander the Great received a prophecy here according to which he was destined to destroy the Persian Empire. In 88 BCE Mithridates VI of Pontus, rebelled against Rome, besieged Patara, and started to cut down a grove of sacred trees at Letoon to use as siege engines. After a nightmare warned him he was committing sacrilege he desisted, but given his subsequent fate perhaps it was already too late. The Letoon remained a religious center well into the 5<sup>th</sup> century when a church was built at the site, doubtless to hasten the Christianization of the local population.

Leto (Latona to Romans) is the daughter of the titans Coeus and Phoebe. She is the goddess of modesty, motherhood, and together with her two children, protector of the young. Leto was an early favorite of Zeus, who impregnated her. As the wife of Zeus, Hera was furious about this love affair and created serious problems for Leto. She was exiled from Olympus and forced to wander the earth looking for a place of refuge to give birth. For fear of Hera, no place would allow her to stay. At this time the mighty Python, a huge serpent monster, lived at Delphi just below Mount Parnassus where he protected the navel of the earth and an oracle. Hera sent the Python to kill Leto before she could deliver her babies. As the mighty Python pursued Leto, Zeus instructed the north wind to carry Leto safely away. Hera prevented Eileithyia, goddess of childbirth, from helping so Leto had to manage her own delivery. After wandering in many countries, Leto finally simply wrapped her arms around a palm tree, knelt down and gave birth to the goddess Artemis near Ephesus. Then Leto arrived on a barren, floating island called Delos. After a difficult nine days in labor Leto, ably assisted by Artemis who rapidly became an expert in midwifery, gave birth to the god Apollo. In gratitude to Delos, Leto anchored the island to the bottom of the Aegean Sea with four indestructible columns. Leto next went to Anatolia where she washed her infant children in the Xanthus River. Then she went to a nearby pond to drink fresh water from a spring. Fearing the wrath of Hera and seeking to keep the pond for themselves, the local shepherds tried to drive her away. They shouted, threatened, and stirred up mud from the bottom of the pond. At this point a pack of wolves came to Leto's assistance and chased the men away. Out of gratitude Leto renamed the region Lycia, from the word for wolf. This spot was the venue of the future Letoon. Leto turned the shepherds who had harassed her into frogs and allowed them to return to the pond where they can be heard to this day. The giant Tityus was an offspring of Zeus with the mortal woman Elara. Years earlier Zeus had hidden Elara from Hera deep inside the earth when she was pregnant. Unfortunately Tityus as an embryo grew so large that he split his mother's womb and she died in childbirth. Hera now enlisted Tityus against Leto and induced the powerful giant to attempt to rape her. By now however, Leto had her two fast developing children, both powerful archers, to protect her. Their arrows dispatched Tityus without difficulty. On another occasion Niobe, a mortal woman, boasted that she was superior to Leto because she had borne seven sons and seven daughters, whereas Leto only had two. This hubris enraged Artemis and Apollo, who fired their deadly arrows at all fourteen of her offspring. Niobe wept so much for her dead children that she turned into a pillar of stone, which can still be seen at Magnesia on the Sipylum. As mother of two powerful gods, Leto eventually returned to Olympus and Zeus's favor despite Hera's disapproval. Leto, together with her offspring, sided with the Trojans during the war and helped heal Aeneas from his wounds. Although Leto was worshiped throughout the Greek-speaking world, she was particularly revered in Lycia.

*Letoon temples: Apollo (nearest), Artemis (middle), Leto (upper)*

**Letoon Site**: Lycians came to the Letoon religious complex along a sacred way to worship at a triad of adjacent temples erected on podiums. To the W the largest and best preserved is the 3$^{rd}$ century BCE temple of Leto (30 x 16 m) surrounded by Ionic columns. The temple of Leto was built of fine, clear colored limestone. An Ionic portico surrounded the cella, which was decorated with a Corinthian colonnade. The Artemis temple in the middle was the oldest (early 4$^{th}$ century) and smallest (18 x 9 m) with the N part of the structure incorporated into a large rock and rough stone blocks. The Doric 4$^{th}$ century BCE temple of Apollo to the E was almost the same size (28 x 15 m) as the temple of Leto and decorated with half-columns. During excavations a remarkable mosaic was unearthed depicting a bow and quiver, a rosette and a lyre, attributes of Apollo. In the immediate vicinity of this temple an important trilingual inscription in Lycian, Aramaic and Greek dating back to 358 BCE was discovered, which decrees creation of a new religious cult and threatens offenders with the wrath of Leto, Artemis, Apollo and the Nymphs. To the SW of the temples was a large $3^{rd}$ century nymphaeum with a semi-circular pool. A sacred spring supplied water to the nymphaeum and the pool was used for religious ceremonies.

Further SW of the temples are ruins of a $4^{th}$ century monastery destroyed in the mid $7^{th}$ century, probably during an Arab Muslim raid. The nave and aisles were decorated with floor mosaics depicting geometric designs and animal figures, including a stork. Archeologists refer to this monastic community as "the drunken monks" because of the large number of drinking vessels uncovered. Further to the N of the complex is the $2^{nd}$ century BCE Hellenistic theatre built into the hillside. This theatre was used to hold religious performances for pilgrims from the entire region. The entrance on the S side is decorated with a row of sixteen carved theatrical masks, including Dionysus, and Silenus.

**Patara** (36° 15′ 37″ N, 29° 18′ 51″ E), 70 km SE of Fethiye along the beach, was a leading Lycian port located in a coastal valley with a 1.6 km long harbor protected from onshore winds by the surrounding hills. Patara was home to the main Lycian League meeting hall with an archive at the temple of Apollo. According to tradition Apollo lived at Delos in summer and at Patara in winter, and a large head of Apollo was discovered SW of the city gate. From the oracle of Patara, Telephos learned that he could only be cured of his wound with the spear of Achilles. Along with the rest of Lycia, Patara welcomed Alexander the Great in 333 BCE. During the $4^{th}$-$3^{rd}$ centuries BCE Alexander's Macedonian successors struggled for control of the city and its strategic naval base. Rome granted Patara and the rest of Lycia independence in 167 BCE. In 88 BCE Mithridates VI, King of Pontus besieged the city. Brutus and Cassius captured Patara in 42 BCE during their campaign to extort funds for use against Mark Antony and Augustus, but did not engage in the slaughter that occurred at Xanthus. Patara was formally annexed by the Roman Empire in 43. Emperor Claudius instructed his newly appointed governor to survey the Lycian road system, which resulted in the massive Stadiasmus Provinciae Lyciae monument with inscriptions listing 67 routes and distances. When the Romans created the province of Lycia-Pamphylia in the latter part of the 1$^{st}$ century, the governor resided in Patara. In 70 Emperor Vespasian visited Patara and commissioned the large baths bearing his name. Emperor Hadrian visited in 129 and opened the large granary, which still stands.

*Hadrian (Antalya Museum)*

**Hadrian (Publius Aelius Traianus Hadrianus Augustus) reigned as Roman Emperor 117-138. He was born in 76 in the Iberian Roman town Italica, a cousin of his predecessor, Emperor Trajan. Hadrian had a strong military background serving along the Rhine frontier, in Athens, in the Dacian war, in the Persian campaign and in Syria. When Trajan died, Trajan's wife claimed he had designated Hadrian as his successor. Hadrian secured the support of the army and the Senate, and became emperor in 117. His policy was to promote peace through military strength rather than undertake new conquests. Hadrian considered certain recently conquered territories, such as Mesopotamia, indefensible and withdrew, which was not popular. He carefully avoided war with Parthia in 121 and negotiated a lasting peace agreement. Hadrian built permanent fortifications and**

watchtowers along the imperial borders, such as the famous wall in N England. He lived with the army and traveled widely, spending more than half his reign outside of Italy.

Hadrian was a philhellene who greatly admired Athens and constructed temples in the E dedicated to traditional gods, as well as libraries, aqueducts, baths and theaters. He generously used imperial funds to rebuild regions devastated by earthquakes. Hadrian developed a passionate relationship with Antinous, a Greek youth whom Hadrian later ordered deified when he drowned under mysterious circumstances in the Nile, which was understandable to Greeks but did not enhance his popularity among the more austere Romans. Hadrian was the first emperor to wear a beard, which then became popular. In 128 Hadrian attended the Eleusinian mysteries and visited Ephesus. In 130 Hadrian decided to rebuild Jerusalem, largely destroyed after the First Jewish Revolt, as a non-Jewish Roman city named Aelia Capitolina, after himself and Jupiter Capitolinus (Zeus). To discourage Christian worship, Hadrian erected a massive temple of Aphrodite on top the structure early Christians venerated as the tomb of Jesus. (Later St. Helena demolished this temple of Aphrodite and built the Church of the Holy Sepulcher on this spot.) Hadrian built a temple of Zeus over the ruins of the Second Jewish Temple.

*Patara: Modestus Arch (right); Baths (left)*

In 132 the Jewish population rose up in the famous Bar Kokhba revolt and even reestablished an independent Jewish state for three years, which many Jews regarded as the beginning of a Messianic Age. In response Hadrian called in troops from as far away as Britain and the Danube and took to the field personally to suppress the revolt. In 135 after three years of ferocious fighting the rebellion was crushed with more than 500,000 Jews killed, and 50 major towns plus at least 900 smaller villages destroyed.

Once the conflict was over the Romans forbade Jews to even enter Jerusalem. Hadrian now attempted to outlaw Judaism because he regarded it as a divisive faith, which turned groups of people against each other, encouraging ethnic conflict. In line with Greek ideals, he viewed Jewish circumcision as a barbaric practice and made it illegal. Hadrian prohibited use of Jewish Torah law in legal disputes and executed recalcitrant Jewish scholars. After protracted illness Hadrian died in 138 at age 62. His successor Antoninus Pius built the Tomb of Hadrian in Rome and had Hadrian formally deified.

Patara is famous in Christian history for being a place St. Paul visited en route to Jerusalem during his third missionary journey. St. Nicholas, Santa Claus and future bishop of Myra, was born at Patara in 270 into a Christian community probably started by St. Paul. In the 6$^{th}$ century Emperor Justinian built a massive city wall to protect the city. Over time the harbor silted up and sand dunes engulfed Patara.

**Patara Site**: The 12 km-long Patara Beach is an easy 10-15 minute stroll from the Patara ruins, encompassed within a national park. Patara's

A Modestus gate
B baths
C Corinthian tomb
D church
E theatre
F Roman street
G Hadrian granary
H temple tomb
I agora

*Patara*

ancient naval and military base fortress, Pydnai, is located at the far W end of the beach. A 10 m high, 19 m long triple-arched triumphal Roman gate, built in 100, marks the entrance to the site from the N. The arch celebrated completion of an aqueduct built by Trebonius Proculus Mettius Modestus, Roman governor of Lycia and Pamphylia. The arch was decorated with statues of the immodest Modestus and his relatives. Modestus went on to become consul in 103. Near the gate are many Roman era sarcophagi. To the S of the arch are the harbor baths, otherwise known as the Date Palm baths, decorated with floor mosaics. To the SW, a city wall Emperor Justinian built in the 6th century runs N-S by what is perhaps the oldest extant road sign, the Stadiasmus Provinciae Lyciae. To the SE at a corner in the wall is the 1st century Marciana Temple Tomb, which a Roman official built to honor his deceased four-year-old daughter. The large 1st century Vespasian Baths (152 x 38 m) lie directly S along the wall. To the W a 12.5 m wide colonnaded street linked the harbor to the agora. The central baths were located at the N end of this street, the agora to the S. On the W side of the agora archaeologists uncovered the bouleuterion used as the assembly hall for Lycian League representatives. Rows of stone seats are arranged in a semicircle; the stone-vaulted main entrances are intact, as is the seat where the elected chairman (Lyciarch) presided.

*Patara Theatre*

S of the bouleuterion the sand-swept theatre dates back to Hellenistic times, but was enlarged and modified under Emperor Antoninus Pius in 147 following a major earthquake. The theatre decorations encompass military symbols, suggesting it was a venue for gladiatorial fights. Near the peninsula jutting out toward the silted up harbor is an unidentified Corinthian style Roman temple (13 x 9 m) with intact walls. As the major Lycian port, Patara played an essential role in the grain trade. Along the W side of the harbor Emperor Hadrian built a large granary (65 m x 32 m) with eight storage rooms, each with a separate door facing the harbor. The structure still stands dedicated with an inscription to Hadrian and his wife Sabina, who are likened to Zeus and Hera. A Corinthian temple tomb was built to the N of the granary. Archeologists recently discovered a round building at the SW corner of the harbor identified as a lighthouse at least 22 m tall. The lighthouse contains many large inscriptions, originally with bronze lettering, dating back to the early 1$^{st}$ century. The Lycian Way hiking trail passes through Patara. Professor Klaus Zimmermann and other German archeologists from the Westfälischen Wilhelms-University of Münster have worked at Patara: http://www.uni-muenster.de/AsiaMinor/projekte/epigr-lykien/index.html

*Patara: Hadrian Granary*

**Antiphellos** (36° 12′ 0″ N, 29° 38′ 6″ E), modern Kaş (eyebrow), is a pleasant fishing and tourist town 168 km W of Antalya. Antiphellos, meaning in front of Phellos, received its name for being the port of the city of Phellos (stony land) located up in the mountains. Over time Antiphellos eclipsed Phellos in importance and became a member of the Lycian League in its own right.

**Antiphellos Site**: To the N of the city in a rock wall are 5th century BCE rock-cut tombs near the point where the Lycian Way passes. One of these Lycian tombs was reused centuries later, as a Latin inscription indicates, by a certain Claudia Regelia Herennio. The symbol of Kaş is a 4th century BCE stone tomb at the upper end of Uzun Çarşı Street in the center of town, the Lion Tomb. The top part of the sarcophagus has two lion heads resting on paws. The short side of the lid is divided into panels with two standing figures. The sarcophagus rests on a stone base and beneath is a second burial chamber. On the side of the 1.5 m high lower chamber is an eight-line inscription written in a non-deciphered form of the Lycian only found elsewhere on the Inscribed Pillar at Xanthus. The well-preserved Hellenistic theatre is built into the hillside on the W edge of town facing S toward the sea along the coast with seats for 4000 people. A 4th century BCE house-type rock-tomb, known as the Doric Tomb for its pillars, is carved out of the hillside 100 m above and to the NE of the theatre. Inside the chamber is a bench decorated with rosettes and oyster shells. A frieze depicts 25 dancing female figures holding hands.

*Tomb in Antiphellos*

**Cyanea** (36° 14′ 45″ N, 29° 48′ 54″ E), meaning dark blue, is an isolated, heavily over grown, and rarely visited ancient city hidden away on back roads near the town of Yavu. Near the base of a hill an ancient path leads past clusters of Lycian tombs up to an acropolis with walls and gates on three sides, a cliff on the fourth. Overgrown remains have been identified as a bath complex, a library and several cisterns. To the W of the acropolis stands the well-preserved theatre. Many different types of Lycian tombs decorated with reliefs and bearing inscriptions lie between the theatre and the acropolis along an ancient roadbed and on the edges of the city.

**Myra** (36° 14' 41" N, 29° 59' 7" E), modern Demre or Kale, is 145 km SW of Antalya, 45 km E of Kaş. A defensive wall around Myra has been dated to the $5^{th}$ century BCE. In the $2^{nd}$ century Myra was one of the six most important Lycian League members. The temple of Artemis Eleuthera at Myra was reportedly Lycia's largest building, built on large grounds with gardens and an inner colonnaded court containing an altar and a statue of Artemis. In 42 BCE, after Brutus had massacred the population at Xanthus he sent Lentulus Spinther to extort funds from Myra for the campaign against Augustus and Antony. Spinther broke the defensive chain across the harbor entrance at Andriace and, fearful of his vengeance with Xanthus in mind, Myra acceded to his demands. Andriace, 5 km SW of Myra, was Myra's port and a major trans-shipment point for ships carrying grain from Egypt to Rome and other parts of the Empire. In 18 the popular Germanicus and his wife Agrippina visited Myra a year before his suspicious death; statutes were erected in their honor at the Andriace. Emperor Hadrian visited Myra in 131 and commissioned a large granary at Andriace, as he had at Patara. The presence of a significant Jewish community at Myra was confirmed by the recent discovery

*Myra Sea Necropolis*

of an ancient synagogue at Andriace. Christianity came early to Myra. In 60 the Romans imprisoned St. Paul and sent him to Rome for trial. On the way from Jerusalem to Rome he stopped briefly at Myra, changed ships and continued their voyage. St. Nicholas, commonly known as Santa Claus, served as bishop of Myra in the 4th century. In the 5th century Emperor Theodosius II made the prosperous city of Myra capital of Lycia. When a terrible plague swept through Anatolia in 542-543, Myra lost a third of its population. Over time as the harbor at Andriace silted up, economic activity declined. In the 7th-8th centuries continuous Arab raids further disrupted commercial life. In 808 Muslim Caliph Harun ar-Rashid besieged and conquered Myra. The Lycian Way passes through the city.

**Myra Site**: 5th-3rd century BCE Lycian rock-cut tombs are carved into the S cliffs of the city acropolis above the theatre 1.5 km N of the center of Demre. There are two separate groups of 4th century BCE Lycian rock-cut tombs at Myra: the sea necropolis and the river necropolis. The sea necropolis NW and NE of the theater is clearly visible and difficult to miss. These rock-cut sepulchers are built in the style of ancient Lycian wooden dwellings and shrines, with doors, windows, and reliefs. Many contain elaborate facades and inscriptions; some depict reliefs of funeral scenes and the daily life of the deceased. A few temple tombs have steps carved out of the rock leading to them. One ground level tomb at the base of the cliff depicts a conflict between two warriors at the point where the one on the left tries to flee but is restrained by the other holding his shield. The river necropolis, 1.5 km to the E from the theater, around the corner facing the Myros River is harder to find. Here is the Painted Tomb, an unusual house-type tomb with a group of eleven life-size figures, presumably depicting the deceased, his family members and friends. To the left a reclining man holds a wine cup and to his right are a woman and two children; on the left stands a magisterial male figure holding a staff with a woman and a girl holding her hand; separately a veiled woman carries a box which she offers to a young man who offers her a flower as a child grips at his cloak. When Sir Charles

Fellows visited these tombs in 1840 they were still painted red, yellow and blue, but now only faint traces of paint remain.

*Myra Theatre*

The theatre cavea was carved directly out of the hillside rock and surrounded with two concentric vaulted galleries used for shops and stairs to access upper areas. This theatre seated 13,000 spectators. Inscriptions are still visible. In the center of the wall above the stairs is a depiction of Tyche with the inscription, "Fortune of the city, be ever victorious, good luck." Another at a shop confirms the "place of the vendor Gelasius." The stage building façade includes numerous theatrical masks and scenes referring to Zeus, as well as Medea with her children.

Medea was daughter of King Aeetes of Colchis (in modern Georgia) from whom Jason and the Argonauts sought the Golden Fleece. King Aeetes agreed to give it to him if he could perform three seemingly impossible tasks. First, Jason had to yoke and plow a field with fire-breathing oxen. Then, Jason had to sow the teeth of a dragon into a field and defeat the army of warriors sprouting from these teeth. Finally, Jason had to overcome a dragon who never slept and guarded the Golden Fleece. Medea fell in love with Jason and gave him an ointment that protected him from the oxen's flames so he managed to plow the field. Then Medea explained how to throw a rock into the crowd of warriors so that they would attack and destroy each other. Finally, she gave him an herbal potion, which he sprayed on the dragon so it fell asleep, enabling him to seize the Golden Fleece. Then the Argonauts and Medea sailed away with King Aeetes and his men in hot pursuit. To elude capture, Medea chopped up her little brother Apsyrtus and threw pieces of his body into the sea. Later as the Argonauts approached Crete, Talos, a huge bronze man guarding the island, hurled boulders at their ship. Talos had one blood vessel running from his neck to his ankle closed with one bronze nail. Medea cast a spell on Talos and then removed the bronze nail so he bled to death.

Eventually Jason and Medea arrived in Corinth, where Jason spurned Medea and decided to marry beautiful Creusa, daughter of the king of Corinth. Infuriated, Medea got her revenge. First she presented Creusa with a beautiful but cursed dress as a wedding gift, which stuck to her body and burned her to death as soon as she put it on. Creusa's father, the king of Corinth, also burned to death trying to save his daughter. Then out of spite Medea killed the two sons she had with Jason. Finally, Medea fled to Athens in a golden chariot driven by dragons sent by her grandfather, the sun god Helios.

At Myra the earliest church of St. Nicholas (36° 14' 41" N, 29° 59' 7" E) was built over the saint's tomb not long after his death in 343. Emperor Justinian refurbished the church after a major earthquake in 529. In the 8$^{th}$ century a basilica was built with a central nave, a side aisle to the N and two side aisles to the S. The tomb of St. Nicholas is in the second S aisle between two pillars behind a marble screen. An

*Church of St. Nicholas interior*

attempt was made to destroy the saint's tomb during an Arab attack on Myra in 808, but the Muslim commander inadvertently smashed another nearby sarcophagus instead, and body of St. Nicholas remained undisturbed. The church suffered another Arab attack in 1034 and was restored in 1043 by Emperor Constantine IX, at which time a walled monastery was added. In 1087, a group of Italian merchants overpowered the local monks, broke open the saint's sarcophagus, and carried his relics away to Bari in Italy, where the Pope presided over placing the relics in a large church, which soon became a major pilgrimage. The church at Myra remained a major Christian pilgrimage destination, even after the relics were stolen. Fragments of the saint's jawbone and skull, which escaped the trip to Bari, remained at Myra and are now safely housed at the Antalya Museum. In the early 12$^{th}$ century cloisters, a courtyard and a second entrance were added. The floor of the church, accessed via a ramp, is 5 m below street level. Mosaics and faded wall paintings decorate the floor and walls throughout the church, including some depicting important scenes from the life of St. Nicholas. In the apse of the central nave are semicircular seats for the clergy and four columns surround the stone altar.

St. Nicholas was born in Patara in 270 into a wealthy and devoutly Christian family. When he was still a child his parents died in an epidemic. The uncle of St. Nicholas, who was bishop of Patara, raised him. From an early age the future saint was very religious and rigorously observed Christian fasts on Wednesdays and Fridays. Nicholas dedicated his life to God and gave up his inheritance to assist the poor. He became a priest and made a pilgrimage to Egypt and Palestine while still a young man. Returning home by sea, his ship was caught in a powerful storm. The terrified sailors watched in amazement as Nicholas calmly prayed and then the fierce wind abated and the waves calmed. One day

*St. Nicholas*

during a time of famine an unscrupulous butcher lured three small boys into his shop and, while they were napping, killed them, cut them into pieces and put them in a barrel of salt to sell them as ham. Nicholas, upon learning of the heinous crime from an angel, resurrected the boys with prayer and returned them safely to their families. On another occasion Nicholas learned of a man from Patara who had lost all his money, and could not afford to support his three daughters. The girls were of marriageable age but their father could not afford the dowry needed for them to find husbands. In desperation the girls soon would be reduced to prostitution. Upon learning of their dilemma, Nicholas took three bags of gold and, under cover of darkness, tossed each bag of gold down the chimney of the man's house. The girls had just washed their stockings and placed them by the chimney to dry. When they went to dress in the morning, each girl discovered a bag of gold in her stocking, and all were able to arrange suitable marriages.

The elevation of Nicholas to bishop of Myra was unexpected. Upon the death of the former bishop, a synod of other bishops gathered in Myra to select a successor. During the night, the senior bishop heard a supernatural voice telling him to observe the church doors the following morning and choose the first person to enter named "Nicholas" as the next bishop. When the time came, the young priest Nicholas from Patara walked through the door and was consecrated as the new Bishop of Myra. His elevation to bishop came at a time when Emperor Diocletian was

*St. Nicholas appears to Constantine in a dream (left); reassures sailors (right)*

cracking down on Christianity as a destructive force endangering the security of the empire by alienating traditional gods. Nicholas, along with many other Christian leaders, was imprisoned and tortured because he refused to renounce his faith. He was released after Emperor Galerius issued the edict of toleration in 311 and resumed his role as bishop. When Constantine became sole emperor in 325 the position of Christians throughout the empire dramatically improved.

Bishop Nicholas worked tirelessly to promote Christianity and to suppress earlier, non-Christian beliefs. Artemis had long been the patron goddess of Myra and her impressive temple was the largest building in the city. Nicholas and his supporters attacked the temple of Artemis with great determination and vigor, destroying it so completely that archeologists have yet to find any trace of it. Later in 325 Emperor Constantine convened the Council of Nicaea, the first ecumenical council. More than 300 bishops from all over the Christian world came to debate and define the nature of the Holy Trinity.

*Council of Nicaea*

Arias of Alexandria taught that the Son Jesus came after God the Father in time and substance. Nicholas adamantly opposed Arianism and tried repeatedly to make Arias see the truth. Finally, in exasperation, Nicholas slapped the unyielding Arias in the face so hard that his bones shook. For this injudicious act, Constantine removed Nicholas from office and threw him in prison. According to tradition, that night both Jesus and the Virgin Mary appeared to Nicholas: Jesus brought him a bible and Mary brought him his bishop's vestment, which had been taken from him. This event is depicted on numerous Eastern Orthodox icons of St. Nicholas. Reinstated, Nicholas resumed his holy work and the Council of Nicaea condemned Arianism.

Myra experienced famine in 333; crops had failed and people

were hungry. Bishop Nicholas learned that ships bound from Alexandria for Constantinople carrying wheat were anchored at Andriace. The bishop went to the harbor and implored the ship captains to unload a measure of grain from each ship so that the people of Myra would not starve. The ship captains demurred, greatly fearing the wrath of the emperor if the grain delivered in Constantinople were to be reduced. Nicholas persisted, promising them in the name of God that they would not suffer for this act, and was so persuasive that the captains relented and allowed a measure of grain to be taken from each ship. When the ships arrived in Constantinople, to their amazement the merchants discovered that the grain shipment had not been diminished despite unloading enough grain in Myra to last that city for two years.

Even after the advent of Christianity corruption and skullduggery were not unknown in the Roman Empire. Once a senior Roman official in Myra accepted a bribe to condemn three innocent men to death. Learning that a miscarriage of justice was about to take place, Nicholas ran to the prison, arrived just in time and fearlessly stayed the hand of the executioner. Nicholas then turned to the corrupt official and furiously reproached him until he confessed his wrongdoing, released the men and begged for forgiveness. Three imperial officers en route from Phrygia to Constantinople witnessed this whole affair, but were not involved. Some time later back in Constantinople the three officers themselves were victims of political intrigue after they inadvertently aroused the jealousy of the prefect Ablavius, who had them imprisoned and sentenced to death on false charges. The three officers remembered the example of justice they had witnessed in Myra and prayed for the help of the bishop of Myra. That night St. Nicholas appeared in a dream to Emperor Constantine and to prefect Ablavius and demanded that the three innocent men be set free. In the morning the Emperor consulted Ablavius and, upon learning they recently had met with Bishop Nicholas, was convinced of their innocence and released them.

St. Nicholas died on December 6, 343 in Myra and was buried in his cathedral church. Even from beyond the grave, the saint protected the people of Myra. Once on the eve of his feast day a band of Arab pirates raided Myra, seized treasure and, kidnapped a young boy named Basilios to serve them as a slave. Back in the home country of the pirates, the local emir selected Basilios as his personal cupbearer, because the boy did not known Arabic and could not repeat what was said to others. For the next year Basilios waited on the emir, bringing him wine in a fine golden cup. The year passed miserably for Basilios' parents, filled with grief at the loss of their only child. At the next St. Nicholas feast day, Basilios' mother prayed devoutly for his wellbeing and safe return. Then as Basilios waited on the emir in a distant land, St. Nicholas suddenly appeared before the terrified boy, blessed him, and miraculously swept him up and set him down back at his home in Myra together with the golden cup. St. Nicholas is the patron saint of Greece and Russia as well as of children, sailors, merchants, scholars, bakers, pawnbrokers, and those unjustly imprisoned.

ANMED describes recent archeological work at St. Nicholas church in Myra and at Myra's port Andriace:
http://www.akmedanmed.com/article_en.php?catID=14&artID=253

http://www.akmedanmed.com/article_en.php?catID=15&artID=290

**Andriace** (36° 13' 34" N, 29° 57' 21" E), modern Çayağzı (meaning mouth of stream), is 3 km SW of Myra. Formerly the port of Myra, the harbor is now silted up. Emperor Hadrian visited Myra in 131 and by 139 had built a substantial granary at Andriace, similar to the one he built at Patara. The eight-room granary (65 x 32 m), used to store local as well as Egyptian grain, still stands complete with busts of the emperor and his wife over the main door. A small relief on the front wall near the second door depicts Serapis standing and Isis reclining with a griffin (a winged creature with the body of a lion) between them. Beside the granary was a large heap of Murex shells, used in the ancient world to make a valuable, much sought after purple dye for royal garments. Archaeologists recently uncovered a 3rd century Jewish synagogue at Andriace on top of a hill overlooking the harbor. This synagogue, only the third yet found in Asia Minor, is located less than a km from the harbor and served Jewish merchants and traders working at the port. The two-room structure was identified from a well-preserved marble plaque on the wall of the larger room, which was supported by two columns and used as a congregational hall. The plaque contained reliefs of a seven-branched menorah; a lulav or closed date palm frond; an etrog, a lemon-like fruit; and a shofar or a ram's horn.

The menorah, perhaps the oldest symbol of the Jewish faith, is a seven-branched lamp stand built based on biblical instructions in the Old Testament book of Genesis. The lamp burned ritually pure olive oil at the temple at Jerusalem perhaps symbolizing enlightenment and creation of the world in seven days, with the center light representing the Sabbath.

*Andriace Synagogue Plaque (Antalya Museum)*

The menorah is also closely associated with the eight-day Chanukah holiday, which celebrates rededication of the temple after the successful 2nd century BCE Jewish revolt against Seleucid rule. Although only enough ritually pure olive oil remained to fuel the temple menorah for one day after its Seleucid desecration, the flame miraculously burned for eight days. Because tradition prohibited use of a seven-branched menorah outside the temple of Jerusalem, Chanukah menorahs have eight branches plus a ninth used to kindle the others.

The shofar is a traditional Hebrew (ram or ibex) horn blown to announce Rosh Hashanah (New Year) and Yom Kippur (the Day of Atonement). The curve in the horn represents contrition and Abraham's willingness to sacrifice his son Isaac. Joshua conquered Jericho when the shofars were blown and the walls of Jericho came tumbling down.

**Sura** (36° 14' 41" N, 29° 56' 39" E), 5 km W of Demre along the bay near Andriace, had an unusual fish oracle of Apollo. According to ancient accounts, a petitioner in search of advice would toss meat or bread into the water. A priest would summon the fish with sound from a pipe and then observe the results. Many varieties of fish, some quite large, would appear. If the fish eagerly tore apart and consumed the meat, it was a good sign; if they ignored the offering, it meant bad luck. The priest provided a more detailed prediction depending on which fish appeared and how they behaved.

**Sura Site**: At the end of a long plain stands a walled acropolis with a rectangular watchtower to the N. Several Lycian sarcophagi are strewn nearby. At the SW corner of a $5^{th}$ century BCE rock-cut house-tomb is a statue-base with a long Lycian inscription. To the S was a house of priests of which only the terrace (15 x 9 m) cut from the rock remains. Carved into the rock of the N and W walls an inscription lists clergy responsible for maintaining the oracle of Apollo. To the W the ground descends sharply toward a marshy inlet and a small Doric temple of Apollo (14 x 7 m). The interior walls are carved with inscriptions from ancient worshippers. Just N above the temple are ruins of a late Roman church, undoubtedly erected to hasten the transition of popular worship from Apollo to Christianity.

**Arykanda** (36° 30' 47" N, 30° 3' 34" E), 111 km SW of Antalya, is an ancient city built on mountain terraces at an altitude of 1000 m near the village of Aykiriçay. As the "anda" ending of its name suggests, Arykanda is one of the oldest Lycian cities. Although the city dates back to the $7^{th}$ century BCE, most ruins are from the $5^{th}$ century BCE through the $3^{rd}$ century. Like other Lycian cities, Arykanda was under Persian rule in the $5^{th}$ century BCE.

Alexander the Great assumed control in 333 BCE and after his death, first the Ptolemies, then the Seleucids, and finally Rhodes ruled the city. Later the city was in the Lycian League. Emperor Claudius imposed direct Roman rule in 43. Christianity arrived as early as the 3$^{rd}$ century. Arykanda survived through late Roman times, until the inhabitants moved to Arif, a separate site S of the modern road, in the 6$^{th}$ century.

**Arykanda Site**: This beautiful and remote site is extensive, rising up several terraces built into the rock face. Near the car park are the remnants of a Sebasteion or imperial cult temple built during the reign of Emperor Trajan. Blocks from this temple were reused to construct a late Roman basilica church

*Tomb at Arykanda*

and bishop's palace in the 5$^{th}$ century, which still contains traces of wall paintings and floor mosaics covered with a modern roof. On the lowest terrace stands a largely intact bath complex supported with arches, converted into a bath-gymnasium after an earthquake in 141, and later refurbished. Higher up between the bouleuterion and the agora, are remains of a small bath and a fountain. Arykanda obtained water from a nearby spring and channeled it to two large cisterns. A necropolis runs along the street above the bath complex to the E with impressive barrel-vaulted monumental tombs, temple tombs and sarcophagi. One temple tomb on a podium contains an inscription and Corinthian façade decorated with a lion relief; another displays winged figures on either side of a bust over the lintel. A second necropolis starts from the cliffs to the W of the city and extends to the spring.

To the N higher up is a wide, flat 4th century agora, once enclosed on three sides with a portico. In the center of

*Theatre at Arykanda*

the agora are the ruins of a temple dedicated to Tyche. On a higher terrace behind the agora are foundations of a temple dedicated to Helios, which had formal entranceways on both sides. Helios was widely revered on Rhodes, which suggests the temple dates from time when Rhodes ruled Arykanda. Archeologists discovered two altars here, one identifying Helios by inscription and the other by a depiction of Helios with a halo.

Helios (Sol to Romans) is the titan god of the sun. His parents were Hyperion and Theia from the first generation of twelve titans, offspring of the earth Gaia and the sky Uranus, displaced by the Olympian gods. During the Titanomachy when the Olympians fought the titans for control of the cosmos, Hephaestus was overwhelmed but Helios rescued him and helped the Olympians. In gratitude, Hephaestus built Helios an underwater golden palace in the E as well as a huge golden cup. Each day Helios emerges at dawn as the sun and rides his flaming chariot across the sky from E to W drawn by his four, fire-breathing, winged steeds: Aethion (fiery red), Asterope (starry eyed), Bronte (thunder), and Phlegon (burning). At the end of each day Helios grazes his horses at the island of the Hesperides (evening) in the W. Then Helios, the chariot and the winged horses board the golden cup and float back overnight from W to E on the Oceanus, the river running around the edge of the world. After the Titanomachy, Zeus decided to divide the world fairly among the gods and loyal Titans. All came

*Bouleuterion at Arykanda*

together and received their shares, except for Helios who was on his daily flight across the sky. Helios remonstrated to Zeus who agreed to let him choose his territory. During his daily journey, Helios had noticed an ideal, fertile island just beneath the ocean waves, which he claimed. Zeus and the other gods agreed, whereupon the island of Rhodes immediately rose above the ocean surface. Helios filled Rhodes with light and made it the brightest island in the Mediterranean Sea. From at least the early 5$^{th}$ century BCE, Rhodes has been a leading place of worship for Helios. In the 3$^{rd}$ century BCE the citizens of Rhodes erected an enormous bronze statue of Helios (35 m high), commonly known as the Colossus of Rhodes, which straddled the entrance of the main harbor and was known as one of the Seven Wonders of the ancient world. Sadly, during the earthquake of 225 BCE, the statue broke apart at the knees and collapsed.

Helios was all seeing. He was the god who informed Hephaestus about Aphrodite's illicit affair with Ares and told Demeter that Pluto had abducted Persephone. Although Helios had a son named Phaethon, the youth lived with his mother Clymene and was adopted by her husband, the king of Ethiopia. Phaethon, a handsome but impetuous young man, eventually learned the identity of his real father. Determined to impress his friends with his true origin, Phaethon boldly presented himself at his father's palace in the E. Helios felt guilty for neglecting his son during his childhood and swore an oath by the sacred river Styx that he would grant Phaethon whatever gift he wanted. Phaethon rashly demanded to drive his father's golden chariot across the sky. Horrified with the presumptuous wish, Helios explained the danger and tried in vain to dissuade his son. Phaethon remained adamant, motivated by an intense desire for greatness. Finally the eager but unskilled youth took the reins and started across the sky, but could not control the horses, lost control and set the earth on fire. To save the earth from destruction, Zeus struck and killed Phaethon with a thunderbolt and regained control of the horses. On another occasion when Odysseus and his surviving crew were returning from Troy, they landed on Helios' island of Thrinacia. Despite being warned by Odysseus, the crew killed and ate cattle belonging to Helios. In response, Zeus destroyed the ship with a lightning bolt, killing the entire crew except for Odysseus. During his Eleventh Labor, a mission to capture the red cattle of Geryon at the edge of the world, Hercules was in such intense heat as he crossed the desert in Libya that he fired an arrow in anger at Helios. Immediately recognizing his mistake, Hercules apologized profusely. Helios took pity on Hercules, forgave him, and even loaned him his golden cup in which to travel through the ocean to the edge of the world.

Although there were already a number of temples in Rome dedicated to Helios, Emperor Aurelian established Sol Invictus, Unconquered Sun, as the favored official cult in 274. Romans celebrated the winter solstice on December 25 as the birthday of Sol and held athletic games every four years in his honor. From Aurelian up to and including Constantine the Great, known as the first Christian Emperor, Roman emperors identified themselves with Sol Invictus on their official coinage. In 315 Constantine erected his triumphal arch in Rome, carefully aligned so that a colossal statue of Sol by the Coliseum would form the dominant backdrop from the main approach to the arch. On March 7, 321, Constantine decreed the day of the sun, "Sunday," as the Roman day of rest during which magistrates and people residing in cities should rest and all workshops were closed. Constantine erected a column with a statue resembling himself as Helios in Constantinople. Perhaps to please Constantine, the early Christian Church used Jesus-

Helios symbolism and adopted December 25 as the birthday of Jesus.

At Arykanda further up is a 2nd century odeon, once elaborately decorated with colored marble. The odeon portico (75 x 8 m) was paved with floor mosaics and led to a triple portal with a statue of Emperor Hadrian (now at the Antalya Museum) flanked by masks of deities.

*Stadium at Arykanda*

At the rear of the odeon were two portals, one leading E to the terrace wall and up to the theatre, the other to the W to the agora. Stairs lead up to the 1st century BCE theatre on the next terrace with 20 rows of seats built into the hillside. The top two tiers bear inscriptions reserving their use and each row still contains holes where poles for a protective awning were once inserted. To the W of the theatre a 137 m long stoa passes 12 shops and leads to the bouleuterion with seats cut out of the NW slope of the mountain. On the next terrace up above the theatre is the half-size 1st century BCE Hellenistic stadium (106 x 17 m) with seats only on N side facing S, cut into the mountainside. A late Roman house between the stadium and the theatre has thick walls and fine mosaic floors. An article in ANMED describes excavations at Arykanda:
http://www.akmedanmed.com/article_en.php?artID=91&catID=11

**Limyra** (36° 20' 35" N, 30° 10' 14" E) is 110 km SW of Antalya, and 6 km inland from the sea. This city first played a significant role in history during the 4th century BCE when the Lycian ruler

Pericles supported a rebellion of satraps (governors) in Asia Minor against the ruling Persians. Persian rule eventually was reestablished with the involvement of Mausolus, the Carian satrap at Halicarnassus. After Alexander the Great ended Persian rule in 333 BCE, much of Lycia including Limyra was ruled by his successor Ptolemy in Egypt, followed by the Syrian Seleucids, then by Rhodes and finally by Rome after 167 BCE. Roman rule brought centuries of prosperity. Limyra has the unusual distinction of commemorating each of these historical periods with a specific monument to: the $4^{th}$ century BCE ruler Pericles, the $2^{nd}$ century BCE period of Ptolemaic rule and finally a cenotaph to a $1^{st}$ century member of the Roman imperial family.

**Limyra Site**: The lower city at the base of the hill encompasses two separate walled areas. A gate in the district to the W leads through to a marshy area and down toward a massive structure standing on a stone podium. This is the cenotaph of Gaius Caesar, grandson and heir apparent of Emperor Augustus. Augustus had adopted Gaius Caesar in 17 BCE and designated him as his heir. At age 21 Gaius Caesar was sent on a political mission to Armenia, which the Parthians had recently invaded. Gaius successfully placed a pro-Roman king on the Armenian throne but was seriously wounded during a subsequent skirmish. On February 21, 4, Gaius Caesar died from his wounds at Limyra during his return to Rome. Although only the basic structure remains *in situ*, reliefs of the exploits of the young prince once graced the cenotaph. A path leads E across a stream to the other walled area containing a large $5^{th}$ century church with a nearby bishop's palace to the S. Back on the modern road further down on the left (N) is the theatre cut into the base of the hill with seating capacity for 8000 spectators. Behind the theatre to the NE is the tomb of Xatabura, a two-tiered sarcophagus with inscriptions, which dates back to 350 BCE and belonged to a close relative of Pericles. The sarcophagus was mounted on an ornamented base decorated with depictions of a traditional mourning banquet and of the judgment of the dead. To the W of the theatre stands a small $2^{nd}$ century bathhouse with a complex heating system, which remained in use until the 5th century. On the W side of the site is the Ptolemaion, a 3rd century BCE round temple tomb with a conical roof on a large square podium (10 x 15 m). This structure is adorned with 2.3 m tall statues of a man and a woman believed to be Ptolemy II Philadelphus, who ruled Egypt 285-246 BCE, and his consort-sister Arsinoë II. During the period after Alexander the Ptolemaic dynasty ruled Limyra from Egypt. Reliefs included lions and a Celtic shield, which suggests that the Ptolemaic rulers protected the city from marauding Celtic Galatians. During the Roman period an 8 m wide colonnaded street linked this monument with the harbor.

*Gaius Caesar Cenotaph*

Up on the acropolis to the N are remains of fortified walls and a late Roman monastery with a 6th century church (23 x 15 m). Near the S wall of the acropolis is the 4th century Heroon of Pericles (10.4 x 6.8 m), a 5.3 m high temple raised on a high podium (19 x 18 m) decorated with statues and reliefs. Eight larger than life Persian style caryatids (female figures serving as columns) wear bracelets with lion heads and carry funerary libation vessels. Friezes (6 m long) depict scenes such as Pericles mounted on his chariot followed by soldiers in Persian and Lycian attire, some on horseback others on foot. The upper pediment shows Perseus after beheading Medusa. In the 4th century BCE this same Pericles fought the Persian satrap in Xanthus, founded the Lycian League and led Lycia in support of the Satrap rebellion against the Persians in 372-362 BCE. Although with the support of Mausolus of Caria, Persia eventually

suppressed the rebellion, the Heroon immortalized Pericles. The necropolis of Limyra extends beyond the theater and contains a vast number of elaborate tombs. For example, to the W of the city wall the two-tiered 4$^{th}$ century BCE Tomb of Tebursseli contains reliefs depicting the 4$^{th}$ century BCE battles led by Pericles against Xanthus, Telmessos and Persians with Lycian explanatory inscriptions. Dr. Martin Seyer of the Austrian Archeology Institute is excavating Limyra as described at:
http://www.oeai.at/index.php/limyra-274.html

**Olympos** (36° 23' 46" N, 30° 28' 26" E), 73 km SW of Antalya, is an ancient Lycian-Roman town along the beach, named for nearby Mount Olympos and encompassed within Olympos National Park. (Olympos is believed to be a pre-Greek word for mountain). Olympos, founded in the 3$^{rd}$ century BCE, was a pilgrimage center for the temple of Hephaestus at nearby Chimaera reachable on a Roman paved road.

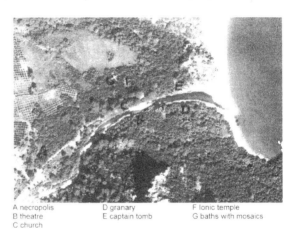

A necropolis    D granary    F Ionic temple
B theatre    E captain tomb    G baths with mosaics
C church

*Olympos*

Olympos was one of the six leading Lycian League cities. Conditions deteriorated in the 1$^{st}$ century BCE, when pirates under the command of Zenicetes took control of Olympos and nearby Phaselis. The pirates disrupted coastal shipping and kidnapped local residents and travelers for ransom or to sell into slavery. In response in 78 BCE the Roman governor of Cilicia, Publius Servilius Vatia, accompanied by the young Julius Caesar, attacked the pirates and besieged Olympos. To avoid capture, Zenicetes burned up himself and his family. Servilius destroyed Olympos and declared the land of Olympos and Phaselis public property available for resettlement. In 67 BCE the area became even more secure after Roman general Pompey the Great decisively defeated the Cilician pirates. When Lycia was formally brought into the Roman Empire as a province together with Pamphylia in 43, Olympos enjoyed a period of prosperity. Emperor Hadrian visited in 129 and constructed the granary on the S side of the river. Christianity developed early in Olympos. The city's bishop Methodius became a leading author and theologian in the early church until he was martyred in 311 under Emperor Galerius. The Lycian Way hiking trail passes through Olympos.

**Olympos Site**: Olympos can be reached from the modern town of Çıralı by a short walk along the beach, or via a long drive around the mountain. Olympus is encompassed within a thick pine forest and bisected by the river, with paths running along both sides. One abutment survives from the ancient bridge across the river. The necropolis on the S side of the river contains chamber tombs cut into the rock. NE of the necropolis lie remains of a small overgrown Roman theatre with an elaborate entrance. NE of the theatre stands a late Roman church.

*Captain Tomb*

The 5 m wide Hellenistic quay on the S bank leads to the ruins of a granary. At the edge of the beach along the mouth of the river are two well-preserved tombs, one with a poetic inscription in memory of an ancient ship captain together with a detailed carving of his beached boat. A path up a steep hill N of the river near the shore leads to the acropolis and an attractive Ionic temple entrance (8 m high, 3 m wide) with classic egg and dart border decorations. A dedicatory inscription on a statue base to Marcus Aurelius confirms that the portal was built in 172. A path leads W to a Roman bath complex containing geometric mosaics.

**Marcus Aurelius** (Caesar Marcus Aurelius Antoninus Augustus) reigned as Roman Emperor 161-180. He was born in Rome in 121, related to Emperor Hadrian. At age 17 he became, together with Lucius Verus, adopted son of future emperor Antoninus Pius, in an imperial succession arrangement. Although he studied literature and rhetoric, from an early age Aurelius was primarily interested in philosophy, particularly Stoicism. During the long reign of Emperor Antoninus Pius, Aurelius was his close advisor and confidant and, in 139, married the emperor's daughter Faustina. In 161 at age 40, Marcus Aurelius became emperor. He immediately arranged, without compulsion, to share power with Lucius Verus, a man more interested in enjoying life than the hard-working, stoical Aurelius. Immediately after the new emperors came to power, a major foreign challenge arose in Armenia, a buffer state along the Roman-Persian border. Parthian King Vologases IV placed his own relative on the Armenian throne, and defeated Roman forces sent in response. To underscore the Roman commitment to Armenia, Lucius Verus went E to confront the Persians supported by the best Roman generals. In 162 Rome launched an offensive, eventually capturing and sacking Seleucia and the Parthian capital at Ctesiphon. In 166 Parthia capitulated and Rome appointed the Armenian king. Unfortunately the triumphant Roman army brought back a devastating plague, most likely a smallpox infection.

*Marcus Aurelius (Ephesus Museum)*

Although an initial invasion of Germanic tribes across the N frontier was repulsed in 162, this threat steadily grew. In 166 a major force of Germanic invaders crossed the Danube while Roman troops were tied up elsewhere. In early 169, the Marcomanni and Quadi tribes reached Italy and besieged Aquileia, the main Roman city in NE Italy. This attack marked the first barbarian incursion into Italy in three hundred years, the end of Pax Romana. Both Roman emperors moved N to confront the invaders, but in 169 Lucius Verus died suddenly, probably from the plague. Aurelius returned to Rome, gave Lucius Verus a royal funeral and then went N to restore order. Barbarian attacks, together with plague and natural calamities such as earthquakes, famine and flooding, caused widespread fear and foreboding. These catastrophes lead to an upsurge in Christian persecution, because many blamed their failure to worship traditional gods as the cause. Although Aurelius was a devout adherent of traditional Roman religion and viewed Christians as obstinate to the point of irrationality, he did not systematically persecute them. Instead, Aurelius continued the longstanding policy initiated under Trajan, under which Christians were not sought out, and, if brought before the courts, legal proof of their guilt was required. In practice this meant that during periods of peace and prosperity they were left alone, but in times of disaster and widespread anxiety, local mobs denounced them and Roman officials persecuted them. This happened repeatedly in Asia Minor, Syria and later Gaul during the reign of Marcus Aurelius. During a campaign in mid-summer 174 N of the Danube, a large force of the Germanic Quadi tribe trapped Aurelius and his army on high ground cut off from any water source. The Romans, unable to escape, were on the verge of collapsing from thirst. This Roman army included the Twelfth or Thundering legion formerly based in Melitene, Armenia, which was largely Christian. After the Christians prayed for deliverance, a powerful thunderstorm arose, frightening the barbarians and enabling the Romans to drive them away. Like the Christians, Aurelius believed their rescue was divinely inspired, but he apparently credited Zeus.

Aurelius is remembered as a philosopher king whose life was devoted to and molded by philosophy, as reflected in his Meditations, written during military campaigns in central Europe 171-175. He often quoted the Stoic philosopher Epictetus, an ex-slave who wrote about: the physical, desires and aversions; the ethical, the impulse to act or not to act; and the logical, freedom from deception and hasty judgment. Epictetus taught that the philosopher should train his desires to be in harmony with nature, control his impulses and reject unwarranted judgments. Meditations can be viewed as Aurelius' private written exercises aimed at clarifying and analyzing his perceptions and then, with abstention and endurance, improving his actions. In 175 Aurelius became quite sick. His doctor Galen, the most renowned physician of the ancient world, regularly gave him opium pills for pain in his stomach and chest. Rumors that Aurelius had died prompted the Roman governor of Syria, Avidius Cassius, to attempt a coup. Cassius, known for his triumphs against the Parthians, seized control of Egypt and most of the E provinces. Aurelius reacted decisively and traveled E, but Cassius was killed by his own troops even before the emperor arrived in Syria. Aurelius then visited Antioch, Alexandria and finally Athens, where he was initiated into the Eleusinian mysteries. In Athens he established four endowed Chairs of Philosophy, one each for Platonism, Aristotelianism, Stoicism, and Epicureanism. Aurelius returned N and gradually regained control by isolating the tribes and defeating them one by one using his superior military command and control capability. In 177, following several successful military campaigns, Aurelius proclaimed his 16-year-old son, Commodus, joint emperor. Aurelius appeared on the verge of bringing long-term stability to the N frontier with the judicious use of force when he fell seriously ill and then died at his military headquarters in 180. His young successor Commodus, who proved a disastrous ruler, entered an expedient peace agreement with the Germanic tribes and quickly returned to a life of luxury in Rome.

ANMED describes excavations the Antalya Museum staff conducted at Olympos and Chimaera:
http://www.akmedanmed.com/article_en.php?artID=114&catID=11

**Chimaera** (36° 25' 53" N, 30° 27' 21" E), modern Yanartaş meaning flaming rock, is 80 km SW of Antalya, 7 km N of Olympos. Here within the Olympos National Park flames burn spontaneously through permanent gas vents 300 m up a mountain slope. These flames are attributable to the presence of the Chimaera, a three-headed monster who breathed flame and battled Bellerophon. At night the flames are visible far out to sea and served as a natural lighthouse for ancient mariners. A temple here dedicated to the worship of Hephaestus, god of fire, was reached via a paved Roman road from Olympos. The Lycian Way hiking trail passes from Çıralı to Ulupınar and on to Chimaera marked in red and white.

**Chimaera Site**: From the car park a 30-minute uphill walk leads to the ruins of the temple of Hephaestus and perhaps a dozen flaming vents in the ground. The nearby area is barren and steeply sloped. Not surprisingly, a late Roman church was built at this venue to discourage non-Christian worship. Fresco traces are still visible at the church ruins.

Hephaestus (Vulcan to Romans) is god of fire, a force of nature found in volcanic districts. He had a major place of worship at this Chimaera site. Hephaestus is son of Zeus and Hera, and unlike all other gods was born weak and physically ugly. As a flame starts with a small spark, the god of fire was weak and delicate at birth. Hera was so disgusted with her ugly baby that she threw him off Mount Olympus to get rid of him. Hephaestus fell and fell for an entire day and finally landed in the ocean near the island of Lemnos. The impact of his fall broke one of his legs and left him permanently lame. His broken body was carried to the shore where the Nereids, Thetis and her sisters, rescued him. Hephaestus lived secretly in an ocean grotto with the Nereids for nine years, fearing the wrath of Hera, as he became a master metallurgist and craftsman. Collecting pearls, gold, silver and coral from the ocean floor, Hephaestus crafted incredibly beautiful jewelry for the Nereids. One day Hera noticed the jewelry Thetis was wearing and demanded to know where it came. Upon learning the jeweler was none other than her long lost son Hephaestus, she decided that perhaps it was time for reconciliation. For his part, Hephaestus was inspired to build a golden throne for his mother and send it to Mount Olympus. Pleased, Hera sat on the throne and was immediately bound with invisible fetters and imprisoned. All the Olympian gods tried to free Hera but none could break the power of Hephaestus' workmanship. Zeus sent Ares, god of war, to bring Hephaestus to Mount Olympus to release Hera. Instead of returning, Hephaestus drove Ares away with flames. Next Zeus sent Dionysus, god of wine, to meet with Hephaestus, gain his confidence and persuade him to return. This tactic worked well and the intoxicated Hephaestus was returned to Mount Olympus passed out, slumped over the back of a mule led by Dionysus. At this time Zeus faced two sources of discord on Mount Olympus: his angry and alienated, yet clearly talented son Hephaestus; and the serious rivalry among the gods for the affections of the newly arrived and highly attractive goddess Aphrodite. To solve both problems Zeus gave Aphrodite as a wife to the delighted Hephaestus, who promptly released Hera from the golden throne. Then one day Zeus developed a terrible, incessant migraine headache. Finally in desperation, Zeus instructed Hephaestus to temporarily split open his head with an axe. When he did, out sprang the fully-grown goddess Athena.

Of all the gods, the deformed Hephaestus created works of the greatest beauty and utility in his underground workshop. He created: a golden girdle for Aphrodite, which made her absolutely irresistible; silver bows and arrows of death for Artemis and Apollo; palaces for each of the twelve Olympians, with unbreakable locks and golden thrones; the breastplate of Hercules; the spear of Athena; the golden chariot of Helios that pulled the sun across the sky; the sickle of Demeter; the shield bearing the head of Medusa; the winged helmet and sandals of Hermes; the bow and arrows of love for Eros (Cupid); and perhaps most importantly the thunderbolts for Zeus. One day the titan Prometheus stole fire from Hephaestus' forge and gave it to mankind for the first time. Zeus punished Prometheus for this infraction by instructing Hephaestus to bind him to a rock where a huge eagle would come every day and devour his liver, after which it would grow back in the night and the process would be repeated. Zeus also decided to punish mankind and instructed Hephaestus to create Pandora, the first mortal woman. Pandora was married to Prometheus' foolish brother, Epimetheus, and her dowry was a jar filled with evils, which she released, much like Eve in the Garden of Eden. During the Trojan War, Hephaestus created an invincible shield and armor for Achilles, at the request of his mother Thetis, who had helped him in his time of need. The river god Xanthus ruled the river on the plain of Troy. After the death of his beloved friend Patroclus, Achilles went on a furious killing spree, filling Xanthus' river with Trojan corpses. In response, Xanthus flooded the plain to drown the heavily armored Achilles. Hephaestus reacted with massive flames to dry up the river and successfully drove back Xanthus, enabling the Greeks to win yet another battle.

Although Aphrodite treasured the many gifts from Hephaestus, she was by nature highly sexually promiscuous. She was particularly attracted to Ares, the manly god of war. Hephaestus learned about Aphrodite's infidelity from Helios, the all-seeing sun god. Hephaestus fashioned an invisible net, so fine and strong no one could escape it. Hephaestus then surprised and trapped Aphrodite and Ares in the act of love with the inescapable net. He summoned the other Olympian gods and subjected the two illicit lovers to the public humiliation of a public viewing while they were naked and wrapped together. Although the other gods roared with laughter at the sight, they proved unwilling to inflict severe punishment and eventually prevailed upon Hephaestus to release them. Hephaestus, however, bore a deep grudge and remained determined to settle the score. The liaison between Aphrodite and Ares resulted in the birth of a daughter, Harmonia. When she grew up and married King Cadmus of Thebes, Hephaestus gave Harmonia a resplendently beautiful necklace as a wedding gift. Unbeknownst to her, although Hephaestus had wrought the necklace so that any woman wearing it would remain eternally young and beautiful, it was cursed to bring disaster. Eventually Harmonia and Cadmus were both transformed into serpents. Their daughter Semele inherited the necklace, then became Zeus' lover but was incinerated when, with Hera's connivance, she demanded that Zeus reveal himself to her in all his glory. Similar disasters afflicted the following generations, enabling Hephaestus to exact full revenge.


**Phaselis** (36° 31′ 26″ N, 30° 33′ 8″ E), meaning chickpea, is 58 km S of Antalya, on an isthmus with three pleasant beaches. Settlers from nearby Rhodes established a colony in 690 BCE. With three separate natural harbors the city soon became a major trading center. Phaselis was incorporated into the Persian Empire in 546 BCE and then conquered by the Athenians under Cimon in 469 BCE. In the 4th century BCE Persian rule was reestablished and Phaselis was allied with the satrap Mausolus. In 333-334 BC, during his campaign against the Persians, Alexander the Great was welcomed at Phaselis where he remained for the winter.

After the death of Alexander, Phaselis was ruled in turn from Ptolemaic Egypt, Seleucid Syria and Rhodes, until 160 BCE when it was absorbed into the Lycian confederacy under Roman domination. Pirates under the command of Zenecites overran Phaselis and Olympos in the 1$^{st}$ century BCE until Rome reestablished control in 78 BCE. During the Roman civil wars, Brutus bullied Phaselis into contributing funds. When Emperor Hadrian visited in 131 Phaselis was adorned with new statues, monuments and buildings in his honor. An alternative route of the Lycian Way hiking trail passes through Phaselis.

**Phaselis Site**:
Phaselis is set in an attractive pine forest within a national park, surrounded on three sides by the sea.

A N harbor
B central harbor
C aqueduct
D S harbor
E necropolis
F Roman street
G theatre
H agora of Domitian
I agora of Hadrian
J gate of Hadrian

*Phaselis*

The necropolis is located to the N of the site, extending beyond the well-preserved aqueduct along the shoreline of the N harbor. Phaselis had three natural harbors.

One was the N harbor where two small islets were joined to the mainland by a causeway and a harbor enlarged enough to accommodate an ancient naval base. The second was a small central harbor E of the car park, which was enclosed with a seawall and could be blocked with an 18 m long chain between towers. A pier extending 183 m from the city walls to protect a third harbor to the S, parts of which can still be seen. A colonnaded, paved 25 m wide ancient street ran 225 m from the central harbor to the Hadrian Gate to the S lined with 2nd century BCE shops and public buildings. The Roman road enters a square shaped area in the middle and alters direction to conform to the topography. Statues once lined the colonnaded street, which also served as a stadium. On the W side of the main street the ruins of a bath-gymnasium complex still contain mosaic fragments. To the S of the bath complex, W of the street is the square-shaped agora of Hadrian, once lined with porticoes and shops. Ruins of a late Roman church lie to the W in this agora. Further S and W of the street is the agora of Domitian (60 x 40 m) built in 93. A dedicatory inscription to Domitian found here on a gate toward the street had his name scratched out after the Roman Senate damned his memory. Next, to the S, stands a later period agora connected to the harbor. An inscription confirms that the Hadrian Gate at the S end of the main street was built in 131 CE in honor of his visit. The 2nd century theatre is located on the W side of the street across from the agora of Hadrian and could hold 2000 spectators. The small gates in the stage building at ground level suggest the theatre was used for gladiator or wild animal fights. The walled acropolis was above the theatre to the W. N of the theatre lie ruins of a 3-4th century bathhouse, including the brick foundations and heating system, a nymphaeum and an ancient latrine. A hillside near the acropolis is believed to contain the scant remains

*Phaselis Aqueduct*

of a 5th century BCE temple of Athena, which, according to ancient writers, once displayed the broken bronze spear of Achilles. Nearby stood a circular 3rd century BCE temple dedicated to Hermes and Hestia.

Hermes (Mercury to Romans) is messenger of the gods, god of merchants, boundaries, thieves and persuasion, as well as guide to the Underworld. The multi-faceted Hermes is the god of travelers, shepherds, orators, poets, athletes, inventors, liars and prostitutes. He wears winged shoes, enabling him to fly, and often helps travelers arrive safely. Hermes is the son of Zeus and Maia, a daughter of Atlas. On the day he was born, Hermes invented a musical instrument, the lyre, and then stole immortal cattle from Apollo. Hermes hid the cattle and covered their tracks. When Apollo confronted Hermes, his mother Maia believed him to be innocent but Zeus confirmed that Hermes was the thief. Hermes, while arguing with Apollo, began to play the lyre. Apollo was so enchanted by the music that he agreed to let Hermes keep the cattle in exchange for the lyre.

*Hermes (Antalya Museum)*

# IX ANCIENT REGION OF PAMPHYLIA

Pamphylia, meaning "land of many tribes," is a coastal region between Lycia to the W, Pisidia and Galatia to the N and Cilicia to the E. According to tradition, Calchas and Mopsus, early seers, founded a number of cities in the region. During the 6$^{th}$ century BCE Lydian King Croesus took control of Pamphylia, followed by Persian King Cyrus the Great in 546 BCE. In 467 BCE the Athenian Cimon with a fleet of 200 ships destroyed a large Persian naval fleet based at the mouth of the Eurymedon River and dominated coastal Pamphylia for several years before Persia reasserted full control. Despite Persian sovereignty, the local language was similar to Greek, trade with the W was strong, and the area was rapidly Hellenized. In early 333 BCE Alexander the Great occupied the Pamphylian coast. Although the local population generally welcomed Alexander, he encountered resistance at **Sillyon** and then at **Aspendos**. He initially agreed to lenient terms for **Aspendos**, but the city reneged on its agreement when he encountered difficulties besieging nearby **Sillyon**. Alexander abandoned his plan to subdue **Sillyon** as not worth the effort, but returned to **Aspendos** in force and imposed harsher terms. Following Alexander's death, his Ptolemaic and Seleucid successors ruled the area. In 188 BCE the Romans drove out the Seleucids and established the nominal rule of Pergamum over the area. **Sillyon** remained independent and as time went on Pergamum came to exercise limited control in Pamphylia. Pergamum formally bequeathed its possessions, including Pamphylia, to Rome in 133 BCE. At first Roman rule was arbitrary and corrupt in Pamphylia. In 79 BCE the Roman statesman Cicero testified against the previous Roman quaestor Gaius Verres for misusing his authority and stealing all moveable wealth, including statues and temple offerings, from **Perge** and **Aspendos**. During the 1ˢᵗ century BCE when Rome was preoccupied with the rise of Mithridates VI of Pontus and his slaughter of Roman citizens to the N, lack of central control encouraged lawlessness and piracy in Pamphylia. Pirate bands ravaged commercial shipping throughout the E Mediterranean. The most valuable contraband trade was in human beings and the city of **Side** became a notorious central slave market. Pirates would capture free people, including Roman citizens, and hold them for ransom or sell them as slaves. Many more respectable citizens migrated away from coastal towns such as **Side** to smaller interior towns beyond pirate control, such as **Lyrbe**. Eventually these egregious actions prompted a Roman military response. In 77 BCE Publius Servilius Vatia led an expedition, accompanied by the young Julius Caesar, to restore order and recapture coastal Lycia and Pamphylia. In 67 BCE Roman general Pompey the Great conducted a major anti-piracy campaign, which finally eradicated the threat.

**Pompey the Great (106-48 BCE), Gnaeus Pompeius Magnus, was a leading Roman military and political figure during the late Roman Republic. Pompey's father was a powerful provincial landowner, politician and military leader. Pompey gained military experience under his father's command and allied himself with Sulla, the first de facto Roman dictator. Pompey commanded troops loyal to Sulla during successful military campaigns in Sicily and North Africa. Although Sulla initially refused Pompey's demand for a formal triumph parade following his victories, he eventually agreed. In 78 BCE Sulla died and Pompey demanded that the Senate appoint him governor in Hispania where another Roman general had been unable to suppress rebellion. Pompey refused to disband his legions until his request was granted. Pompey served in Spain 76–71 BCE, eventually defeating the rebellion and putting into place an efficient provincial administration. At this time Crassus, the richest man in Rome, was suppressing a major Spartacus-led slave rebellion in Italy. Pompey, returning with his army from Spain to Italy in 71 BCE, encountered and defeated remnants of Spartacus' army. Much to the fury of Crassus, Pompey then claimed credit for the final elimination of the Spartacus threat. The highly popular 35-year old Pompey received a second formal triumph parade and was overwhelmingly elected Consul, together with Crassus, despite not having followed the traditional career path.**

As Roman military prowess overwhelmed traditional powers, such as Carthage, the Seleucids and Rhodes, there were no local naval forces to maintain law and order on the high seas. As a result of this power vacuum, Mediterranean cities collaborated with pirate chieftains, paid tribute, and provided services and facilities to avoid being terrorized and plundered. During the Mithridatic Wars, the situation deteriorated further as Mithridates VI fought the Romans on the land while pirates under his influence raided coastal settlements. By the third Mithridatic War, well-organized pirates operated more like hostile military fleets than disparate bands of robbers, capturing coastal towns and stealing treasure from temples. Pirates menaced commerce throughout the Mediterranean, intercepting Roman grain shipments from Africa and even plundering Rome's principal port Ostia. Historians estimate as many as 1,000 pirate ships were raiding as many as 400 Mediterranean cities along major transport routes. Pirates even seized senior Roman officials and held them for ransom. It was during this period that young Julius Caesar was kidnapped. During this period of history, slavery was largely circumstantial in that middle class people traveling abroad could be kidnapped and sold into slavery. Unless they had the financial ability and connections to arrange and pay a large ransom, they could be sold on slave markets and permanently lose their freedom. Pirates captured tens of thousands of slaves and many ended up as agricultural laborers on large Italian estates. One effect of widespread piracy and disruption of the grain trade was to raise the price of agricultural produce to the detriment of the Roman majority but the benefit of the Italian landed gentry. Pirate bases were concentrated along the remote Cilician and Pamphylian coasts where the rugged coastline riddled with small bays and enclaves provided refuge.

In 67 BCE the Senate passed a law to eradicate piracy, granting Pompey absolute authority in all the seas within the Pillars of Hercules (Gibraltar) and the adjacent mainland up to about 70 km inland. The Senate authorized and funded Pompey to commission 270 ships, and to raise 120,000 troops, and 4,000 cavalrymen. Twenty-four senators with military experience were appointed to assist Pompey in the anti-piracy campaign and all Roman allies were told to accept his authority. When these measures were announced, prices of agricultural goods immediately stabilized. Pompey devised a plan under which the Mediterranean was divided into thirteen districts with one Roman commander responsible for confronting and destroying the pirates in each district. His fleet was large enough to assign ships to each district and retain sixty ships under his direct command as a mobile force dedicated to finding and eliminating pirate ships. Within three months by monitoring the entire sea at the same time, Pompey swept away the pirates in the western

Mediterranean. Those who survived fled east to Cilicia. Pompey completed this first stage of his campaign in only 40 days, then turned E. Pompey's name and reputation so terrified pirates that he encountered little resistance. Pompey followed a clever and effective policy of granting clemency to those pirates who surrendered to him personally, rather than his district commanders. This policy encouraged many pirates to surrender their ships, their families and themselves to Pompey. From these prisoners, Pompey gained valuable intelligence about where others were hiding. The remaining pirates made a stand against Pompey at Coracesium (modern Antalya). Pompey blockaded the town and won a decisive victory, completely eliminating the piracy threat in just 89 days during the summer of 66 BCE. Pompey offered surviving former pirates an alternative life as farmers in new settlements established in depopulated areas along the coast.

The success of the anti-piracy campaign guaranteed Pompey his next assignment as Roman commander in the third war against Mithridates VI of Pontus. At Pompey's approach, Mithridates withdrew his forces. Tigranes the Great of Armenia refused Mithridates refuge, so he retreated to Pontus. Pompey first reached agreement with Tigranes, and in 65 BCE set out after Mithridates. He advanced into Colchis (Georgia) and then decisively defeated Mithridates, leading the latter to eventual suicide. Pompey absorbed Pontus into the Roman Empire, and in 64 BCE deposed the Macedonian ruler of Syria, adding Syria and Phoenicia (Lebanon) to the Empire. Pompey then intervened in a Judean civil war on behalf of Hyrcanus II, supported by the Pharisees sect, against Aristobulus II, supported by the Jewish Sadducees. Pompey and Hyrcanus II besieged Jerusalem, capturing the city after three months. Despite the long tradition that access to the inner sanctum of the temple was limited to Jewish high priests, Pompey entered but did not seize or damage its contents. The next day Pompey ordered the temple priests to make the traditional Jewish offerings to God and restore the high priesthood to Hyrcanus.

Roman control now extended N from Palestine through Phoenicia and Syria throughout Asia Minor to the eastern Black Sea coast. Back in Rome in 61 BCE, Pompey celebrated a magnificent third triumph parade on his 45th birthday. The Senate, fearful of Pompey's popularity, resisted granting Pompey's retiring veterans the public lands he had promised them and hesitated to approve the political settlements Pompey had negotiated with the eastern potentates. Although Pompey and Crassus distrusted each other, political expediency led them to form an alliance with Julius Caesar, known as the First Triumvirate. Pompey and Crassus used their influence to make Caesar Consul in 59 BCE, ensuring Pompey's veterans received their promised lands. To seal the alliance, Pompey married Caesar's daughter Julia, which resulted in a surprisingly happy marriage. The three allies agreed Pompey and Crassus would stand for the consulship in 55 BCE, while Caesar would command Roman forces in Gaul for five more years.

In 54 BCE Julia died in childbirth along with the baby, an incident with profound historical consequences. Although Pompey and Caesar shared a common grief, their family connection was broken. The following year the third member of their alliance, Crassus, launched a disastrous campaign against the Parthians, which resulted in his death and the annihilation of a major Roman army at Carrhae in SE Asia Minor. In 52 BCE, the Senate named Pompey sole Consul with sweeping powers to restore order. While Caesar was conquering Gaul, Pompey enacted legislation to weaken Caesar's position, by prohibiting Caesar from standing for the consulship in absentia and requiring him to relinquish control of his armies upon returning to Rome. In 49 BCE, Caesar crossed the Rubicon and invaded Italy. Pompey abandoned Rome and went E with an army. After an inconclusive series of skirmishes, Pompey failed to pursue Caesar at a critical moment and lost the chance to destroy his smaller army. Under pressure from Caesar's forces, the leading Republican senators and Pompey fled to Greece. In 48 BCE at the Battle of Pharsalus Caesar decisively defeated Pompey's significantly larger army. Pompey and his entourage then fled to Egypt where Pompey was treacherously assassinated as he disembarked from a ship. Caesar mourned Pompey's death and executed his assassins.

Eventually more stable Roman rule in Pamphylia led to considerable prosperity and economic growth, particularly in the 2nd-3rd centuries. Christianity came early to Pamphylia as Saints Paul and Barnabas visited the region as well as Pisidia to the N on their missionary journeys. Following the 4th century conversion of Constantine Christianity reigned supreme in the region. By the mid-7th century continuous Arab raids caused economic decline and forced many inhabitants to abandon the major cities. Substantial remains exist of four major cities in Pamphylia: **Perge**, **Sillyon**, **Aspendos** and **Side**, as well as more remote **Lyrbe** up in the mountains. The Saint Paul Trail, a 500 km long marked walking trail, starts at **Perge** and loops N past numerous ancient ruins, including Pednelissos, and then across Lake Egirdir all the way up to Antioch in Pisidia. Hikers retrace their route as far as Adada and then proceed S on a different leg of the trail past ancient Selge to **Aspendos**. Kate Clow's excellent book St. Paul

Trail provides very specific trail descriptions complete with GPS coordinates and much practical advice for hikers.

**Perge** (36° 57' 38" N, 30° 51' 15" E), a popular mass tourism site, is located in the E outskirts of Antalya 12 km inland on the navigable Kestros River. According to tradition and ancient inscriptions, the seers Calchas and Mopsus founded Perge after the Trojan War.

Calchas was the son of a priest of Apollo and the most famous soothsayer among the Greeks during the Trojan War. He had the gift of interpreting the flight of birds and correctly reading entrails. Calchas was the seer who told Agamemnon that to placate Artemis and set sail from Aulis, he would have to sacrifice his daughter Iphigenia. Calchas correctly predicted the siege of Troy would last ten years. Later during the war Agamemnon enslaved the beautiful Trojan woman Chryseis and refused to ransom her to her father, a priest of Apollo. When the Greeks were then stricken with a terrible plague, Calchas told Agamemnon that he must return Chryseis to her family to appease Apollo and stop the plague. Agamemnon released Chryseis but then took another beautiful Trojan woman, Briseis, away from Achilles as compensation.

Unlike Mopsus, Calchas proved unable to state the number of figs on a wild fig tree or predict the number of pigs a particular sow would give birth to. Having failed to best Mopsus he died of disappointment. This disastrous move infuriated Achilles who then refused to fight the Trojans. Later Calchas endorsed the plan of Odysseus to build the Trojan Horse. He also foresaw that

A Roman gate  F N-S street  J palestra
B agora  G E-W street  K baths
C temple of Tyche  H church  L theatre
D Hellenistic gate  I nymphaeum  M stadium
E Demetrius-Apollonios arch

*Perge*

Aeneas would survive the battle and found another city. After the fall of Troy, Calchas remained in Asia Minor and continued to practice divination. An oracle predicted he would die if he were ever outdone in prophecy by a greater seer. After founding various cities, Calchas claimed the right to administer the oracle at Claros, but the seer Mopsus also claimed this role. Mopsus was a son of Apollo and a mortal woman Manto, daughter of the blind seer Tiresias.

Perge is where St. Paul and St. Barnabas landed in 46 at the start of their first missionary journey and then walked N to Antioch in Pisidia, as modern hikers can do following the Saint Paul Trail. In the 4$^{th}$ century during the reign of Constantine the Great Perge became an important Christian center, represented at the council of Nicaea in 325 and at the council of Ephesus in 431. Although Perge remained a significant imperial city in the 5$^{th}$-6$^{th}$ centuries, it was eventually abandoned in the mid-7$^{th}$ century in the wake of continuous Arab raids.

**Perge Site**: Much of Perge is encircled with walls dating as far back as the 3$^{rd}$ century BCE, although the theatre and stadium were built during the Roman period and lie outside the walls. Visitors enter Perge through the Roman Gate, built during the reign of Septimius Severus in 193-211. To the right is a large 4$^{th}$ century agora (75 x 75 m). The central courtyard and shops were surrounded with a wide grey granite stoa. At the center of the agora was a round 2$^{nd}$ century temple of Tyche. On the S side of the agora are remains of the first church built in Perge. In front of one of the stores on the N portico a playing board is carved into the stone for a popular ancient game. Note a butcher's sign with a hook and a knife at the NW corner of the agora. Ahead is the 3$^{rd}$ century BCE Hellenistic city gate, designed to protect the city with two high cylindrical towers. Around the arch are a dozen inscriptions which refer to a remarkable 2$^{nd}$ century woman, Plancia Magna, daughter of a Roman governor, and a major benefactor of the city. In 120-122 she redesigned the courtyard, adding Corinthian columns and statues of gods, as well as Roman emperors with their wives from Nerva through to Hadrian. Many of these fine statues survive and are on display at Antalya Museum. When Plancia Magna died she was buried in a tomb next to the Hellenistic Gate, which still stands.

*Perge Agora*

Plancia Magna was an aristocrat born and raised in 1st-2nd century Perge. Her father Marcus Plancius Varus served as Proconsul (governor) of Bithynia and Roman senator. Although she was not a practicing Jew, she was descended on her maternal side from King Herod the Great of Judea. King Tigranes VI of Armenia was also a maternal grandfather. Plancia Magna married Gaius Julius Cornutus Tertullus, a man from another

*Main N-S street at Perge*

prominent family in Perge and had one child, a son named Gaius Julius Plancius Varus Cornutus. Plancia Magna inherited and managed her family estates in Galatia and Pamphylia. In 120-122 she remodeled much of Perge, erecting statues of the imperial family and beautifying the Hellenistic Gate. Plancia Magna also was high priestess at the temple of Artemis, the most important temple in town, as well as high priestess of the imperial cult. Inscriptions record that the city council honored Plancia Magna both as "Founder" and "Demiourgos," its highest title, confirming her dominant role in civic life.

At Perge visitors pass through the Hellenistic Gate and courtyard to enter a broad, colonnaded main street, extending N-S 300 m from the main gate to the N nymphaeum on the acropolis. The street is 20 m wide, divided in two by a 2 m wide water channel running down the middle with shops on both sides flanked by statues of prominent citizens. Marble paving on the street still shows ruts from ancient wagon wheels. Columns near the middle of the main street are decorated with small reliefs: Artemis holding a gigantic torch as well as her bow and arrows; a figure in a Roman toga, probably Calchas, pouring a libation on an altar; and the goddess Tyche, wearing the city as a crown. To the left (W) of the main street are ruins of the 5th century Christian basilica. At the N end of the main street is the nymphaeum where the water channel originates. The large 2nd century nymphaeum (21 x 38 m) consists of a wide pool with a two-storey carved façade dedicated to Artemis, Emperor Septimius Severus, his wife Julia Domna, and their sons. Statues of the emperor

*Perge Stadium*

and his wife found here are now in the Antalya Museum. A reclining, headless statue of a river god Kestros still presides over the nymphaeum at the foot of the acropolis.

Further up the acropolis are Roman foundations of a temple, perhaps dedicated to Leto. Another major ancient street running E-W intersects the main street at the arch of Demetrius Apollonius. At the W end of this street are remains of a large rectangular palaestra, which date back to the year 50 and were dedicated to Emperor Claudius. Remains of the N baths and the necropolis are W of the palaestra. Further S, W of the Hellenistic gateway, is the large and relatively complete S marble-coated baths complex, built during the reign of Emperor Hadrian. At the caldarium visitors can see, due to the partial collapse of the pavement, the hypocaust (heat from below) system. To the SW of the main complex, the stadium of Perge lies outside the city walls, reached on a path through the woods from the parking lot. This huge, well-preserved $2^{nd}$ century structure (34 x 234 m) is shaped like a horseshoe on the N end and open to the S, once entered via a monumental wooden door. The stadium contained shops, and inscriptions list the names of shopkeepers and types of goods sold. The stadium seated 12,000. In the $3^{rd}$ century after gladiatorial and wild animal combat became popular, the N end of the stadium was transformed into an arena for these activities. The Greco-Roman theatre stands to the SW on the other side of a paved road built into the hill with capacity for 14,000 spectators. On the outer façade of the $2^{nd}$ century stage building was a 12 m high nymphaeum. The inner façade was decorated with a frieze of the

*Perge Theatre*

river god Kestros; various nymphs; the life story of Dionysus; and Tyche holding a cornucopia and accepting bulls for sacrifice. Istanbul University archeologists have been working at Perge since 1946 and have uncovered a large number of magnificent sculptural works, particularly from the $2^{nd}$ and $3^{rd}$ centuries, which can be seen at Antalya Museum. Several of these works depict gods, as well as temporal rulers.

ANMED describes recent archeological work at Perge: http://www.akmedanmed.com/article_en.php?catID=15&artID=293

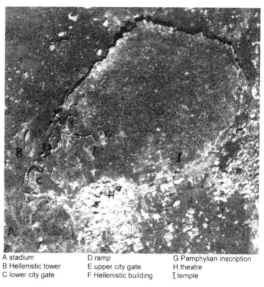

A stadium
B Hellenistic tower
C lower city gate
D ramp
E upper city gate
F Hellenistic building
G Pamphylian inscription
H theatre
I temple

*Sillyon*

**Sillyon** (36° 59′ 34″ N, 30° 59′ 13″ E) was an important ancient mountain stronghold 10 km NE of Perge. Greek settlers founded the city perhaps as early as the $11^{th}$ century BCE. In 333 BCE Alexander the Great initially besieged Sillyon but abandoned the attack upon realizing the enormous cost and effort that would be required to overcome determined local resistance. Sillyon was prominent during the late Roman period as a fortified town.

**Sillyon Site:** At this remote rural site visitors first encounter the horseshoe-shaped lower city gate with two towers and a courtyard. Nearby remains of an ancient stadium are difficult to discern. An impressive Hellenistic tower stands to the N of the lower gate. Ancient ramps lead up the only accessible side to the SW of the acropolis. Near the top is the upper city gate. Buildings

on the acropolis include a late Roman building with arched windows in the upper storey, a Hellenistic public hall and a smaller Hellenistic building directly to the NE, which contains the longest extant inscription in the Pamphylian language (its meaning remains obscure). On the SE side of the city erosion and consequent landslides have pulled huge chunks of the theatre down a steep cliff side into the plain below. To the E of the site are ruined dwellings and remnants of a small Hellenistic temple (11 x 7 m). ANMED describes recent archeological work at Sillyon:
http://www.akmedanmed.com/article_en.php?catID=15&artID=314

**Aspendos** (36° 56' 26" N, 31° 10' 8" E) is 16 km inland on the Eurymedon River, 49 km E of Antalya. According to tradition, the seer Mopsus founded Aspendos in the 13$^{th}$ century BCE. During this period the Eurymedon River was navigable as far as Aspendos, which protected the city from pirates, who had difficulty making surprise attacks and escaping uickly along a river.

*Aspendos Aqueduct*

Aspendos was under Persian rule until 467 BCE when Athenian commander Cimon with a fleet of 200 ships destroyed a large Persian naval fleet based at the mouth of the Eurymedon River. Aspendos became a member of the Athenian-dominated Delian League until Persia recaptured the city in 411 BCE. In 333 BCE Alexander the Great occupied Aspendos. Following the death of Alexander, Perge, like the rest of Pamphylia, was ruled by his various Macedonian successors, then Pergamum and finally Rome after 133 BCE. During the initial period of Roman misrule Romans under Gaius Verres pillaged Aspendos, as they had Perge. However, the city eventually prospered during the Roman imperial period, particularly in the $2^{nd}$-$3^{rd}$ centuries. Aspendos was badly damaged by Arab incursions in the $7^{th}$ century. However, later Selçuk rulers during the $12^{th}$-$13^{th}$ centuries refurbished ancient structures, particularly the theater.

**Aspendos Site**: Aspendos, a mass tourism site, has one of the best-preserved ancient theaters in the former Roman Empire. The theatre, partially built into the hillside, can seat 20,000. The architect Zeno, a native of the city, built the theater during the reign of Emperor Marcus Aurelius in 161-180. The most prestigious seats were at the lowest level, although this theatre is famous for excellent acoustics and there was an elegant sheltered arcade for the top seats.

*Aspendos Theatre (above); Dionysus (below)*

The two-storey stage building had five doors and sculpture in niches along the back wall. In the center of the colonnaded upper floor a relief still depicts Dionysus. The smaller doors at orchestra level belonged to long corridors, which led to compartments where wild animals were kept.

The $13^{th}$ century Selçuk restoration, for use as a royal caravansary, is attested by geometrical red zigzag decorations on the right side of the stage. Further to the N at the same level as the theatre are remains of a large stadium (250 x 30 m). On the acropolis to the NW of the theatre and through the E gate are foundations of a triple-nave basilica (27 x 105 m) with a large central hall surrounded by smaller chambers. W of the basilica was the agora and a 70 m long row of twelve shops. N of the agora is a 3$^{rd}$ century nymphaeum (33 m wide, 15 m high) with a two-level façade containing five niches at each level. To the W of the nymphaeum is the 3$^{rd}$ century odeon (39 x 30 m) where the city council met. Down the hill to the S of the theater are scant remains of a gymnasium-bath complex.

*Aspendos Nymphaeum*

From the acropolis visitors can see the huge 2$^{nd}$ century Roman arched aqueduct (15 m high), which dominates the skyline and runs for more than one km N of Aspendos along the paved road. At both ends of the aqueduct water was collected in 30 m high towers for distribution to the city. Aspendos is the terminus (or starting point) for the Saint Paul Trail, which goes up and inland initially following the line of the aqueduct through rural farm country to the village of Akbas. Professor Veli Köse of Hacettepe University in Ankara directs Aspendos archeological work involving several universities described at: http://www.aspendosproject.com/

**Side** (36° 46' 5" N, 31° 23' 26" E), meaning pomegranate, is on a small N-S peninsula near Manavat and Selimiye, 75 km E of Antalya. Although Greeks colonized Side in the 7$^{th}$ century BCE, they assimilated with the local population and adopted the Sideian language as attested by numerous inscriptions dating back to the

3rd-2nd centuries BCE. After Alexander the Great occupied Side in 333 BCE the population adopted Hellenistic culture. During the 1st century BCE, Side became a pirate stronghold and major slave-trading center. In 67 BCE Roman general Pompey defeated the pirates and brought Pamphylia under Roman control, ushering in a period of prolonged prosperity. The city's population reached 60,000. Two inscriptions found at the site suggest a significant Jewish population in the late Roman period. Side declined in the 7th century following repeated seaborne Arab raids.

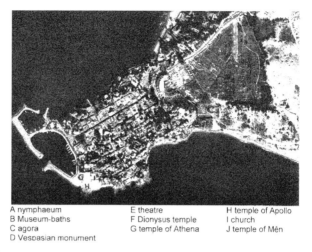

A nymphaeum
B Museum-baths
C agora
D Vespasian monument
E theatre
F Dionysus temple
G temple of Athena
H temple of Apollo
I church
J temple of Mên

*Side*

**Side Site:** The ruins span a one km long, 400 m wide flat peninsula jutting out into the sea, integrated into a major tourist resort. Well-preserved 2nd century BCE city walls remain in place on the landward side. Outside the city wall is an elaborate three-storey nymphaeum, which distributed water brought via aqueduct from 32 km away. The 5th century Roman baths were converted into an impressive museum displaying ancient statues and sarcophagi. Archeologists believe the reliefs of weapons and shields at the museum, formerly at the city's E gate, commemorate a 2nd century BCE

*Ixion in Tartarus*

victory of Side over Pergamum.   In the museum is a relief of Ixion, King of Thessaly, condemned by Zeus to spend eternity bound to a fiery wheel.

Ixion was king of the Lapiths in Greece and a descendant of the god Ares. Ixion married Dia, a daughter of Eioneus, and promised his father-in-law a substantial bride price.  However, Ixion reneged on the payment, so Eioneus seized Ixion's horses in retaliation.  Ixion concealed his resentment and lured his father-in-law into a trap by inviting him to dinner.  Eioneus arrived, fell into a hidden pit of burning coals and died.  Ixion was so cursed for this gross violation of the host-guest relationship that no mortal could cleanse him.  Zeus took pity on Ixion and purified him.  Zeus even invited Ixion to Olympus as a guest, where he sat at the table of the gods.  Ixion, as the ultimate ingrate, then attempted to seduce the goddess Hera, wife of Zeus.  Zeus, incredulous that anyone could so completely violate the terms of the guest-host relationship, created a cloud in the form of Hera.  Ixion impregnated the cloud, which bore the monster Centaurus.  Zeus punished Ixion, binding him to a flaming winged wheel spinning through Tartarus for eternity.  For his part, Centaurus mated with the mares of Mount Pelion in Magnesia and became the progenitor of the race of centaurs.

At Side across the street from the museum are the foundations of the large 2$^{nd}$ century square agora (91 x 94 m), once the city's main slave-trading venue.  In the center of the agora are ruins of a circular Corinthian style 2$^{nd}$ century BCE Tyche temple.  An ancient library stands to the E.  The road from the museum passes through a monumental Roman arch next to a second nymphaeum with two basins in front and a niche where a statue of Emperor Vespasian, dated to 74, once stood. The

*Theatre with Library (left)*

large 2nd century Roman theater seated 17,000 and was supported with arches. The podium (7 x 18 m) of an early temple of Dionysus lies just NW and adjacent to the theater.

At the harbor to the SW are ruins of two 2nd century temples surrounded with Corinthian columns. The temple of Apollo (16 x 30 m) to the E was slightly smaller and still displays standing columns adorned with a frieze of Medusa heads above.

*Side Temple of Apollo*

The larger temple of Athena (18 x 35 m) to the W was once presented with a golden statue of Emperor Caracalla by the emperor himself. The 5th century ruins of an adjacent Christian basilica, built on the foundations of the temple of Athena, can be seen directly to the E. Slightly further E along the coast are the ruins of a 2nd century temple of Mên, an Anatolian moon god, consisting of a surviving podium (2.2 m high), which once supported semi-circular cella approached up a flight of stairs.

**Mên is a Phrygian lunar god connected with fertility, healing, and punishment. He was widely worshiped in Asia Minor and Attica during the 3rd century. Mên is depicted as a male figure with a crescent moon on his shoulders, wearing a Phrygian cap, carrying a pinecone in his right hand with his left hand on a sword, often accompanied by bulls and lions. His symbols were the pinecone, the peacock and the**

pomegranate. A temple of Mên also has been excavated at Pisidian Antioch.

From 1952 to 1956 Professor Paulo Verzone of Istanbul University and the Italian Archeological Mission excavated Side:

http://www.archmuseum.org/Gallery/Photo_15_2_archeology2-side.html

Professor Hüseyin Sabri Alanyali of Anadolu University in Turkey currently directs site excavations at Side:
http://www.akmedanmed.com/article_en.php?catID=15&artID=296

**Lyrbe** (36° 52' 26" N, 31° 28' 31" E) was founded in the 3$^{rd}$ century BCE and stands 23 km NE of Side further N along the road that runs by the Manavat waterfalls. Access is via the town of Sihlar and requires driving a considerable way on a steep, primitive dirt road. After pirates occupied Side in the 2$^{nd}$ century BCE, many townspeople migrated here. An inscription found in Greek and the Sideian language enabled archeologists to identify the city as Lyrbe. Few tourists visit this remote site.

*Lyrbe (above and below)*

**Lyrbe Site:** The site is situated on a hilltop with steep cliffs to the N, E and W, providing a strong defensive position. The ruins are hauntingly beautiful, overgrown with a mature pine forest. Approaching the city from the S visitors encounter ruins of a gate (5 m high) flanked with two towers (9 m high) in the city wall. Further up the hill stands the agora, containing a row of two and three-storey building facades and four entrances. In the N stoa archeologists found a floor mosaic representing the story of Orpheus. Ruins at the site include a semicircular palace, a heroon, and a number of structures believed to have been dwellings. Artifacts found at the site include an Asclepius head, a Leto figurine and a bronze statue of Apollo (now at the Antalya museum). SE of the agora stands the odeon with six rows of seats. NW of the agora is a late Roman era chapel. Remains of a temple of Apollo lie 20 m N of the agora. To the W on the slope are remains of a sacred cave and, further W, ruins of a Roman bath complex with floor mosaics. To the SW of the baths is a large basilica with colored marble slabs on the floor and sarcophagi beneath. Given its remote, mountainous location, the site has not been robbed of building materials. The site appears abandoned and largely unexcavated.

# X ANCIENT REGION OF PISIDIA

Pisidia is between Phrygia to the N, Pamphylia to the S, Caria to the W and Cappadocia to the E. Pisidia encompassed the Taurus mountain range, and several warlike, independent-minded tribes. In 334 BCE **Selge** concluded a pact with Alexander the Great against **Termessos** and **Sagalassos**. Alexander first laid siege to Termessos, but when this city proved to be impregnable, he shifted to Sagalassos. Although the Sagalassians valiantly resisted and succeeded in beating back the first attack assisted by archers from Termessos, they were ultimately overwhelmed and conquered. After Alexander's death nominal rule over Pisidia passed to his Macedonian successors, including the Seleucids, and then to the Pergamum in 188 BCE. In 133 BCE Rome inherited the kingdom of Pergamum and its territories. The archeological record suggests that the local population was rapidly Hellenized. During the $1^{st}$ century BCE Pisidia suffered from an extortionist Roman tax contracting system, trade disruption caused by an outbreak of piracy along the coast to the S, and the chaos of the Mithridatic wars in 89-63 BCE. Stability returned in 39 BCE under the rule of Roman client-King Amyntas of Galatia and continued after his death in 25 BCE when Rome imposed direct rule. During the Pax Romana, Augustus established several Roman colonies in Galatia and Pisidia and constructed a good road system, including the Via Sebaste linking Pisidian Antioch with the Pamphylian ports. The $2^{nd}$-$3^{rd}$ centuries were a period of prosperity and economic growth. Major ancient sites in Pisidia include: **Termessos**, **Selge**, **Antioch**, and **Sagalassos**.

**Termessos** (36° 59' 18" N, 30° 28' 4" E) was a Pisidian city built at an altitude of 1050 m on the SW side of Solymeus Mountain (modern Güllük Dagi) 38 km NW of Antalya. The ancient city and its natural pine forest comprise Termessos National Park. The original Pisidian inhabitants were indigenous to Anatolia and known as Solymians after Solymeus, an ancient Anatolian mountain god who through syncretization eventually became Zeus Solymeus. The founder of the city was Bellerophon, sent by King Iobates of Lycia to fight the Solymians after defeating the monster Chimaera. Termessos long profited from charging transit duties on goods passing from the coast to the interior through their valley N of Solymeus Mountain. In 333 BCE Alexander the Great briefly besieged the city but did not conquer it. In 319 BCE during the power struggle following the death of Alexander, Termessos provided refuge to the Macedonian general Alcetas, but then agreed to relinquish him to his rival Antigonus Monophtalmos to avoid war. Termessos had friendly relations with Pergamum King Attalus II, who built a two-storey stoa at Termessos to commemorate an alliance. During the Roman period Termessos enjoyed considerable independence as one of the few cities to support Rome during the Mithridatic wars. The population abandoned Termessos in the 5$^{th}$ century, perhaps after a major earthquake destroyed an aqueduct and cut off the city water supply.

A gateway
B gymnasium
C colonnaded street
D agora
E heroon
F odeon
G temple of Zeus
H theatre
I founder house
J Alcetas tomb

*Termessos*

**Termessos Site**: From the steep road up to the city visitors can see Hellenistic period walls. Right by the parking lot are the remains of an elevated ancient gate, part of a temple dedicated to Artemis and Emperor Hadrian built in the lower part of the city. The main ruins are 500 m further, higher up a steep path through

*Termessos Theatre*

the woods. Visitors encounter a watchtower at the lower city walls and remnants of a $2^{nd}$ century street. On the inner side of the gateway walls 4-5 line inscriptions report a dice oracle, including numbers thrown, the name of the god consulted and the prediction made. Steps (to the NE) lead up to ruins of a $1^{st}$ century, two-storey Doric style gymnasium. The agora was raised on stone blocks surrounded on three sides by stoas, including to the NW the two-storey Doric stoa of Pergamum King Attalus II.

To the SW of the agora stands a heroon, commemorating an unidentified dignitary, with niches on the side and stairs up to square platform on the top. To the E of the agora stands the 4,200-seat, $2^{nd}$ century theatre, carved out of the rock and perched at the edge of a steep cliff with a spectacular view. Some seats bear carved names of prominent citizens reserving their places. The stage building had a long narrow room connected to the podium via five doors through an ornamental façade. Animals were kept in five small rooms under the stage for wild beast shows. A colonnaded street lined with shops and statues of successful athletes ran N-S through the city. A $1^{st}$ century BCE odeon with 10 m high walls and seating capacity of 600 stands S of the theatre. Inscriptions cut into the N wall record

*Necropolis at Termessos*

names of victorious athletes.  Directly to the W of the odeon are scant remains of a temple of Zeus Solymeus (6 x 7 m), the city's chief god.  SE of the odeon is an early $3^{rd}$ century smaller temple of Artemis (6 x 6 m), which an inscription notes was donated by one Aurelia Armasta and her husband.  To the E are the remains of a larger temple of Artemis with six by eleven Doric columns, where archeologists uncovered a relief depicting the sacrifice of Iphigenia at Aulis.  W of the agora stands a well-preserved Roman period house, with an inscription above a Doric order doorway stating the house belonged to a founder of the city.  An ancient helmet relief is well preserved.  On the edge of the city a vast necropolis contains hundreds of $2^{nd}$-$3^{rd}$ century rock-cut tombs and sarcophagi.  Along a separate path to the NW, the $4^{th}$ century BCE tomb of Alcetas displays a relief carved out of solid rock depicting the Macedonian general as a mounted warrior.  Lower down to the right of the Alcetas relief his helmet, shield and sword are depicted.

**Alcetas (died 320 BCE) was one of Alexander the Great's generals during his Indian expedition.  Following the death of Alexander in 323 BCE, Alcetas' brother Perdiccas became regent of the empire.  Attempting to consolidate power, Perdiccas invaded Egypt to attack Ptolemy and left his loyal brother Alcetas to deal with rivals in Asia Minor.  Then in 321 BCE the officers under the command of Perdiccas rebelled, killed him and joined Ptolemy.  Meanwhile Alcetas joined forces with Attalus against**

rival Antigonus, but in 320 BCE they were defeated in Pisidia. Fourteen years after Alexander the Great unsuccessfully besieged Termessos, Alcetas fled to that city remembering how defensible it was. Antigonus followed him to Termessos and surrounded the city with a huge army. Although Alcetas was their guest and had their sympathy, the elder Termessians refused to go to war for the sake of a foreigner and his hopeless cause. The younger Termessians considered Alcetas a great warrior and supported his cause, but were overruled. When Alcetas learned the elders had decided to betray him, he took his own life rather than be taken alive. The city elders presented his corpse to Antigonus who was mollified and departed leaving the desecrated and unburied corpse. The younger Termessians retrieved Alcetas' corpse, and buried him with full honors in a magnificent tomb, which has survived into the 21$^{st}$ century.

*Selge Theatre*

**Selge** (37° 13' 45" N, 31° 7' 39" E), 40 km N of Aspendos, is located at an altitude of 950 m above sea level at a beautiful and remote point area where the Eurymedon River passes S through the Taurus Mountains. Like other cities in the region, Selge claimed the ancient seer Calchas as its founder. Although ancient Selge had a population of at least 20,000, minted its own coins, fielded a fierce army of 2,000 and was a leading Pisidian city, the current impoverished village of Altinkaya has only about 1,000 people. Given its remote mountainous location, Selge was naturally protected from invaders. When Alexander the Great passed through Pisidia in 333 BCE, Selge cooperated with him. Although nominally under Pergamum rule after 133 BCE, Selge appears to have been effectively independent and prosperous during the period of Roman control in Pisidia. Roman engineers built an aqueduct to help Selge obtain adequate water supplies, a major challenge currently facing Altinkaya. In 339 Selge was strong and determined enough to defeat a band of marauding Goths. On the way up to Selge from the coast, the road crosses a well-preserved Roman Bridge (37° 11' 31" N, 31° 10' 52" E) over the Eurymedon river valley 5 km N of Beşkonak village in a sparsely settled area popular with white water rafters. The one lane bridge (14 m long, 3.5 m wide) was built in the $2^{nd}$ century.

**Selge Site**: At the time of writing, there was no entrance fee at the site but rather many importuning local women aggressively selling handicrafts, such as necklaces and shawls. The town has been incorporated into a national park and is on the Saint Paul Trail. About 350 m of the original wall encircling the village remain. The most dramatic extant part of the ancient city is the $2^{nd}$ century theatre partially built into the hillside with 30 rows of seats for 10,000 people. Remnants of the stadium adjacent to the theatre are incorporated into the town with houses built inside and one stadium wall forming a main village street. At the far end of the stadium are ruins of a bath complex, the necropolis lies to the E, and a ruined late Roman church lies on a hilltop SW of the theatre. Up a hill to the W were two temples: the larger one a $3^{rd}$ century BCE temple of Zeus (17 x 34 m); the other a temple of Artemis.

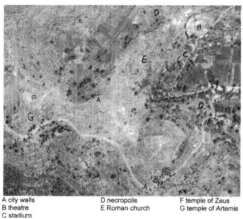

A city walls   D necropolis      F temple of Zeus
B theatre      E Roman church    G temple of Artemis
C stadium

*Selge*

**Antioch in Pisidia** (38° 18' 14" N, 31° 11' 28" E) is an ancient city one km NE of modern Yalvaç. The Seleucid successors to Alexander the Great founded the city in the 3rd century BCE on a plateau outcrop 1200 m above sea level near a strategic road juncture. Early inhabitants were Greeks, Jewish immigrants the Seleucids brought in from Galilee and Phrygians. In 25 BCE Emperor Augustus assumed direct Roman control and established at Antioch the largest of several Roman military colonies connected via a system of roads. Augustus settled 3,000 Latin-speaking Roman veterans in Antioch and granted them land to farm. During his reign the city was divided into seven quarters analogous to the seven hills of Rome. Unlike other cities in Asia Minor, Latin was the official language of Antioch and remained so until the latter part of the 2nd century. Imperial support for Antioch led to the construction of baths, colonnaded streets, a stadium, a nymphaeum, aqueducts, temples and roads. Westerners poured into the city: retired soldiers, merchants and farmers seeking more land and greater opportunity than available in Italy. Antioch hosted Roman festivals and games and had strong ties with the imperial capital. In 46 St. Paul and St. Barnabas came to Pisidian Antioch, perhaps at the behest of an influential convert they made in Cyprus, the Roman proconsul Lucius Sergius Paulus.

Roman Proconsul Lucius Sergius Paulus met Saint Paul at Pathos in Cyprus in 46. In response to the proconsul's request, Paul, accompanied by Barnabas and John Mark, spoke to Sergius about the life of Jesus. Then as the Jewish magician Elymas criticized the Jesus followers, a cloud of darkness miraculously blinded him, which prompted Sergius to embrace Christianity. A boundary stone discovered in Rome confirms Sergius was appointed a Curator of the Tiber River in 47. Sergius apparently served as Proconsul in Cyprus 43-46, and then returned to Rome. An inscription dated to 70 named Sergius as a Consul in Rome, the first from an eastern province to hold that position. He was the first of six successive senators named Lucius Sergius Paulus from Pisidian Antioch. Sergius' family had large land-holdings in the area of Pisidian Antioch, and a stone inscription discovered here in 1912 displays his name. Saints Paul and Barnabas went from

Cyprus to Pisidian Antioch. Sergius Paulus may have asked them visit to his family and friends, and probably gave them a letter of introduction.

The New Testament Book of Acts records that St. Paul delivered his first and longest recorded sermon at the Jewish synagogue in Antioch.

Paul the Apostle (5-67), originally Saul of Tarsus, grew up in a strict Jewish family descended from the tribe of Benjamin. His parents were Greek-speaking Roman citizens living in Tarsus. Paul enjoyed privileged legal status with respect to property and governance because he was a Roman citizen. Paul's family worked as tent-makers, a trade that Paul followed throughout his ministry. Paul was not one of the original Twelve Apostles. After studying in Jerusalem with Gamaliel, a leading theologian and Pharisee rabbi, Saul initially supported mainstream Jewish religious authorities in opposing the Jesus movement. He even took part in the murder of Saint Stephen, the first Christian martyr, by guarding the cloaks while Stephen was stoned. Then in the year 35 while en route to Damascus Paul saw a blinding light and heard the voice of Jesus ask him, "Saul, Saul, why do you persecute me?" From that moment on, Paul was a devoted Christian. He went to Damascus, where a Christian named Ananias healed his blindness and baptized him. Paul then spent a couple of years in Damascus and other parts of Arabia, learning about Christianity and preparing himself for his future missionary work.

In 37 Paul made his first trip to Jerusalem where he spent 15 days meeting Jesus' brother James, Peter and other leaders of the nascent church. Paul returned to Tarsus where he preached the Christian faith for the next five years until the year 43 when Barnabas recruited him to work for the church at Antioch on the Orontes (not Antioch in Pisidia). A year later during a famine in Palestine, Paul and Barnabus were sent to bring alms to the Christian poor in Jerusalem. Paul brought material support to Christians in Jerusalem from various churches he had founded. Then in 47-49 Paul, Barnabas and John Mark embarked on the first missionary journey and went to Cyprus, Perge, Antioch in Pisidia, and Lycaonia. They established churches at Antioch in Pisidia, Iconium, Lystra, and Derbe. Their first stop at each new city was the Jewish synagogue, because Christianity at this time was essentially a Jewish sect. At Paphos in Cyprus, Paul converted the Roman proconsul Sergius Paulus, a major triumph. The monotheistic religious communities Paul founded worshiped the God of Israel and adhered to the Judaic moral code, but abandoned the rituals of Mosaic Law, and included people of non-Jewish ancestry. The pressing question became whether non-Jews would have to undergo circumcision and follow Kosher dietary laws to be Christians. Early church leaders met in Jerusalem in 49 to consider the question. Paul and Barnabas, representing the Christians of Asia Minor, argued that the Christian converts should be exempt from these requirements. Peter, John and James eventually agreed to Paul's position. After the Jerusalem Council concluded, Paul, accompanied by Silas, Luke and later Timothy undertook a second missionary journey, first revisiting established churches in Asia Minor, and then reaching Galatia. At Alexandria Troas Paul had a vision of a Macedonian, which he interpreted as a call from God to evangelize Macedonia. Paul then sailed to Greece and preached in Philippi, where men unhappy about the conversion of their slaves complained to the authorities and had Paul and Silas imprisoned. After a miraculous earthquake, the prison gates fell apart freeing Paul and Silas and convincing their jailor to convert. The missionaries continued to Athens where Paul preached to Jews and non-Jewish God-fearers in the synagogue, and then separately to Greek intellectuals at the acropolis. In 50-52, Paul spent 18 months in Corinth and met Aquila and Priscilla, a couple who became faithful Christians. This couple followed Paul and his companions to Ephesus where they remained, founding one of the strongest and most faithful churches. In 52, Paul sailed to Caesarea in Palestine and then traveled N to Antioch on the Orontes where he stayed for about a year. In 53 Paul began his third mission traveling all around Galatia and Phrygia, then to Ephesus where he stayed for three years, healing people, casting out demons, and organizing missionary activity in the hinterlands. To earn his living he worked several hours every day making tents. Paul left Ephesus in haste after a local silversmith prompted a large-scale pro-Artemis riot. Then Paul went through Macedonia into Achaea, and visited Corinth for three months in 56. Paul and his companions visited Philippi, Alexandria Troas, Miletus, Rhodes, and Tyre.

St. Paul's four most famous Epistles (letters) were written during this third mission: the first to the Corinthians from Ephesus; the second to the Corinthians from Macedonia; then to the Romans from Corinth; and finally to the Galatians. In 57 Paul returned to Jerusalem with money collected for the Christian community there. Paul continued to preach against circumcision, Jewish dietary restrictions, and other requirements of the Torah. When Paul appeared at the temple in Jerusalem, he escaped the wrath of the crowd only when he was arrested. Paul was held prisoner for two years in Caesarea until a new governor considered his case in 59. When accused of treason, Paul claimed his right as a Roman citizen to appeal to the emperor and face trial in Rome. Paul's journey to Rome as a prisoner was slow and difficult as the boat followed the coasts of Syria, Cilicia, and Pamphylia. At Myra in Lycia the prisoners were transferred to an Alexandrian vessel bound for Italy, but the ship was wrecked at Malta, where Paul remained for three months. Paul finally reached Rome in March 60 where he preached for two years from a rented home while awaiting trial. Scholars believe that at the end of the two years St. Paul was released from his Roman imprisonment, traveled to Spain, and then back to Rome, where he was imprisoned a second time. Emperor Nero blamed the great fire of Rome in 64 on the Christians. Tradition says that Paul, as a Roman citizen, was beheaded, a more merciful death than crucifixion, in Rome in 67.

At Antioch in Pisidia, according to the Acts of Paul and Thecla, St. Thecla was condemned and had her miraculous deliverance.

St. Thecla was born in 16 to a prosperous, non-Christian family in Iconium (modern Konya). The Acts of Paul and Thecla, one of the 2$^{nd}$ century New Testament Apocrypha, is the story of St Paul's relationship with the young woman Thecla. In 34 Paul traveled to Iconium proclaiming, "the word of God about abstinence and the resurrection." Paul is described as, "a man of middling size, and his hair was scanty, and his legs were a little crooked, and his knees were projecting, and he had large eyes and his eyebrows met, and his nose was somewhat long, and he was full of grace and mercy; at one time he seemed like a man, and at another time he seemed like an angel." At this time Thecla was betrothed to a man named Thamyris. Although Thecla's mother Theokleia prohibited her from going to hear Paul, Thecla could hear his preaching from her bedroom window. For three days and nights Thecla sat and listened to Paul's preaching and his call for chastity. Realizing Thecla was becoming enchanted with Christianity, Theokleia and Thamyris went to the Roman governor and demanded that Paul be silenced. In response to their complaints and others, the governor imprisoned Paul. When Thecla learned of Paul's arrest she secretly went to the prison, bribed her way in to see him, and entered Paul's prison cell. She knelt before Paul, kissed the chains binding his hands and feet, and stayed all night listening to his message. When her family found her, both she and Paul were brought before the governor. Paul was beaten and expelled from Iconium.

When the governor asked Thecla why she had come to Paul and now refused to marry her fiancé, she announced she was determined to remain a virgin for the sake of Christ. Horrified, her enraged mother asked the governor to threaten Thecla. The governor admonished Thecla for her foolishness and told her she would be burned at the stake unless she renounced Christianity. When Thecla refused to recant, she was taken to an arena, stripped naked and tied to the stake. At this moment she had a vision of Jesus, which gave her the strength needed to face the flames. The fire was lit, but as the flames approached Thecla a thunderstorm suddenly developed and a torrent of rain extinguished the flames. The embarrassed and somewhat anxious Roman authorities released Thecla, but demanded she leave Iconium immediately. Still strongly attracted to Paul and his message, Thecla disguised herself as a man and rejoined Paul at the outskirts of the city. She recounted her miraculous escape from the flames and asked him to baptize her. Paul refused, saying that this would be accomplished in God's own way and time. Paul and Thecla then departed Iconium together and traveled to Antioch in Pisidia.

As they entered Antioch in Pisidia, a rich and powerful young man named Alexander saw Thecla and desired her. He first offered Paul money for Thecla, then tried to seize her by force. Thecla valiantly fought him off, publically humiliating Alexander in front of his friends and the amused bystanders. The enraged Alexander prevailed upon the Roman authorities to arrest this vagrant girl for assault. As her Christian beliefs became apparent, Thecla was condemned to face wild beasts in the arena unless she submitted to Alexander and abandoned her beliefs. Thecla's treatment aroused considerable sympathy among the local women and came to the attention of Antonia Tryphaena, an influential woman from a powerful family. Tryphaena was the daughter of Roman client rulers in Pontus, a direct descendant of Mark Antony and a distant cousin of Roman Emperors Caligula, Claudius and Nero. Although Tryphaena served as a priestess in two imperial cults, she was interested in the preaching of Paul. In the <u>New Testament</u> (Romans 16:12) Paul sends greetings to "Tryphaena" and notes that she works in the Lord's service. Tryphaena took Thecla home to protect her from sexual assault before she would have to appear in the arena. The next day, however, the authorities accused and convicted Thecla of sacrilege, dragged her into the arena, where she was stripped naked. A fierce, hungry lioness was released. To the amazement of the crowd, the lioness only licked Thecla's feet and then sat down beside her. Next the authorities released a large bear, but the lioness rose up and killed the bear before he could touch Thecla. Then other ferocious animals were released and a large male lion approached. Again the lioness rose to her defense, killing the attacking lion but being mortally wounded in the process. Fearing she would now die without being baptized, Thecla jumped into a pool of water and proclaimed, "In the name of Jesus Christ do I baptize myself on this last day." A miraculous fire then appeared, protecting Thecla from the remaining beasts and shielding her nakedness from public view. At this point, the nervous authorities stopped the persecution of Thecla and released her. Thecla went to the home of Tryphaena where she stayed eight days, converting Tryphaena and her entire household to Christianity. When Thecla left Antioch, Tryphaena gave her gifts of gold and precious jewelry. Thecla "yearned for Paul" and caught up with him at Myra, declaring she was now a baptized Christian. She gave Paul all her gold and jewelry to distribute among the needy. Paul gave her his blessing but told her it was best that she not accompany him further on his mission. Instead, he encouraged her to preach the Gospel on her own, so she moved S to Silifke, established a nunnery, worked as a healer and spent the rest of her long life as a nun.

At Antioch in Pisidia, an early Christian community was established. Although Pisidian Governor Valerius Diogenes actively persecuted Christians in the early 4th century, by 381 Antioch had a bishop and was represented at the Council of Constantinople. After the arrival of Muslim Arab invaders the city was besieged four times between 640 and 713, and then abandoned.

**Antioch in Pisidia Site**: The acropolis covers a large area surrounded with fortified defensive walls. Visitors enter the site via the W side by a triple-arched gate, decorated with weapons and garlands and dedicated to Emperor Hadrian during his 129 visit. The decumanus maximus (E-W street) leads past the theatre to intersect the

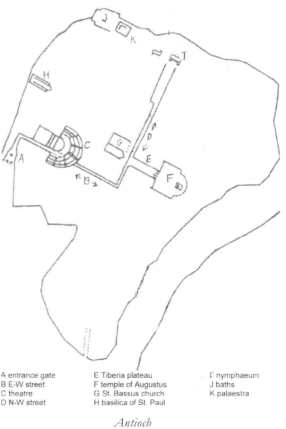

A entrance gate
B E-W street
C theatre
D N-W street
E Tiberia plateau
F temple of Augustus
G St. Bassus church
H basilica of St. Paul
I nymphaeum
J baths
K palaestra

*Antioch*

cardo maximus (N-S street) at a right angle. Shops lined colonnaded streets. Ancient vehicle ruts worn in stone, game boards etched in the pavement and remnants of the drainage system are still visible. The Romans enlarged the original Greek theater in 311-313 to reach a seating capacity of 15,000 with the decumanus maximus passing through a tunnel on the S side. To the E of the cardo maximus was the 1$^{st}$ century Tiberia platea, a colonnaded walkway leading up 12 steps to the E through a three-arched triumphal gateway (propylon) to the imperial temple of Augustus. A bronze dedicatory inscription on the gateway read, "for the emperor Caesar Augustus, son of a god, pontifex maximus… father of the country." Carved into the propylon was the Res Gestae Divi Augusti (record of the Augustus' accomplishments) in Latin, one of only three to survive. The propylon was decorated with statuary and reliefs commemorating the victories of Augustus, such as a naked Pisidian captive with hands tied behind his back. Other symbols of victory here (and at the Yalvaç Museum) included reliefs of weapons, armor and tritons representing naval triumphs. On a rocky outcrop at the highest point of the city Emperor Augustus built an imperial cult temple, completed by his successor Emperor Tiberius in the year 25. The sanctuary area (85 x 100 m) contained a semicircular two-storey portico carved into the hillside out of bedrock. In the center is the fairly small temple podium with steep steps and Corinthian columns (8 m high). Friezes of bulls decorated with garlands and fruit stand at the site.


**Augustus (Gaius Julius Caesar Augustus), meaning revered one, reigned as the first Roman Emperor 27 BCE-14 CE. Augustus profoundly changed the world, not as a military genius like Alexander the Great, but rather as a brilliant administrator. Augustus was born Gaius Octavian on September 23, 63 BCE. His father served as senator; Julius Caesar's sister Julia was his maternal grandmother. During his youth the political fabric of the Roman Republic was torn apart as politicians used violence to achieve their objectives, with riots, assassinations and civil war**

*Temple of Augustus at Antioch*

becoming commonplace.  In 46 BCE young Octavian accompanied Julius Caesar on his triumphal procession following his victory over Roman opponents in Africa.  In 45 BCE young Octavian boldly joined Caesar in Spain where he was fighting supporters of Pompey.  On March 15, 44 BCE Julius Caesar, recently declared dictator for life, was surrounded by the conspirators at the Senate and stabbed 23 times.  Although the aristocratic assassins regarded themselves as liberators, the common people loved Caesar and rioted, prompting the liberators to flee Rome.  At this time power seemed firmly in the grasp of Mark Antony, Caesar's right-hand man.  However, Caesar's will named 18-year old Octavian his chief heir and adopted son.  Against the advice of his family, Octavian went to Rome to claim his perilous inheritance.  Mark Antony held Caesar's papers and assets and refused to relinquish any funds.  Caesar's will included substantial bequests to the public, which Octavian struggled to pay for as best he could.  Without a patronage network of his own, Octavian was forced to appeal directly to the masses, including Caesar's former troops and supporters.   Octavian traveled the countryside where military colonies of Caesar's veterans were located and managed to win over troops loyal to the memory of Caesar, raising a private army perhaps 10,000 strong. Cicero, Rome's elder statesmen, underestimated Octavian and took up his cause as a foil to limit Antony's power. Encouraged by Cicero, the Senate granted Octavian the rank of senator, broke with Antony and compelled him to withdraw to Gaul. After various military skirmishes around Italy, Octavian marched on Rome, was elected consul, paid out remaining donations from Caesar's will, revoked the amnesty for Caesar's assassins and convicted them in absentia.

In 43 BCE Octavian formed a ruling triumvirate with Antony and another leading general, Marcus Lepidus, to punish Caesar's assassins, particularly Brutus and Cassius who occupied the E provinces of the empire. First, using a tool devised by Sulla, the triumvirate "proscribed" and slaughtered thousands of political enemies, including at least 300 senators and 2,000 equestrians (knights), seizing their property in the process. At Antony's insistence, the unfortunate Cicero had his hands and head cut off and placed on public display in the Forum. Then in 42 BCE at the Battle of Philippi Antony decisively defeated Brutus and Cassius. The triumvirs divided up the Roman world: Antony, senior partner, received the entire E; Octavian received most of the W; and Lepidus N Africa. To strengthen the agreement Antony married Octavian's sister Octavia in 40 BCE. Antony agreed to provide Octavian 120 ships, in return for 20,000 soldiers for Antony's war against the Persians. Antony sent the ships, but Octavian only supplied 2,000 soldiers. At about this time the third triumvir, Lepidus, unsuccessfully challenged Octavian and was forced out of politics. Octavian now spent considerable funds in Rome rebuilding basic services, such as the sewer and water systems, and restoring temples. He also launched a major public relations campaign depicting Antony as having "gone native" in Egypt, because he wore non-Roman clothing and schemed to make Cleopatra queen of Rome. Antony played into Octavian's hands when in 34 BCE he declared Cleopatra "Queen of Kings" and her son by Julius Caesar, Caesarion, "King of Kings," as well as dividing the E Roman provinces among Cleopatra, Caesarion, and his own children. In 32 BCE Antony divorced Octavia and Octavian seized and publicized Antony's confidential will, held by the Vestal Virgins in Rome, which confirmed his dynastic commitment to Cleopatra. In late 32 BCE, the Senate declared war on Egypt. In 31 BCE the Roman Navy under the brilliant military commander Agrippa defeated the combined fleets of

Antony and Cleopatra at Actium in Greece. Antony's men defected to Octavian en masse. Within a year both Antony and Cleopatra committed suicide and Rome annexed Egypt.

By 27 BCE Octavian, now known as Augustus, methodically created the Principate, a system in the form of Republican government, which actually kept him in control. He reduced his legions from 60 to 28, using Egyptian funds to resettle soldiers. He established the Praetorian Guard, and discretely stationed it towns around Rome. (The Praetorian Guard were special troops primarily responsible for the protection of the ruler.) Well aware of the danger of assassination, Augustus carefully avoided the trappings of kingship and continued as Rome's first citizen. He followed a modest lifestyle, treated the Senate with respect, and skillfully manipulated Roman politics. The Senate evolved from being the chief organ of the state into a subordinate entity made up of respected administrators at the disposal of Augustus. The provinces benefited enormously from Augustus's reign due to both peace and good governance. Roman governors had no incentive to extort huge sums of money from their provinces as they had during the Republican era because career success now depended on the emperor's favor rather than buying electoral victories in Rome. In the E, with its long tradition of ruler worship, an imperial cult of Augustus began shortly after Actium. The greatest challenge to Augustus and the Principate was the succession issue. Augustus spent considerable time and effort preparing for dynastic continuity and stability, attempting to create a pool of legitimate succession candidates. When through attrition Tiberius was clearly the strongest candidate, Augustus dutifully gave him equal status and power to ensure smooth succession. Augustus died peacefully on August 19, 14; on September 17 the Senate formally deified him. The Res Gestae Divi Augusti (Achievements of the Divine Augustus) is an ancient first-person inscription listing his achievements, which can still be seen today in Ankara and in part at Antioch in Pisidia. Augustus established Pax Romana, which introduced unparalleled prosperity, shaped modern Europe and ultimately enabled the empire to survive for more than 1400 years.

At Antioch to the W of the cardo maximus across from the Tiberia Platea are the remains of the Central or St. Bassus Church built in the 4th century. The church was built on the axis of the Platea, the propylon, and temple of Augustus.

*Church of Saint Bassus*

St. Bassus was an early Christian martyr, believed to have been a Roman courtier under Emperor Diocletian. In 303 Emperor Diocletian confronted St. Theopemptus, Bishop of Nicomedia, and demanded that he worship an idol representing the god Apollo. Theopemptus refused and was thrown into a fiery furnace, but did not burn. Then the emperor deprived Theopemptus of food and drink for 22 days, but he remained alive and healthy. Bassus and a number of others were impressed by the bishop's determination and were baptized as Christians. Diocletian, however, then tortured and beheaded Theopemptus. Similarly, Bassus was buried in the ground up to the waist, and then his upper body was cut to pieces.

Archeologists found a large iron seal at Antioch's St. Bassus Church depicting three martyrs from the period of Diocletian: Neon, Nikon and Heliodorus.

Nikon, Neon, and Heliodorus lived in Asia Minor during the reign of Emperor Diocletian (284-305) at the beginning of a campaign to persecute Christians. One day Mark, a shepherd in

Pisidian Antioch, openly announced his Christian faith.

*Church of Saint Paul*

Mark discussed his faith with thirty soldiers who were then persuaded to convert to Christianity. In response Emperor Diocletian beheaded the thirty soldiers at Nicaea, and sentenced Mark to be tortured for being a bad influence. Mark refused to renounce his faith and was eventually beheaded in a Galatian town known as Claudiopolis. When the Roman soldiers carried the severed head of St. Mark into a temple of Artemis, all the temple idols miraculously fell down and broke apart. Nikon, Neon, and Heliodorus, were three young men at the Artemis Temple who witnessed these events and in response became Christian converts. As a result, they too were executed for their faith when they refused to recant.

The Antioch cardo maximus terminated to the N at the U-shaped 1st century nymphaeum, which distributed water to the entire city from a 1st century aqueduct. From the nymphaeum the remains of the ancient aqueduct are visible in the distance. NW of the nymphaeum lie the remains of a palaestra and a well-preserved bathhouse. SW of the nymphaeum along the W wall is the basilica of St. Paul, Antioch's largest church, built in the late 4th century. A baptism font found at the site reads, "Saint Paul" as well as, "The voice of the Lord is over the waters" and "Jesus Christ is victor." The large church (70 x 27 m) is oriented E-W. Most walls are gone, but mosaics (now covered) and inscriptions remain on the floors. One of the mosaic inscriptions refers to Optimus, the bishop who attended the Council of Constantinople in 381. Another mosaic from the Septuagint Psalm 43 reads, "Then I will go unto the altar of God." Archeological evidence suggests that the wall foundations at the S side of the basilica belonged to the synagogue where St. Paul first preached. Hikers can take the St. Paul Trail from Pisidian Antioch S via Adada to Perge or Aspendos. During the early 20th century W. M. Ramsay of Princeton University and F. W. Kelsey of the University of Michigan excavated Antioch in Pisidia. The University of Michigan and Kelsey Museum have good websites covering the excavations and history of Antioch in Pisidia:

http://sitemaker.umich.edu/late-antiquity/pisidian_antioch

http://www.lsa.umich.edu/kelsey/antioch/

Since the 1980s the Yalvaç Museum has excavated the site:
http://www.yalvac.bel.tr/index.php?p=349&l=2

**Sagalassos** (37° 40' 41" N, 30° 31' 17" E) was an ancient mountain city near modern Ağlasun 110 km N of Antalya. Sagalassos is built on S-facing terraces at altitudes 1400-1700 m above sea level with a panoramic view of the surrounding mountains and valley. Sagalassos first became part of a Phrygian kingdom in the 9th-7th century BCE and then the Lydian kingdom until it was incorporated into the Persian Empire in 546 BCE. In 334 BCE Sagalassos was one of the wealthiest cities in Pisidia with a population of a few thousand when Alexander the Great

A site entrance  E heroon  I temple of Apollo
B Neon library  F bouleterion  J baths
C nymphaeum  G macellum  K city gate
D theatre  H odeon  L temple of Antoninus Pius

*Sagalassos*

overwhelmed fierce local resistance and conquered the city. In 25 BCE, Sagalassos was incorporated into the Roman Empire. At about this time the city became a major pottery producing and exporting center. Sagalassos did well under Roman rule with a significant increase in trade and building construction during the $1^{st}$-$3^{rd}$ centuries. Emperor Hadrian favored Sagalassos, making it the provincial capital and center of the imperial cult, which included hosting annual festivals and games involving thousands of visitors. Sagalassos had a bishop in the $4^{th}$ century who went to Council of Constantinople in 381. Christianization provoked internal conflict and in about 400 led to the destruction of the Neon Library. Early in the $5^{th}$ century the first basilica church was built in Sagalassos. At this time Isaurian raids necessitated construction of a new city wall. In 590 an earthquake leveled the town, after which it was largely abandoned.

**Sagalassos Site**: Sagalassos was well preserved because of its remote mountain location and a thick erosion layer, which protected the city from plundering and decay. At Sagalassos archeologists have effectively applied anastylosis, a scientific method to rebuild the site as much as possible using original elements. The visitor parking area is to the E of the site and signage is good. In the NE part of the city the theatre, with seats for 9000, was built in the Hellenistic tradition into the mountainside. The one-storey stage building was erected in 180-210. To the E of the theatre a ceramic production center was discovered with ten kilns, workshops and thousands of defective pots, which was active from the 1st century BCE through to the 6th century. To the W of the theatre is the Neon Library, built by prominent local citizen Flavius Seberanus Neon in 120, with a fine mosaic floor. Further W is the Antoninus Pius nymphaeum, built in 160-180 with a 4th century, single-storey façade (27 m long, 8 m high) adorned with Medusa heads.

*Dancing Maidens on Heroon*

The 1st century NW heroon is a monument (14 m high) built with stone blocks to commemorate an as yet unidentified hero. Three steps on top of a podium led to a frieze section depicting fourteen dancing girls holding hands. Above the dancing girls a temple-like heroon contained a small cella with four Corinthian columns in front carrying a pediment. A 1st century BCE Doric temple of Zeus was built on the highest terrace W of the upper agora. In about 400 the temple was transformed into a watchtower and incorporated into the city fortifications. The 1st century BCE bouleuterion, a rectangular structure with tiers of seats facing the center from three directions, was built to the W of the upper agora. Some of the seats in the lowest row were

*Nymphaeum with Heroon (upper left)*

decorated with lion paws. In the 5th century the bouleuterion was transformed into a church forecourt. The area of the original portico was subdivided into several shops and workshops. To the SE, a 2nd century paved quadrangular courtyard (21 x 21 m) contained a food market, bordered on three sides by shops behind Corinthian columns. In the middle a round building sheltered a basin where live fish were kept for sale. Just to the N of the lower agora was an odeon with seats for 3,000. The well-preserved Hadrian nymphaeum, constructed 128-134, is to the N of the lower agora on a terrace above the public square. The fountain has a two-storey façade (17 m long, 6 m wide) with a rectangular basin in front. The lower podium was decorated with figures of the Muses, reclining river gods and Nereids standing on seaborne creatures on pillars. A statue of Apollo (5 m high) stood in a large niche on the lower storey flanked to the E by a satyr, Aphrodite and Poseidon. Reliefs of Tritons blowing horns and a Medusa head decorated the center of the façade.

Poseidon (Neptune to Romans) is god of the sea, rivers, earthquakes, and horses, as well as an elder brother of Zeus. During the Titanomachy he played a key role using his trident along with Zeus and his other brother Pluto to defeat the titans and confine them to Tartarus. When Poseidon drew lots with Zeus and Pluto for dominion over the cosmos, he received the oceans. The consort of Poseidon was Amphitrite, daughter of Nersus and one of the fifty Nereids. Amphitrite bore Poseidon a son named Triton, with the upper body of a human and the lower body of a fish, who serves as his father's herald. On one occasion King Minos of Crete called upon Poseidon to send him a bull from the sea in order to make a special sacrifice to honor the god. Poseidon acceded to this request, sending Minos a fine white bull. Upon seeing the bull, Minos decided to keep it and sacrifice another one instead. This ingratitude infuriated Poseidon who prevailed upon Aphrodite, and her son Eros (Cupid), to make the king's wife Pasiphae fall in love with the bull. This unfortunate love triangle eventually produced the flesh-eating monster known as the Minotaur, who was half human, half beast.

At one point Poseidon was enamored with the virgin goddess

Athena, who spurned his advances. Later, perhaps out of spite, Poseidon seduced a beautiful mortal priestess of Athena named Medusa and they made love in a temple of Athena. Athena, furious over the defilement of her temple, transformed Medusa into a hideous monster with a petrifying glance and turned her beautiful hair into writhing snakes. Once Poseidon was strongly attracted to the beautiful sea nymph Scylla. Amphitrite found out about the relationship and threw magic herbs into the water while Scylla was bathing, which transformed her into a hideous, six-headed sea-monster with three rows of teeth and 12 feet. Scylla then lived by snatching human sailors off their ships and eating them alive. Poseidon had sired a beautiful and loyal sea nymph daughter named Charybdis with Gaia (mother earth). Charybdis pushed the ocean onto the shore and submerged so much coastline to make it part of her father's ocean kingdom that she eventually provoked Zeus, who angrily turned her into a monstrous whirlpool. The result of these two actions was a highly dangerous narrow channel of ocean, perhaps between Sicily and the Italian mainland, where Charybdis lay on one side and Scylla on the other. Once the queen of Ethiopia, Cassiopeia, boasted that her daughter Andromeda was more beautiful than the Nereids. To punish the queen for this hubris, Poseidon sent the sea monster named Cetus to ravage the Ethiopian coast. After a great deal of damage had been done, the desperate king of Ethiopia consulted an oracle of Apollo, who revealed that the king would have to sacrifice his daughter beautiful Andromeda to the monster Cetus. Andromeda was accordingly chained naked to a rock along the coast. Fortunately, the hero Perseus was flying home after slaying Medusa and spotted the girl chained to the rock. Perseus managed to kill Cetus and took Andromeda as a wife.

At one point Poseidon and the other Olympian gods plotted a rebellion against Zeus and managed to immobilize him. However, Zeus escaped, regained control, banished Poseidon and Apollo from Olympus for a year and compelled them to build the walls of Troy, which explains why they were so sturdy. Not knowing who they were, Trojan King Laomedon foolishly refused to pay them when they were done. Not surprisingly Poseidon favored the Greeks during the Trojan War, although at one point he rescued Aeneas from certain death. Poseidon also gave the Greek hero Odysseus a very difficult time to punish him for blinding the Cyclops, one of his offspring.

In Sagalassos to the W of the agora stood a 1st century BCE temple of Apollo, which was converted into a Christian basilica in the late 5th century. On a slope to the W are numerous sarcophagi. To the E of the lower agora are 2nd century imperial baths. Underneath these baths archeologists discovered an earlier, smaller bathing complex (33 x 40 m) built during the reign of Augustus in 10-30. When Hadrian selected Sagalassos as the center of the Imperial cult in Pisidia and venue for the related festivals and games, thousands of visitors came to town and much larger imperial baths were built over the earlier structure. A 165 inscription at the later baths is dedicated to co-rulers Lucius Verus and Marcus Aurelius. Here archeologists have uncovered finely carved, colossal heads from statues of: Emperor Hadrian; Faustina the Elder, wife of Antoninus Pius; and Emperor Marcus Aurelius. These huge statues (4-5 m high) were carved in sections, fitted together onsite and displayed in the largest room in the baths. The entrance to the city was from the S via a 280 m long, 9 m wide colonnaded street. Steps led down from the lower agora to a temple (27 x 14 m) of Antoninus Pius and the gods of the city.

**Antoninus Pius (Titus Aelius Hadrianus Antoninus Augustus Pius) reigned as Roman emperor 138-161. He was born in 86 to a wealthy Roman family and held various imperial offices, including regional judge in Italy. Then he served as governor of Roman Asia 133-136. Antoninus was tall and handsome, physically strong, with the ability to speak well. He followed the example of Hadrian and wore a beard. After his return to Rome, Antoninus served on Emperor Hadrian's imperial council. In 138 Hadrian's designated successor died unexpectedly. The ailing Emperor Hadrian then named Antoninus his adopted son and successor on condition that Lucius Verus and Marcus Aurelius be adopted and designated joint heirs of Antoninus. Antoninus became emperor in 138 and the Senate awarded him the title Pius, meaning dutiful and respectful, because he insisted on the posthumous deification of Hadrian despite the fact that Hadrian was widely unpopular. The long reign of Antoninus was peaceful and prosperous. Antoninus strengthened the Senate and the imperial bureaucracy. Although unnecessary wars were avoided, the Romans acted forcefully to maintain order. Rebellion in Britain was suppressed,**

and in 142 the 58 km long Antonine Wall was built and extended Roman control 140 km further N beyond Hadrian Wall into Caledonia (modern Scotland). Marauding Germanic and Scythian tribes were confronted along the N border in central Europe. In 150 a Berber rebellion was suppressed in North Africa. Local rebellions were put down in Egypt in 154 and then in Dacia in 158. Antoninus even wrote to Vologases, King of Parthia, and persuaded him to desist from plans to attack Armenia. Pax Romana encompassing perhaps 150 million people was maintained by a Roman military of about 350,000 soldiers. Although Antoninus was devoted to traditional polytheistic worship, he continued Trajan's relatively tolerant policy of not actively seeking out Christians for persecution. Antoninus' only surviving daughter, Faustina the younger, married Marcus Aurelius in 145. He elevated Marcus Aurelius to be joint ruler in 146. Antoninus lived to age 74, ruling longer than Trajan or Hadrian, and died a popular man in 161, enthusiastically deified by the Senate.

Marc Waelkens of Katholieke University Leuven in Belgium is director of site excavations at Sagalassos: http://www.archaeology.org/interactive/sagalassos/

http://www.sagalassos.be/nl

# XI ANCIENT REGION OF PHRYGIA

Phrygia borders Galatia to the E, Pisidia to the S, Lydia to the W and Bithynia to the NW. The first known Phrygians came from Thrace in the late 2nd millennium BCE and their language was related to those spoken in the Balkans. **Gordium** was established as the capital of Phrygia in the 9th century BCE. In 738 BCE the Phrygian King Midas, known from Greek legend and contemporary Assyrian sources, came to power. Midas was the first non-Greek king to make offerings to the oracle at Delphi, and to adopt Hellenistic culture. Eventually nomadic Cimmerians overwhelmed Phrygia and burned Gordium in 696 BCE. Lydia dominated Phrygia from this time until Persian King Cyrus the Great conquered Lydia in 546 BCE and incorporated Phrygia into the Persian Empire. A Persian garrison remained in Gordium from that time until 334 BCE when the forces of Alexander the Great captured the city. After the death of Alexander in 323 BCE, Antigonus first ruled Phrygia, until 301 BCE when Phrygia came under Seleucid rule. During the 3rd century BCE Celtic Galatians dominated the region. In 189 BCE Roman general Manlius Vulso sacked Gordium, defeated the Galatians and destroyed the city. Pergamum seized control with Roman support in 188 BCE and in 133 BCE Phrygia was incorporated directly into the Roman Empire. From shrines at **Pessinus** Phrygian worship of the mother goddess Cybele and the first decoration of pine trees as part of a religious holiday passed to the Greeks and spread throughout the Roman Empire. The spread of early Christianity in Phrygia during the 2nd century was largely due to St. Paul. Major ancient Phrygian cities include: **Gordium**, **Pessinus**, **Hierapolis**

(Pamukkale) and **Laodicea**. The Phrygia region encompasses the tomb of the 8th century Muslim Arab warrior Abdullah al-Battal (695-740), known by the honorific **Seyitgazi**, who died in 740 at the Battle of Akroinon when late Roman Emperor Zeno thwarted a major Muslim invasion.

**Gordium** (39° 39′ 10″ N, 31° 59′ 48″ E), 82 km SW of Ankara, was the capital of ancient Phrygia located where the Royal Road of Persian Kings crossed the Sangarius River, now known as Yassıhüyük or "flat mound." In 1893 the site of Gordium was rediscovered when German archeologist Alfred Körte visited engineers working on the Berlin–Baghdad Railroad and correctly identified the Phrygian capital based on descriptions from ancient writers in Greek and Latin. The most famous Phrygian king was Midas who ruled from 738 to 696 BCE.

Midas was the son of Gordias, a poor peasant who became king of Phrygia and tied the original Gordion Knot. Midas promoted worship of the mother goddess Cybele and Dionysus. Once Dionysus found his old schoolmaster and foster father, the satyr Silenus, missing. Silenus and Dionysus had just returned from the E where they had been introducing cultivation of the grape. The old satyr had been drinking too much wine, wandered into a rose garden belonging to King Midas and fell asleep. Local Phrygian peasants discovered Silenus, bound him in wreaths of flowers and carried him before King Midas. Midas recognized Silenus and treated him with the utmost hospitality for ten days and nights, while Silenus delighted Midas and his friends with stories and songs. On the eleventh day, Midas returned Silenus to Dionysus in Lydia. In gratitude Dionysus offered Midas his choice of whatever reward he would like. Midas asked that whatever he might touch would turn into gold, and, somewhat reluctantly, Dionysus granted his wish. Midas rejoiced in his new power, turning twigs and stones into valuable gold. However, later in the day when he grew hungry Midas was horrified when his food and drink turned into gold before he could consume it. Realizing his mistake, Midas beseeched

Dionysus to deliver him from starvation. Dionysus consented and instructed Midas to bathe in Pactolus River to free himself from his gold-creating power. Midas did so with the result that the Pactolus River was endowed with sands of gold, which later was the basis of the wealth of Lydian King Croesus. On another occasion, Midas was chosen as one of the judges of a musical competition between the satyr Marsayas and the god Apollo. Although the other judges awarded victory to Apollo for his beautiful lyre playing, Midas dissented, preferring the music of Marsayas. The vengeful Apollo then changed Midas' ears into donkey ears. After this disfigurement, Midas wore a Phrygian cap to cover his ears and avoid ridicule. In time the Phrygian cap, a soft wool headdress with a pointed crown curling forward, came to represent people from the E, and eventually was adopted as a symbol of freedom by emancipated slaves. More recently 18$^{th}$ century French revolutionaries adopted a red Phrygian cap as their symbol of liberty.

Archeological evidence in Gordium confirms nomadic Cimmerians destroyed the city at the end of the reign of Midas. The scant remains of ancient Gordium include city walls, terraces buildings, megarons, and temples. (A megaron was an early rectangular great hall in a palace complex with an open hearth used for feasts, sacrifices, worship, and a royal guesthouse.) The ancient Phrygian kings built perhaps a hundred tumuli tombs near Gordium, of which at least 35 have been excavated. The tombs consisted of a timber-frame burial chamber in the form of a

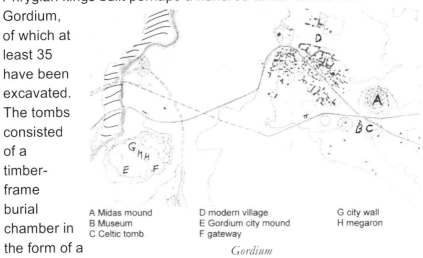

A Midas mound
B Museum
C Celtic tomb
D modern village
E Gordium city mound
F gateway
G city wall
H megaron

*Gordium*

house, roofed over and then covered with a protective layer of clay and earth as deep as 65 m, which made them difficult for grave robbers to find. One of these barrow tombs even contained a young prince together with toy wooden animals.

**Gordium Site**: The largest tomb, known as the Midas Mound, contains a cedar wood structure surrounded with juniper logs buried under a 53 m high, 300 m wide tumulus. This tomb is the oldest wooden structure in Turkey, and perhaps the world, dating back to the 8$^{th}$ century BCE. In the NW corner of the tomb were remains of the royal occupant: a man 1.59 m tall, about 60 years old in an open log coffin resting on twenty rich purple and gold textiles. The tomb contained remains of a funeral feast, several ornate tables, 178 bronze vessels, three giant copper cauldrons decorated with figurines, leather belts with bronze attachments, and 70 bronze "safety pin" pieces of jewelry. An alphabetic script found on five bronze vessels suggests that the Phrygians obtained the first alphabet from Phoenicia and passed it on to Greece. This tomb is now believed to predate the death of King Midas and may have been for his father, King Gordias. Guests at the funeral banquet, dated to the second half of the 8$^{th}$ century BCE, ate lamb or goat stew and drank a mixed fermented beverage. Visitors can access the tomb via a long narrow tunnel. Adjacent to the tomb a museum complex displays maps, city walls and foundations, an ancient mosaic and numerous statues all with explanatory signs. Particularly noteworthy is an ancient Celtic Galatian tomb on the museum grounds. Another nearby structure is believed to have been a temple where the Gordian Knot was kept.

The Gordian Knot of Phrygian Gordium often serves as a metaphor for an intractable problem solved by a bold stroke. Once upon a time during a period of political discord and confusion in Phrygia, an oracle predicted a poor man would ride into Gordium on an ox cart and become ruler. Shortly thereafter, a poor farmer named Gordias rode into town in an ox cart and, as a sign of divine approval, an eagle alighted on his cart. In response to this sign and to solve their political succession problems, the Phrygians chose him as king.

In gratitude King Gordias placed his cart in the temple of Cybele, the mother goddess, and tied the reins together in such an intricate knot that neither end was visible. Gordias was the father of Midas, who became king when he died. Long after Midas, the ancient ox-cart remained in place and the belief developed that whoever could successfully untie the knot would rule Asia. Alexander the Great heard the story and came to Gordium in 334 BCE at which time Phrygia had been reduced from a kingdom to a satrapy (province) within the Persian Empire. Alexander attempted to untie the knot but could not find the end needed to unbind it. Instead he took out his sword, severed the rope and solved the problem. Although Alexander went on to conquer Asia, some say he would have lived and ruled Asia longer had he patiently found a way to untie the knot without cutting it.

Archeologists from the University of Pennsylvania Penn Museum, formerly led by Professor Rodney Young and then Professor Mary Voigt have conducted excavations at Gordium as described at the excellent website:

http://sites.museum.upenn.edu/gordion/

The Museum of Anatolian Civilizations in Ankara provides information about Gordium in Turkish at:

http://www.anadolumedeniyetlerimuzesi.gov.tr/belge/1-54426/gordion-muzesi.html



**Pessinus** (39° 20′ 2″ N, 31° 35′ 3″ E), modern Ballıhisar, is 120 km SW of Ankara. The Archeological Center displays artifacts dating from the Phrygian and Roman eras at ancient Pessinus, a major cult center for the mother goddess Cybele. When the Galatians occupied Phrygia in 275 BCE Pessinus became a major trading center. After Hannibal successfully invaded Italy in 217 BCE during the second Punic War, the Romans decided a new form of divine intervention was needed. They consulted their Sibylline Books and the oracle at Delphi, and concluded that the foreign foe could only be defeated if the mother goddess Cybele were brought from Pessinus to Rome. Cybele had fallen from the sky as a stone, and the name Pessinus means, "castle where the fall has taken place." With the support of Attalus I of Pergamum, the leading Roman surrogate in Asia Minor, the Romans removed from Pessinus both the primary statue of Cybele and the black meteorite personifying her, and brought them to Rome. After they built a temple for her on Palatine hill and established a festival with athletic games in her honor, Hannibal was defeated.

Cybele, the Great Mother goddess, was first known during the 5$^{th}$ century BCE in Phrygia. Cybele represents universal motherhood, embodies the fertile Earth. She is the goddess of nature, presiding over caverns, mountains and wild animals, particularly lions and bees. Cybele often appears with a mural crown, seated on a throne accompanied by two lions. One day at Pessinus her lover Attis was just about to wed the daughter of the local king, when Cybele jealously appeared in her full glory. In shock Attis then castrated himself and bled to death. Cybele grieved for Attis and brought him back to life as a pine tree. Cybele and Attis were worshipped in emotional, and bloody fertility rituals

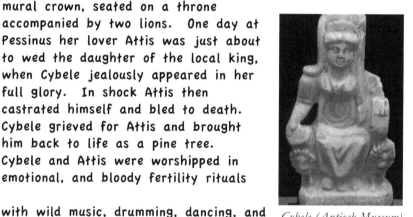

with wild music, drumming, dancing, and drinking, which included sacred

*Cybele (Antioch Museum)*

prostitution. The priests of Cybele, known as galli, followed the sacrifice of Attis and willingly castrated themselves upon entering her service, then wearing women's clothing and assuming female identities. Because most male Roman followers of Cybele were not prepared to make as extreme a sacrifice as her original priests, an alternative initiative rite was established. A candidate would enter a pit underneath a wooden floor where a bull would be sacrificed. Blood would run down and drench the initiate, thereby cleansing and reenergizing him – a practice Mithraism later adopted. The goddess Cybele was very popular with the Romans. Her worship spread throughout the Empire and continued until the 4th century. Cybele even plays an important role in Virgil's Aeneid, Rome's epic foundation story, when she provides Aeneas and his men with indestructible ships from her sacred trees. The tradition of decorating pine trees in memory of Attis was adopted by Christian competitors and is the origin of the Christmas tree ritual. Early Christians condemned the cult as demonic and the New Testament Book of Revelation refers to her as the "Mother of Harlots who rides the Beast."

In 133 BCE Attalus III of Pergamum bequeathed his kingdom, including Pessinus, to Rome. By 25 BCE Pessinus was a major Greek-Celtic trading city.

**Pessinus Site**: In 25-35 Emperor Tiberius built the Sebasteion (39° 19' 55" N, 31° 34' 52" E), a Corinthian temple dedicated to the imperial cult, which is still visible today. Archeologists discovered a small temple of Cybele (8 x 8 m) nearby in 1967. Next to the temple was a theater, which also served as the stairs leading to the temple.

*Theatre at Pessinus*

During the reign of Emperor Hadrian the theatre was repaired and embellished. Below the theatre a colonnaded agora was built at the time of Emperor Claudius. In 362 Emperor Julian, on his march from Constantinople to Antioch to confront the Persians, worshipped at the temple of Cybele in Pessinus. Although Emperor Julian tried to revitalize Cybele's declining cult, Christianity already had a strong hold in Phrygia at that time.

From the 1960s archeologists from the University of Ghent in Belgium, led by Professor John Devreker, have excavated at Pessinus: http://www.archaeology.ugent.be/pessinous/

In 2009 Professor Gocha Tsetskhladze of the University of

Melbourne in Australia began excavations at the site:
http://kristalflemming.wordpress.com/

**Hierapolis** (37° 55' 29" N, 29° 7' 30" E), modern Pamukkale, meaning cotton castle, is 22 km N of Denizli. Hierapolis is famous for natural hot springs and distinctive travertines, snow-like white terraces created over millennia from calcium bicarbonate minerals deposited by flowing water.

A sacred pool
B Museum-baths
C temple of Apollo
D church
E theatre
F Plutonium
G Domitian gate
H N Byzantine gate
I Philip Martyrium
J baths

*Hierapolis*

Hierapolis became part of the Pergamum kingdom after Romans and Pergamum defeated Antiochus the Great at the Battle of Magnesia in 190 BCE. Eumenes II of Pergamum established Hierapolis, meaning "sacred city," as a religious center honoring the local sun god Lairbenos, later identified with Apollo, as well as Apollo's mother Leto, a deity identified with the mother goddess Cybele. Hierapolis was ceded to Rome in 133 BCE along with the rest of the Pergamum Kingdom. Hierapolis grew from being a religious center into a cosmopolitan city with thousands of inhabitants, including a substantial Jewish community, as evidenced by numerous tomb inscriptions. This sizeable Jewish community facilitated the early spread of Christianity. St. Paul is believed to have founded the first

Christian Church at Hierapolis on his third missionary journey with Barnabas and Silas. Epaphras, one of Paul's companions mentioned in the New Testament, was an early Christian leader who supported Christian churches at Hierapolis, as well as at the nearby cities of Colossae and Laodicea. The Apostle Philip was also associated with the first Christian community at Ephesus, as was Papias, an early bishop and disciple of the Apostle John. The city was repeatedly damaged by earthquakes and rebuilt with Roman financial support. The city reached its greatest prosperity at the end of the $2^{nd}$ century under Emperor Septimius Severus and his son Emperor Caracalla.

**Hierapolis Site:** The ancient site is 200 m above the surrounding plain with hot springs and semi-circular pools in shelves along the upper third of the slope. Entering from the S visitors pass through the S Gate and proceed N to the center of Hierapolis. At the bath-gymnasium complex and the Sacred Pool visitors have a unique opportunity to swim in pleasantly warm water from hot springs amidst submerged ancient columns. To the W lie the travertine cliffs with a panoramic view of the valley. The $2^{nd}$ century Roman bath complex has a large courtyard at the entrance followed by an enclosed, rectangular palaestra (36 x 52 m). A large athletic gymnasium ran along the W side of the palaestra and led into the frigidarium and then the caldarium. The E Bath adjoining the main hall now houses the museum, which contains statuary and reliefs once used to decorate the theatre. One decorative frieze shows the coronation of Emperor Septimius Severus together with his wife, Julia Domna, and his two sons, Caracalla and Geta.

**Septimius Severus (Lucius Septimius Severus Augustus), founder of the Severan dynasty, reigned as Roman Emperor 193-211. He was born in 145 in Roman Africa at Leptis Magna into a wealthy, distinguished family of Italian Roman ancestry on his maternal side and Libyan-Punic ancestry on the paternal. Severus grew up in Leptus Magna, spoke the Punic language fluently and was educated in Latin and Greek. As a young man he advanced steadily through several imperial offices in Rome and elsewhere during the reigns of Marcus Aurelius and Commodus. In 187**

*Coronation of Septimius Severus with Nike above*

**Severus married Julia Domna, a member of a noble Syrian family descended from high priests of the local sun god Elagabal. In 193 Severus seized power after the death of Emperor Pertinax during the Year of the Five Emperors. However, the legions of Syria proclaimed his rival, Pescennius Niger, emperor. Severus moved E, defeated Niger at the Battle of Issus and devoted the following year to consolidating his position in the E. Then, in 197 at the Battle of Lugdunum in Gaul, Severus defeated another rival and secured full control over the Empire. At this point Severus launched a war against the Parthian Empire, sacked the Parthian capital at Ctesiphon, annexed the northern half of Mesopotamia and expanded the Empire's eastern frontier to the Tigris River. In 202-203 Severus campaigned in North Africa. He expanded and fortified the entire southern frontier of Roman Africa to ensure that desert nomads could no longer raid the territory with impunity and escape back to the Sahara. Then in 208 he traveled to Britain, strengthened Hadrian's Wall and attempted to conquer Caledonia (Scotland). By 210 the Roman campaign in Caledonia had achieved significant territorial gains, despite dogged guerrilla resistance from the local population and heavy Roman casualties. Then Severus became seriously ill and died at York (ancient Eboracum) early in 211, succeeded by his sons Caracalla and Geta.**

One relief at the Hierapolis museum depicts the Titanomachy. Several reliefs in the museum depict the life of Apollo, patron deity of the city, including his birth; a procession and sacrifice honoring his sister the goddess Artemis; the punishment of Niobe and her children by Artemis and Apollo; and the musical contest between

Marsyas and Apollo, followed by the punishment of Marsyas.

Marsyas the satyr discovered a flute Athena made and discarded, and became an expert flute player. He became so impressed with himself that he foolishly challenged Apollo to a musical contest. Although Marsayas won the first round, Apollo then turned his lyre upside down and played the same tune, which Marsayas could not do. Marsayas lost, was flayed alive, and hanged from a pine tree for having the hubris to challenge a god. Many nymphs, gods and goddesses mourned his death, and their tears created the Marsayas River in Phrygia, a tributary of the Meander River.

E of the Hierapolis museum are the remains of the 6th century cathedral built by Emperor Justinian with a semicircular apse, large central nave and two side aisles with a small chapel at the end, as well as a baptistery with a circular baptism font. A 4th century nymphaeum, adjacent to the swimming area and accessible from the street, was both a shrine to the nymphs, and a monumental fountain used to distribute water to city residences. This elaborately decorated U-shaped structure included a large basin and five niches decorated with statues.

*Temple of Apollo with entrance to Plutonium*

Also to the E of the museum is the temple of Apollo whose foundations date back to late Hellenistic times. The upper temple structure was reconstructed using recycled blocks from an older temple during the 3rd century, probably following an earthquake.

This temple (18 x 14 m) sits on a podium (2.5 m high) and was approached via a broad flight of steps. The well-preserved walls of a $3^{rd}$ century rectangular fountain in front of the temple were adorned with statues and columns and the lower terrace is surrounded with a Doric marble portico. The temple of Apollo was built over a cave called the Plutonium, a cavern of religious significance and the oldest cult center at Hierapolis. One of the theatre reliefs at the museum depicts Pluto's abduction of Persephone. In 1964 archeologists discovered on the S edge of the temple of Apollo the semi-circular marble Plutonium entrance, which leads to an underground cavern where carbon monoxide collects. Several ancient writers describe the Plutonium and how it functioned to awe ancient worshippers. Within the cavern fast flowing hot water released enough lethal carbon monoxide through a deep crack in the rock to kill any living thing. Pluto was believed to be responsible for sending this instant death. Ancient priests sold birds and small animals used as sacrifices to demonstrate Pluto's power as they died immediately when exposed to the carbon monoxide. These same priests learned how to avoid breathing the gas, descended into the Plutonium and then emerged unscathed, impressing visitors with their superior powers and divine protection. Not surprisingly, worshippers would pay well for advice from these divinely favored priests. During the $4^{th}$ century as Christianity suppressed older religions, the Plutonium was filled with stones. In 2009 archeologists uncovered a marble statue of Pluto, god of Tartarus, the underworld realm of the dead.

*Pluto*

**Pluto, also known as Hades (the unseen), ruled the dead in the underworld realm of Tartarus. He was the eldest son of the Cronus and**

Rhea making him, together with his younger brothers Zeus and Poseidon and his three sisters, Demeter, Hestia, and Hera, one of the six original Olympian gods. During the Titanomachy, the divine war for control of the universe, the three brothers obtained fantastic weapons to help win the war: Zeus the thunderbolt, Pluto the helmet of darkness, and Poseidon the trident. The night before the first battle, Pluto put on his helmet, became invisible, then went to the titan camp and destroyed all their weapons. This act had a major impact and the Olympian gods eventually emerged victorious. Although Zeus was proclaimed ultimate ruler, he and his brothers drew lots to decide who would rule which realm. Zeus got the sky, Poseidon got the seas, and Pluto received underworld Tartarus, an unseen realm where the dead go upon leaving the world. Later Pluto abducted his niece Persephone, Demeter's daughter, to serve as his wife and queen. Persephone was taken by force while picking flowers in the fields of Nysa. In fury, Demeter cursed the earth and caused great famine. One by one, the gods asked Demeter to relent before the human race perished, but she remained adamant that the earth would stay barren until she was reunited with her daughter. Finally, Zeus intervened and sent Hermes, the messenger god, to ask Pluto to relinquish Persephone. Pluto complied but only after Persephone had eaten a pomegranate, which bound her forever to Pluto and underworld Tartarus. A compromise was reached under which Persephone would spend the winter with her husband, and the rest of her time with her mother.

The Hierapolis theatre, up the hill E of the temple of Apollo, was first built in 60 during the reign of Emperor Vespasian, was rebuilt again in 129 when Emperor Hadrian visited, and finally renovated by Emperor Septimius Severus in 206. The theater had two entrance passages, each with statues in niches flanked by marble columns, and could seat 13,000. Hierapolis was built on a rectangular grid of streets with a long main street N of the Sacred Pool running NW-SE for more than one km from the Gate of Domitian to the S Byzantine gate. This main road (13 m wide), known as Frontinus Street, was colonnaded, and paved with large limestone blocks. At the city's N entrance the monumental Gate of Domitian still stands with a triple arch flanked by two round towers. An inscription in Latin and Greek originally stated that Julius Sextus Frontinus, Roman proconsul of Asia in 82-83, built the monument dedicated to Emperor Domitian. The erasure of this Greek and Latin dedication is an example of the *damnatio*

*Gate of Domitian*

*memoriae* procedure whereby the Roman Senate condemned Domitian and ordered his name removed. Nearby to the NW of the Domitian arch is the tomb of Flavius Zeuxis, a 1st century merchant who, according to an inscription, successfully sailed 72 times to Italy. The tomb has a Doric frieze ornamented with rosettes. In the late 4th century, a defensive wall built from scavenged materials enclosed the N, S and E sides of Hierapolis. The N Byzantine Gate stands at the point where Frontinus Street intersects this later-period wall. The S Byzantine

*House tomb*

Gate, a four-towered 5th century structure, was the city's S entrance. In the area between the main street and the mountain to the E are remains of the 2nd century agora (170 x 280 m).

The main necropolis at Hierapolis lies N of the city's walls and encompasses about 1200 limestone or marble tombs lying one km on either side of the main road beyond the Gate of Domitian. Most date from the late Hellenistic period, some from the Roman and early Christian periods. The tombs are of three principal types: tumuli, house-shaped tombs, and sarcophagi. The tumulus tombs are circular mounds with a small narrow, passage connecting to a round, vaulted chamber inside and are the oldest, dating back to the 2nd and 1st centuries BCE. House-shaped tombs have walls arranged on a raised square or rectangular temple-like structure. During the Roman imperial period, tombs were often constructed with gabled roofs and contained marble sarcophagi and decorative reliefs in which the occupant is sometimes depicted. Inscriptions often

*Tumulus Tomb*

name the deceased, and mention the profession and good works he or she performed while alive, as well as warning not to desecrate the tomb. Many inscriptions and symbols suggest the presence of a large Jewish community. For example, Tomb 148B is inscribed with a menorah, a lulav (palm branch) and a shofar (ram's horn) and belonged to a Jew named Marcus Aurelius Philoumeno Strenion. Further along the road a sarcophagus lid near a group of tumuli tombs is carved with a menorah and lion head inscribed to read "of the Jews." Another 2nd century tomb bears an inscription of the Aurelii family described as Ioudaioi (Jewish). During the 4th century, Christian inscriptions began to appear engraved with crosses and the Greek letters alpha and omega (first and last letters of the alphabet) representing Christ as the beginning and end of the world.

The martyrium of Philip the Apostle stands on top of a hill NE of the city where the Apostle was, according to tradition, martyred. This early 5th century building has a central 20 m diameter octagonal structure, originally under a lead plate dome set on a wooden frame but now open to the sky. The sides were covered with brick vaults interspersed with wooden roofs. The octagon was enclosed in a rectangular portico, consisting of 28 small

*Martyrium of Apostle Philip*

square rooms. The outer rooms connected to the octagonal area. Within the octagon were eight chapels, which led to four triangular courtyards in the corners of an outer rectangle. Four rectangular rooms were used as entrances to the church under arches marked with ancient crosses. All together the structure has a double cruciform shape. Although crosses and other Christian symbols were carved over the arches, no altar or burial site was found at the Martyrium, which suggests it was used primarily as a pilgrimage and procession site. After Christianity became the state religion and the 4th century Acts of Philip were published, the site of the saint's martyrdom became a major pilgrimage destination. Pilgrims approached along a great processional route up from the ruined temple of Apollo, stopping to purify themselves at a small bath complex, and then proceeding up a long stairway. After ascending the final flight of steps, pilgrims spent the night in the small square rooms of the octagonal martyrium before they entered the great octagon holding the relics of the Apostle Philip.

Archeologists have found religious mementos, which commemorated visits to the holy site. For example, a $6^{th}$ century bronze bread stamp, found at Hierapolis (now at the Virginia Museum of Fine Arts in Richmond) was used to mark loaves of bread during rites held in honor of the saint. The stamp depicts a full-length illustration of the Apostle Philip, identified as Hagios Philippos, standing on the monumental staircase between two churches. Italian archeologists recently discovered what they believe is the actual Apostle's tomb in a $5^{th}$ century church 40 m away from the martyrium. The ancient bread stamp suggests that the building on the right is the martyrium, and the one on the left is the $5^{th}$ century church built around the saint's tomb. The Apostle's grave may have been moved from the Martyrium to the new church during the $5^{th}$ century following an earthquake.

**Philip the Apostle, one of the original twelve, came from Bethsaida in Galilee and was originally a follower of John the Baptist. Philip convinced Bartholomew to follow Jesus and is mentioned at the feeding of the five thousand. During the last discourse Philip asked Jesus to show them the father, to which Jesus replied, "He that sees me sees the father." Philip preached the Gospel in Greece and then Phrygia. According to ancient tradition, Philip settled in Hierapolis with his daughters before the destruction of Jerusalem in 70 and was martyred in 80. Much of what is known about the Apostle Philip is based on a $4^{th}$ century text known as the Acts of Philip, considered apocryphal by many Christians and not included in the New Testament. The most complete version of the Acts of Philip was discovered in 1974 at the Xenophontos Monastery library at Mount Athos in Greece.**

While proselytizing in Greece, Philip went to Athens and three hundred Greek philosophers assembled to meet him. Philip told them the good news about Jesus and how he had commanded his twelve chosen disciples, filled with the Holy Spirit, to preach salvation. The assembled Greek philosophers knew this message was beyond the reach of their philosophy and, since Jesus and the Apostles were Jews, they decided to ask the Jewish High Priest in Jerusalem about Philip. Upon receiving a letter from the Greeks, the High Priest of Jerusalem, Ananias, was infuriated, consulted with the Pharisees, and then decided to go to Athens with five hundred devout Jewish supporters to confront Philip. After they arrived in Athens, Ananias and his entourage of five hundred joined the three hundred Greek philosophers to meet Philip. Ananias accused Philip of being a deceptive sorcerer, and explained to the Greeks that Jesus was a heretic who had violated Jewish religious law and was crucified as a result. Ananias claimed the disciples had stolen the body of Jesus and then falsely proclaimed that he had risen from the dead. Then Ananias further asserted he would drag Philip back to Jerusalem where the Jewish King Archelaus would put him to death. Ananias then reached out to seize Philip but miraculously his hand was paralyzed and he went blind, as did his entire entourage of five hundred. Then the heavens opened up, all the idols of Athens fell down, and Jesus appeared with lightning. His face was shining seven times more brightly than the sun. A powerful earthquake ensued and the frightened crowd begged Philip for mercy. Then Philip graciously gave Ananias back his sight, but still the high priest remained obstinate. The earth then swallowed up Ananias as far as his knees, but still he would not repent. Philip warned Ananias that he would sink further into the abyss if he remained adamant in unbelief. Philip now restored the sight of the five hundred Jews from

*Stairway to Martyrium*

Jerusalem who, together with the three hundred Greek philosophers, became Christian believers. Philip then brought a prominent young man back to life at the request of his father. Although the others became believers, Ananias obstinately remained committed to the religion of his ancestors and was finally swallowed up by the earth. Philip remained in Athens for two years, appointed a Christian bishop and then went on his way.

Later in life Philip settled in Hierapolis at the home of a Christian believer named Stachys, accompanied by the early Christians Mary Magdalene and Bartholomew. Philip preached the good news about Jesus to the multitudes and particularly condemned a popular snake worship cult at Hierapolis. One day Nicanora, wife of the Roman Proconsul (governor), heard the Apostle Philip and his teaching. Nicanora suffered from various diseases, particularly a serious eye infection. She went to the house of Stachys, became a believing Christian and was completely cured. However, Nicanora's husband, the Roman Proconsul, arrived at the house enraged that his wife had become a Christian. His men seized Apostle Philip, Bartholomew and Mary Magdalene, and dragged them before his court, where he ordered them to be beaten. Next their feet were tied and they were dragged through the streets to the gate of the popular serpent temple. A large crowd assembled, amazed at the patience and calm the Christians displayed as they were violently dragged along and mistreated. The Proconsul ordered his men to strip Mary Magdalene naked to humiliate her in front of the crowd. When the men started to strip Mary Magdalene, a cloud of fire appeared so no one could see her body and all fled from her. The angry Proconsul ordered Philip to be hanged upside down from iron hooks through his ankles and heels on a tree across from the serpent temple. Bartholomew was stretched out opposite Philip with his hands nailed to the wall of the temple gate. Then Apostle John arrived and forcefully condemned the ignorance of snake worshippers and the wrongful punishment of the Christians. The snake priests attempted to seize John but their hands immediately were paralyzed. Although John said to Philip, "Let us not render evil for evil" and Bartholomew and Mary Magdalene attempted to restrain him, Philip lost patience with his tormentors and cursed them in Hebrew. Suddenly an abyss opened in the earth, swallowing up the Proconsul, the viper temple, and the hostile crowd of about seven thousand. However, the Apostles, Stachys, the wife of the Proconsul, and a multitude of Christian believers remained unscathed. Jesus appeared to Philip and admonished him for being unmerciful, and for having cursed his enemies in wrath. As punishment for having done evil to those who did evil to him, Philip would have to remain outside of paradise for an extra forty days and nights after which time Archangel Michael would admit him. Then Jesus stretched out his hand, and marked a cross in the air, which became a ladder. All the people who had fallen into the abyss due to Philip's curse climbed up the ladder and were saved, except for the Proconsul. They attempted to rescue Philip, still hanging, but he told them not to release him, but rather to release Bartholomew and Mary Magdalene. After Philip died, Bartholomew and Mary Magdalene took down his body, buried it at the site, built a church in his honor and appointed Stachys bishop of Hierapolis.

In 1957 Professor Paulo Verzone of the University of Istanbul, began the work of the Italian Archaeological Mission at Hierapolis, later continued under Professor Francesco D'Andria:
http://www.archmuseum.org/Gallery/Photo_15_4_archeology4-hierapolis.html

Archeologists from the University of Oslo in Norway also participate in the Hierapolis excavations:
http://www.hf.uio.no/iakh/english/research/projects/hierapolis/

**Laodicea on the Lycus** (37° 50' 9" N, 29° 6' 37" E) was built on the river Lycus 10 km S and within sight of Hierapolis. Laodicea was founded as a Seleucid city in the mid $3^{rd}$ century BCE on a square-shaped strategic plateau rising 35 m above the Lycus valley floor along a major trade route. The Macedonian ruler of Syria, Antiochus II Theos, named the city in honor of his wife

Laodice. Pergamum gained control in 188 BCE, followed by Rome in 133 BCE. Laodicea, unlike most Greek-speaking cities in Asia Minor, refused to support Mithridates VI of Pontus against the Romans in 88-85 BCE. A prosperous Jewish colony existed well before the

A Syrian gate
B Hierapolis gate
C Aphrodisias gate
D church
E Ephesian gate
F Roman bridge
G nymphaeum
H theatre
I water tower
J stadium
K agora

*Laodicea*

Christian era. Cicero reports that in 62 BCE Roman governor Flaccus confiscated 20 pounds of gold from Laodicea bound for Jerusalem as an offering at the great Jewish Temple. The amount of the offering suggests a large Jewish population of at least 7,500 adult Jewish freemen, as well as many more women and children. The matter was resolved and an extant letter from the local authorities to a Roman magistrate confirms that the former would refrain from molesting the Jews in their religious

*Laodicea Main Street*

observances and customs, including sending donations to Jerusalem. Given the large Jewish community, Christianity came early to Laodicea. The city was one of the seven churches Apostle John mentioned in the <u>New Testament</u> Book of

Revelation, although he criticized its residents for being "lukewarm" in their Christian commitment. While St. Paul was preaching at Ephesus, Epaphras, an early Christian from nearby Colossae, is believed to have spread Christianity to Laodicea as well as Hierapolis. Following a devastating earthquake during the reign of Emperor Focas in 602-610 Laodicea was finally abandoned.

**Laodicea Site:** Visitors enter the site from the E near the Syrian gate. The main street runs through the city flanked with a colonnade and numerous pedestals with an underlying drainage system. The original city was built on a grid with four gates: the $1^{st}$ century Syrian gate to the E; the Hierapolis gate to the N; the Aphrodisias gate to the SW and the triple-arch Ephesian gate to the NW, which leads W to a Roman bridge across the Asopos River. Later, during the $4^{th}$ century the so-called Byzantine gates and walls, still visible on the E perimeter, were built closer in to defend a smaller city. Archaeologists discovered a 1500-year old cloth-dyeing factory on the E side of the city. To the N of the main street in the center of the plateau are remains of a $3^{rd}$ century monumental nymphaeum once decorated with a large statue of the goddess Isis. At the nymphaeum archeologists also discovered part of a column engraved with a menorah, a shofar (ram horn) and lulav (palm branch) and a cross above, confirming the presence of early Jewish and Christian communities. On the NE slope of the plateau are remains of two theatres not far apart with the ruins of a $5^{th}$ century church between them. The larger Greek-style theatre faces NE and has 15,000 seats, some engraved with the names of associations and leading families. The older, smaller theatre faces NW with seats for 8,000.

On the SW edge of the city are remains of an aqueduct, which brought water 8 km to a water tower (5 m high) on the S slope of the plateau. Nearby to the W is the large stadium (275 x 75 m) dedicated in 79 to Emperor Vespasian. It was used for athletic and gladiatorial contests and had capacity for 40,000 spectators, with another 15,000 on the adjacent hillside. NE of the well-preserved 1st century stadium (275 x 75 m) is the large, well-preserved bathhouse (133 x 75 m) dedicated in 124 to Emperor Hadrian and his wife Sabrina. Archeologists are carefully reconstructing and restoring ancient Laodicea. Although there is always a question of what time period reconstruction work should target given continuous modification over at least one thousand years, the authorities appear to conscientiously distinguish restored masonry from the original by using lighter colored masonry for the restoration.

The director of Laodicea archeological excavations is Professor Celal Şimşek of Pamukkale University: http://www.world-archaeology.com/features/laodicea/

**Seyitgazi** (39° 26' 41" N, 30° 41' 41" E), 43 km S of Eskişehir, contains the tomb of the 8th century Muslim Arab warrior Abdullah al-Battal (695-740). Al-Battal, known by the honorific Seyitgazi, died battling the late Romans nearby in 740 at the Battle of Akroinon. In 1208 his tomb was encompassed within an Islamic mosque complex. The Seyyid Battal Gazi shrine is a popular religious pilgrimage site where visitors can see the tomb as well as a later 13th century madrassa

*Tomb of al-Battal*

(religious school). Abdullah al-Battal is remembered as Sayyid Battal Ghazi, a folk hero of Arab and later Turkish epic poetry, further immortalized in a series of 20th century Turkish films. Al-Battal participated in the unsuccessful second Arab Siege of Constantinople in 718 and later was the Umayyad commander martyred at the Battle of Akroinon. His romanticized stories demonstrate the active role of Islam in Anatolia long before the

Turkish victory at the Battle of Manzikert in 1071.

The ancient Seyitgazi tomb and the early 13$^{th}$ century mosque complex is described on the ArchNet website:
http://archnet.org/library/sites/one-site.jsp?site_id=11441

**The Battle of Akroinon in 740 was a major turning point in relations between the late Roman Empire and the Umayyad Arab Caliphate. Following a disastrous defeat at the Battle of Sebastopolis in 692 in Cilicia, the Romans were reduced to a defensive strategy in confronting regular Arab raids from the S into Anatolia. Although the Arab siege of Constantinople in 717-718 failed, the Umayyad rulers conducted regular large-scale raids, plundering the countryside without making permanent conquests. In 737 after a major military victory over the Khazars in the Caucasus, the Umayyad Arabs focused their efforts against the Romans, capturing Ancyra in 739. Then in 740, Caliph Hisham launched the largest expedition of his reign with a massive force of 90,000 men. The Umayyad force was divided into three armies: 10,000 attacked the W coast of Asia Minor; 60,000 attacked the Christian settlements in Cappadocia; and 20,000 commanded by Abdullah al-Battal attacked Phrygia. Roman Emperor Leo III the Isaurian led his forces against the 20,000 Arabs invading Phrygia at the Battle of Akroinon and secured a decisive victory. Abdullah al-Battal was killed and most of his army destroyed, with fewer than 7,000 surviving. The other two Arab armies devastated the countryside but were unable to capture any major towns or fortresses. The invading Arabs suffered from severe hunger and deprivation, eventually withdrawing back to Syria. The Battle of Akroinon was a critical Roman victory and marked the last major Arab incursion for thirty years. From this time onward the Umayyad Caliphate was beset with internal problems and the beginning of the Abbasid revolt. Roman Emperor Leo interpreted his victory as divine vindication for his iconoclasm policy.**

# XII ANCIENT REGION OF BITHYNIA

Bithynia is a forested, mountainous region with fertile valleys, named after the Bithyni, an ancient tribe from Thrace. Bithynia borders the Sea of Marmara, the Bosphorus, and the Black Sea, as well as Paphlagonia to the E, Phrygia to the S, Galatia to the E, and Mysia to the SW. In 560 BCE Croesus, King of Lydia conquered Bithynia. Six years later Bithynia was incorporated into the Persian Empire, along with Lydia. In 334 BCE Alexander the Great occupied Bithynia and after his death in 323 BCE Macedonian general Antigonus I seized the province. Antigonus I founded Nicaea (now Iznik) in 316 BCE. A dynasty of Bithynian kings ruled from in the $3^{rd}$ -$1^{st}$ centuries BCE. During the reign of the last King of Bithynia, Nicomedes IV, Mithridates VI of Pontus became a major threat to regional stability. In 89 BCE the Bithynian army, together with two allied Roman legions, invaded Pontus but were decisively defeated. Mithridates drove Nicomedes IV out of power and in the following years slaughtered 80,000 Roman citizens in Anatolia. Eventually the Romans restored Nicomedes IV to power and he developed an unusually close relationship with young Julius Caesar. In 74 BCE on his deathbed Nicomedes bequeathed Bithynia to Rome, which triggered a third war with Mithridates VI. Pompey the Great took command of the Roman campaign against Mithridates in 67 BCE and five years later the defeated Mithridates was dead. The Romans ruled Bithynia together with Pontus as a combined province. Christianity developed early here. Apostle Peter addressed his first epistle (letter) to Bithynia. In 110-112, Pliny the

Younger served as governor and asked Emperor Trajan for guidance on how to deal with the new and peculiar religious sect know as Christians. Trajan advised leniency, a "don't ask, don't tell" policy that did not actively seek to ferret out Christians or act in response to anonymous accusations. People formally accused of practicing Christianity would be given the opportunity to repent and be pardoned if they made sacrifices to the traditional gods, punished only if they refused. Pliny followed these instructions regarding Christians, focused his efforts on effective financial management and infrastructure improvement and proved to be an effective administrator. Much later Emperor Diocletian, who ruled 284-305, established the seat of imperial government in Nicomedia largely as a military command center to fend off barbarian attacks from the N. Not much remains of ancient Nicomedia. The primary extant ancient site in Bithynia is **Nicaea**.

**Nicaea** (40° 25' 45" N, 29° 43' 13" E), modern Iznik, was the venue in 325 of the First Council of Nicaea, which was critically important in creating the early Christian church.

The First Council of Nicaea took place in 325 during the reign of the first Christian Emperor, Constantine I. The Council defined the concept of the Trinity, developed the Nicene Creed and settled a debate among early Christians about the divinity of Christ. In Alexandria the popular Christian preacher Arius had taken the position that Jesus was a figurative Son of God, like the other Biblical "sons of God," and was essentially a messenger from the one God. Arius claimed that the Son of God was a created being and could not be considered divine. The First Council of Nicaea rejected his position (by a vote of 250 to 2) and affirmed the divinity of Christ as the one true God together with the Father. Arius himself was highly unpopular with many leading bishops, such as St. Jacob of Nisbis, who prayed for his death, and St. Nicholas of Myra (Santa Claus) who struck Arius across the face during council proceedings. Arius died suddenly and painfully in 326 either struck down by divine intervention for his heresy, or poisoned by his opponents. This First Council of Nicaea established the transcendently important precedent that councils (synods) of Bishops could meet to define unity of belief for the community of Christian believers throughout the Roman Empire.

**Nicaea Site**: Ancient Nicaea was strategically situated on the E edge of Lake Ascania (now Lake Iznik), a body of water too large to besiege. The ancient city was surrounded with a wall built in the 3$^{rd}$-4$^{th}$ centuries, which remains largely intact. Three of the original four massive gates have survived: Istanbul Gate to the N; New City Gate to the S built by Emperor Claudius II Gothicus in 268-270; and Lefke Gate to the E. Roman governor Marcus Plancius Varus built the original Istanbul and Lefke gates during the reign of Emperor Vespasian in 69-79. After an earthquake in 120, Emperor Hadrian rebuilt both gates, and the Lefke Gate was rededicated to him in 123.

A Istanbul gate  C Lefke gate  E Hagia Sophia
B New City gate  D theatre

*Nicaea*

Beyond the Lefke Gate stands a 6$^{th}$ century Roman aqueduct. In 110-112 Roman governor Pliny the Younger, who resided at Nicaea, built the theatre, which still stands within the city wall to the SW with seats for 15,000 spectators. In the 6$^{th}$ century Emperor Justinian built a church here, the first Hagia Sophia, which was rebuilt in the 11$^{th}$ century and then converted into a mosque in 1331. This structure still stands in the center of town in a park. Visitors can still see an ancient floor mosaic from the original church, as well as ancient murals with the outlines of hallowed saints on the upper walls. In 787 the Second Council of Nicaea met in this church to confront the Iconoclastic Controversy, which caused massive destruction, civil conflict and death among early Christians. At this council the participating bishops determined that veneration of icons as holy images in Christian worship was not idolatry.

**The Iconoclastic Controversy** was a major 8th-9th century dispute among Christians over the use of religious images, known as icons. Iconoclasts rejected icon worship as violating the Ten Commandment prohibition on worshiping graven images, and viewed this as the reason Christians suffered defeats by Muslim armies. In 730 Emperor Leo III the Isaurian forbade the use of icons and ordered them removed from churches. Soldiers carried out his orders, provoking disturbances throughout the empire. Figurative images were banned and existing church icons were destroyed or plastered over. Leo's son and successor Constantine V (741–775) persecuted icon worshippers even more severely. Iconoclasts also applied this principle to relics, breaking open shrines and burning the bodies of saints buried in churches. Monasteries were destroyed, monks banished, tortured, or put to death. In 754 Constantine V summoned a synod to remove recalcitrant bishops and to confirm the widespread destruction. Churches now were only decorated with crosses, flowers, fruit, and birds. In 767 the emperor actively tried to abolish monasticism and murdered large numbers of rebellious monks. When Constantine died in 775, his son Leo IV continued his father's iconoclasm in a milder form. However, Leo IV's wife Empress Irene favored icons and, when Leo died in 780, she set about restoring pictures and relics to churches and reopening monasteries. In 787, Empress Irene convened the Seventh Ecumenical Council at Nicaea, which

*Nicaea Hagia Sophia*

formally condemned Iconoclasm and reinstated the use of images. Sadly, 27 years later the cycle of iconoclastic persecution repeated itself after a Bulgar army inflicted a major defeat on Emperor Michael I, who was forced to abdicate in favor of Leo V the Armenian, a rabid iconoclast. Again holy pictures were destroyed, their defenders fiercely persecuted. Two succeeding emperors continued this policy until Emperor Theophilus died in 842 and his wife Empress Theodora, an icon sympathizer, released imprisoned monks, and recalled exiled icon supporters. Theodora sponsored a synod, which confirmed the legitimacy of decisions reached at the Second Council of Nicaea in 787 and excommunicated the Iconoclasts. To this day each year in February on the first Sunday of Lent the Orthodox Christian church celebrates this 842 return of icons with the "Feast of Orthodoxy."

Professor Bedri Yalman of Uludağ University in Turkey excavated the Roman theatre at Nicaea as described on the website of the University of New England in Australia:
http://www.une.edu.au/cat/sites/izniktheatre.php

# XIII CONSTANTINOPLE

After successfully reuniting the Roman Empire, Emperor Constantine established a new imperial capital in 330 at the small Greek city of Byzantium with perhaps 35,000 inhabitants on the European side of the Bosphorus. He chose this strategic point because military headquarters needed to be closer to the frontiers to deal with the type of barbarian incursions commemorated with the $3^{rd}$ century **Monument of the Goths**. Constantine was determined to establish the New Rome as a ritual capital with approving crowds for whom he greatly expanded the **Hippodrome** where he erected the ancient **Serpentine Column** from Delphi. To honor the new capital he built the **Column of Constantine** and put in place the **Milion stone** to mark the origin point for imperial roads. Constantine built the **Great Palace** linked to the two basilica churches **Hagia Eirene** (Holy Peace) and **Hagia Sophia** (Holy Wisdom), as well as the no longer extant Church of the Apostles, designed as a final resting place for future emperors. During his reign the Hormisdas Palace, later known as the **Bucoleon Palace**, was built for a Persian prince. In the mid-$4^{th}$ century Emperor Theodosius I re-erected at the Hippodrome an ancient **Obelisk of Theodosius** taken from Luxor in Egypt. An enormous population increase to at least 300,000 by the mid-$4^{th}$ century necessitated construction of the **Valens aqueduct**. The strategically essential **Theodosian Walls** were built during the reign of Theodosius II, as was the **Walled Obelisk**. His successor, Emperor Marcian, is honored with the mid $5^{th}$ century **Column of Marcian**. The $7^{th}$ century **Church of St. Euphemia** was built from the remains of the $5^{th}$ century Antiochos palace near the Hippodrome. The Stoudios Monastery with its $4^{th}$ century **Church of John the Baptist** once played a major role in developing early Christian thought and monastic practice. By the 6th century the population had doubled again to at least 600,000, making Constantinople by far the largest city in the Christian world. At this time the aristocrat Anicia Juliana built the Church of **St. Polyectus**, which may have prompted Emperor Justinian to build the Church of Saints Sergius and Bacchus, now known as **Little Hagia Sophia Mosque**. Justinian also built the **Basilica Cistern** and completely rebuilt the **Hagia Sophia**. Although the **Eyüp Mosque** dates from the 15th century, it is the holiest Islamic shrine in Istanbul, built over the 8th century tomb of the last Companion of Mohammed.

Although Turks had long used the name "Istanbul," derived from the Greek phrase "istimbolin" meaning "to the city," it only became the sole legal name of the city in 1930. Although Kemal Ataturk named Ankara the capital in the early 20th century, Istanbul remains by far the country's largest and most important city. Modern Istanbul is a vast city of perhaps 13 million people with innumerable things to do and places to visit. This work describes and provides coordinates for more than twenty extant ancient sites within the city from before the year 800. When Mark Twain visited Constantinople in 1867 he stopped by sites tourists still frequent, such as the **Binbirdirek (Thousand and One Columns) Cistern** (41° 0' 27" N, 28° 58' 28" E); the 19th century marble mausoleum of Sultan Mahmoud II (41° 0' 30" N, 28° 58' 21" E), the 30th Ottoman Sultan who ruled 1785-1839; the Grand Bazaar (41° 0' 38" N, 28° 58' 5" E); and a Whirling Dervishes show. In his book he includes an amusing and clearly apocryphal description of a slave girl market, written as though it were the Chicago commodity exchange. Mark Twain's account is most striking in his lengthy and disparaging remarks about the **Hagia Sophia**, clearly the city's leading tourist attraction in his day as it is now.

The **Column of the Goths** (41° 0' 52" N, 28° 59' 8" E) is a 3rd century Roman victory column (18.5 m high) at the highest point in Gülhane Park, just N of Topkapi Palace. This monolithic granite pillar is crowned with a Corinthian capital decorated with a coat of arms depicting eagles. An almost invisible Latin inscription at the base states, "To Fortuna, who returns for victory over the Goths." The monument commemorates the victory of Emperor Claudius II Gothicus over the Heruli Goths in 269 at Naissus and precedes the founding of Constantinople. Two years earlier in 267 this tribe had sacked the city of Byzantium, as well as Athens and Sparta. According to ancient sources, a statue of Byzas, the eponymous city founder, once stood on this column.

**Byzas: When Zeus fell in love with Io he transformed her into a cow to protect her from the wrath of Hera. Io crossed the Bosphorus and then gave it the name "Bosphorus," which means cow-ford. Eventually she resumed her original form and gave birth to a daughter, Keroessa. When Keroessa grew up she caught the eye of Poseidon and the result was a son named Byzas. In the 7$^{th}$ century BCE Byzas was chosen to lead a group of Dorian Greek colonists from the city of Megara. Before settling out on his mission, Byzas consulted the oracle of Apollo at Delphi, who instructed him to settle opposite the "Land of the Blind." The colonists then landed where the Golden Horn meets the Bosphorus and flows into the Sea of Marmara, opposite Chalcedon. Byzas determined the Chalcedonians were blind not to recognize the advantages of the European shore of the Bosphorus over the Asiatic side and founded Byzantium.**


The **Column of Constantine** (41° 0′ 31″ N, 28° 58′ 16″ E), also known as Burnt Column or Çemberlitaş (stone with hoops), was dedicated on May 11, 330 in the center of the Roman forum, a large oval-shaped square on top of the second hill of the new capital. In 325-328 Constantine assembled this column using nine cylindrical, 3 m diameter blocks taken from the temple of Apollo in Rome. Constantine placed a statue of himself at the top, depicted as the sun god Helios clasping a javelin in one hand and a cross in the other. A hidden sanctuary at the base of the column reportedly contained early relics Constantine's mother St. Helena brought from the Holy Land such as: soil from tomb of Jesus, nails and fragments of the True Cross, the staff of Moses, the axe Noah used to build the ark, Mary Magdalene's flask of anointing oil, the menorah of Solomon, baskets from the loaves and fishes miracle, and a wooden statue of Athena from Troy, as well as the ancient protecting statue (palladium) of Rome. To strengthen the column, Theodosius I later encircled it with iron bands. In 1106 a powerful storm toppled the statue and the three upper cylinders. In the 12$^{th}$ century a huge cross was placed on top of the column, which was removed after the 1453 Muslim conquest. The Constantine column currently stands 35 m high and bears scorch marks from a 1779 fire, which destroyed the surrounding neighborhood.

**Constantine I the Great (Flavius Valerius Constantinus), born February 27, 280 in Moesia (now Serbia), was the first Roman emperor to profess Christianity. He was the son of Helena, an unmarried innkeeper's daughter, and Flavius Constantius, a senior Roman army officer. When Emperor Diocletian raised Constantius to the rank of Caesar in 293, as part of a Tetrarchy (rule of four) governing the empire, Constantius abandoned Helena to marry Theodora, daughter of Maximian, another Tetrarch. Young Constantine was sent to the care of Emperor Diocletian where he did well fighting as a soldier but witnessed severe persecution of Christians beginning in 303. After receiving advice from the oracle of Apollo at Didyma, Diocletian acted and 3,000 Christians were martyred, with many more tortured and imprisoned. Constantius apparently was more tolerant in his realm in Britain, Gaul and Iberia. When Emperor Diocletian voluntarily retired in 305, which was unprecedented, Constantius became one of four senior rulers of the empire and Constantine joined his father in Britain for a campaign against the Picts. In 306 Constantius died at Eboracum (York) and his troops proclaimed his son Constantine their new emperor. To strengthen his political legitimacy, Constantine abandoned his mistress, took their son Crispus, and married Maximian's daughter Fausta in 307.**

**By 311 four competing Roman tetrarchs remained: Constantine and Maxientus in the W, Licinius and Maximinus Daia in the E. In 312 Constantine boldly invaded Maxentius' Italian territories. Despite persecution, perhaps 20% of the empire's population had adopted Christianity by this time. On the night before a fateful**

battle with Maxentius at Milvian Bridge near Rome, Constantine had a dream, in which he saw the cross of Christ, shining above the sun. The following morning Constantine ordered his soldiers to paint the cross on their shields. Then Constantine decisively defeated the larger army of Maxentius, who drowned in the Tiber River together with thousands of his soldiers as they tried to escape. Constantine became ruler of the entire W Roman empire. To commemorate this battle, he erected a victory arch in Rome, built largely from earlier monuments, which associates Constantine with earlier Roman emperors and gods and notes he was inspired by the divine, but lacks Christian iconography. In 313 Constantine and Licinius, emperor of the E, met at Mediolanum (modern Milan) where Licinius married Constantine's sister Constantia and agreed to the Edict of Milan, which decreed religious toleration of Christians and restored their confiscated property. For at least a decade Constantine's coinage depicted the sun god Helios, known to the Romans as Sol Invictus (unconquered). In 321 Constantine decreed the day of the sun, "Sunday," as a Roman day of rest during which magistrates and urban people should rest and all workshops were closed. Imperial unity must have been a primary concern for Constantine and he may have sought to unite his subjects in worship of the one monotheistic sun god subsuming the Christian Father-God and other widely popular beliefs, such as Mithraism. Constantine released Christians from prisons and mines; abolished the penalty of crucifixion; outlawed gladiatorial contests; prohibited Jews from owning Christian slaves; built and adorned churches; and granted Christian clergy considerable fiscal privileges and judicial functions. Unsurprisingly, Christianity flourished as more and more ambitious courtiers converted to the favored faith. Over time, Constantine's relations deteriorated with Licinius, who had defeated his rival Maximinus Daia and resumed Christian persecution. In 324, civil war erupted and Constantine defeated Licinius at Hadrianopolis, while Constantine's son Crispus won a major naval victory against Licinius. Then Licinius fled across the Bosphorus, but Constantine and Crispus pursued and decisively defeated him at Chrysopolis. Licinius was executed in 325 and Constantine emerged as sole emperor of the Roman world.

In 325 Constantine convoked at Nicaea the First Ecumenical Council of the church to resolve Christian theological disputes. The Council condemned Arianism as heresy and adopted a unified Nicene Creed for all Christians. In 326, on suspicion of adultery or treason, Constantine executed his heir apparent, Crispus. Perhaps Constantine's wife Fausta, determined to secure the succession for her own three sons, accused Crispus of sexual assault. Perhaps after the execution Saint Helena, Constantine's mother, convinced the emperor that Fausta's accusation had been false. Not long afterwards, Constantine had his wife Fausta put to death. The following year, Saint Helena embarked on a pilgrimage to the Holy Land. In Jerusalem she discovered the wooden cross Jesus had been crucified on 300 years earlier and found his tomb, where Constantine built the Church of the Holy Sepulcher.

On May 11, 330 Constantine established Constantinople as the new imperial capital at a site more suited to the strategic needs of the empire than Rome. Constantinople remained the imperial capital for more than 1100 years. Constantine intended to be baptized as a Christian in the Jordan River, following the example of Jesus. However, he fell seriously ill in 337, and realized it was now or never. Ironically, an Arian bishop baptized Constantine shortly before he died on May 22, 337. Constantine was buried in the Church of the Holy Apostles in Constantinople surrounded with memorial steles for the Twelve Apostles, suggesting he was the thirteenth. His three Christian sons, Constantine II, Constantius II, and Constans, first engaged in a bloody purge of all family members seen as possible rulers; then divided up the empire and fought continuous civil wars until finally in 355 Julian the Apostate emerged as ruler from the carnage.

The **Milion** (41° 0' 29" N, 28° 58' 41" E) was an early 4th century tetrapylon, i.e., a square structure with four arches surmounted with a dome, which marked the starting point of all imperial roads. Emperor Constantine built the Milion for his new Rome modeled on the Milliarium Aureum Emperor Augustus built in Rome. Statues of Constantine and his mother, St. Helena, with a cross, stood looking E, with a statue of Tyche behind them. In the 6th century Justinian added a Sundial, and his successor Justin II added statues of his wife Sophia, his daughter Arabia and his niece Helena. During the first half of the 8th century, paintings of ecumenical councils adorned the structure, replaced with scenes from the Hippodrome during the Iconoclastic Age. After the

Muslim conquest in 1453, the structure remained intact for another 50 years, and then disappeared. During the 1960s the Milion foundations were rediscovered in the Cağaloğlu neighborhood, to the N of the Aya Sophia, close to the Basilica Cistern. Visitors today can see one long stone fragment of an original Milion arch.

The **Hippodrome** (41° 0′ 23″ N, 28° 58′ 33″ E) or horseracing track was a stadium, a place for popular assembly in ancient Constantinople. In modern Istanbul, the Sultanahmet Park follows the ground plan and dimensions of the Hippodrome. The course of the ancient Hippodrome is indicated with paving, although the actual track is buried 2 m below the surface. The park lies next to the Blue Mosque and Hagia Sophia. The first Hippodrome was built during the Hellenistic age when this was the provincial town Byzantium. In 324 Emperor Constantine greatly expanded the Hippodrome and adorned it with artwork from all over the Roman Empire. The Hippodrome was 117 m wide and 480 m long with 40 rows of seats for as many as 100,000 spectators. Although two and four-horse chariot races were the main events, entertainment included musicians, dancers, acrobats and animal trainers. Chariot races were run for seven laps around the central axis of the Hippodrome, and the emperor awarded the winner a laurel wreath and gold. Statues of successful charioteers, such as Porphyrius, lined the Hippodrome. As many as eight chariots, two chariots per team, competed in each race, with huge bets placed on the outcome. The four chariot racing teams, Blues, Greens, Reds, and Whites, attracted enormous popular support, particularly the first two. Blues were associated with the upper and middle classes, more orthodox in religion and politics, while the Greens were viewed as more egalitarian and radical. Rivalry between the Blue and Green factions often deteriorated into hooliganism and occasionally into civil strife. Fragments of the original Hippodrome survive, including ruins of the curved end of the U-shaped structure to the S of the park and three remaining ancient columns in the center of the Hippodrome. The Emperor's box once stood to the E of the track and could be accessed directly via a passage from the palace. Four magnificent bronze horses once adorned its roof but were stolen during the Fourth Crusade in 1204 when western Christians sacked the city. These bronze horses can now be seen on the W facade of St Mark's Basilica in Venice.

**Porphyrius, the most famous 6th century Roman charioteer, had seven statues erected in his honor by different teams at the Hippodrome. He was born in Africa (modern Libya) in 480 and grew up in Constantinople, where he began racing with while still very young. At this time chariot racing was at its height; charioteers were celebrities, super stars. Porphyrius was the only charioteer to twice within one day win the diversium, an event in which a charioteer first wins a race with one team, then switches and wins again with the team that previously lost. In 507 Porphyrius led an attack on the Jewish synagogue in the Antioch suburb of Daphne, plundered and set fire to it, and massacred many worshippers. Although the financial or religious motives for this attack remain obscure, he does not seem to have been punished. In 515 Porphyrius rallied the Green team to support Emperor Anastasius and was instrumental in suppressing a popular rebellion. He was still racing in his sixties, apparently retaining his flamboyance and popularity. The decorative bases of two of his seven Hippodrome statues survive and are on display at the Istanbul Archaeological Museum. Among the images preserved are: Porphyrius in his quadriga holding a palm branch; Nike, the goddess of victory; Tyche the goddess of fortune carrying a cornucopia and wearing a mural crown; the emperor watching the races; and team members dancing, playing the flute and waving banners.**

The **Walled Obelisk** or Orme Column (41° 0' 19" N, 28° 58' 29" E) is 32 m high and built from cut limestone blocks. Although originally built in the 5th or 6th century, in 944 Constantine VII extensively repaired and adorned it with gilded bronze plaques, which portrayed victories of his grandfather Emperor

Basileios I. A Greek inscription on the base states, "The four-sided column marvel of the uplifted, now Emperor Constantine and his son Romanos restored this now ruined glorious quadrangular monument to a state better than the original; the column was a wonder in Rhodes, this is now a wonder here." In 1204 during the disastrous Fourth Crusade the western Christians removed these bronze plaques and melted them down into coins.

The **Serpentine Column** (41° 0' 20" N, 28° 58' 30" E) or Yilanli Sutun was originally built to commemorate a Greek victory over invading Persian forces at the battle of Plataea in 479 BCE. Thirty-one Greek city-states melted captured bronze Persian weapons into a column made of three intertwined serpents with twenty-nine spirals whose open jaws supported a golden sacrificial tripod. It stood before the temple of Apollo at Delphi and had the names of all the cities involved in the war inscribed on its base. Emperor Constantine brought the serpentine column to the Hippodrome in 324. In 1700 the column collapsed and the three serpent heads were removed; one can be seen still be seen at the Istanbul Archeology Museum.

The **Obelisk of Theodosius** (41° 0' 21" N, 28° 58' 31" E) is the oldest monument at the Hippodrome, originally carved from red granite in 1490 BCE at the Karnak Temple at Luxor, in Upper Egypt. Egyptian Pharaoh Thutmose III is depicted offering a sacrifice to the sun god Amon-Ra. Each of the four obelisk faces contains a hieroglyphic inscription based on the Pharaoh's victories in 1450 BC: to the E "owner of the Upper and Lower Egypt, Pharaoh Thutmose III, conqueror of the all seas and rivers, built and erected this column in the 30$^{th}$ festival year of his empire"; to the W: "Thutmose III, son of the Sun who carries the crowns of Upper and Lower Egypt on his head, built this monument out of respect for his father the god Amon, to enlighten the universe with the strength and fortune granted by Horus"; to the S: "the owner of the favor of the god Horus, Emperor of Upper and Lower Egypt, and the son of the sun, Thutmose III went through Mesopotamia in front of his soldiers, and fought great battles at the Mediterranean"; and to the N: "after Thutmose demonstrated his respect to the god Amon-Ra, he successfully expanded his country's boundaries to Mesopotamia with the strength and the might granted by Horus." In 357 Emperor Constantius II ordered this obelisk and another similar one removed from Luxor and transported to Alexandria. The other obelisk was brought to Rome to celebrate 20 years of Constantius' reign, where it stands today as the famous Lateran obelisk, Rome's largest. In 360 Emperor Julian brought the second obelisk to Constantinople using a boat specifically built for the purpose. Although the Lateran obelisk is 30 m high, this obelisk is only 18.5 m high, probably truncated to facilitate transport. In 390 Emperor Theodosius I ordered this obelisk erected at the center of the Hippodrome next to the Serpents' Column. The obelisk stands 25.6 m tall on four bronze cubes over a marble base (6 m high) decorated with $4^{th}$ century reliefs. The white marble base depicts Emperor Theodosius I: to the N he is watching the obelisk being erected; to the S he watches chariot races with his family: to the E he holds a laurel leaf crown of victory and stands between his sons Arcadius and Honorius in front of spectators, musicians and dancers; and to the W barbarian Goths are kneeling before him offering tribute. The column bears the Latin inscription: "Once it was difficult to conquer me, but I was ordered to obey mild masters and to carry the subdued tyrants' palm. Everything cedes to Theodosius and his eternal descendants. Thus conquered I was tamed in thrice ten days. When Proculus was judge, I was erected to the skies." A Greek inscription states, "This column with four sides which lay on the earth, only the emperor Theodosius dared to lift again its burden; Proculus was invited to execute his order; and this great column stood up in 32 days." This 3500-year old obelisk has stood here for more than 1600 years.

The **Valens Aqueduct** (41° 0' 57" N, 28° 57' 20" E) was completed in 368 during the reign of Emperor Valens. Because Constantinople was built, like Rome, on seven hills, and arches were needed to carry water over valleys, particularly where the aqueduct spans the section between the third and the fourth hill near Istanbul University. The surviving aqueduct is about 920 m long reaching a maximum height of about 29 m with a constant slope of 1:1000. To meet the needs of the population, the water collection system expanded to 250 km with two aqueduct lines from the NE and one from the NW. Constantinople could store enough water in reservoirs and cisterns within its walls to withstand a prolonged siege (over one million cubic meters).

**Valens (Julius Valens Augustus) served as Roman emperor in the E 364-378. When Emperor Julian died in 363 fighting the Persians, Jovian, commander of his bodyguards, succeeded him. In a short and unimpressive reign, Emperor Jovian made a disastrous peace during his hasty retreat from Persia, restored Christian worship and then died from smoke inhalation near Ancyra. Emperor Valentinian I, a capable soldier, was chosen in 364 to succeed Jovian. Within a month of his succession, Valentinian appointed his younger brother Valens as co-emperor to rule the E. Valens was born in 328, also served in the army but lacked his older brother's extensive military experience. Although he was a Christian, Valens was an adamant Arian Christian who did not accept the Nicaean creed. The first challenge Valens faced was from Procopius, a distant relative of Emperors Julian and Constantine. While Valens was in Antioch, two military units in Constantinople proclaimed Procopius emperor, and Procopius cleverly played up his dynastic claims using the widow and daughter of deceased Emperor Constantius II. However, Valens managed to retain the loyalty of the bulk of the army and in 366 defeated and executed Procopius. Valens next waged war on the Goths, who had aided Procopius and were poised to invade Thrace. In 367 and again in 369 Valens led his army across the Danube River and successfully engaged and defeated various groups of Goths. Valens then turned E to face the Persians and attempted to reverse the territorial concessions of Jovian, particularly in Armenia. Valens supported the**

Armenian prince Pap after the Persians deposed and imprisoned his father. In 371 the Romans defeated a Persian army in Armenia, which led to a five-year truce while the Persians were forced to deal with problems on their other frontiers. The young Armenian King Pap turned out to be an unreliable ally, prompting Valens to arrange for his execution and replacement with another Armenian prince, Varazdat. In 375-377 Valens suppressed serious rebellions in Isauria and in Palestine. Valentinian I died in 375, succeeded in the W by his two sons: Valentinian II and Gratian. During this period large numbers of Goths pushed across the Danube, essentially ancient illegal immigrants driven by aggressive Huns further to the NE. The few Roman officials along the Danube exploited and mistreated the arriving Goths, but were soon overwhelmed by huge numbers of invaders. The Goths rebelled, ravaged the Balkans and broke down remaining Roman controls along the Danube border. Valens returned from the E with his army to confront the invaders and appealed to the co-emperors in the W for support. Although the Romans in the W agreed to help and another army was en route, Valens made the disastrous decision to attack the Goths before reinforcements arrived. With an army of about 15,000 he confronted the Goths at Adrianople in Thrace on August 9, 378. The result was a catastrophic defeat for the Romans, largely because the Goths had far more cavalry and used them effectively to divide the Roman force. Valens perished, his body was never found, and at least two-thirds of his Roman army was killed.


The **Theodosian Walls** (41° 0' 44" N, 28° 58' 34" E) of Constantinople have had a more profound effect on world history than any other known architectural structure. Constantinople developed one of the most complex and elaborate defensive systems ever built, which undoubtedly contributed to the decline of the Roman Empire in the W as numerous barbarian invaders from the N were deflected in that direction. In 324 Emperor Constantine began construction of a wall with towers at regular intervals 2.8 km W of the existing $3^{rd}$ century wall and extending along the coast. In 413 the regent for Emperor Theodosius II extended the walls of Constantine to cover new districts. These new walls were 15 m high, strengthened with double wall, 110 towers and trenches on the landward side. The wall started on the shores of the Sea of Marmara and extended 5 km up to the Golden Horn shore. Eventually the 6.5 km long triangular-shaped system of city walls came to be known as the Theodosian Walls. In 447 an earthquake severely damaged the walls, but the city enlisted 16,000 citizens in a massive effort to rebuild and they finished within two months, highly motivated by the steady advance of Attila and his Huns, who eventually arrived but were deflected W. The Theodosian walls (12 m high) were 5-6 m thick and made of solid limestone blocks augmented with a 2 m thick outer wall (8.5 m high). About 20 m further from the outer wall was a 20 m wide, 10 m deep moat with another defensive wall (1.5 m high) on the inner side. Along the walls were 96 towers 15–20 m tall placed at irregular intervals, depending on terrain. The Theodosian walls had nine main gates and many smaller posterns. Seaward walls enclosed the city on the sides of the Sea of Marmara and the gulf of the Golden Horn. A heavy chain supported by floating barrels was stretched across the mouth of the inlet as needed to block enemy access to the walls facing the Golden Horn. On the Marmara coast strong currents precluded enemy ships from approaching. When the city finally fell to Muslim besiegers on May 29, 1453, gunpowder siege cannons had rendered the fortifications more vulnerable and the defenders were desperately short of manpower. Many parts of the walls survive in modern Istanbul flanked with parkland.

**Theodosius II (Flavius Theodosius Junior Augustus), only son of Emperor Arcadius, served as Roman emperor in the E 408-450. When his father died in 408 Theodosius was seven and praetorian prefect Anthemius served as regent. In a peculiar agreement Emperor Arcadius had asked the Persian King Isdigerdes to ensure the succession of Theodosius by threatening war if anyone else took the throne. In part due to this guardian role, Rome and Persia remained at peace until Isdigerdes died in 421. With the accession of his son, Vararanes V, hostilities broke out, motivated in part by allegations of Persian persecution of Christians. A military stalemate resulted in a peace agreement, which remained in effect with one brief exception for the rest of the century. During the previous century, and even as recently as 408,**

Germanic or Hunic tribes repeatedly overran Thrace and threatened Constantinople. Although Theodosius' name is associated with the impregnable defensive wall around Constantinople, credit for this effective response should actually go to Anthemius who in 413 completed the indomitable circuit wall around the city and built a massive underground water supply. After 414, Theodosius' powerful older sister Pulcheria replaced Anthemius as regent. Pulcheria exercised enormous moral authority over her younger brother, educating him in statecraft and Christian morality. Pulcheria, in her brother's name, enacted strict laws against non-Christians, including Jews and heretics. During a visit to Syria in 428, Theodosius met the preacher Nestorius and appointed him Patriarch of Constantinople.

Pulcheria convoked an ecumenical council at Ephesus in the summer of 431, condemned Nestorius and his compromise doctrine that Jesus embodied two separate persons: one human, the other divine. The orthodox Nicaean creed was upheld; Nestorius was deposed and exiled; and Nestorianism was declared heresy. In an attempt to assist the Roman Empire in the W, Constantinople sent armies in 431 and again in 441 against the Vandals, who occupied most of Roman Africa. On both occasions, the Vandals were too strong for the imperial forces and could not be dislodged. However, the gravest threat to the empire's security came from the Huns, fierce steppe-dwelling nomads from Central Asia recently united by Rua and his nephew Attila. Under enormous military pressure, in perhaps 425 Constantinople began to pay protection money to the Huns, 350 pounds of gold each year. When Attila replaced his uncle, he successfully demanded twice as much tribute. After the Huns defeated imperial forces in 443, the annual tribute was raised to a staggering 2,100 pounds of gold, with an additional punitive payment of 6,000 pounds due immediately. In 448, Attila demanded even more and the emperor complied, a disastrous fiscal policy of abject appeasement. On July 28, 450, Theodosius II fell from his horse in a hunting accident and soon died, after purportedly naming the soldier Marcian his successor.

The **Column of Marcian** (41° 0' 56" N, 28° 57' 1" E), erected in 455 in honor of Emperor Marcian, is a two-piece red-grey granite structure with a Corinthian column on top of a quadrilateral base of white marble decorated with Christian Chi-Rhos on three sides and two female figures holding a globe. The Chi Rho is an early symbol for Christ formed by combining the first two Greek letters from the word Christ, chi (X) and rho (P). An inscription on the N side of the base reads, "Observe this statue of the prince Marcian and its base dedicated by the prefect Tatianus." This column, now in Fatih Square, has remained *in situ* for more than 1500 years.

**Marcian (Flavius Marcianus Augustus) served as Roman Emperor 450-457.** Marcian was born in 392 in Thrace, son of a soldier, and spent his early career in the E Roman army. He was sent to fight the Persian Sassanids in 421–422 as a unit commander, but fell seriously ill in Lycia and convalesced at Sidyma. Marcian recovered and went to Constantinople, where he became military assistant to the army commander-in-chief, Aspar. In 431-434 Marcian fought with Aspar against the Vandals in North Africa. At one point, he was captured and brought before Vandal King Geiseric. The Vandal king released Marcian after he took a solemn oath never again to take up arms against the Vandals. Marcian returned to Constantinople and, with the support of Aspar, first was promoted to captain of the guards and later to senator. In 450 while out hunting on horseback, Emperor Theodosius II fell from his horse, injured his spine, and died two days later from the injuries. With his death the imperial succession was thrown open to question because Theodosius had left no male heir. As a foreign-born German and Arian Christian, Aspar could never be emperor himself, but supported Marcian as his surrogate. Theodosius' sister, Pulcheria had been the eldest child of Emperor Arcadius and had long assisted her much younger brother Theodosius II to run the empire. Pulcheria, recognized as a saint by the Catholic and Eastern Orthodox Churches, was responsible for building numerous churches, hospitals, and houses for pilgrims. In 438 she brought the bones of St. John Chrysostom, who had died in exile, back to Constantinople to the church of the Apostles. Pulcheria also interred the relics of the Forty Martyrs of Sebaste at a church. Although Saint Pulcheria was in her sixties and had taken a religious vow of chastity, she agreed to marry Marcian on the condition that he respect her chastity and support religious orthodoxy. The Senate and the army supported this arrangement and on August 25, 450, Marcian became emperor.

Marcian's reign began with an immediate policy change toward Attila the Hun, the "scourge of god." Under Theodosius II, the E Romans had paid tribute to the Huns. Marcian ended this unpopular policy. Given the formidable defenses of Constantinople, Attila turned his attention W and ravaged Gaul in 451 and Italy in 452. Attila died suddenly in 453, supposedly of natural causes after a night of drunken revelry following his marriage to a beautiful young maiden. However, in The Night Attila Died: Solving the Murder of Attila the Hun, Michael Babcock develops a cogent case that Marcian was responsible. After a dream, Marcian reported that he saw Attila's bow broken before him; shortly thereafter Constantinople received word of Attila's death. Without Attila the empire of the Huns quickly disintegrated and a major threat disappeared. Marcian reformed imperial finances, reduced extravagance, shifted revenues from public spectacles to essential public works, and provided additional funds to communities hard-hit by earthquakes. Marcian and Pulcheria worked tirelessly to condemn Nestorius and the Monophysite doctrine. In 451 they assembled the fourth ecumenical Council of Chalcedon with 600 bishops in attendance, which rejected Monophysitism, the doctrine that Christ had one divine nature, and upheld the orthodox doctrine that Christ had two natures, divine and human. Instead of encouraging compromise and reconciliation, Marcian enforced the decrees of the Council and imposed heavy penalties on those who disputed them. This policy produced doctrinal uniformity in Constantinople, but could not be enforced successfully in Syria and Egypt. When Palestinian monks rose in revolt in 453, Marcian sent in soldiers to quell the insurrection. At about this time Marcian sent soldiers to Egypt to enforce orthodox views and install a like-minded archbishop of Alexandria. The Council at Chalcedon greatly exacerbated the theological split between E and W, which ultimately enabled Islam to triumph. Marcian died in early 457 and was buried in the church of the Holy Apostles together with Pulcheria.

The **Church of St. Euphemia** (41° 0' 27" N, 28° 58' 30" E) was built in the early 7th century and survives in ruins viewable through railings in a public park. In the early 5th century Antiochos, a courtier who served at the imperial court during the early reign of Emperor Theodosius II, built a palace NW of the Hippodrome. In 620 the original Church of St. Euphemia at Chalcedon was destroyed during a Sassanid Persian invasion and a hexagonal hall in the S section of the Antiochos palace was converted into the Church of St. Euphemia to house the saint's relics. On the SW wall of the church behind a protective glass frescos can be seen narrating the martyrdom of St. Euphemia and of the Forty Martyrs of Sebaste.

St. Euphemia was born in Chalcedon, across the Bosphorus from Byzantium in 290, daughter of the prominent senator Philophronos and his wife Theodosia. In 304, during the reign of Emperor Diocletian, the Roman governor Priscus required everyone to demonstrate their loyalty by making sacrifices to Ares, traditional god of war. Euphemia together with 48 other Christians went into hiding together, worshipping Jesus instead. Their hiding place was discovered and the Christians were brought before Priscus. The governor focused his attention on Euphemia, who was the youngest at age 15, intending to break her resistance first so the others would follow. Priscus separated her from the others, at first offering her material rewards. Then he ordered her tied to a huge wheel with sharp knives, which cut her body. The wheel suddenly refused to move and her wounds were miraculously healed. Next the governor ordered two soldiers, Victor and Sosthenes, to throw Euphemia into a red-hot oven. As the soldiers started to carry out the order, they saw two angels in the midst of the flames, became Christian believers on the spot, refused to carry out the order and, after declaring their faith, were promptly executed. Euphemia was then thrown into the red-hot oven by other soldiers, but miraculously emerged unharmed. Priscus ordered a pit dug and filled with upturned knives, but Euphemia miraculously walked over the pit and did not fall into it. After nineteen days Priscus sentenced her to be devoured by wild beasts at the circus, but none of the beasts set loose in the arena attacked her. Finally, once she had strengthened the resolve of her companions and served as an example for all the non-believers who would listen, one of the female bears in the arena came over and gave her a small wound on the leg, from which she died immediately on

March 16, 307. An earthquake occurred at the time of her martyrdom, enabling her parents to recover her body as the terrified soldiers and spectators ran away.

Eventually, following the triumph of Christianity, a fine Church of Saint Euphemia was built at the spot of her martyrdom. In 451 the Fourth Ecumenical Council of Chalcedon met in this church to resolve the Monophysite controversy. Among the 630 Christian bishops both Monophysite and Orthodox believers were represented and fairly evenly divided. After several meetings when no consensus could be reached, the Patriarch of Constantinople suggested they submit the decision to the Holy Spirit, acting via Saint Euphemia. Both parties wrote down their interpretation of the nature of Jesus and placed two documents in the tomb of the St. Euphemia. Emperor Marcian sealed the tomb and placed it under strict guard for three days, during which council participants fasted and prayed. Then the tomb was opened and the Orthodox document was in St. Euphemia's right hand while the Monophysite document was at her feet. The issue was thus resolved and the Monophysite position condemned. When the Persians threatened Chalcedon in 620, the relics of St. Euphemia were transferred to Constantinople and placed in her church along the Hippodrome. During the Iconoclast heresy, Emperor Zeno ordered her relics thrown into the sea, but they were recovered by two pious fishermen, Sergius and Sergonos, and taken to the island of Lemnos, until they were returned to Constantinople in 796.

The Forty Martyrs of Sebaste were Christian Roman soldiers serving in Armenia in the Legio XII Fulminata who were martyred in 320. Roman Emperor Licinius began actively persecuting Christians in the eastern empire after 316. His Roman prefect condemned forty openly Christian soldiers to be exposed naked in a frozen lake on a bitterly cold night, so that those who did not recant would freeze to death. Any who renounced Christianity would be forgiven and allowed to warm themselves in a hot bath prepared nearby. As the night went on, the resolve of one of the Christian soldiers weakened and he abandoned his companions and his faith, going to the hot bath. At that moment, one of the Roman guards at the lake experienced a miraculous vision, proclaimed himself a Christian, threw off his clothes and joined the thirty-nine freezing soldiers. At dawn the frozen bodies of the forty martyrs were burned and their remains cast into a river. However, other Christians managed to collect their remains as sacred relics and distributed them to other cities, founding many churches dedicated to the Forty Martyrs.

The **Church of John the Baptist** (40° 59' 46" N, 28° 55' 43" E), later known as the Imrahor Ilyas Bey Mosque, was built in 454-463 as part of the monastery founded by a Roman patrician named Stoudios. The Stoudios monastery was highly influential in developing the procedures and doctrine of early Christianity, with many of its monks suffering for their defense of icons during the iconoclasm controversy. In its 9th century heyday perhaps seven hundred monks lived here, translating and protecting documents and books, developing calligraphy, composing chants and religious poems and searching for spiritual salvation. The monastery contains the tomb of Kasım, son of Sultan Beyazıt, who was a guest visiting Constantinople when he contracted the plague in 1417 and reportedly converted to Christianity on his deathbed. After the Islamic conquest, the church was converted into the Imrahor (stable master) Ilyas Bey mosque. Although to this day impressive 13th century floor mosaics remain *in situ*, many architectural elements have been removed, such as an ancient limestone sarcophagus depicting the entrance of Jesus into Jerusalem, which is on display at the Istanbul Archeology Museum. The exterior of the church of John the Baptist is visible but entry requires permission from the museum.

John the Baptist led a baptism movement on the Jordan River, part of a long tradition of Hebrew prophets who lived austerely, challenged sinful rulers, called for repentance, and promised divine justice. John anticipated a messianic figure greater than himself and many of Jesus' early followers had been followers of John. The New Testament Gospel of Luke includes an account of the Archangel Gabriel foretelling Zachariah that he would have a son named John. According to Luke, Jesus and John the Baptist were relatives because their mothers were cousins. John recognized Jesus as the Messiah, and at Jesus' request, baptized him, an act marking the beginning of Jesus' ministry. As the New Testament relates, King of the Jews Herod Antipas had John imprisoned at Machaerus for denouncing his marriage, and then beheaded him. John the Baptist is known as Yahya in the Koran, a prophet of the righteous coming to confirm the word of God.

The **Church of St. Polyeuctus** (41° 0' 50" N, 28° 57' 11" E) was built 524-527 by Anicia Juliana, the descendant of several Roman emperors, and dedicated to Saint Polyeuctus. This church was the largest in Constantinople at the time and replaced an earlier church built by Juliana's great-grandmother Eudocia, wife of Emperor Theodosius II, which enshrined the saint's skull. Historical sources attest to an extraordinarily rich two-storey interior with colonnades, mosaics, galleries and marble sculptures and walls. The narthex contained a depiction of the baptism of Constantine. (The narthex is the entrance area of a church at the far end from the church altar, often separated from the rest of the church by a screen or rail. Its original purpose was to allow those not yet part of the congregation to hear the service.) The church introduced Sassanid Persian decorative elements, such as friezes of palm trees, pomegranates, lilies and peacocks in geometric patterns. Ten relief plaques bore images of Christ, the Virgin Mary and the Apostles. In a 76-line inscription in the church, Juliana compared herself to past emperors Constantine I and Theodosius II as a monumental builder, and stated that the proportions of the church were based on the ancient Jewish Temple of Solomon as specified in the Bible. It was a square basilica (52 x 52 m) with a central nave, two side aisles, with a narthex preceded with a long atrium. Foundations confirm the suggestion that this church introduced the use of a dome on top of a basilica. The magnificence of the building challenged peasant-born Emperor Justinian to undertake his massive reconstruction of the Hagia Sophia. The church survived until the 11$^{th}$ century and was built over during the Ottoman period. In the 1960s, archeologists from the Istanbul Archaeological Museum and the Dumbarton Oaks Institute rediscovered and excavated the site, directly across from the Istanbul City Hall. The scant ruins are now preserved for visitors in a small park.

Saint Polyeuctus was an early Christian martyr. Although Melitene, a major base for Roman troops in Armenia, was known for producing a great many martyrs, Polyeuctus was the first. He was a wealthy Roman army officer who served under the Emperor Decius and later Emperor Valerian. Polyeuctus led a virtuous life, but was a non-believer until he befriended Nearchos, a fellow-soldier and a Christian. When the anti-Christian persecution of Valerian began, Nearchos sadly told Polyeuctus they would soon be separated, that he would be taken away and tortured, and that Polyeuctus would renounce their friendship. Instead Polyeuctus told Nearchos that in a dream Jesus had taken away Polyeuctus' soiled military cloak and dressed him in a radiant garment. Polyeuctus announced he was now ready to serve the Lord Jesus Christ. Polyeuctus went to the city square and tore up an official edict requiring everyone to make sacrifices to traditional gods. Shortly thereafter, he encountered a procession carrying twelve idols through the streets of the city. Polyeuctus pulled down the idols and trampled them underfoot. His father-in-law, the Roman magistrate Felix, who was responsible for enforcing the imperial edict, was horrified at what Polyeuctus had done. Felix angrily announced that this action was punishable by death and told Polyeuctus to bid farewell to his wife and children. His wife Paulina and his children tearfully begged him to renounce Jesus for the sake of his loved ones, but he refused. Then the Roman authorities tortured him, but still he refused to repent. Even his father-in-law Felix wept, but Polyeuctus remained steadfast in his resolve. When he was formally sentenced to death, he responded with such cheerfulness and joy, and exhorted all to renounce the traditional gods with so much energy, that many others were drawn to Christianity. As a Roman citizen, he was to be beheaded – a merciful death. With joy he bent his head beneath the sword of the executioner and was baptized in his own blood on January 10, 259. Nearchos gathered his blood in a cloth, and afterwards wrote down the story of Polyeuctus. Christians buried Polyeuctus at Melitene, and later when Christianity triumphed during the reign of Constantine, churches were built in his honor at Melitene and later in Constantinople.

**Binbirdirek Cistern** (41° 0' 27" N, 28° 58' 28" E), also known as the 1001 Columns Cistern or Philoxenus Cistern, dates from 330. Senator Philoxenus built this cistern during the reign of Constantine I under the Antiochos palace. This 66 x 56 m cistern, second largest in the city after the Basilica Cistern, is now dry but has 224 columns in 16 rows. As a guide pointed out to Mark Twain in 1867, visitors can still see a 4th century cross on one of the columns.

The **Great Palace Mosaic Museum** (41° 0' 16" N, 28° 58' 36" E) at the lower part of the Sultanahmet Mosque contains many wall and floor mosaics often *in situ*. The Great Palace, on the SE end of the peninsula, was first built by Constantine in 330 and greatly expanded under Justinian after the Nike riots in 532. The palace was located between the Hippodrome and Hagia Sophia. Although it served as the imperial residence 330-1081, much was demolished under early Ottoman rule.

**The Church of Holy Peace** (41° 0' 35" N, 28° 58' 52" E), or Hagia Eirene, stands in the outer Topkapi Palace grounds. Although the exterior is visible, it only opens to the public for concerts. Constantine first built the church in the 4th century, then Justinian rebuilt after it burned down during the Nike riots in 532 and finally it was again rebuilt after a 7th century earthquake.

During the Iconoclastic period, a large mosaic cross was constructed in the dome above the narthex in place of the traditional image of Christ. In 381 the Second Ecumenical Council of Constantinople met here to confirm the Nicene Creed and condemn the Arianism doctrine. The 100 × 32 m church was enlarged in the 11$^{th}$–12$^{th}$ centuries.

**Little Hagia Sophia Mosque** (41° 0' 10" N, 28° 58' 19" E), formerly the Church of Saints Sergius and Bacchus, was built 527-536 near the Hippodrome and the Sea of Marmara. Emperor Justinian assigned the project to the mathematician Anthemius of Tralles and the geometrician Isidore of Miletus, future builders of the larger Hagia Sophia. This church pioneered the octagonal design later used on a much larger scale to build the Hagia Sophia. In front of the building stand an Ottoman era portico and courtyard containing a fountain and small garden. Small rooms surround the courtyard and were once dervish lodges, and are now book and artisan shops. The umbrella-shaped dome contains eight flat sections alternating with eight concave ones, supported with eight wide arches on eight wide pillars forming the octagon. Twenty-eight marble columns span the space between the pillars, some of which still bear the monogram of Justinian and Theodora. A late Roman era marble floor is preserved in the SE corner covered with glass. After 1504 the church was converted to a mosque and four minarets were added. The interior is decorated and furnished as a mosque, with Arabic calligraphy, and red, yellow and blue spirals, as well as tiny black flowers painted on white walls. A two-storey colonnade runs along the N, W, and S sides, and still bears the following inscription dedicated to the Emperor Justinian, Theodora, and Saint Sergius in Greek hexameters: "Other sovereigns have honored dead men whose labor was unprofitable, but our ruler Justinian, fostering piety, honors with a splendid abode the Servant of Christ, Begetter of all things, Sergius; whom not the burning breath of fire, nor the sword, nor any other constraint of torments disturbed; but who endured to be slain for the sake of Christ, the God, gaining by his blood heaven as his home. May he in all things guard the rule of the sleepless sovereign and increase the power of the God-crowned Theodora whose mind is adorned with piety, whose constant toil lies in unsparing efforts to nourish the destitute." The building is open to visitors, but remains a working mosque and visitors should dress appropriately.

**Sergius and Bacchus** were young, high-ranking Roman military officers stationed on the Syrian frontier at the beginning of the 4$^{th}$ century. They were renowned for their bravery and favorably known to Emperor Maximian, one of four rulers of the empire during Diocletian's Tetrarchy. While serving in the E, Sergius and Bacchus had secretly become Christians. During one of Maximian's visits in 303, Sergius and Bacchus attempted to avoid entering a Temple of Jupiter with their fellow officers, where they would be obliged to make offerings to Zeus. At this point their Christian faith was discovered and the outraged emperor demanded they recant. When they refused they were stripped of their military uniforms and paraded around town in heavy chains dressed in women's clothing. When they continued their refusal to renounce Christianity, they were severely tortured. Maximian then sent them to a prison in Resafa near the Euphrates River where an old friend of Sergius, Antiochus, was in command. Although Bacchus was beaten so severely that he died, Antiochus tried to reason with Sergius and explained that by renouncing the traditional gods he was putting everyone in jeopardy. Bacchus then appeared to Sergius as an angel wearing military garb and encouraged him to remain steadfast. The next day Sergius again refused to renounce his faith and was beheaded. With the advent of Christianity following the 4$^{th}$ century conversion of Constantine, the two soldiers were recognized as patron saints of the Roman armed forces. A shrine was built at their tombs in Resafa (in modern Syria), which was renamed Sergiopolis and became a major Christian pilgrimage site. During the reign of Emperor Anastasius in 517, the future Emperor Justinian was a young man accused of conspiring against the emperor on behalf of his uncle, and condemned to death. Saints Sergius and Bacchus then appeared to Emperor Anastasius in a dream and convinced him

Justinian was innocent and should be pardoned. Needless to say, when Justinian came to power in 527 he remained a strong devotee of the two saints, expanded the church at Resafa and built the Little Hagia Sophia Church in their honor.

The **Basilica Cistern** (41° 0' 29" N, 28° 58' 40" E), or Yerebatan sarayi (Sunken Palace), lies just 150 m SW of the Hagia Sophia, accessible via stairs down from a small building next to the tramline. Emperor Justinian built the cistern in 532 underneath the Stoa Basilica, a grand late Roman public square. The 70 m wide, 140 m long underground reservoir contains 336 columns taken from non-Christian temples, each 9 m high and arranged in 12 rows. The reservoir is surrounded with a 3.5 m firebrick wall coated with waterproof mortar and can hold 80,000 cubic m of water, which was distributed via pipes at different levels on the E wall. At the back of the Cistern a column with an upside down Medusa head and another Medusa head placed sideways symbolize the ancient triumph of Christianity. Walkways and lighting were installed in 1987.

**Justinian I (Flavius Anicius Justinianus), born in 483 into a Latin-speaking peasant family in Tauresium (modern Macedonia), served as Roman Emperor in Constantinople 527-565. From 521 Justinian assisted his uncle Emperor Justin I, an army-installed ruler, and then became emperor in his own right in 527. Justinian married Theodora in 523, a former dancing-girl and beautiful courtesan of humble origins who exercised enormous power as queen. Another influential figure was Belisarius, a former member of Justinian's bodyguard who became a highly talented general and married a close friend of Theodora. The ancient historian Procopius worked for Belisarius. Justinian sent Belisarius to confront Persian aggression along the Euphrates River and in 530 he won a major victory at Dara, near Nisbis, which lead to a peace treaty recognizing Roman suzerainty over the Christian Lazica (in modern day Georgia). In 532 the Nike (Victory) Revolt almost brought down Justinian. The incident began when Constantinople authorities arrested seven hooligans for murder, including both Green and Blue team chariot racing team supporters, and ordered them hanged. Two escaped, a Blue**

and a Green, and thousands of supporters of the normally rival teams came together during races at the Hippodrome to demand clemency. Justinian initially ignored these demands until the angry crowds rioted, shouting out "Nike," which prompted Justinian and his entourage to flee the Hippodrome. Over the next several days the city was engulfed in rioting and arson. Early on Sunday Justinian returned to the Hippodrome, repented and promised amnesty. Sensing weakness, the angry mob proclaimed as emperor a relative of a previous emperor. Justinian retreated and seriously considered fleeing, but Theodora adamantly insisted they stay and respond with force. Belisarius lead loyal troops into the Hippodrome, where his men slaughtered 35,000 unarmed rioters and restored order. Arson had destroyed much of central Constantinople, giving Justinian an opportunity to rebuild the city, particularly the Hagia Sophia, his most impressive lasting monument with its incredible pendentive dome. Hagia Sophia inspired construction of domed churches across the Roman world. Justinian also promulgated a major legal reform, the Body of Civil Law, which encompassed scattered decrees of previous emperors and formed a clear, well-organized imperial law code.

Justinian envisioned a restoration of the W Roman Empire, which had fallen fifty years earlier and was now ruled by independent Vandal and Goth kings. Tensions were exacerbated because these rulers were Arian Christians, which the Roman Church considered heretical. First, taking advantage of a Vandal succession dispute in 533, Justinian sent Belisarius with a fleet of about 500 vessels and 18,000 men to conquer N Africa. Belisarius defeated the Vandals near Carthage, took the Vandal king prisoner, conscripted 2,000 Vandals into the imperial army and reincorporated the Vandal kingdom into the empire, including N Africa, Sardinia, Corsica, and the Balearic Islands. In 535 Belisarius took on the Goths in Italy, conquering Sicily and then defeating a Gothic garrison at Naples. He marched on to Rome, where the Italians sympathized with the imperial forces rather than the ruling Goths, and occupied the city without a fight. The Goths mobilized larger forces and unsuccessfully besieged Rome for more than a year until 537, when a second general, Narses, arrived from Constantinople with reinforcements. The Goths in 540 were so hard pressed that in desperation they offered to proclaim Belisarius emperor. As a ruse to seize the Gothic capital at Ravenna, Belisarius accepted their offer, later revealing himself loyal to Justinian. In 540 the Persians took advantage of the Italian conflict to invade and loot Roman cities in Syria, Armenia, and Mesopotamia, including the major imperial city of Antioch. The Persians then invaded Lazica, but withdrew when Belisarius arrived with an army at the Persian frontier. After protracted military conflict in Armenia and Edessa, a temporary truce was agreed, followed in 561 with a more comprehensive peace treaty.

In 551, Justinian intervened in a Spanish dynastic dispute among Visigoths and obtained a portion of the Spanish coast. In Italy fighting continued until 562 when imperial forces decisively defeated the Goths and controlled the entire peninsula. Justinian's successes were undermined by Bubonic plague, carried by rats and fleas, which first struck Constantinople in 542, spread throughout the empire and returned to the capital again in 558. At one point the city of Constantinople may have lost half its population to plague within six months. Due to plague, the population of the empire in the year 600 is estimated at only 60% of what is was in 500. Plague halted economic growth and limited imperial military recruitment, while dispersed nomadic barbarians to the N were much less affected. In 559 a horde of Kotrigur Huns, joined by Bulgars and Slavs, broke through the frontier and threatened Constantinople. Belisarius was called out of retirement, mustered the civilian population and, together with 300 veterans, ambushed and defeated the barbarian horde. During Justinian's reign non-Christian "pagans" were persecuted, barred from government and teaching jobs and threatened with loss of property. It was a capital crime for baptized Christians to return to "paganism" or to secretly worship traditional gods. Judaism remained legal although fanatical local Christian clergy could be problematic. However, the Samaritans, who considered themselves descendants of the Israelite tribes and constituted a large part of the population in Palestine near Mt. Gerizim, suffered when Justinian enacted rules to demolish their synagogues and prevent them from bequeathing property to non-Christians. The Samaritans revolted in 529, but their uprising was crushed, their leader beheaded and 20,000 Samaritans were sold into slavery. In 556, the Samaritans again rebelled with some Jewish support, but were mercilessly suppressed. The most serious and intractable theological challenge Justinian faced was the Monophysite schism. Monophysite Christians predominated S and E of the Taurus Mountains in Georgia, Armenia, Syria and Egypt. During her wayward youth Theodora, while in Egypt, became a committed Monophysite. Until her death in 548, Monophysites believed they had a champion in Constantinople and remained loyal to the empire. Theodora promoted Jacob Baradaeus of Edessa as a roving Monophysite bishop; he consecrated 27 bishops and an estimated 100,000 clergy. When Justinian died in 565, a separate Monophysite Christian hierarchy existed and the prospect for reconciliation was lost. Although Justinian succeeded in reestablishing imperial control over perhaps half of the W Roman Empire, plague and the high cost of these conquests made them unsustainable and most were lost within a generation.

**Bucoleon Palace** (41° 0′ 12″ N, 28° 58′ 28″ E) is a ruin near the shore of Marmara Sea, formerly known as Hormisdas after Hormizd, third son of Sassanid Persian King Hormizd II and brother-in-law of King Shapur II. In 323 Hormizd escaped from prison in Persia and made his way to Constantinople, where Emperor Constantine I accepted his services and gave him a palace on the shore of the Sea of Marmara. In 363, Hormizd served with Emperor Julian in war against Persia, and his son later served as a Roman proconsul. The palace, rebuilt in the 5$^{th}$ century, was the residence of Justinian before he became emperor and is near the site where chose to build the Little Hagia Sophia. Later queen Theodora used the Bucoleon Palace to house and to protect her favored clergy during the Monophysite controversy and even extracted a promise from Justinian on her deathbed that they be allowed to remain unmolested, which was granted. Only fragments of this 5$^{th}$ century structure remain, including one wall with three windows.

**Monophysite controversy:** A fundamental cause of the ultimate Islamic victory in the E territory of the Roman Empire about a century after Justinian was Christian disunity. Since the 4$^{th}$ century rule of Emperor Constantine the imperial church had sought to establish uniform Christian doctrine.  Under Emperor Marcian in 451 Christian bishops met at the Council of Chalcedon and determined Christ had two natures united in one person.  Monophysites rejected this determination and believed Christ had one nature composed of both divine and human elements.  While Christological dispute may seem absurd to a modern reader, this Monophysite schism had an enormous historical impact.  Christians in Armenia, Syria, and Egypt were committed Monophysites and, as a result, were subjected to sustained and brutal persecution from the mainstream church and various emperors in Constantinople.  During the reign of Justinian a separate Monophysite Christian hierarchy came into being.  Continuous theological conflict severely weakened any lingering loyalty Christians in the E felt toward Constantinople.  With the advent of $7^{th}$ century Islam, Christians in Egypt, Syria, and Armenia came to prefer rule by the Muslim Caliph to persecution by fellow Christians in Constantinople.


The **Hagia Sophia** (41° 0′ 31″ N, 28° 58′ 48″ E) or Church of Holy Wisdom is the most outstanding ancient monument in Istanbul, dating back to the $6^{th}$ century.  Mark Twain famously describes Hagia Sophia as "the rustiest old barn in heathendom" and says, "all the interest that attaches to it comes from the fact that it was built for a Christian church and then turned into a mosque, without much alteration, by the Mohammedan conquerors."  He even complains that, "they made me take off my boots."  Hagia Sophia is "unsightly enough" and the "dirt is more wonderful than the dome, though they never mention it."  The "hundred and seventy pillars" taken from ancient temples are "battered, ugly and repulsive" and "were a thousand years old when this church was new" so "the contrast must have been ghastly."  Inside the dome a "monstrous inscription" looks "as glaring as a circus bill" with "battered and dirty" marble balustrades and a perspective marred by "a web of ropes" and "countless dingy, coarse oil lamps."  On the floor of the mosque, "squatting or sitting in groups" were "ragged Turks reading books, hearing sermons or receiving lessons like children."  He notes "more of the same sort of bowing and straightening up, bowing again and getting down to kiss the earth, muttering prayers the while, and keeping up their gymnastics till they ought to have been tired" and "everywhere was dirt, and dust, and dinginess and gloom." Twain asserts there was "nothing touching or beautiful about it" and "people who go into ecstasies about St. Sophia must surely get them out of a guidebook." In retrospect, it is difficult to say whether this refreshing perspective is a reaction to what he regarded as ignorant blind faith, or simply Twain's contrarian response to glowing contemporary guidebook descriptions. In the 19$^{th}$ century non-Muslims were, in theory, required to obtain a "firman" (permit) from the Ottoman authorities, which Twain sarcastically reports could be handled for a small bribe. The Christian mosaics the modern tourist sees were only uncovered after Kemal Ataturk transformed the mosque into a museum in 1935 and would have been plastered over at the time of Twain's visit. Conditions are different now that Hagia Sophia is a museum, not a house of prayer, and Christian and Muslim symbols stand side by side.

Before Emperor Justinian built Hagia Sophia in 537, two earlier churches at this site were burned down during periods of political turbulence: the first when Emperor Arcadius exiled the popular Patriarch John Chrysostom in 404, the second in the Nike revolt against Emperor Justinian in 532. Marble blocks from the main entrance of the second church survive, including reliefs depicting twelve lambs symbolizing the twelve apostles. Procopius describes in his book Of the Buildings of Justinian how shortly after the Nike revolt was suppressed, Justinian planned to build a larger and more majestic church. He assigned the task to mathematician-physicist Anthemius of Tralles and professor of geometry and mechanics Isidore of Miletus, after they had proven their ability building the Church of Saints Sergius and Bacchus. They brought building material from all over the empire: columns from the temple of Artemis at Ephesus and the temples of Baalbek (in modern Lebanon), porphyritic rock from Egypt, green marble from Thessaly, black stone from the Bosphorus, and yellow stone from Syria. Ten thousand people worked on the project for five years.

**Procopius of Caesarea (500– 565) was a prominent late Roman historian from Palestine who wrote: the Wars of Justinian, the Buildings of Justinian and his incredible Secret History. He is a primary historical source for the reign of the Emperor Justinian. His Buildings of Justinian describes and celebrates Justinian's extensive building program, particularly the churches, fortifications and water supply system. The infamous Secret History covers the same years as the History of Justinian's Wars and was clearly written secretly and meant for posterity. The scathingly critical Secret History expresses deep disillusionment with Justinian, as cruel and venal; Theodora, as lustful and mean-spirited; and Belisarius, as misguided. The Secret History only came to light in 1623 when it was discovered in the Vatican Library, and was the source for much of Robert Graves' excellent book Belisarius.**

On December 27, 537 Justinian inaugurated the Hagia Sophia Church, famously exclaiming "Oh Solomon! I have outdone you!" The enormous building, which remained the largest cathedral in the world for a thousand years, contained a large central nave and two side aisles, separated by columns, apse, inner and outer narthex. The most impressive feature is the 31 m wide dome above the square nave, an architectural marvel floating above 40 arched windows admitting natural light over 30 million gold colored tesserae, or mosaic tiles, covering the dome interior. Four massive pendentives, inverted triangular forms, transfer and distribute weight in an aesthetic transition from the round dome to the walls of the square nave and massive piers below. The pendentive form was first fully realized at Hagia Sophia and had a major impact on subsequent architecture. Earthquakes in 553, 557 and 558 first cracked and then caused the main dome to collapse. Justinian chose Isodorus the Younger to rebuild the dome. Isodorus used lighter materials, hollow bricks from Rhodes, and raised the dome 6.25 m into a stronger more elliptical form to reach its current height of 55.6 m. In 1346 supports were added and the structure was further buttressed during the Ottoman period. A horseshoe-shaped upper gallery, reached via ramps, encloses the nave as far as the apse and was traditionally reserved for the empress and her court. A round, green stone in the center of the upper gallery marks the spot where the throne of the empress once stood. In a side aisle to the NE of the imperial door is a brass-clad pillar containing the relics of St. Gregory the Miracle-Worker. If worshipers place their fingers in a designated hole in the pillar and they become moist, they will be cured of ailments.

Saint Gregory the Wonderworker was born in 210 into a prominent non-Christian family in Neocaesarea (modern Niskar) in the Pontus region of N Asia Minor. Originally named Theodore, he studied law and traditional Greek and Roman classics at Neocaesarea. In 233 Theodore and his brother accompanied their sister to Palestine where her husband had been appointed assessor, i.e., legal counsel, to the Roman Governor at Caesarea. Theodore and his brother intended to continue on to study at the leading ancient law school in Beirut. Instead, Theodore encountered Origen, an early Christian theologian, and studied philosophy for several years in Caesarea. Origen was a popular teacher of dialectics, physics, and ethics, who approached Christianity from a theoretical perspective compatible with Hellenistic thought. Theodore gradually converted to Christianity and adopted the name Gregory as part of a new Christian identity. Gregory returned to Neocaesarea in 238, intending to practice law, but instead the seventeen local Christians elected him bishop of the city. He became an eloquent, persuasive preacher. Although his training was in abstract theology, Gregory was concerned with practical applications of Christian faith and made many converts. He had tremendous healing power with his touch, which often cured patients and led them to convert. Gregory was so renowned for miraculous powers that he became known as Gregory Thaumaturgus, or wonderworker. During construction of a church for his growing congregation, work was stopped when the builders encountered a huge buried boulder. Gregory miraculously moved the rock aside to make room for the church foundation. On one occasion two brothers in Gregory's congregation disputed an inheritance of land with a large lake and resolved to settle the matter by force. The night before their fight, Gregory prayed for a peaceful solution. During the night the lake dried up, leaving easily divisible dry land and a compromise was reached. On another occasion Gregory acted to restrain the Lycus River, which had often overflowed its banks and destroyed surrounding communities. Gregory planted his staff in the ground at a point near the riverbank and prayed that the river would never again rise past that point. The staff took root, grew into a large tree, and the river never again flooded above the tree. Another time two local men heard of Gregory's generosity and decided to con the bishop. One lay along the road where Gregory was walking and pretended to be dead while the other begged Gregory for money to bury his friend. Gregory had no money but threw his cloak over the prostrate man and told the other to sell the cloak to cover the burial costs. After Gregory left, the conman found that his friend was actually dead.

In 250 when Emperor Decius actively persecuted Christians, Gregory and his congregation fled into remote mountain areas to escape the authorities. An informer told the Roman soldiers where Gregory and his followers were hiding. As their pursuers approached Gregory told the Christians to pray and remain completely still; the soldiers saw only trees where the Christians were standing and passed right by. The amazed informer repented his ways and also became a fervent Christian. During this period plague struck the region and then Goths invaded and sacked Neocaesarea. As soon as the persecution ended, Gregory returned and devoted all his efforts to assisting the suffering population. At this stage of history numerous divergent and contradictory Christian beliefs existed, particularly concerning the Holy Trinity. Gregory had the first recorded vision of the Virgin Mary when she and <u>John the Baptist</u> appeared to him and motivated his principal work, <u>The Exposition of Faith</u>, a statement of doctrine on the Trinity which was used at the 264 synod of Antioch to condemn rival Christian interpretations. Gregory was the first bishop to organize feast days to honor particular martyrs, which he used as a way of attracting non-Christians accustomed to religious ceremonies accompanied by large feasts. At the time of his death from natural causes in 270 he had converted to Christianity all but seventeen inhabitants of Neocaesarea. In the 6$^{th}$ century the Hagia Sophia contained his relics, although some were reportedly taken to Calabria in Italy.

After Kemal Ataturk transformed Hagia Sophia into a museum in 1935, several original mosaics, which had been plastered over during the Ottoman period, were uncovered. However, due to religious sensitivity and the importance of early Islamic calligraphy, the mosaic restoration process has been largely confined to the upper gallery. Many of the earliest mosaics were altered or destroyed during the 726–843 Iconoclastic period. Extant Hagia Sophia mosaics date from the 9$^{th}$ century or later although some reproduce earlier work. For the sake of completeness, these mosaics are identified below. Located above the Imperial Gate is a late 9$^{th}$ century mosaic of Leo VI the Wise bowing down before Jesus, who is seated on a jeweled throne, giving His blessing and holding an open book in His left hand. The text on the book reads, "Peace be with you; I am the light of the world." To the left is the Archangel Gabriel, holding a staff, and to the right the Virgin Mary. Above the SW entrance is a famous 10$^{th}$ century mosaic of the Virgin Mary and Child Jesus flanked by Emperors Justinian and Constantine. The Virgin sits on a throne with her feet resting on a pedestal embellished with precious stones, while Jesus sits on her lap, giving a blessing and holding a scroll. To the left stands emperor Constantine presenting her a model of the city with the inscription, "Great Emperor Constantine of the Saints." To the right stands Emperor Justinian presenting a model of the Hagia Sophia. At the E end up on the half dome of the apse is a mosaic of the Virgin Mother and Child inaugurated in 867, a reconstruction of a 6th century mosaic destroyed during the iconoclastic era. Archangels Gabriel and Michael (largely destroyed) flank the Virgin.

Archangel Gabriel plays an important role in Judaism, Christianity and Islam. He is God's messenger, first mentioned in the Book of Daniel in the Old Testament, where he appears as a man to assist Daniel to understand his visions. In the New Testament book of Luke, Gabriel appears to the parents of John the Baptist and foretells the birth of a son. Later

Gabriel appears to the Virgin Mary, tells her she is blessed by God and will conceive a son to be called Jesus. Muslims share the belief that Gabriel informed the Virgin Mary she would give birth to Jesus. In Islam, Gabriel appears as the heavenly angel by whom God reveals the Koran to Mohammed. Gabriel is the angel who accompanied Mohammed on his night ride to Heaven.

Archangel Michael appears repeatedly in Jewish, Christian and Muslim belief. He commands the armies of God, responsible for vanquishing evil in heaven and on earth. In the Book of Daniel in the <u>Old Testament</u> Michael is identified as protector of Israel. The <u>New Testament</u> states that Michael and his followers defeated Satan in a great war, and expelled him from heaven. Michael stopped Abraham from sacrificing his son Isaac on Mount Moriah. In Islam Michael was so shocked by the sight of hell when it was created that he never laughed again. Michael helped the Muslims win their first significant military victory in Arabia in 624. He dwells in the seventh heaven, and has wings of beautiful emerald green. He is an angel of good, bringing peace and prosperity to mankind. Michael is works together with Archangel Gabriel, as when he purified Mohammed's heart before his night journey to Heaven.

On the second floor of Hagia Sophia in a dark corner of the ceiling is a mosaic depicting Emperor Alexander holding a scroll in his right hand and a globus cruciger (globe with a cross on top symbolizing Christ's majesty of the world) in his left hand. On the E wall of the S gallery is the 11$^{th}$ century Empress Zoe mosaic. Jesus, clad in the dark blue robe, is seated in the middle of a golden background, giving his blessing with the right hand and holding the <u>Bible</u> in his left hand. To the left Constantine IX Monomachus offers a purse as symbol of donations made to the church; to the right Empress Zoe holds a scroll, also to symbolize donations. The emperor's head was scraped off and replaced, because it first depicted Zoe's previous husband. On the E wall of the S gallery is the 1122 Comnenus mosaic. The Virgin Mary stands in the middle in a dark blue gown holding Jesus on her lap. He gives a blessing with his right hand while holding a scroll in his left hand.  To the left stands emperor John II Comnenus holding a purse as a symbol of imperial donations.  To the right stands the blonde Empress Irene offering a document.  Their youthful eldest son Alexius Comnenus stands nearby.  In the imperial enclosure of the upper galleries the third panel holds the 1261 Deësis mosaic, which marked the end of 57 years of Roman Catholic control of Hagia Sophia.  The Virgin Mary and John the Baptist both seem to implore Jesus to show mercy to humanity on Judgment Day.  Above the upper gallery below two rows of windows high up on the N tympanum are mosaics of St. John Chrysostom and St. Ignatius the Younger standing, clothed in white robes with crosses, blessing with their right hands and holding richly jeweled bibles in their left hands.

Saint John Chrysostom was born in 347 in Antioch, son of a high-ranking military officer, and raised by his widowed Christian mother.  John first studied law and theology, eventually giving up this profession to become a hermit-monk, then a priest.  John became known as a great preacher, deeply concerned with the spiritual and temporal welfare of the needy and oppressed.  The zeal and clarity of his preaching strongly appealed to the common people and earned him his title "Chrysostom" meaning golden-mouthed.  In 398 Chrysostom was named patriarch of Constantinople, a position the Second Ecumenical Council of 359 had claimed to be on a par with the Pope in Rome in terms of Apostolic succession.  During his first year in Constantinople he greatly reduced expenses of the clergy and built a hospital with the money saved.  John imposed the primacy of the Patriarch of Constantinople over leading bishoprics in Asia Minor and the Aegean and established an extensive patronage system.  He appropriated the Virgin Mary from Ephesus, site of a church founded by St. Paul and Mary's former residence, and made her patron saint of Constantinople, where there had been virtually no Christians in the $1^{st}$ century.  John actively supported missionary work and destroyed non-Christian temples, such as the temple of Artemis at Ephesus.  He further strengthened the role and independence of the Patriarch of Constantinople in relation to the imperial government.  John spoke plainly and clearly with a genius for applying Scripture to everyday life and making a moral point in each sermon. Chrysostom frequently preached against the extravagance of the rich, and particularly the expensive clothing upper class women wore. Constantinople aristocrats were not accustomed to such rebuke. In 403 Eudoxia, the powerful wife of Emperor Arcadius, conspired with Theophilus, patriarch of Alexandria, and discredited John with trumped up charges at a synod of bishops. Emperor Arcadius banished Chrysostom, but soon reversed his decision in the face of popular outrage and reinstated him. In 404 Empress Eudoxia was infuriated when Chrysostom reportedly complained about a silver statue of her erected in front of the cathedral. Under intense pressure from his wife, Arcadius again signed a decree sending Chrysostom into exile. In response an angry mob burned down the cathedral, the Senate-house, and other buildings. Chrysostom was taken to Cucusus, a secluded and rugged place on the east frontier of Armenia, where he continued to be active and influential. His enemies arranged for him to be sent to an even more remote location on the Black Sea boundary of the empire near the Caucasus. His military escort forced him to make long marches toward this destination and his health rapidly deteriorated. John died at Comana in Pontus on September 14, 407. His body was returned to Constantinople with full honors, entombed in the Church of the Apostles.

At Hagia Sophia in the late 10$^{th}$ century six-winged Seraphim were painted on the pendentives, one of which had its face restored in 2009.

Seraphim, the plural of Seraph, are high-ranking angels, which the Old Testament states the prophet Isaiah saw as attendants at Yahweh's court. In the Book of Isaiah the Seraphim have six wings, guard the throne of Yahweh, and proclaim, "Holy, holy, holy." One Seraph flew to Isaiah and purified his lips with a burning coal so that henceforth he was consecrated to make inspired utterances. In the New Testament Book of Revelation, Seraphim are the highest rank of angels, caretakers of God's throne.

During the Fourth Crusade Latin Christians turned against their coreligionists in Constantinople and seized the city, which they ruled for 57 years. The tomb of Enrico Dandolo, the Doge of Venice who commanded the 1204 seizure and sack of the city, can still be seen in the Hagia Sophia. The Latin Christians stole numerous religious relics from Hagia Sophia, including a stone from the tomb of Jesus, the shroud of Jesus, and the bones of several saints. In 1453, the Ottoman Turk Mehmet II finally conquered the city. Muslim soldiers immediately battered down the doors and entered Hagia Sophia, slaughtering or enslaving the remaining Christian worshippers. Mehmet transformed the building into a mosque and removed bells, altar and sacrificial vessels. On June 1, 1453 Mehmet II attended the first Friday Muslim prayer service at the Hagia Sophia. Christian mosaics were plastered over and the Islamic mihrab (prayer niche facing Mecca), minbar (pulpit), and eventually four minarets were added. Over time many Ottoman royal tombs were placed around the building. The chandeliers hanging low above the floor are Ottoman additions, as are the large $19^{th}$ century medallions inscribed with the names of God, Mohammed and the early caliphs Ali and Abu Bakr in Arabic lettering.

The **Eyüp Sultan Mosque and Mausoleum** (41° 2' 52.61" N, 28° 56' 1.63" E) is on the N end of the Golden Horn on the European side of Istanbul outside the original city walls. Mehmet the Conqueror built a mosque at this spot in 1458, the first major mosque constructed following the 1453 conquest. Although the extant structure itself dates from 1800, it was erected at the site of the $7^{th}$ tomb of Abu Ayyub al-Ansari, also known as Eyüp Sultan, the last surviving close companion of the Prophet Mohammed. Ayyub al-Ansari was an Arab chieftain who died during the unsuccessful 670 Arab attack on Constantinople. This tomb is the holiest Islamic shrine in Istanbul. Devout Muslims have long sought final burial near the tomb, causing a proliferation of nearby cemeteries. For generations, Ottoman rulers traditionally began their reign here during a ceremony in which they would receive the sword of Osman Gazi, the founder of the dynasty. Throngs of pilgrims visit the site to view the tomb, particularly on Fridays and during Ramadan. Young boys wearing white satin suits with spangled caps and red sashes emblazoned often stop here en route to their circumcision ceremonies. Many arrive by ferry, the most convenient mode of arrival. The outer courtyard of the Eyüp Sultan Mosque has two gates opening to the street. A marble gateway decorated with Arabic inscriptions leads to an inner courtyard, which is shaded by a large sycamore tree and contains a fountain. The rectangular mosque has galleries on three sides with a vaulted mihrab, or niche in the front wall toward Mecca, and a marble pulpit. The mosque dome is 17.5 m in diameter and there are two minarets. An Ottoman hamam, or bathhouse, is attached to the complex. The outer and inner walls of the mausoleum are covered with fine glazed blue tiles. The mausoleum hall and the tomb chamber are adorned with silver decorations, crystal chandeliers, and elaborate calligraphy acquired over centuries. The single-domed tomb has an octagonal shape with the silver enclosed sarcophagus separated from the rest of the hall. The sarcophagus lid is decorated with symbolic inscriptions and protected with finely carved silver shields. A marble footprint of the Prophet Mohammed framed in silver and embedded in the wall points toward Mecca. Visitors walk backwards leaving the room to avoid turning their backs on the tomb.

**Abu Ayyub al-Ansari (597-676)** also known as Khalid ibn Zayd ibn Eyüp was born in Medina, a member of the Banu Najjar tribe. He was a close companion, known as an Ansar or early helper, of the Prophet Mohammed. When Mohammed arrived in Medina on the Hijra or migration to Medina in 622 all the Muslim inhabitants offered to host him. Mohammed decided to let his camel Kusva carry him around Medina and then stay at the house where the camel stopped, which turned out to the home of Abu Ayyub. The Prophet stayed with Abu Ayyub for seven months. Abu Ayyub became a committed soldier of Islam and fought courageously in Mohammed's battles. After the death of Mohammed in 632, Abu Ayyub continued his military service under the Caliphs, serving with distinction in the 639-642 Muslim conquest of Egypt. Even when he was almost eighty years old and was perhaps the last surviving companion of Mohammad, Abu Ayyub continued to fight. In 676 Umayyad Caliph Muawiyah launched an Arab siege of Constantinople, lead by his son Yazid. Abu Ayyub pressed ahead to the front lines, where he was mortally wounded in battle and realized he would soon be bound for paradise. When Yazid approached him, Abu Ayyub told him to say farewell to the troops and asked to be buried at the furthest point of the Muslim military advance, so that eventually he would hear the sounds of victory from beyond the grave. Abu Ayyub then passed away. The Muslim army fought furiously and pushed back the Roman forces until they reached the walls of Constantinople, where they buried Abu Ayyub in accordance with his final wishes. Almost eight hundred years later, in 1453, the location of the tomb of Abu Ayyub was revealed in a dream to Ak Şemsettin, spiritual advisor to Mehmet the Conqueror. Mehmet constructed the first purpose built mosque in Constantinople at the tomb.

**Arab Siege of Constantinople:** During the 7th and 8th centuries Umayyad Caliphs twice almost conquered Constantinople. In 676 Yazid, son of Caliph Muawiyah and future Caliph, brought a large Muslim army all the way to Constantinople, which besieged the city and blockaded the Bosphorus. The Arabs were unable to breach the Theodosian Walls. Fortunately for the Christians they had just recently developed a powerful new weapon, a napalm-like substance known as Greek fire. In 678, the late Roman navy used this Greek fire to decisively defeat the Umayyad navy in the Sea of Marmara and lift the siege. Forty years later in 717 Umayyad Caliph Sulayman ibn Abd al-Malik tried again to conquer Constantinople with a huge army of 80,000 men led by his brother Maslama, supported by a fleet of 1,800 Arab warships. Once again the massive Theodosian walls blocked the initial Arab advance and the Roman navy effectively used Greek fire to prevent the Umayyad navy from proceeding up the Bosphorus. As time wore on plague and an unusually harsh winter decimated the ranks of the massive Arab force besieging the city. While Constantinople continued to receive supplies via the Black Sea, the Arab attackers suffered terribly from disease and starvation and, reportedly, were forced to eat camels, horses, donkeys and even the bodies of the dead to survive. Finally another Umayyad fleet of about 750 ships brought in supplies and reinforcements, but despite repeated valiant attempts the attackers failed to overcome the city's defenses. Many of the Umayyad sailors were recently enslaved Christians who deserted whenever the opportunity presented itself. The death of Caliph Sulayman in 717 and the consequent leadership change undermined Maslama's ability to obtain additional resources for the siege. Then the dramatic arrival of Christian Bulgar troops from the N in support of Constantinople turned the tide against the Arabs. Caught between Roman soldiers attacking from the city and Bulgars attacking in the rear, the position of the Arab besiegers became untenable. In July and August 718 the Arabs lost as many as 32,000 men and were forced to withdraw. Part of the Arab army escaped by land through Anatolia to the S while the rest boarded the remaining Umayyad ships. Then a fierce storm struck the Umayyad ships, sinking all but five and drowning much of the Arab army. The Umayyad failure to conquer Constantinople was a major event in world history with enormous ramifications for the political, cultural and religious development of Europe and the western world.

# Appendix I: Chronological Order of Historical Figures Identified and Discussed in Reference to Sites:

(see index for page number)

King Midas ($8^{th}$-$7^{th}$ century BCE)

King Croesus (595-547 BCE)

Herodotus (484-420 BCE)

Hippodamus of Miletus (498-408 BCE)

Socrates (469-399 BCE)

Mausolus (337-353 BCE)

Alexander the Great (356-323 BCE)

Aristotle (384-322 BCE)

Alcetas (350-320 BCE)

Menander (342-291 BCE)

Lucius Cornelius Sulla (138-80 BCE)

Pompey (106-48 BCE)

Julius Caesar (100-44 BCE)

Cleopatra VII (69-30 BCE)

Marcus Vitruvius Pollio (70-15 BCE)

Emperor Augustus (63 BCE-14 CE)

Germanicus Julius Caesar (15 BCE-19 CE)

Strabo (63 BCE-23)

John the Baptist ($1^{st}$ century)

Emperor Tiberias (42 BCE-37)

54 Emperor Claudius (10 BCE-54)

John the Apostle $1^{st}$ century

Virgin Mary $1^{st}$ century

Paul the Apostle (5-67)

Lucius Sergius Paulus ($1^{st}$ century)

Apostle Philip (1st century)
Mary Magdelene 1st century
Emperor Nero (37-68)
Emperor Vespasian (9-79)
Emperor Domitian (51-96)
Saint Thecla (16-100)
Emperor Trajan (53-117)
Emperor Hadrian (76-138)
Emperor Antoninus Pius (86-161)
Emperor Lucius Verus (130-169)
Emperor Marcus Aurelius (121-180)
Galen (129-200)
Diogenes of Oinoanda (1st-2nd century)
Plancia Magna (1st-2nd century)
Emperor Septimius Severus (145-211)
Saint Gregory (210-270)
Saint Polyectus (3rd century)
Saint Euphemia (290-307)
Emperor Constantine the Great (280-337)
Saint Nicholas (270-343)
Emperor Valens (328-378)
Emperor Theodosius I (379-395)
Saint Bassus (4th century)
Saints Sergius and Bacchus (4th century)
Saint John Chrysostom (347-407)
Emperor Theodosius II (401-450)
Emperor Marcian (392-457)
Emperor Justinian (483-565)
Procopius of Caesarea (500-565)

Porphyrius 6th century
Abu Ayyub al-Ansari (597-676)
Sir Charles Fellows (1799-1860)
Heinrich Schliemann (1822-1890)
John Turtle Wood (1821-1890)
Sir Charles Newton (1816-1894)
Carl Humann (1839-1896)
Otto Benndorf (1838-1907)

## Appendix II: Deities in Context of Ancient Sites:

(see index for page number)

Zeus (Jupiter): supreme god, ruler of Olympus and the sky

Hera (Juno): wife of Zeus, first lady of Olympus

Pluto (Hades): brother of Zeus, ruler of the underworld realm of the dead, Tartarus; husband of Persephone

Poseidon (Neptune): brother of Zeus, ruler of the oceans, rivers, and earthquakes

Hestia (Vesta): goddess of hearth and home, sister of Zeus

Aphrodite (Venus): goddess of erotic love and beauty; mother of Eros (Cupid), ancestor of the Romans

Hephaestus (Vulcan): god of fire and craftsmanship, son of Zeus and Hera, husband of Aphrodite

Athena (Minerva): goddess of wisdom, industry and strategic thinking in war, daughter of Zeus, virgin goddess

Helios: titan god of the sun, all-seeing

Leto: goddess of modesty, protector of the young, lover of Zeus and mother of the Apollo and Artemis

Artemis (Diana): goddess of wild animals and the hunt, virgin goddess, twin sister of Apollo

Apollo: god of health, oracles and music, twin brother of Artemis

Asclepius: god of medicine and healing, son of Apollo

Hygeia: goddess of hygiene, daughter of Asclepius

Telesphorus: Celtic dwarf god of physical recovery, adopted son of Asclepius

Dionysus (Bacchus): god of wine, vegetation, theatre, and ecstasy; son of Zeus

Hercules (Herakles): son of Zeus; born an incredibly strong and daring man, eventually given immortality

Demeter (Ceres): goddess of agriculture, seasonal rebirth; mother of Persephone

Hermes (Mercury): god of travelers, merchants, thieves and prostitutes, messenger of the gods, visitor to Tartarus, son of Zeus

Cybele: Anatolian mother goddess, appears seated on throne with two lions, brought to Rome to save Roman republic from Hannibal

Hecate: goddess of black magic, often takes triple form

Tyche (Fortuna): goddess of fortune and prosperity, particularly for city-states

Nike (Victoria): goddess of victory

Serapis: god of fertility, healing, and life after death from Ptolemaic Egypt

Isis: goddess of motherhood and devotion, appears with baby Horus, consort of Osiris or Serapis, from Egypt

Harpocrates: originally Egyptian Horus, transformed into youthful god of silence and secrecy

Anubis: god of embalming and the dead, head of a jackal from Egypt

## Appendix III: Time Management – Origin of Days and Months

During the 1st-3rd centuries the Romans developed a system in which each day of the week was named for one of the gods. Following in the footsteps of the Babylonian astrologers, each god was associated with a heavenly body. The Roman seven-day week was based on gods in this order: Sunday, or day of the sun and associated with the sun god Helios or Sol; Monday, day of the moon associated with moon god Selene (or Sin); Tuesday, derived from day of Mars or Ares, god of war (in English Mars was transformed over time into Tiwaz a Germanic war god); Wednesday, derived from day of Mercury or Hermes, messenger of the gods who visited Tartarus (in English Mercury was transformed into Woden, an Anglo Saxon god who carried the dead to the underworld); Thursday, derived from day of Jupiter or Zeus (in English Jupiter was transformed into Thor, god of thunder in the Norse pantheon); Friday, derived from day of Venus or Aphrodite, goddess of love and beauty (in English Venus was transformed into Frigg, the beautiful Germanic goddess and spouse of Woden); and Saturday, derived from day of Saturn, father of Jupiter.

The Romans also gave us our months. January is named for Janus, Roman god of gates, doorways, beginnings and endings in time. He had two heads facing opposite directions: one looking back at the past year, the other on to the new. During war the gates of the temple of Janus were opened; they were closed only during peacetime. February is from Februus, Roman god of the dead and purification; a festival of washing and cleaning associated with heavy rain held at this time of year. March is from Roman god of war Mars, and was the time to launch military campaigns. April is from Aphrilis or Aphrodite, goddess of love. May is from the Greek goddess Maia, a lover of Zeus and mother of Hermes. June is from Juno (Hera), wife of Zeus (Jupiter), and goddess of marriage, which is one reason June is considered a fortuitous time to marry. The Roman Emperor Augustus named July in honor of Julius Caesar and August in honor of himself. Before Julius Caesar established a 12-month calendar in 46 BCE, September, October, November and December were simply the last four ordinal names of the original ten months Roman year: septem (seven); octo (eight); novem (nine); and decem (ten).

# Appendix IV: List of Maps

Ancient regions 4

Troy 10

Alexandria Troas 12

Pergamum acropolis 22

Pergamum 30

Pergamum Asclepium 36

Ephesus and Selçuk 58

Ephesus upper city 60

Ephesus lower city 81

Magnesia 88

Priene 89

Miletus 98

Sardis 114

Aphrodisias 119

Herakleia 138

Kaunos 141

Knidos 145

Labranda 149

Iasos 152

Halicarnassus 155

Alabanda 159

Tlos 180

Xanthus 185

Letoon 191

Patara 197

Olympos 219

Phaselis 227

Perge 235

Sillyon 240

Side 244

Termessos 250

Selge 254

Antioch in Pisidia 261

Sagalassos 269

Gordium 277

Hierapolis 282

Laodicea 295

Nicaea 301

# INDEX

(includes main reference or definition)

Achelous 69

Aedile defined 62

Aeneas 9

Aeolia 39

Agora defined 18

Al-Ansari, Abu Ayyub 342

Al-Battal, Abdullah 297

Alabanda 159

Alcetas 252

Alexander the Great 12

Alexandria Troas 11

Alinda 161

Amazonomachy 87

Amos 147

Andriace 209

Androclus 78

Andron defined 149

Antalya Museum 35, 91, 95, 122, 158, 195, 205, 210, 216, 223, 229, 237, 239, 240, 248

Antioch in Pisidia 255

Antiphellos 199

Antoninus Pius 273

Anubis 92

Aphrodisias 119

Aphrodite 120

Apollo 103

Apse defined 34

Arab Siege of Constantinople 343

Archangel Gabriel 337

Archangel Michael 338

Architrave defined 18

Ariadne 70

Aristotle 16

Artemis 51

Arykanda 211

Asclepium defined 36

Asclepius 38

Aspendos 241

Assos 15

Athena 95

Atlantes defined 34

Atlas 34

Augustus 262

Austrian Archeological Institute 85, 102, 219

Bacchus (see Dionysus)

Babcock, Michael 319

Baptistery defined 84

Basilica Cistern 328

Battle of Akroinon 298

Bellerophon 177

Benndorf, Otto 85

Binbirdirek Cistern 325

Bithynia 299

Bouleuterion defined 10

British Museum 21, 48, 49, 94, 102, 145-147, 155, 187-190

Bucoleon Palace 331

Byzas 306

Calchas 235

Caria 118

Caryatids defined 34

Cave of Seven Sleepers 57

Cavea defined 39

Cella defined 43

Centaur defined 38

Ceres (see Demeter)

Chimaera 223

Church of Baptist John 322

Church of Holy Peace 325

Church of Holy Wisdom 332

Church of Saints Sergius and Bacchus 326

Church of St. Polyeuctus 323

Claros 44

Claudius 128

Cleopatra 76

Clow, Kate 172, 234 (see: Lycian Way; St. Paul Trail)

Colonnade defined 18

Column capital defined 19

Column of Constantine 306

Column of Marcian 317

Column of the Goths 305

Constantine the Great 307

Constantinople 304

Consul defined 33

Corinthian Order 23

Cornucopia defined 69

Croesus 109

Cyanea 200

Cybele 280

Cyme 39

Demeter 167

Diana (see Artemis)

Diazoma defined 26

Didyma 102

Diogenes of Oinoanda 175

Dionysus 165

Domitian 65

Doric Order 18

Eleusian Mysteries defined 168

Endymion 139

Entablature defined 18

Ephesus 46

Ephesus Museum (Selçuk) 76, 79

Ephesus Museum (Vienna) 78, 79, 85

Ephesus Temple of Artemis 50

Ephesus Tomb of St. John

53

Erotes defined 78

Erythrai 42

Etrog defined 96

Euromos 156

Eyüp Sultan Mausoleum 341

Fellows, Sir Charles 188

Fethiye Museum 172, 181

First Council of Nicaea 300

Fluting defined 18

Fortuna (see Tyche)

Forty Martyrs of Sebaste 321

Frieze defined 19

Galen 36

Germanicus 45

German Archeology Institute 34, 38, 97, 102, 177

Gordian Knot 278

Gordium 276

Great Palace Mosaic Museum 325

Hades (see Pluto)

Hadrian 195

Hagia Eirene (see Church of Holy Peace)

Hagia Sophia (see Church of Holy Wisdom)

Halicarnassus 153

Harpocrates (Horus) 92

Harvard University 116

Hecate 169

Heliodorus 266

Helios 213

Hephaestus 224

Hera 31

Herakleia 136

Hercules 136

Hermes 229

Herodotus 153

Heroon defined 22

Hestia 64

Hierapolis 282

Hippodamus of Miletus 98

Hippodrome of Constantinople 310

Horus (see Harpocrates)

House of Virgin Mary 55

Humann, Carl 21

Hygeia 37

Iasos 151

Iconoclastic Controversy 302

Ionia 40

Ionic Order 93

Isis 90

Istanbul Archeological Museum 189, 311, 312, 322, 324

Italian Archeological Institute 39, 55, 152, 247, 294

Ixion 244-245

Judaism 79, 80, 89, 96, 97, 100, 109-113, 124, 129, 135, 143, 181, 196, 197, 201, 210, 233, 244, 255-258, 282, 289, 292-296, 311, 317, 330

Julius Caesar 61

Juno (see Hera)

Jupiter (see Zeus)

Justinian 328

Kaunos 140

Kibyra 116

Knidos 144

Labranda 147

Laodicea on the Lycus 294

Leda 134

Leto 191

Letoon 191

Limyra 216

Louvre 87

Lucius Sergius Paulus 255

Lucius Verus 79

Lulav 96

Lycia 170

Lycian Way 172, 184, 199, 220, 227 (see Clow)

Lydia 108

Lyrbe 247

Magnesia on the Meander 85

Marcian 318

Marcus Aurelius 221

Marsayas 285

Mary Magdalene 49

Mausolus 154

Medea 203

Medusa 24

Megaron defined 277

Melbourne University 282

Mên 246

Menander 70

Menorah 210

Mercury (see Hermes)

Metropolitan Museum of Art (New York) 116

Midas 276

Miletus 98

Milion 309

Minerva (see Athena)

Monophysite Controversy 331

Münster University 15, 199

Muses 61

Mylasa 150

Myra 201

Mysia 20

Narthex defined 323

Nave defined 54

Neandria 12

Necropolis defined 12

Neon 266

Neptune (see Poseidon)

Nereids 189

Nero 131

New York University 121, 136

Newton, Sir Charles 155

Nicaea 300

Nike 68

Nikon 266

Nymphaeum defined 61

Nysa on the Meander 162

Obelisk of Theodosius 312

Octavian (see Augustus)

Odeon defined 10

Oinoanda 173

Olympos 219

Orestes 69

Palaestra defined 59

Pamphylia 230

Pamukkale (see Hierapolis)

Patara 194

Pediment defined 101

Penthesileia 134

Pergamon Museum (Berlin) 20, 25, 34, 38, 101

Pergamum 20

Pergamum Asclepium 36

Pergamum Temple of Serapis 33

Perge 235

Peristyle defined 22

Persian tomb 41

Pessinus 279

Phaselis 226

Phocaea 41

Phrygia 275

Pinara 182

Pisidia 249

Plancia Magna 237

Pluto 286

Pompey 231

Porphyrius 311

Portico defined 33

Poseidon 271

Praetorian Guard defined 265

Priene 89

Proconsul defined 61

Procopius of Caesarea 334

Propylon defined 45

Proskynesis defined 14

Prytaneum defined 64

Quaestor defined 62

Sagalassos 268

Saint Bassus 266

Saint Euphemia 320

Saint Gregory 335

Saint John Chrysostom 339

Saint John the Apostle 54

Saint John the Baptist 322

Saint Luke 59

Saint Nicholas 205

Saint Paul 256

Saint Philip the Apostle 291

Saint Polyeuctus 324

Saint Thecla 258

Saints Sergius and Bacchus 327

Sardis 109

Sarpedon 187

Satyr defined 30

Schliemann, Heinrich 11

Selge 253

Septimius Severus 283

Seraphim 340

Serapis 35

Serpentine Column 312

Seven Sleepers 57

Seyitgazi 297

Shofar 210

Side 243

Sidebottom, Harry 41

Sidyma 183

Silenus 30

Sillyon 240

Socrates 71

Stoa defined 26

Strabo 162

St. Paul Trail 234-236, 243, 254, 268 (see Clow)

Sukkot 96

Sulla, Lucius Cornelius 67

Sura 211

Syrinx 49

Telephos 28

Telesphorus 37

Telmessos 172

Teos 42

Termessos 250

Tetrapylon defined 121

Theodosian Walls 315

Theodosius I 74

Theodosius II 316

Three Graces 122

Tiberius 124

Titanomachy 27

Tlos 177

Torah defined 96

Trajan 23

Triptolemus 167-168

Triton 71

Troad 5

Trojan War 5

Troy 8

Tübingen University 10-11

Twain, Mark 1, 4, 5, 48, 49, 55, 59, 305, 325, 332, 333

Tyche 73

University of Michigan 268

University of New England 170, 303

University of Oslo 294

University of Pennsylvania 10, 279

University of Southern Denmark 156

University of Wisconsin 116

Uppsala University 150

Valens 314

Valens Aqueduct 314

Venus (see Aphrodite)

Vespasian 142

Vesta (see Hestia)

Victoria (see Nike)

Virgin Mary 56

Vitruvius, Marcus 43

Walled Obelisk 311

Wood, John Turtle 48

Xanthus 185

Yalvaç Museum 262, 268

Zeus 157

BIBLIOGRAPHY

Aksit, Ilhan, Ancient Ephesus, 1995

Akurgal, Ekrem, Ancient Civilizations and Ruins of Turkey, 2007, ISBN 9754791104

Bainbridge, James, Lonely Planet Turkey, 2009, ISBN 9781741049275

Bayhan, Suzan, Priene, Miletus, Didyma, 1997, ISBN 9757559172

Bean, George, Lycian Turkey, 1978, ISBN 0393057089

Blake, Everett, Biblical Sites in Turkey, 1994, ISBN 9754130582

Brosnahan, Tom, Istanbul, 1999, ISBN 0864425856

Brosnahan, Tom, Turkey: Lonely Planet Travel Atlas, 1997, ISBN 0864422725

Bulfinch, Thomas, Bulfinch's Mythology, 1979, ISBN 0517274159

Bunson, Matthew, A Dictionary of the Roman Empire, 1995, ISBN 0195102339

Cesaretti, Paolo, Theodora, Empress of Byzantium, 2004, ISBN 0865652376

Cimok, Fatih, Pergamum, 1998, ISBN 9757528722

Clow, Kate, St. Paul Trail, 2004, ISBN 0953921816

Clow, Kate, The Lycian Way, 2009, ISBN 9780953921867

Delicotopoulos, Athan, St. Paul's Journeys to Greece and Cyprus, 2001, ISBN 9602263865

Demirsar, Metin, Insight Guides Turkish Coast, 1990, ISBN 0887297889

Dortluk, Kayhan, Side, Aspendos, Perge, 2010, ISBN 9757559784

Erim, Kenan, Aphrodisias, 1993, ISBN 9754790639

Fagan, Garrett, The History of Ancient Rome, Parts 1-4 (The Teaching Company, Great Courses DVD), 2001, ISBN 1565855736

Fant, Clyde, A Guide to Biblical Sites in Greece and Turkey, 2003, ISBN 9780195139181

Farmer, David, Oxford Dictionary of Saints, 2004, ISBN 0198609493

Gibbon, Edward, The Decline and Fall of the Roman Empire, 1960

Goldsworthy, Adrian, In the Name of Rome. 2007, ISBN 9780753817896

Grant, Michael, The Founders of the Western World, 1991, ISBN 0684193035

Harl, Kenneth, Great Civilizations of Asia Minor, Parts 1&2 (The Teaching Company, Great Courses CD), 2001, ISBN 1565853377

Harl, Kenneth, The World of Byzantium, Parts 1&2 (The Teaching Company, Great Courses DVD), 2001, ISBN 1565855957

Hawkes, Jacquetta, Atlas of Ancient Archeology, 1974, ISBN 007027293X

Hawting, G.R., The First Dynasty of Islam, 2005, ISBN 0415240735

Heather, Peter, The Fall of the Roman Empire, 2006, ISBN 9780195325416

Keskin, Naci, Ephesus, 2000, ISBN 9757559482

King, Charles, The Black Sea: A History, 2005, ISBN 019928394X

Kravitz, David, Who's Who In Greek and Roman Mythology, 1975, ISBN 0517527464

Lassus, Jean, The Early Christian & Byzantine World, 1967

Levine, Amy-Jill, The Old Testament, Parts 1&2 (The Teaching Company,

Great Courses DVD), 2000, ISBN 1565855507

Lloyd, Seton, Ancient Turkey: A Traveler's History, 1989, ISBN 9780520220423

Macrone, Michael, It's Greek to Me, Brush Up on your Classics, 2001, ISBN 0062700227

McDonagh, Bernard, Blue Guide Turkey, 1995, ISBN 0393311953

Mehling, Marianne, Editor, Turkey: A Phaidon Cultural Guide, 1989, ISBN 0714825301

Murray, Alexander, Who's Who In Mythology, 1995, ISBN 1858910684

Norman, Bruce, Footsteps: Nine Archeological Journeys of Romance and Discovery, 1988, ISBN 0881623245

Norwich, John, A Short History of Byzantium, 1997, ISBN 0679772693

O'Donnell, James, The Ruins of the Roman Empire, 2009, ISBN 9780060787417

Ozeren, Ocal, Ephesus, 1992, ISBN 9757559032

Payne, Robert, The Gold of Troy, 1959, ISBN 070904285X

Perowne, Stewart, Roman Mythology, 1969, ISBN 0600033473

Ring, Trudy, International Dictionary of Historic Places: Volume 2 Southern Europe, 1995, ISBN 1884964028

Robinson, Charles, Plutarch Eight Great Lives, 1960, ISBN 0030094305

Russell, Francis, Places in Turkey, 2010, ISBN 9780711230613

Stoneman, Richard, A Traveler's History of Turkey, 2006, ISBN 1566566207

Sumner-Boyd, Hilary, Strolling Through Istanbul, 2010, ISBN

9781848851542

Tadgell, Christopher, Imperial Space, 1998, ISBN 0823003795

Tamturk, Jessica, Istanbul & The Turkish Coast, 2010, ISBN 9781598801750

Taskiran, Celal, Silifke and Environs, 1993, ISBN 9789944626415

Tatlock, Jessie, Greek and Roman Mythology, 1917

Tomlinson, Richard, From Mycenae to Constantinople: The Evolution of the Ancient City, 1992, ISBN 0415059984

Trefler, Caroline, Fodor's Turkey, 2009, ISBN 9781400008155

Tucker, Alan, The Berlitz Travellers Guide to Turkey, 1993, ISBN 2831517168

Twain, Mark, The Innocents Abroad, 2010, ISBN 9781840226362

Vandiver, Elizabeth, Classical Mythology, Parts 1&2 (The Teaching Company, Great Courses DVD), 2000, ISBN 156585568X

Wilson, Mark, Biblical Turkey: A Guide to Jewish and Christian Sites of Asia Minor, 2010, ISBN 9786055607357

Wood, Michael, In the Footsteps of Alexander the Great, 1997, ISBN 0520213076

# ABOUT THE AUTHOR

Jack Tucker is a former diplomat who has worked and traveled for many years in the Middle East and Central Asia. He currently lives in Maryland. The author is entirely responsible for all errors and omissions in the text and would be most grateful for corrections or suggestions sent to tuckjack2@yahoo.com via email. The author is very interested in changes in the websites listed and additional websites providing comprehensive information regarding these ancient sites.

Made in the USA
San Bernardino, CA
03 March 2014